London: A Travel Guide Through Time

London: A Travel Guide Through Time

MATTHEW GREEN

MICHAEL JOSEPH
an imprint of
PENGUIN BOOKS

MICHAEL JOSEPH

UK | USA | Canada | Ireland | Australia
India | New Zealand | South Africa

Michael Joseph is part of the Penguin Random House group of companies
whose addresses can be found at global.penguinrandomhouse.com.

Penguin
Random House
UK

First published 2015

001

Text copyright © Dr Matthew Green, 2015
Maps and illustrations copyright © Alice Smith, 2015

The moral right of the author has been asserted

Set in 11.5/13.5 pt Garamond MT Std
Typeset by Jouve (UK), Milton Keynes
Printed in Great Britain by Clays Ltd, St Ives plc

A CIP catalogue record for this book is available from the British Library

HARDBACK ISBN: 978-0-718-17976-2

www.greenpenguin.co.uk

For Marianne

Acknowledgements

Penning a time-travelling guide to a city that contains 'all that life can afford', faster than Dr Johnson did his dictionary, has been a colossal task, so I would like to thank all of those who have made it such an exhilarating and rewarding experience.

First, my commissioning editor Fenella Bates, who not only came up with the brilliant idea in the first place, but also infinitely enriched the writing and editing experience with her bundles of enthusiasm, insight and understanding. Much gratitude, too, to my agent and occasional drinking partner Chris Wellbelove who has been, at every turn, both a rock of good counsel and a wellspring of ideas, and to the superhuman Alice Smith, who has furnished the book with witty and wonderful illustrations and maps, responding cheerfully and with good grace to our urgent and ever-stranger picture requests.

I would also like to thank Helen Coyle, whose laser-guided comments greatly enhanced the manuscript; my copy-editor, Trevor Horwood, who streamlined the writing and reined in some of my more self-indulgent flourishes; and Fi Crosby, for her incisive input.

My friends have been a reassuring and bounteous source of encouragement, help and ideas in this, as in my other historical pursuits, and I would like to extend my heartfelt thanks to Daisy Leitch, Keiran Goddard, David Heales, Ed Fornieles, Jessie Huth, Will Hammond, Edward Shawcross and Duncan Brown, the latter two being kind enough to read and comment upon some early drafts of chapters. I would also like to express my gratitude to Ian Spurr, who helped with the research for the

Victorian chapter, and patiently proofread much of the manuscript; the staff of the British and London Libraries; and Tina Baxter for taking me on a tour of medieval London.

I would never have been in a position to write this book if it weren't for my tutors at Oxford University. Of all the academicians who haunt those hallowed quadrangles, I would like to single out my undergraduate tutor, Dr Faramerz Dabhoiwala, and my doctoral supervisor, Dr Perry Gauci, a font of wisdom and generosity. They not only instructed, but inspired me, then as now. I am grateful to Dr Gauci for casting his eye over the eighteenth-century chapter (though any mistakes there, as in all the chapters, are firmly of my own making).

What follows is essentially a series of guided tours through time and as such the book is an evolution – and, in parts, distillation – of the immersive historic tours that I lead, both digitally and in person, through historic London for Unreal City Audio, an organisation I co-founded with Duncan Brown and Edward Shawcross in 2012. I thank everyone who has ever been on a tour (and stomached our gritty seventeenth-century-style coffee). We are honoured to have so many loyal and enthusiastic followers, but would be nothing without our tireless troupe of actors and musicians, above all the inestimable Mr Jonathan Hansler.

But the biggest thanks of all are reserved for my mother and father, whose unwavering and unconditional support of my pursuits over the last two decades has been the stuff of dreams, my many brothers and sisters, and my one and only fiancée, Marianne, who has had little choice but to be my partner in time travel, making brilliant suggestions at every turn, and putting up with endless midnight meals. This book is for her.

Dalston, 2 May 2015

Contents

Introduction   1

1603: A Whirlwind Tour of Shakespearean
    London   5

1390: A Descent into Medieval London   67

1665: A Mournful Walk through Plague-struck
    London   157

1884: Depravity and Wonder on a Tour of
    Joseph Merrick's London   243

1957: London Rising – A Tour of the
    Blitzed City   313

1716: Four Days in Dudley Ryder's London   361

Falling Back to Earth   447

Notes   451

Further Reading   479

Introduction

In London, we are all time travellers, however unwitting. Thanks to its habitual juxtapositions of historic and modern buildings, evocative place names and kaleidoscopic diversity of tone and energy, we are liable to find ourselves transported to a different place just by walking round a corner and stumbling across the unexpected. A perfectly preserved Georgian house next to a stark council estate, a fragment of the Roman walls in the hullabaloo of the City. London is peppered with portals into historical worlds – you just need to know where to look.

The following chapters will take you on a joyride through 600 years of London's history, soaking up the sights, sounds, smells and tastes of the greatest city in the world, and meeting a plethora of memorable characters, some well known, some not, all of whom capture the zeitgeist of each age. As we slide through time, we'll watch London crack out of its Roman shell in the medieval period, spread its tentacles in the seventeenth and eighteenth centuries and, in the Victorian period, evolve into 'a human awful wonder of God' – the biggest city the world had ever seen. We will witness some of London's darkest hours as the Grim Reaper swings his scythe during the Great Plague and vast swathes of the city are razed to the ground the following year. But we'll also see her resurgent, rising from the ashes, whether of the Great Fire or the incendiaries of the Blitz.

How does it work?

You are the time traveller, I am your guide. Hello. I'll be narrating your experiences and dispensing wisdom as we go. In terms of the mechanism, don't expect to find any wormholes, tears in the space–time continuum, police call-boxes or whatever else people use to hurtle through time these days. Our time machine is wrapped in the skin of the city, and it will be sensitive to your touch.

The six chapters that follow will begin with you wandering the streets of the present-day city. But then you will find something – it could be a building, a street name, a blue plaque – that will act as a portal into London's past. When you open your eyes, you will find yourself in an alien world, surrounded by strange buildings, mysterious sounds and, more often than not, hideous smells. You will be informed of the year and the month and sometimes the exact date. From there, you will have to work your way through hazardous landscapes populated variously by killer rats, religious pyromaniacs, flying pigs, cocky watermen, executioners, vengeful saints, blood-baying xenophobes, bloodthirsty bears, tenacious pornographers, slimy lawyers, the Elephant Man, sharpies, cullies and conniving link boys amongst others.

Our metaphorical time machine is a cranky, capricious thing. You will have no say where you land. You could be spun into any number of worlds. Nor will the chapters be arranged in strict chronological order. Where would be the fun in that? You will have no idea where you are going to land next, and experiencing London in different periods will invite some unexpected juxtapositions and synergies that might otherwise go undetected. Think of each journey as a series of historical quantum leaps into mirror universes, a whirlwind tour of some of the darker and more offbeat sides of London's history.

Please remember – you're not setting out on an information-gathering mission to observe every last facet of London's society and culture at various moments; to do so would rapidly become a chore, and the book would spill into thousands of pages. There are plenty of brilliant history books for such comprehensive and scholarly approaches already and I would direct you to the bibliography for this. Each chapter takes the form of a guided tour, exploring between eight and twelve places within the space of a day or two, or four in the case of the final journey.

Sadly, we can't cover the whole city, especially not after the dawn of the nineteenth century, when the population of London expanded into the millions and its physical extent sprawled ever-outwards to consume meadows and suburbs like a giant squirming octopus. To keep up the pace and maintain a sense of cohesion, we will confine our tours largely to central London, what are called Zone One and Zone Two on the Underground today, though there will also be the odd foray further afield. Remember that for much of her history, London consisted solely of the City of London, Westminster and Southwark; places that we think of as part of London today were, before the mid-eighteenth century, technically separate towns and villages. At the end of each tour, you will be catapulted back into the here and now via an epilogue, in which we will look for echoes of the past in the present.

Don't worry about money or clothes. When you are parachuted into each new world, take a look at yourself in the nearest glass or mirror, and you'll see that you're dressed in period fashion, so will melt seamlessly into the city – unless you do something stupid, that is. And you will find that you always have sufficient money for your stay in your pouch – sufficient, mind, not infinite.

Though fantastically exciting in its own right, remember there is a philosophical dimension to time travel too. By visiting alien worlds, we can hold up a mirror to the nature of our own society: how we live, interact, what we believe, what we aspire to, how we build and rebuild our cities. Perhaps you will come away from this experience wondering what a future time traveller would make of modern London if he or she were to travel back from a distant and opaque future.

Reel in your inhibitions, buckle up and get ready.

It's going to be quite a ride.

1603
A Whirlwind Tour of
Shakespearean London

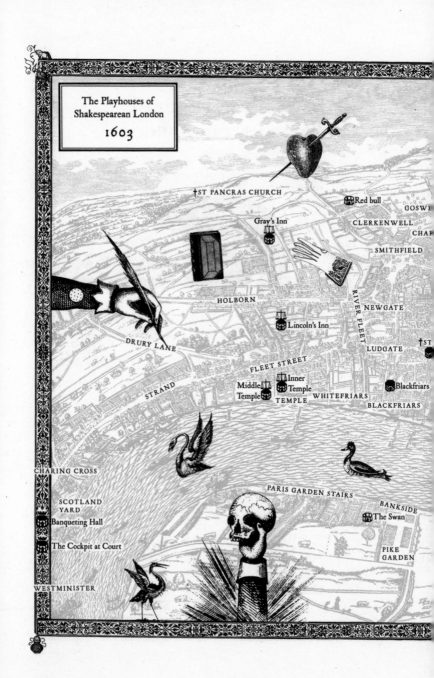

The Playhouses of
Shakespearean London
1603

†ST PANCRAS CHURCH

Red bull

GOSWE

Gray's Inn

CLERKENWELL

CHAR

SMITHFIELD

HOLBORN

RIVER FLEET

NEWGATE

Lincoln's Inn

LUDGATE

†ST

DRURY LANE

FLEET STREET

Middle
Temple

Inner
Temple

Blackfriars

STRAND

TEMPLE

WHITEFRIARS

BLACKFRIARS

PARIS GARDEN STAIRS

CHARING CROSS

BANKSIDE

SCOTLAND
YARD

The Swan

Banqueting Hall

PIKE
GARDEN

The Cockpit at Court

WESTMINISTER

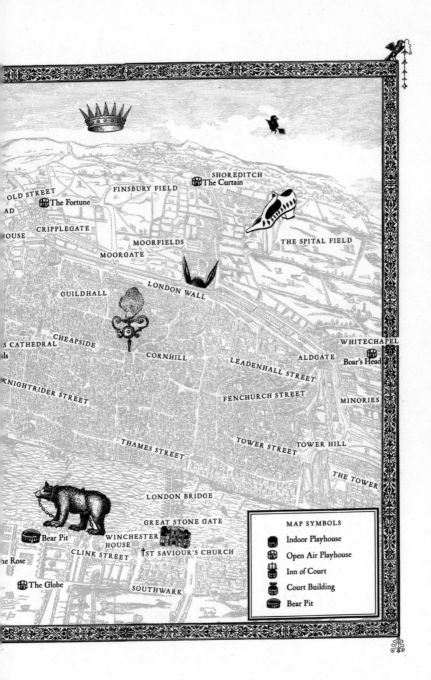

OLD STREET

The Fortune

CRIPPLEGATE

HOUSE

FINSBURY FIELD

SHOREDITCH
The Curtain

MOORFIELDS

MOORGATE

THE SPITAL FIELD

LONDON WALL

GUILDHALL

CHEAPSIDE

S CATHEDRAL
ls

CORNHILL

WHITECHAPEL

LEADENHALL STREET

ALDGATE

Boar's Head

KNIGHTRIDER STREET

FENCHURCH STREET

MINORIES

THAMES STREET

TOWER STREET

TOWER HILL

THE TOWER

LONDON BRIDGE

Bear Pit

GREAT STONE GATE

WINCHESTER
HOUSE

CLINK STREET

ST SAVIOUR'S CHURCH

e Rose

The Globe

SOUTHWARK

MAP SYMBOLS

Indoor Playhouse

Open Air Playhouse

Inn of Court

Court Building

Bear Pit

On a fresh spring evening, there's nowhere better to go for a walk and soak up the city than the South Bank. Walking towards Southwark Bridge, you'll find languid lovers draped over benches, the city glittering across the water, and the resurrected Globe playhouse on your right. Despite the best efforts of historians, archaeologists and architects it still looks fake, almost computer-generated. As you dodge choleric cyclists and thickets of drunken men, you pass a narrow cobbled alleyway leading away from the promenade. If you weren't seeking it out, the chances are you would miss it. But this evening, you *are*. A strange prowling motion in the shadows has caught your eye.

As you veer into the alleyway, the bustle of the pedestrians, the lapping of the Thames and the wails of buskers on the South Bank retreat into the distance. Ahead of you there are no pigeons, no cars, no people. In the twilight, the flick-flick-flickering of street lamps is the only sign of life. You look back. Up high, towards the promenade, there is a new-looking street sign, with black and red block capitals on a crisp white background. It reads: BEAR GARDENS.

Just then the calm is pierced by offensively out-of-tune bagpipes accompanied by an ungodly shrieking coming from the end of the alleyway. You whisk round to make out the unmistakable silhouette of a bear being dragged past, a rope around his neck. Clinging on for dear life to his back is a frenzied baboon, who is treading a fine line between being bitten by the bear and shrugged off into the street. The creatures are followed by a ruddy-faced man playing a set of bagpipes that appears to be growing out of his bushy beard. The endless warehouse-style blocks of the city have dissolved into bushy trees, green fields, ditches and a ribbon of sprawling timber-framed houses over-looking the Thames. The air hangs heavy with the noxious fumes of tanneries and is lacerated by the growls of animals and the hopeful cries of prostitutes.

Welcome to Shakespearean Southwark.

'Go, dog! Go, bear!'

Southwark, which formerly lay outside the jurisdiction of the City of London, has traditionally been a whirl of pleasure and leisure, a cornucopia of indulgent activity. Look out for the prostitutes – they can be identified by their long gowns, peri-wigs and starched blue ruffs, giving them something of a ghostly presence as they walk the streets or stand outside ale-house on the game. Elsewhere this afternoon you will see citizens dancing jigs in taverns, munching sweetmeats, drinking themselves into oblivion, firing arrows at heads carved into tree stumps, and you might hear them unleashing their pent-up sexual urges in the Bankside stews. And why not? For most people the Bankside provides succour from the thankless and, for many, hellish grind of the working week and it is no won-der that they intend to live life to the full, whatever the Puritans have to say about spending one's time in a more pious and pro-ductive manner.

One of Londoners' favourite pastimes – in fact the city's earliest surviving organized spectator sport – is an outlandishly cruel instance of contrived torment known as bull and bear baiting. Going to the bull and bear-baiting arena in this world is akin to going to watch a football match or see a film in the twenty-first century – but much more violent.

As you trudge your way along the muddy path, the foul cries of the watermen rising in the air behind you, a large amphitheatre comes into view. It looks like a rickety timbered caricature of the Roman Colosseum. A series of small flags fly from the overhanging roof, indicating that a baiting match is in progress. Before you reach the entrance, though, you have to navigate across a shit-strewn field oozing with festering offal from Newgate Shambles – dinner for the hundred or so mastiff dogs leaping from their kennels around the edge of the enclosure; you'll be thankful they're on leashes as they snarl and bark at you. At the north-west corner of the field you'll notice two bigger, sturdier sheds, barricaded shut. A deep snoring comes from within; the sheds seem to rattle and quake to its rhythm. This is where the bulls and bears are kept.

You join a long queue. From what you can gather from the chattering spectators, the mourning period for the late Queen Elizabeth has just been lifted, which is why the playhouses and bear pits have reopened. But the new king, James Stuart, has delayed his entrance into his capital city owing to anxieties about the return of the plague. The year, then, must be 1603. And from the fresh, warm air, it feels like spring.

As you reach the entrance, a distraught blood-spattered man rushes out cradling a yelping, dying mess of a thing, tears streaming down his face as his dear dog (and occasional source of income) lies dying in his arms.

Go in.

It is the noise that hits you first. The bellowing, bawling, screaming and shouting of frenzied spectators is ear-splitting, and you can understand why 'bear garden' has entered the English language as an idiom for a place of riotous disorder. The capacity of the amphitheatre is around a thousand and you see most of these spectators standing around the ring. A thatched roof protects you from the elements. A standing ticket costs a penny but for 2d you have the privilege of a seat in one of the galleries, up to three tiers high – although looking at the rotting wooden scaffolds creaking under the weight of so many people you may well wonder how much of a privilege this actually is. Nonetheless, if you don't fancy rubbing shoulders with pickpockets and reeking fishmongers you'd be well advised to clamber your way up the ladder and settle down next to some more genteel customers – the blood sports are of enormous appeal to all sections of society, men and women alike – whom you'll find drinking bottled ale and spitting out apple pips in the stalls.

From this excellent if wobbly vantage point you can see, in the centre of the ring, a magnificent bull pawing the sand, scanning the area for predators. His collar is chained to an iron stake deeply planted in the ground about fifteen feet away, limiting his room for manoeuvre. The tips of his gleaming white horns are splattered with blood. Around the perimeter of the ring are a number of men with mastiff dogs, holding them by the collar and psyching them up with blood-baying incitements. Suddenly, three dogs are released from their masters' grip; the game is on! The crowd comes alive: now 'Dog!' now 'Bull!' as they cheer for each side. Many spectators have money riding on the outcome of the fight.

What happens next is colourfully documented by tourists. 'The bull circulates to watch his enemy,' observes one such. '[The] dog, if right, will creep upon his belly that he may, if possible, get the bull by the nose; which the bull as carefully strives to defend by laying it close to the ground, where his horns are also ready to do what in them lies to toss the dog; and this is the true sport.' And tossed the dogs will be, high through the air like pancakes: 'He made short work of them,' observed a German tourist after watching a young bull hold his ground against three mastiffs, 'goring them and tossing them high in the air above the height of the first storey.' 'And when they are tossed,' writes another observer, 'the men above strive to catch them on their shoulders.'

If this sounds implausible, we have the testimonies of two of the most credible seventeenth-century diarists to fall back upon. 'And after dinner with my wife and Mercer to the Bear Garden,' writes Samuel Pepys in 1666, 'and saw some good sport of the bull's tossing of the dogs – one into the very boxes.' Visiting four years later, the diarist John Evelyn is astonished to see one of the bulls toss 'a dog full into a lady's lap as she sat in one of the boxes at considerable height from the arena' (her response is not noted). With this in mind, you might want to see if you can catch any flying dogs – you'll be sure to get a cheer from the crowd.

Not for nothing is the English mastiff considered the perfect London guard dog, renowned for its nobility, courage, savagery and strength. That said, expect the bull to make mincemeat of his valiant opponents who, inured to their fate, will continue to hurl themselves towards certain death like lemmings. Amidst the pandemonium, you'll see many dogs perish in agony – to the cries and lamentations of those spectators who have placed bets on them – only to be immediately replaced by fresh dogs. Note the presence of men with long poles rushing around trying to break the dogs' fall, their tips being covered in thick leather to prevent the dog being skewered. Beyond tossing them, the bull has several other strategies at his disposal: he might gore the dogs or simply 'stamp their guts out'. For its part, the dog usually tries to attack the bull's head – according to Horatio Busino, chaplain and private secretary to the Venetian ambassador, the most audacious move for a dog to make is to seize the bull's lip, followed by the eyebrows, then the ear. The move that will delight the crowd most, though, is for the dog to 'hold the bull by the nose till he roars, which a courageous bull scorns to do'; dogs are known to have their teeth ripped out as the bull swings them around with all his might.

After fighting off several volleys of dogs, the bull will be led out of the arena. You will barely have time to gather your thoughts before a grizzly bear, no less, is led in and shackled to the same stake. Round two. Attending a bear baiting in 1575, the mercer Robert Laneham describes 'the bear, with his pink eyes leering after his enemies' approach' and 'the nimbleness and wait of the dog to take his advantage'. The dog would fling himself at the bear and try to sink his teeth into its thick pelt. But the enraged bear, 'with biting, with clawing, with roaring, tossing, and tumbling', would do everything in his power to shake off his canine aggressor. Fearlessly, the mastiffs would come back for more, thus revealing, for Swiss medical student Thomas Platter in 1599 and for many others, their 'excellent and fine temper'.

The owners of the dogs, for their part, are keen for them to survive the experience, so if they think their hounds are in mortal danger, they rush forwards and prise open their muzzles with long sticks to which a broad iron piece is attached – though they don't want to get too close to the bear, of course. Being attacked on multiple fronts, the easiest move for the bear is to lacerate the dog with its sharp teeth and claws but, as Platter notes, the bears tend to have their teeth broken short to prolong the sport. The bear's only real option, then, is 'to hug the dogs with their paws so tightly, that, unless the masters come to assist them, they would be strangled by such embraces'. From the gallery, you'd almost be forgiven for mistaking this for a cuddle – until you see the dog's lifeless body slump to the ground and the bear shaking his head in victory, his muzzle smeared in slobber and blood. To spice things up, once the young, virile bear has fended off a decent number of dogs he will be carted off and replaced by an old blind bear tied to a stake and whipped without mercy by five or six men standing in a circle. In 1554 one such bear had the last laugh: breaking free from his stake, he dived into the crowd and bit off a man's leg.

By the time the blind bear is cowering under a storm of lashes, you'll probably be pretty disgusted with the whole affair. But unless you want to draw attention to yourself as an outsider – not a good idea in Shakespeare's London – you'll keep mum and sit still, perhaps even laugh, clap and cheer like all the other spectators. That's right, do not expect anyone to show these enslaved creatures the slightest flicker of compassion; as far as the audience goes, they are all – blinded bears included – perfectly legitimate fodder for your entertainment. The humanist intellectual Erasmus, writing at the beginning of the sixteenth century, couldn't muster any words of disapproval and the Venetian merchant Alessandro Magno considers the baiting 'a fine sight'; for him, the more dead dogs the better. In 1583 the Privy Council itself called bull and bear baiting 'a sweet and comfortable recreation fitted for the solace and comfort of a peaceable people'.

Some, admittedly, worried that the bull- and bear-baiting arenas were breeding grounds for plague and prostitution, and of course the Puritans hated any profanation of the Sabbath. But the only significant criticism on grounds of cruelty and animal welfare comes from the fire-and-brimstone Puritan polemicist Philip Stubbes, who seamlessly absorbs animal baiting into his litany of 'devilish pastimes' that made Londoners so ungodly. 'What Christian heart,' he laments, 'can take pleasure to see one poor beast to rent, tear and kill another, and all for his foolish pleasure?' If you abuse someone else's dog, he conjectures, then its owner will consider it an attack on their person and retaliate; attacking God's creatures, by the same logic, is asking for trouble. But there isn't the faintest shred of evidence that anyone actually heeded his words and by the 1580s, bull and bear baiting was entrenched as London's most popular spectator sport.

However has this come to pass? Some form of animal baiting has been taking place in London since at least the twelfth century. Initially, these baits took place in the open fields but specific references to a Bankside arena appear from the 1540s in official documents and ambassadorial reports. Baiting enthusiasts dead and alive can count Queen Mary, Queen Elizabeth and King James amongst their number, further legitimizing the sport. There is even an official Master of the Bears with the authority to press the dogs of London into service for the entertainment of royalty, even against the wishes of their owners. Two bird's-eye-view maps of London published in the 1560s and 1570s reveal two purpose-built Bankside arenas due east of Paris Gardens in the Liberty of the Clink: the westerly one for bull baiting, the easterly for bear baiting, surrounded by kennels and ponds.

In 1583, however, disaster struck. In one of the arenas the rotten scaffolds collapsed mid-game, killing eight spectators and maiming many more. Seeing the hand of his Maker, Puritan Philip Stubbes savoured every last detail, writing of 'a most wonderful and fearful confusion' in which 'some had their brains dashed out, some their heads all to squashed . . . so that you should have heard a woeful cry even piercing the skies . . . marvellous to behold'. But Londoners took no notice of this apparent warning and the structure was promptly rebuilt and fortified; in 1599 Queen Elizabeth herself paid a visit to the very spot in which you now find yourself (she never bothered to visit the Globe).

What has made such a ferocious sport so popular? In an age with no sense of animal welfare – it will be ninety years before the philosopher John Locke suggests that animals have feelings and casual cruelty towards them is self-debasing – the sport, with its flying dogs and noble bulls, serves as a visually arresting mini-drama of courage and sacrifice. The fiercest and most valiant beasts emerged as London celebrities. Sackerson the bear caught Shakespeare's attention and is mentioned in *The Merry Wives of Windsor*; other bear-celebrities are Harry Hunks, George Stone, Tom of Lincoln, Ned of Canterbury, Don Jon and Blind Robin. Some exceptionally resilient bulls have also become famous; the Star of the West, for example, who lost his horn and will never fight again.

There are more prosaic reasons too: Londoners believe that baited bulls make for tastier and more digestible beef; any butcher discovered selling unbaited beef is in fact liable to pay a fine. In a city of increasing sophistication with ruff starchers, playhouses and a booming book trade, bull and bear baiting is a powerful reminder of the trenchant brutality and hot-bloodedness of the age. A London audience will quite happily watch a philosophically searching play such as *Hamlet* one afternoon, then the carnage at the Bear Gardens the next; indeed, the goriness of so many of Shakespeare's plays is informed by the long-standing tradition of watching blood sports. Sometimes the two traditions collide – the reeking Hope Theatre, which will open in 1614 near the Globe, will be host to both plays and bear baiting, and Act III of Shakespeare's *The Winter's Tale* contains the immortal stage direction 'Exit, pursued by a bear' – though this may wisely have been an actor in a costume.

There's one treat left. In the words of the Spanish ambassador, who in 1544 found the whole scene highly amusing: 'A pony is baited, with a monkey on its back, defending itself against the dogs by kicking them.' In 1562 Alessandro Magno watched in glee as 'the horse run[s], kicking and biting, and the monkey grip[s] the saddle tightly and scream[s], many times being bitten'. Usually this ends with the dogs dangling from the ears and neck of the dying pony. Magno thinks it 'a very fine sight to see' and so did the audience around him. For added drama, lit squibs are tied to the monkey; he shrieks as they fizzle and explode.

When you walk back across the field look out for other famous bears frolicking in the ponds, clambering up trees and basking in the sunshine on purpose-built scaffolds, resigned to their fate.

Shakespearean London will harrow you with fear and wonder – and that's before you've seen the ghost of Hamlet's father at the Globe. For the metaphysical poet John Donne, the city is 'a place full of danger and vanity and vice' yet for others, such as the Swiss medical student Thomas Platter, it's 'brimful of curiosities', 'so superior to other English towns that London is not said to be in England, but rather England to be in London', anticipating James I's remark that 'soon London will be all England'. The population of the City wards has reached approximately 140,000 and the growing suburbs (including Southwark and Westminster), 40,000 [by 1600], though the combined total could be closer to 200,000. London is now one of Europe's five most populous cities, a far cry from the days around 1400 when it was smaller in population than Florence and Prague. Since the rate of burials outstrips births, London sucks in around 5,000 migrants a year. Many of these newcomers hope to follow in the fabled footsteps of Dick Whittington and become rich, but in reality London is a ruggedly unequal society with pockets of glittering wealth sitting cheek-by-jowl with grinding poverty.

'Looking one way you see a beautiful virgin,' writes one observer in 1612, 'another way, some deformed monster' and the metaphor resonates through every last street, alley, wharf and gibbet of this vast and sprawling metropolis. You'll see beauty – palaces of glass glistening in the sunlight, ladies in spectacular jewel-laden ruffs peering out of coaches, their chalk-white faces dotted with ornamental patches in the shape of suns, stars and moons; the towers and spires of over a hundred churches rising into London's skies. But prepare yourself, too, for prisoners' jaundiced fingers, emaciated to the bone, wriggling out of grilles in the street begging for alms without which they will perish; men in the pillory with their ears sliced off or noses slit; sexual miscreants kneeling barefooted in the pouring rain in the marketplace wearing a paper hat saying 'fornicator'; a camel going about his day's business on London Bridge; a dozen liverymen removing their caps every time their master's horse stops to urinate in the street; and endless stray swine rummaging through mounds of rubbish, oinking.

However much you feel like an imposter don't, whatever you do, give anyone cause to suspect that you are one. 'Foreigners are ill regarded not to say detested in London,' cautions Horatio Busino in his travel journal, describing how one hapless Spaniard once incurred the wrath of a resourceful swivel-eyed woman. 'She urged the crowd to mob him, setting the example by assaulting him herself with a cabbage stalk and calling him a Spanish rogue.' In no time at all, the mob swarmed around, and the Spaniard found himself 'foully smeared with a sort of soft and very stinking mud, which abounds here at all seasons, so that the place better deserves to be called Lorda [Italian for filthy] than Londra'. The xenophobic zeal of the London mob was never in question – 'had not the man saved himself in a shop, they would assuredly have torn his eyes out'. It could almost have been a scene from *Monty Python and the Holy Grail*. But a number of other foreigners leave similarly harrowing – if less tragicomic – accounts of confrontations with an insular

London multitude who 'believe the world beyond England is boarded off,' as Thomas Platter puts it, 'and that no nation can compare with England for virtue and comeliness'.

A few further things to bear in mind – you should find a plenteous supply of currency in your purse but if you fall prey to a pickpocket or cutpurse in the crowd don't even think about robbing in turn. As many foreigners observe, the justice system is severe and retributive. Don't expect a jot of New Testament mercy: 'The slightest theft is punished with death,' observes a Venetian visitor. 'A few months ago a lad was seen on his way to the gallows merely for having stolen a bag of currants.' Finally, kissing. The English love to kiss. If you are charming enough to be invited into a house for dinner, remember first to kiss all the women on the lips – or you'll be considered 'badly brought up'. Then, during the meal, 'it is the custom to slap men on the shoulders and cry out "frolic!" . . . and to pat women on the belly' (at least it is according to Alessandro Magno).

With that, it's time for our second stop: St Paul's Church-yard. Walk along Bankside to Paris Garden stairs and hail one of London's two thousand or so water ferries. Your destination is Whitefriars Stairs on the north bank.

Glancing westwards to Westminster, see the stretch of riverside palaces along the Strand, including Arundel House, Somerset House, Durham House and, of course, almost directly to your left, Whitehall Palace, home to the royal court. Many of these were originally home to medieval bishops and archbishops but, following the Protestant Reformation in the mid-Tudor period, are now in the hands of peers. The Crown's seizure of monastic land and wealth was the second biggest land grab in English history (after the Norman Conquest), stimulating a property boom and the rise of a new breed of aristocratic landlord as property was dished out to royal cronies, further fuelling the expansion of London's population. Of the twenty-three religious houses within the city before the Reformation, the vast majority have been sold off, although those that performed crucial social functions – like the lunatic asylum St Mary of Bethlehem (later known as Bedlam) outside Bishopsgate and St Bartholomew's Hospital in Smithfield – were saved. When you alight at Whitefriars Stairs, you are about to set foot in a city where the Church is no longer 'the single most disciplined and authoritative director of the city's affairs'.

Books and brimstone at Paul's Cross

Clamber onto the bank of the river, make your way up Water Lane, and head east, over Fleet Bridge. When you reach the crumbling Roman walls at Ludgate, the watchmen, all being well, will beckon you into the city. Soon you'll feel the presence of St Paul's Cathedral (a far cry from Sir Christopher Wren's successor with which you are doubtless familiar) weighing down upon you in all its Gothic splendour – almost all: it looks a little shorn of its majesty since a lightning strike in 1561 burned down the spire (no one has bothered to rebuild it).

Cross the busy, wagon-strewn junction of Ave Maria Lane and Creed Lane and make your way under a tight crenellated archway. You'll emerge into the wide open space of Paul's Churchyard, gulls swirling above the Cathedral's turrets. To your right is Peter's College, a former monastic property now occupied by the ever more powerful Stationers' Company. The publication of the Gutenberg Bible in Germany in the 1450s sent shockwaves through Europe and in the last fifty years, the printer's movable type has eclipsed the scribe's aching hand in the production of books; though scribal books are not yet extinct, the Stationers have effectively become a printers' guild.

The first man in England fully to realize the commercial and communicative potential of print was a shrewd alien called Wynkyn de Worde, who had been the apprentice of William Caxton, the first Englishman to print books, in the late fifteenth century; 'Worde' is a suspiciously opportune corruption of either Wörth am Rhein or Woerth-sur-Sauer, one of which was presumably Wynkyn's hometown near the Rhine. Following the death of his master, Wynkyn set up a printing shop in one of his houses in St Bride's Churchyard off Fleet Street, around 1500. He chose his shop sign carefully, a wiry sun, establishing what would prove a long-standing tradition equating the printed word with the enlightenment of the public (we still have it in the twenty-first century – *Sun* and *Star* are found in newspaper titles the world over). A lover of seductive title pages and loud woodcuts, not to mention the first man to use italics in the English language, Wynkyn believed in targeting a much broader readership than the more conservative Caxton – hence his decision to operate from Fleet Street, a whirl of commerce, rather than the more aristocratic Westminster.

It paid off. On Wynkyn's watch print became useful, accessible and fun (and more affordable); no longer were books just a vehicle for obsequious poems dedicated to noble patrons or arid theological debates. In the dark, cramped surroundings of his house, Wynkyn and his apprentices thumped, squelched and hammered out over 400 different titles – and double the number of editions – in a wobbly Gothic font (this was deliberate: in the early years of print, stationers wanted their typeface to resemble handwriting as closely as possible to give things a reassuringly familiar feel). His lists were diverse, spanning Chaucer, children's books, horror, recipes for horse medicines, books on etiquette, little encyclopaedias of gods and goddesses and even *The Horse, the Sheep and the Goose* (a smash hit). Mistakes, of course, crept in. Entire pages were skipped at crucial junctures, derailing plots and baffling readers. Illustrations could be woefully inappropriate for the subject matter; struggling to produce a woodcut of beautiful Greek goddesses, Wynkyn just went with an existing one from one of Caxton's editions of *The Canterbury Tales*, in which the women look anything but divine and ethereal. But in spite of these infelicities, Wynkyn's business flourished and he inspired a dozen or so printers to follow in his footsteps for which, some time later, he was posthumously christened the Father of Fleet Street.

By the time of your jaunt through Shakespearean London, the publishing trade has enjoyed over 125 years of continual growth and the Stationers' Company on your right now holds a monopoly on printing. Each new publication – and there will be 259 this year, including two of Shakespeare's masterpieces, *Hamlet* and *Richard III* – has to be approved and entered into the Stationers' Register. Anything considered offensive or disrespectful to Church or state is likely to be rejected. If anyone is foolish enough to publish something illegally, without the approval of the company – and a surprising number of people are – the author and printer, if caught, can expect the Bishop of London or even the Archbishop of Canterbury to come down on them like a ton of bricks. Printing can be a dangerous game. Twenty-eight years from now, the notorious 'Wicked Bible' with the seventh commandment misprinted as 'thou shalt commit adultery' will land the two royal printers with a ruinous £300 fine imposed by Star Chamber, the highest legal court in the land, and the loss of their printing licence (the Wicked Bible also includes the gem 'the Lord our God hath shewed us his glory and his great asse', misprinting 'greatness', from Deuteronomy).

But where are all these books actually sold? To find out, veer left under one of the churchyard's few trees and make for

Pardon Churchyard beyond the Bishop of London's palace. You'll find yourself in Paul's Cross, an open-air preaching ground to the north-east of the cathedral with stairs leading up to a low-walled pulpit with an octagonal roof surmounted by a big golden cross which gleams in the sunlight. This is one of the most public places in London. It is here that banned books are burned and, each Sunday morning, preachers who have been carefully vetted by the Bishop of London deliver al fresco sermons to large crowds. But mention Paul's Cross (or Paul's Churchyard) to an educated Londoner and chances are it won't be sermons that spring to mind. It will be books.

The whole vicinity is jam-packed with booksellers' shops and stalls; you can see them propped up against Dean's Wall, which marks the northern boundary of Paul's Churchyard, clustered around Old Change in the east and sprouting from the cathedral wall further west. The ground may be strewn with rotting apple cores and the ribcages of eaten birds, but nonetheless you're walking into a realm of knowledge and ideas, some of which will come to challenge the monopoly on truth so jealously guarded by the institution opposite. The shops are distinguishable by their fantastical signs, some evocative of the romances and dramas purveyed within. Against Dean's Wall you'll find the Brazen Serpent, Holy Ghost, Love and Death and Green Dragon, where *The Merchant of Venice* was on sale three years ago – and still might be. There is also the Black Bear, which will be one of the first places to sell an anthology of Shakespeare's comedies, histories and tragedies in 1632. Against the cathedral wall on the west of Paul's Cross, you have the Tiger's Head and the Fleur-de-lis, where *The Merry Wives of Windsor* has been stocked for the past three years. Over the wall on the southern side of Paternoster Row (which will emerge as a centre of bookselling in its own right in the seventeenth and eighteenth century) are the Mermaid and the

Golden Anchor. And the White Lion and White Horse, so ethereal sounding, ply their trade from Pissing Alley, which you'd do well to avoid on your way out.

Why here? For a start, tradition. Even before the eruption of print, clergymen had been amongst the most literate members of society. They had to understand the Bible in Latin, teach and preach, and as the record keepers of society register births, marriages and deaths in parish records. So stationers – parchminers (vendors of parchment to write on), paper sellers, scriveners, binders and limners (illustrators) – thrived around medieval St Paul's with its chantries (where prayers are said for the souls of the dead), monastic colleges and priest houses. And then there was the impact of Protestantism. After the dissolution of monastic property in the 1530s, much space in Paul's Churchyard was freed up and, given that it was already such an enclave of literacy, the stationers and booksellers came flooding in. But more fundamentally, the reformed faith emphasized the importance of understanding the Word of God rather than performing endless ritualistic good works and going to confession, as was native to the Catholic faith. This stimulated a huge public demand for bibles in the vernacular, which had a knock-on effect on literacy rates. Being able to read has taken on an existential importance.

As you leave St Paul's Churchyard, why not pause a while on a street corner, close your eyes and listen to the sounds of the city.

Church bells chime in the distance but you can also hear little jingling bells on harnesses closer by, warning pedestrians to make way for horses. In the road, you hear the clopping of hooves, a splash of puddle water and the screeching of an iron-shod wheel on freestone. Further up the street, a painted wooden sign creaks and groans in the wind and cheering and laughter waft from an open tavern window. Further down the street there are the 'ritualized cadences' of tradesmen, one singing 'Ripe chest-nuts ripe! Ripe chest-nuts ripe!' another 'Soop, chim-ney soop!' (promoting a chimney-sweeping service) and another 'Was-sail, was-sail, jolly was-sail!' And someone is playing the flute.

But although the city is ebullient and full of sound, you might be surprised by how much quieter Shakespearean London seems compared to modern cities. The loudest noises you are likely to hear are the pealing of church bells, clapping of thunder and, if you're unlucky enough to get caught up in a siege, which you won't be, cannon fire.

Without the continuous roar of automobile traffic, which drowns out lower-frequency sounds, your 'acoustic horizon' (as the literary historian Bruce Smith puts it) is broader, giving you more of a sense of space within which you can hear a wider range of sounds. Some are a good way off – like that shoemaker up the road tapping on leather in his open-fronted shop or the dull thud of a first-floor printing press behind you.

The most alien feature of the Shakespearean soundscape is just how clear and omnipresent are *voices*. Conversations taking place a hundred feet away may still be audible, as in modern cities with historic, traffic-free centres like Bologna. The city's physical fabric amplifies this phenomenon – wood, plaster and clay, from which most houses are built, are reflective surfaces (as is glass) and the tall, narrow and tightly packed arrangement of the houses is conducive to reverberation. As you move through the Shakespearean city, you'll find yourself suspended in up to half a dozen conversations at any given moment. The only way to ensure privacy is to lower your voice or whisper.

'The holy herb'

As you wind your way towards Cheapside, with St Paul's brooding behind you, don't be surprised by the throngs of people smoking. Horseback journeymen sitting in traffic jams, blades as they gad about, husbands and wives shopping, even little children chasing pigeons in the street – they're all puffing away.

'The English are constantly smoking the Nicotian weed, which in America is called Tobaca,' observed a German visitor in 1598. 'They always carry the instrument on them and they light up on all occasions,' wrote Thomas Platter the next year, 'at the play, in the taverns, or elsewhere . . . and it makes them riotous and merry and rather drowsy.' 'Even at night,' according to Busino, 'they keep the pipe and steel at their pillows and gratify their longings.' 'Nay, it is even stated,' writes an early-twentieth-century historian, 'that the very children in school took a pipe of tobacco instead of breakfast' – you might want to peep through the window of a grammar school tomorrow morning to verify this.

To meet this insatiable demand for the 'holy herb', you'll notice the streets of London are flooded with tobacco shops and tobacco houses, pretty alien-seeming to modern eyes, the closest point of reference perhaps being the shisha pipe dens of Edgware Road in the twenty-first century. In the first two decades of the seventeenth century, chroniclers and pamphleteers counted 7,000 such places, which, if that figure is reliable, utterly dwarfed the number of both alehouses and taverns. (The rounded figure is suspicious too; but in any case, read: a lot.)

Find one on Cheapside. It shouldn't take you long, just look out for the sign of the three pipes swaying in the wind. Inside you can expect to see dangling from a hook a drum-shaped rack with dozens of pipes sticking out. It looks a bit like a deformed disco ball. Help yourself to a pipe. On the walls are lopsided shelves of tankards, jugs, goblets and decanters of wine and ale – this is a drinking house too – and parcels of uncut tobacco for sale, mainly bought from the Spanish, who own plantations in South America (although there are some modest efforts to grow tobacco in Gloucestershire and Worcestershire). Tobacco vendors like to flaunt the exoticism of the new drug by displaying statues of befeathered American Indians, usually with implausibly jet-black skin, puffing giant pipes (or just twisted leaves). You might be surprised by some of the people queuing up to buy the herb – pregnant women, groaning men clutching their joints, scarred scrofula victims, melancholics with dreary, downcast eyes – all hoping to find some smoky succour. The main smoking area is curtained off behind the counter. From inside, you can hear the muffled sound of chortling, coughing, clinking, creaking and sighing. (If you are a female time traveller, this is as far as you can go without getting some very odd looks.)

As you whisk open the curtains, prepare to be lost in a world of smoke. Through watery eyes you'll make out a small row of respectable smokers (or tobacconists as they are known) in ruffs and floppy hats sitting behind a table propped up by bar-rels of tobacco. The customers should be friendly enough and might even shoot you a quick 'God save you, sir' as you take your seat on a spare stool. They'll be keen to show off their elaborate smoking paraphernalia: clay pipes with long and slen-der necks – the finest with mouthpieces of silver (a Winchester pipe was a mark of highest quality though most pipes were manufactured in Stepney, Southwark and Westminster) – maple blocks to shred the leaf, richly decorated tobacco cases, tongs for carrying the embers to the pipe, a gleaming pick for cleaning the head, not to mention silver porringers to receive gentrified spittle.

What you will find most striking, though, in an age when smoking is still a novelty, is the sheer wonder of your fellow tobacconists as they heave in the smoke, hold it for a good long while and then, in a state of rapture, blow it out through their nose along with 'plenty of phlegm and defluxion from the head', as a German observer put it in 1598 (we'd probably just say snot). Before you light up yourself, two things to bear in mind. Number one, unless you want to be identified as an alien, don't make any reference to 'smoking' tobacco – in this world, you 'drink' tobacco. Number two, even if you're a smoker, this stuff will be purer and quite possibly stronger than what you're used to, so prepare for one of the biggest head rushes of your life.

Thought to have been introduced into England from Florida by the merchant adventurer John Hawkins in 1565 and subsequently popularized at court by Queen Elizabeth's one-time favourite Sir Walter Raleigh, tobacco took a while to filter into the mainstream of society. It was only from the 1590s that people began to talk of a London tobacco craze (although at 3d a pipeful, it remains an extravagance for the working classes: building labourers earn only around 8d per day; building craftsmen, around a shilling, or 12d). This could never have happened without the vocal support of London's medical establishment, who, echoing the shamans of Mayan civilization and themselves hankering after an infallibly prophylactic herb, embraced tobacco, with tragic irony, as a miracle cure for just about every ailment and affliction they could dream up.

According to Anthony Chute's *Tabaco* (1595), the 'precious herb' is the perfect antidote for coughs, colds, headaches, fatigue, insomnia, festering wounds, scrofula, melancholy, ripped-off fingernails *and* poisoned cats. So useful. During outbreaks of plague, the dying are routinely informed that their symptoms have been brought on by not smoking enough, which must be cold comfort. Enthroned in the Mermaid Tavern on Friday Street, the greatest literary minds of the age follow suit, eulogizing the miraculous herb in their plays and poems. For Edmund Spenser it is 'divine tobacco'; for Ben Jonson, 'the most sovereign and precious weed that ever the earth tendered to the use of man'.

According to the Four Humours Theory, the classical medical theory to which virtually everyone subscribes, the 'hot and dry' qualities of tobacco counteract colds and other illnesses brought on by an excess of watery humours like rheumatism, which are particularly common in cold, dank countries like England. Furthermore, it's believed that inhaling the heat of tobacco works on the 'cold and moist' humours of the brain, kindling a deft and lyrical wit, allowing smokers to unlock their divinely apportioned creative faculties and bringing them closer to God (as the physician Roger Marbecke explained last year in his *Defence of Tobacco*). The Mermaid wits are thus the first generation of chain-smoking intellectuals.

Not everyone is convinced. For some, tobacco 'makes your breath stink like the piss of a fox'; the speaker, a character in Thomas Dekker's *The Honest Whore* (1604), is probably referring to the unsavoury practice of seasoning tobacco in urine to give it a 'sophisticated scent'. When he eventually arrives in London, the new king, James I, is absolutely horrified by the 'stinking and unsavoury vice', lamenting how 'a man cannot heartily welcome his friend now, but straight they must be in hand with tobacco'. Frothing with anger, he reaches for his quill, dips it in an inkwell of fury, then inveighs against the 'precious stinke' with all his sarcastic Scottish might in his *A Counterblaste to Tobacco* (1604), a strange mixture of rage, reason and patriotism. In it, the king argues that tobacco, a bewitching drug cultivated by 'barbarous . . . beastly . . . godless and slavish' Indians in the wilds of the New World, is invading smokers from within in an insidious process of reverse colonization. The weakening of the physical body, he goes on, will soon spill over into the weakening of the body politic, making England ripe for invasion (always a worry in this period). It is his responsibility, as king, to make sure that this doesn't happen.

This isn't just idle talk: following publication of this *Counterblaste* James increases the tax on tobacco by 4,000 per cent, which ultimately does very little except line the pockets of smugglers. Recognizing defeat and, grudgingly, the value of the tobacco from the new English colony in Virginia, James lowers the tax, controls his temper and lets things rest. This year, 25,000lb of tobacco are deposited at Customs House; in 1628, this skyrockets to 370,000lb; by 1700, 38 million. In the face of this rising tide, he capitulates. (James distinguishes himself as a monarch who declared war on tobacco and witches rather than actual countries.)

Back in the tobacco house, the customers pouring tar into their lungs may not be entirely unaware of the health risks. Suspicious of the claims of his fellow physicians, a freethinking London physician called Philaretes (presumably not his birth name) pens a pamphlet called *Work for Chimney Sweepers; or, a Warning against Tobacconists* (1602), which he hawks for maximum impact by the Great North Door of St Paul's Cathedral. Remarkably, many of the nefarious effects of tobacco smoking, as will be proven by modern science, are portended by Philaretes in 1602, even though his reasoning is mired in the fallacious Four Humours Theory. Somehow he correctly surmises, for instance, that tobacco hardens the arteries, stunts the growth of young people, brings on weight loss (considered a bad thing in the seventeenth century), is shot through with poisonous chemicals, contributes to infertility and damages the health of passive smokers. 'I am told the inside of one man's veins after death was found to be covered in soot just like a chimney,' writes Thomas Platter, the Swiss medical student visiting London in 1599, and five years later King James himself notes 'an unctuous and oily kind of soot' lining the insides of dissected smokers, implying at least a modicum of scientific inquiry into the nefarious effects of the herb.

By now, you're probably choked by the fumes of the 'nasty puffing-engines' and longing to visit somewhere fresher and sweeter smelling. How about taking a turn in Drapers' Hall Gardens, one of the liveliest and most lavish of any of London's inner-city gardens. It even has a maze.

Bees, bowling and a turn in the maze

Cheapside is one of the widest and grandest streets in London. To the east of the ornate Cheapside Cross, one of the twelve crosses erected by Edward I to mark the resting places of his queen's body on its journey to Westminster, you'll find Goldsmith's Row. Here 'inexpressibly great treasures and vast amounts of money may be seen'. Horatio Busino lodged with a goldsmith's family on Cheapside and, for him, this was by far the finest part of the city: 'the houses have many storeys and all the fronts are glazed so that the windows fill the entire space'. Glass – so often described as beautiful in this era – was formerly used mainly as stained glass in churches and cathedrals; it has been widely available only since the 1570s and is now a powerful status symbol. Many poorer and colder dwellings still use greased paper or cloth behind a lattice to let in light but in Crutched Friars, to the north of the Tower, there is a fantastic gargoyle-and-glass mansion: apart from the decorated timber beams, it is made entirely from glass, mesmerizing passers-by.

If you need to cross the road to admire anything, look out for private coaches. When these richly decorated vehicles first appeared in the 1560s, Londoners were suspicious, viewing them as effete and alien; some men would even trail their wife's coach on horseback. But by now they have been accepted as an intrinsic feature of urban transport and an assertion of superiority for wealthy families. Though the rambling, shoddily paved (if paved at all) and rubbish-strewn streets are hardly suitable for these conveyances, their numbers are proliferating. 'The world runs on wheels with many whose parents were glad to go on foot,' wrote the London topographer and antiquarian John Stow in 1598, and in a couple of years, Thomas Dekker will note the thundering of coaches on every street corner. Passengers are likely to be rattled out of their skull though.

Keep walking down Cheapside. Look out for the Great Conduit ahead, a battlemented stone structure with taps on the lower walls, channelling spring water from the River Tyburn through lead and timber pipes. Some water-bearers have laid down large tubs – or 'tankards' – in the middle of the street, which are doing a fine job of obstructing the traffic. Take the last turning on the left before the Conduit, onto Ironmonger Lane.

The population of the ancient walled city (as opposed to the City wards) has swelled to proportions that no one could have envisioned in the Middle Ages, now approaching something in the order of 100,000 residents compared to the 20,000 or so in Chaucer's time. You'll soon discover just how keen Londoners are to protect their gardens from the beady eyes of property developers. Green-fingered statesman and philosopher Sir Francis Bacon speaks for many Londoners when he writes,

'God Almighty first planted a garden. And indeed it is the purest of human pleasures. It is the greatest refreshment to the spirits of man; without which, buildings and palaces are but gross handyworks'. The more the city grows, the more urgent the need for gardens as no one can hope to keep their wits about them in the fast-paced urban world without frequent recourse to nature. Some gardens, such as those attached to the Inns of Court, Whitehall Palace and the riverside mansions of the Strand, are elaborate and grandiose; others are mournful relics of state-sponsored pillage with weeds thickening where churchyards and cloisters once stood; yet others are domestic herbal gardens for culinary and medicinal use tucked away behind unprepossessing frontages.

Fork right down Cateaton Street. You'll pass the boisterous Windmill tavern on your right and then, further down, Grocers' Hall. Look out for an unusual coat of arms with three clouds, each wearing golden crowns, radiating sunbeams in a blue sky – a cryptic reference to the Virgin Mary.

Stop.

You should be standing outside a three-storey brick building with three oriel windows bulging above a large gateway. There's an imperiousness to it; this was formerly the townhouse (or rather complex – it had over fifty rooms) of Henry VIII's Lord Chancellor, the deadly and Machiavellian Thomas Cromwell. The estate, which sprawls into the dissolved monastery of Austin Friars next door, was bought by the prosperous Drapers' Company in 1543, an ideal location right behind the Royal Exchange, the centre of commerce in London. There is a series of interconnected gardens, much developed by Cromwell and irrigated by an ancient underground stream. Technically you have to be a member of the company to gain admission but actually it's pretty easy to sneak in; all the servants drying their masters' washing on the mini-hedges inside the garden are testament to that. I'm sure you'll have no trouble.

Walking down the long, dark passageway you'll hear cavorting and carousing coming from within the walled garden and as you emerge into the late afternoon light, the Great Garden will unfurl in all its Brueghelian wonder. In one corner, a giant beehive rumbles (should the bees cling to their hive, bad weather is on its way, or so people believe). In another, two master drapers curl bowls along a narrow, candlelit green. In the middle, a group of women climb up to a gallery where they will sip wine, munch sweetmeats and admire the garden. Ahead of you there are six large rectangular plots, bordered with tightly clipped privet hedges, five containing knot gardens and the sixth a maze. By the turf-covered benches, archers take turns to fire arrows at a popinjay – a sculpted parrot on top of a long stem (you can hear the ones that miss clattering off the garden wall).

The association of gardens with innocence and virtue certainly isn't lost on Bible-reading contemporaries, but much of the activity here is of a distinctly fallen nature. Young lovers canoodle, carving their initials into the bark of mulberry trees, and apprentices pour beer down their throats and mimic bawdy jigs they've seen at the playhouses. You might witness a fight break out when young men point blank refuse to yield to the masters of the company on the bowling green. Presiding over all this activity – or not, if an official complaint from the master drapers in 1607 about the visitors' disregard for rules is anything to go by – is a ruddy-faced gardener clutching the neck of a bulbous, pear-shaped pot made from clay and shot through with holes from which water sprays as he tramples over the flowerbeds. This is an early watering can, though 'showering can' might be a more appropriate term.

Were it not for the throngs of people, the garden's high

stone walls would give it an exclusive even hermetic air, echoing the garden's original identity as a space of religious contemplation. One need only glance at surviving manuscript illustrations to see that most medieval gardens – those attached to royal fortresses as well as monasteries – were intended to keep a dangerous and politically unstable world at bay; they depict figures lying down, eating fruit and relaxing, safe behind thick walls. But the sort of garden you're in today is more socially porous, transposing the kinds of interactions intrinsic to city life into a greener and more natural setting.

The shift came in 1485 with the conclusion of the Wars of the Roses and the accession of the Tudors, who brought relative political stability. Tudor England evolved from a land of fortresses and moats into one of palaces and mansions. This allowed gardening to blossom into a sophisticated art form influenced by the ideas of the Italian Renaissance. It may not be immediately obvious, but almost everything in this garden, in this work of art, is rich in symbolism and an ostentatious display of the status of its owners.

Take the knot gardens – the most conspicuous feature of the Great Garden. These consist of symmetrical square plots of evergreen 'hedge ribbons' of clipped yew, boxwood and privet interwoven in intricate patterns, filled in with coloured gravel and sand or with flowers of a particular colour and sweet-smelling herbs, which are cultivated for culinary and medicinal use. They are scythed through by straight paths, with a grand marble fountain at a central intersection. The circular, square and triangular hedge patterns are tightly knotted like the coils of a brain. The more intricate or 'enknotted' the garden, the more impressive, and at Hampton Court Palace you can find centaurs, nymphs and sirens woven into the beds. In the Drapers' Garden, as elsewhere, the whole effect is best appreciated from the aforementioned viewing gallery, where a small group can gaze down in satisfaction upon the landscape they have tamed. And that's what this is all about: man foisting order and symmetry upon the chaos and caprice of nature. 'So curious and cunning are our gardeners,' observed chronicler William Harrison in 1586, 'that they presume to do in manner what they list with nature, and moderate her course in things as if they were her superiors'. Even the range of exotic herbs and plants convey a message about England's growing colonial might, manifesting her mastery of the secrets of newly discovered lands.

And then there is the maze, a quintessential feature of any Elizabethan or Jacobean garden worth its salt, and an apt visual trope for the labyrinthine city. With hedges at knee height and the plot relatively compact, if you're accustomed to the thrill of getting lost in the giant maze at Hampton Court in the twenty-first century, walking the Drapers' maze in the early seventeenth can feel a little tame. But what it lacks in scale it more than makes up for in metaphor; the aim is to lose yourself not in physical space but in thought. It draws upon the earlier tradition of the painted floor labyrinth, a common sight in European cathedrals in the Middle Ages, in which worshippers would crawl on their hands and knees towards the 'salvation' of the centre in a kind of surrogate pilgrimage (they were also known as *chemins à Jerusalem*), the twists and turns representing the challenges and crises of faith encountered in the course of a typical Christian's spiritual journey. Unlike labyrinths, which originally followed one marked path, mazes offer any number of possible routes, only one of which brings success, thus introducing free will into the equation.

As you wind your way through the maze, you might find yourself contemplating the truths it conveys – how a single misstep or misturn can knock your entire life off course or how sometimes we need to distance ourselves from something before we can hope to understand or get close to it. These are powerfully evoked; as the twenty-first-century author Rebecca Solnit puts it, 'when you seem farthest from your destination is when you suddenly arrive is a very pat truth in words, but a profound one to find with your feet'.

An alien church

Over the wall of the garden, you'll be able to see the nave and tower of what was formerly the monastery of Austin Friars and is now the Dutch Church, the focal point of one of the largest groups of aliens in London. In 1603 a 'foreigner' is an out-of-towner or someone from a different part of the country whereas an 'alien' is someone from a different country altogether – and, the past being a different country, you fall into that category. We can say with conviction that there were over 7,000 such resident aliens in 1593 when a comprehensive 'Return of Strangers' was conducted by the alderman of each London ward; the figure ten years later is probably only marginally different, so aliens form around 3.5 per cent of London's population. (That the government wouldn't make any serious efforts to conduct a census of the native population for another 300 years shows how seriously the alien 'problem' is regarded.)

The authorities at Guildhall and Whitehall feel it is only right to shelter their Protestant brethren, even if they do hail from hostile or aggressive states (with the concomitant danger that they might actually be spies). They are allowed to worship freely at the Dutch Church and the French Church in nearby Threadneedle Street. The two strictly disciplined churches look after the welfare of their congregants, providing spiritual, financial and legal assistance. But London isn't exactly a blissful haven and they are subject to a welter of protectionist legislation. Alien shopkeepers, to take one example, are not allowed to have shopfronts opening onto the street; they must obscure their windows with lattices and work in the darkness or by candlelight. Aliens cannot join livery companies either. Even so, the mere presence of aliens sometimes fosters resentment amongst the population of London, particularly at times of economic distress. In the bleak and miserable years in the twilight of Queen Elizabeth's reign, when harvest after harvest failed, immigrants (including 'blackamoors') stood accused of undercutting wages and more.

'Rapists, Anabaptists, libertines, drunkards, common women and brothel keepers . . . murderers, thieves and conspirators' is how one government spymaster stereotypes immigrants in the 1570s, begging the Privy Council to allow him the resources to implement his own solution to 'the alien problem' (one that involved him becoming extremely rich). One very common bone of contention is that while aliens are quite happy to reap the benefits of English society, they give little back in return; they are, to borrow a phrase beloved of twenty-first-century tabloids, benefit scroungers. In the opinion of Sir Walter Raleigh, immigrants shouldn't be entitled to receive poor relief (the welfare system administered by each parish church in which wealthier householders are taxed to support the poor); these should rightly flow only to true-born Englishmen.

Not everyone is so cold-hearted. Acts of great generosity are not unknown – after the horrendous St Bartholomew's Day Massacre in Paris in 1572 and subsequent slaughter of thousands of provincial Protestants, mothers and babies included, the Bishop of London donated £320 to the French Church in Threadneedle Street. And certain incomers, usually the very wealthy or the very talented, do flourish in London society. Only the most xenophobic of Londoners are blind to the ways such aliens have enriched society and culture.

As you return to the dim passageway leading back to the

street, steal one last glance at the Great Garden, for if you return here in the twenty-first century you'll find it obliterated by a fourteen-storey office block (called Drapers' Gardens, Throgmorton Avenue) and the much-rebuilt Drapers' Hall inconspicuous in a world of grey office blocks.

Now, before the light dies, it's time to cross what has been described as one of the miracles of the world.

'That darksome street': London Bridge

Walk up Threadneedle Street then turn right onto Gracechurch Street, which becomes Great Fish Street. The fisherwomen are out in full force, balancing their shops on their heads, bellowing out their wares in their distinctive cadences. To your right, rising above a row of rickety timber-framed houses, is Fishmongers' Hall, the headquarters of fish since 1444. Not to be outdone by the other livery companies, at the annual Lord Mayor's Show the master fishmongers like to parade through the city in their finery with gigantic, horse-drawn effigies of salmon and sturgeon, a sight that wouldn't look out of place in a Hieronymus Bosch hellscape, and which must have haunted the dreams of many a child. Incidentally, if you have long hair, beware of people trying to lure you into dark alleys to chop it off. Since long, sweeping locks are in fashion, there is a booming black market for human hair, especially for brides-to-be.

As you walk past the ancient church of St Magnus the Martyr on your left you'll find yourself on an oppressively narrow and 'darksome' street flanked by tall townhouses – some of the grandest you've seen – all casement windows, pilasters and murals of the infant Jesus and Virgin Mary etched into the gables. The street, though, is unpleasant. You have to squeeze your way between the wooden counters protruding from each shopfront, where obstreperous apprentices hawk their wares – books, toys, stationery, jewellery, fancy hats, arrows and silk. Giving way to a flock of geese waddling up the street, you're forced to rub uncomfortably close to the frayed doublet of an unsavoury-looking man who is eyeing your money pouch. You're probably beginning to wonder where on earth this famous bridge has got to, then *bang* – there you are, on it – showered in daylight, fork-tailed red kites chasing sparrows above your head, water gushing beneath your feet. Looking back, you realize that you've already been on the bridge for a good five minutes or more. Spread against the sky is one of the most extraordinary sights you'll ever behold.

Tracing the contours of the northern bank westwards (upriver), you see the grand arches of St Paul's, the narrow turrets of Baynard's Castle, the vast riverside mansions of the Strand, the rambling complex of Whitehall, Westminster Hall, St Stephen's Chapel, the meeting place of the House of Commons, Westminster Abbey and, beyond them, hills. Downriver, the Tower looms under a powerful leaden sky, a stark reminder of royal authority in a city so proud of its independence. The Thames is dotted with wherries, barges and elegant swans (plucked once a year for the mattresses and pillows of the royal household and, according to one possibly gullible tourist, so tame you can feed them out of your hand – but don't try it).

Masted trading vessels and lighters snake in from the high seas towards Customs House and Billingsgate Fish Market, to the west of the Tower. The ships recede almost as far as the eye can see, to the wharves of St Katherine's and Wapping, past Ratcliffe, around the future Isle of Dogs, past Greenwich Palace, and beyond. With their thin masts, the ships look like a colony of spiders creeping towards the city. There is a furious current against which the boatmen upriver seem to be fighting a losing battle. Passengers cling to each other's arms as the river heaves their little defenceless ships towards the fast-flowing rapids under the silted-up archways where the water level drops a couple of feet; the Thames snakes and swirls about its piers as an intrepid boatman, showing off to his fellow wherrymen, prepares to 'shoot the rapids'. Let's hope he has his pig's bladder float on him, which can be inflated, if need be, by blowing into it; otherwise, he may well join the legion of folk who've perished under the arches of London Bridge.

Looking at the grey, opaque and deadly river, it takes a warm imagination indeed to translate it into the 'silver streaming Thames' of poetic lore, let alone the crystalline, impossibly turquoise oasis that would appear in the paintings of Giovanni Canaletto. It is, nonetheless, a powerful sight to behold, the lifeblood of London, her 'liquid history' as the politician-turned-historian John Burns described it in 1929. Notice how the houses on the north bank, their handsome timber beams plastered in by a grey wattle-and-daub (a far cry from the high-contrast black and white of 'restored' Tudor houses you may be familiar with from the twenty-first century) seem abruptly to give way to the watery chasm. From some houses, short ladders and stairs shoot straight into the water, allowing the inhabitants to clamber into small boats moored for private use. The Bankside opposite, presided over by St Saviour's church, looks like a cliff of mud.

And then there is the bridge itself: 900 feet long, made of stone, on a pier of nineteen arches protected from the full force of the river by twenty oval-shaped starlings (bulwarks shielding the bridge's piers from erosion and detritus) driven into the riverbed by piles. What will impress you the most, in all likelihood, is the hundred or so houses lining the street – a rag-tag bunch, barely two the same – making this a so-called city on a bridge as opposed to a mere crossing. It feels sturdy enough but looks a little precarious: timber beams shoot out from the piers to prop up ground-floor storeys bulging out over the river like peascod bellies. With its clumsy elevations, cleaved-on extensions and motley assemblage of towers, cupolas and chimneys, the street is a hotchpotch of architectural styles and colours, a palimpsest of changing fashions and, frankly, a mess. But a glorious one, a fitting microcosm of the two places it straddles – Southwark and the City of London. It even has its own north/south divide – you'll find bookshops and milliners near the City end but more odorous pursuits like tanning, dying and twining towards the Southwark end.

Along most of the bridge, the upper storeys of the houses are gabled, kissing above the street, forming a high, dark tunnel. Yet the overall impression is one of grandeur, of 'quite splendid, handsome, and well-built houses, occupied by merchants of some consequence', as the Duke of Württemberg put it in 1592 – a sort of Shakespearean Bond Street, to borrow the words of Bill Bryson. Sneak a peak over the iron railings – the starlings look like waffles with their crisscross beams. The arches, you'll see, are far from evenly spaced; Renaissance painters had far more regard for symmetry than did medieval builders working under lethal conditions.

As you plough through the next section of the cavern-like street, voices ricocheting from the walls in a brouhaha of commerce, see if you can find a grocer's warehouse that smells of cheese. It's towards the end, on a starling that is fatter and longer than the others. This was once an octagonal chapel dedicated to St Thomas à Becket, the 'turbulent' archbishop of Canterbury who was infamously slaughtered in 1170 after King Henry II insinuated he wanted rid of him. Becket had been baptized at the church of St Mary Colechurch in Cheapside, where, in 1176, an ambitious priest with a flair for architecture named Peter de Colechurch worked. At the time, there was a rickety wooden bridge across the Thames, the latest

43

incarnation of something that always seemed to collapse, burn or be ripped down before too long. Quite possibly inspired by a new stone bridge across the River Lea, it was Peter who first pitched to the king the idea of doing something similar across the Thames.

A chapel to the freshly canonized Becket was integral to Colechurch's scheme, something that appealed to a now penitent king. What could be better! Pilgrims crossing the bridge on their way to Becket's shrine in Canterbury could drop in and pray for a safe deliverance – as could pious fishermen who'd tie up their boats each night and clamber into the chapel, dripping river water over the candles no doubt, to request divine assistance in navigating the icy, choppy waters. Yes, said the king, who was persuaded to impose a tax on wool to help fund the enterprise (whence the saying 'the bridge's foundations rest on woolpacks'). At Colechurch's insistence the Church also dug deep into its pockets but there was still a massive shortfall for the costs of construction and future maintenance, which was expected to be pretty hefty. So the developers hit upon the idea of packing the bridge with houses so the rents could, in the words of King John (1199–1216), 'be for ever appropriated to repair, maintain and uphold the same'. Bridge House, the administrative body, in fact ended up doing quite a lot more than this, growing into one of the biggest landowners in London, channelling its income from rents, tolls, taxes and bequests into a vast property empire. (It still exists over 800 years later, awarding £15 million annually to charitable projects across greater London.) Working without a cofferdam (a watertight enclosure drained of river water), fully exposed to the violent caprices of the river, in the end the bridge took thirty-three years to complete, with the loss of around 150 lives. Peter de Colechurch never saw his vision realized, dying four years before its completion; his remains were buried in the chapel.

Where is it now, the chapel? In the late 1530s Henry VIII, every bit the 'Humpty Dumpty of nightmare' of his final years, objected to the glorification of a man – saint or no saint – who'd so wantonly challenged royal authority back in the twelfth century. And so, history repeating itself, the poor priest was once more eliminated by an English king – this time from the collective, increasingly Protestant, consciousness. In 1543 the devotion of the chapel was suddenly transferred to the much less turbulent Virgin Mary; during the iconoclastic reign of Henry's son Edward VI, it was defaced and pillaged; by 1553 it was a shop; by 1603, the bland storeroom in front of you.

You'll find the shopkeepers on the bridge used to tourists. They'll tell you all about the chequered history of Old London Bridge; perhaps mentioning how, in 1014, the battleships of the Norwegian invader Olaf Haraldsson ripped down houses in Southwark, engineered canopies from the wood (to shield them from the defenders' arrows), then sailed right underneath the bridge. Tying ropes around its piles, they rowed with all their Viking brawn in the direction of the tide, yanking the bridge away and plunging hundreds of soldiers to their watery deaths.

The families living on the bridge might even invite you in and offer to show you round. You can expect to find, behind the street-facing counter, a counting house then, up the stairs, in a room overhanging the river, that rare thing – a kitchen with a private water supply (in this case, cooks lowering buckets into the river). In 1615 a visiting Icelander describes how all eating houses on the bridge have a trapdoor in the floor, through which fish are caught, hoisted up and served to the customers, giving whole new meaning to the concept of fast food. In these wealthy households you can also expect to see gaudy wainscotting (or if they're really à la mode, leather panelling which doesn't accrue cooking smells), tapestries, floors covered in springy mats of rushes, even, perhaps, wooden chairs with arms.

When you emerge from a stretch of overhanging houses, you'll find yourself right in the middle of the bridge. Turn round, and brace yourself for a spectacular architectural explosion. Towering over you is the jewel in the crown of London Bridge, Nonsuch House, a wildly eccentric, garishly painted, meticulously carved Renaissance palace made entirely from wood. Four storeys high, built across both sides of the street and bulging over the pier, it is easily the biggest building on the bridge and really, there is nonsuch like it anywhere else in London. Remarkably, it was prefabricated in Holland, shipped across the North Sea and erected from August 1577 without the use of a single nail (wooden pegs were preferred) as a kind of fiendishly complex jigsaw puzzle.

The building is lavish; the portico and pilasters on the upper levels give it a finely crafted majesty and the first three storeys are packed full of windows in carved archways, flooding the chambers with light and affording some of the best views in London (with prevailing winds and a natural sewer, the street is also less foul-smelling than elsewhere). Here, the wealthy occupier of the house can spring out of bed, open the curtains and gaze out at the metropolis shimmering in the morning light. What could be better for the soul? There are meringue-shaped porticos on all four sides of the house but it is the turrets that will impress you the most, soaring the full height of the town-house and topped with tulip-bulb cupolas, bringing a touch of Russia to London.

Twenty-seven years ago Nonsuch House replaced the medieval Drawbridge Gate. That something so outlandish should replace what had once been an important defensive structure is a testament to the self-confidence and stability of the state and a totem of the burgeoning economic might of the city. To put it in perspective, the year before Nonsuch House was built, another big Protestant city, Antwerp, was sacked by Spanish troops resulting in 6,000 deaths and the destruction of 800 houses; five years earlier, at least 3,000 Protestants were slaughtered in Paris during the St Bartholomew's Day Massacre. London, on the other hand, is enjoying an uninterrupted period of peace and doesn't need to worry about garrisons; instead its citizens can swagger about and indulge in frivolous tastes with gleeful abandon.

You emerge from the next tunnel of housing two arches from the southern end of the bridge, opposite the Great Stone Gate, a crenellated tower with a large entrance defended by a portcullis. Look up. A shiver slithers down your spine as you catch the eye – or the eye-socket – of a human head on a spike. Then another. And another. Over thirty in total. As Thomas Platter explained in 1599, 'at the top of one tower ... were stuck on tall stakes more than thirty skulls of noble men who had been executed and beheaded for treason'. Skewered on long wooden spears that protrude diagonally, the heads resemble gruesome human lollipops. They are the first thing visitors approaching the city from Southwark see, a little reminder of what lay in store if you were deemed a traitor to the Crown. William Wallace (of *Braveheart* fame), the rebels Wat Tyler and Jack Cade, humanist and statesman Sir Thomas More, conspirator Guy Fawkes, and many more – all would end up smiling down from this gate.

Don't expect to see people stopping and gawking, though – native Londoners are hardened to a practice that has been going on since 1305 and will last until the Popish Plot of 1678; indeed, for most people, the heads inspire a certain sense of satisfaction rather than terror. Even noblemen confronted with their own ancestors grinning down at them apparently take a perverse pride in it, eagerly pointing them out to their friends and relatives 'believing that they will be esteemed the more because their antecedents were of such high descent that they could even covet the crown', as a bemused Platter observed in 1599.

The heads are parboiled and sautéed in pitch, a sticky resinous substance distilled from tar that hardens in the cold, effectively waterproofing the skulls. One Tudor manuscript claims that the head of Bishop Fisher, one of Henry VIII's many *personae non gratae*, showed no signs of decomposing after a fortnight, 'so that in his life time he never looked so well'. In fact, the sixty-six-year-old's faded youth appeared to have returned – obviously a miracle. Fearing a martyr's cult, Fisher's head was unceremoniously plunged into the Thames, where, ironically, he became food for the fishes.

The Keeper of the Heads, based at Bridge House, is an important office. It is the Keeper's responsibility to maintain the heads, fending off the vultures – and not just the avian ones: it is falsely believed by some people, not least the Royal Mint workers in the Tower, who are exposed to arsenic fumes as they melt down debased coins, that drinking from a dead man's skull is an antidote for poison and a cure for cancer. Hence sometimes the skulls are thieved in the dead of night and made into cups.

As you leave the bridge, note the public jakes to your left (the lavatory's sewage shooting straight into the Thames, naturally), the fences and chains marking the limits of the City of London and, close by Pepper Stairs on your right, the medieval Bear Tavern. This was opened in 1319 by one Thomas Drynkewater. It is distinguishable by the sign of a white bear with a collar and chain, probably a reference to a polar bear given to Henry III by the King of Norway in 1252 that lived in the royal menagerie at the Tower, about whom we'll hear more in due course.

Only once you've crossed it can you finally fathom why the 'city on the bridge' makes such a huge impression on everyone who sees it for the first time, with tourists variously describing it as 'a noble bridge', a 'beautiful bridge' and even, in the effusive words of one veteran traveller, 'worthily to be numbered among the miracles of the world'. Plainly these are not tributes to its beauty, nor particularly to its convenience as a crossing. Although the bridge is twenty feet wide, the actual walkway in each direction is no more than six feet across; on bad days it can take up to an hour to traverse. But all marvel at how the bridge resembles 'a continual street', at how the houses are 'as great and as high as those on firm land', as though the raging Thames is no match for the ingenuity and determination of man. De Colechurch's bridge would endure for well over 600 years, to be ultimately dismantled by parliamentary consent in 1832. And don't forget, time traveller, without the bridge there may have been no London, since the Romans, needing to cross the Thames in AD 43, picked the most appropriate bridging point; the city trailed in its wake.

By now you must be shattered. Time to retire to an inn. If you walk south, you'll find yourself on a street called Long Southwark, lined with 'fair inns, for the receipt of travellers', as John Stow puts it. Why not try the George Inn? Just look for the sign of St George on horseback, slaying a grisly green dragon. The innkeeper will be charged with looking after your personal effects and, if you're willing to pay, you will get a lockable room with a roaring fire. Supper will be a simple but convivial affair at the common board at six o'clock. Expect meat, cheese, bread and beer and the opportunity to swap tales with the other guests.

Sleep well.

The fading timbers of the Golden Hinde

One of the most popular attractions in the vicinity of London is a good four miles to the south-east of London Bridge. So, after a wholesome breakfast which is basically just the leftovers of last night's meal – washed down with weak ale – why not head to the nearest stairs and hail a wherryman. If the sound of the oars slicing through the water and the breeze on your face lulls you off to sleep, be warned that in about forty minutes you're going to be awoken by hammering, the whack of wood on water and a chorus of grunting and swearing. Welcome to the Deptford dockyard, established in 1513 in the reign of Henry VIII to serve the king's insatiable demand for warships to fight the French (on his watch the Navy Royal swelled from five to fifty-eight ships). Ships of war and armed merchant vessels are built, repaired, docked and eventually chopped up for firewood and the beams of new houses.

In front of all the commotion of Mast Dock, with its swivelling wooden cranes, look out for a dry-walled dock in which sits, forlorn, an emaciated little ship with people crawling over her hull like ants. This, believe it or not, is the *Golden Hinde*, the famous vessel in which the 'noble pirate' Sir Francis Drake sailed around the world in 1577–80. He was the first Englishman to do so, returning with untold riches, but only a tiny fraction of his original crew. It's named after the golden deer on the family crest of Sir Christopher Hatton, one of Elizabeth's leading courtiers and co-financier of the voyage, whom Drake wished to appease after executing one of his servants at sea; its original name was the *Pelican*, rich in maritime and religious connotation. The ship has been preserved as a monument to Drake's pioneering achievement on the orders of Queen Elizabeth I, who knighted him on board at a spice-laden banquet near this very spot in 1581 – though preserved is perhaps not the best choice of word since visitors to the *Hinde* seem to feel it's their God-given right to break off pieces of the ship as souvenirs. Her masts – ironically, since they're literally withering away – stand as tokens of England's ever-growing maritime might, the apogee of which we will see in Victorian London.

Looking at her now, it can be hard to imagine the *Hinde* riding the ocean waves in the bloom of her youth. But it was in this vessel that Drake scoured the high seas for a Spanish ship called the *Nuestra Señora de la Concepción*, which was laden with a vast hoard of New World gold and silver bullion bound for Seville. Sighting it on the horizon on 1 March 1579, Drake showered it with cannonballs and arrows, and eventually sailed off with a tidy £126,000 – approximately ten thousand times the annual wage of the kind of carpenter who might have helped build his ship (and around half the English Crown's annual revenue – certainly the biggest treasure plunder in English maritime history – to the absolute delight of the Queen, who got to pour some of it into her depleted coffers. As a delicious coup de grâce, after plundering his ship, Drake summoned the crestfallen Spanish captain to his quarters and bestowed upon him some pathetic little trinkets as 'compensation' for his epic oceanic heist before allowing him to sail off in disgrace.

As you clamber aboard, you'll soon realize that this is no *Mary Rose* or HMS *Victory*. Weighing little more than a hundred tons and with a keel of no more than seventy feet, it seems too vulnerable and diminished to have sailed the world. But remember: Drake didn't set out to traverse the globe – he did so mainly to evade the Spanish and Portuguese vessels prowling around the coast of Chile and Peru baying for his blood. Still, it's amazing to think that only the rotting planks of wood beneath your feet separated the crew from the sea. In January 1580, in the dead of night, they crashed into a long and sinuous reef a mere seven feet below the water near the Makassar Strait off Indonesia. With the sea surging into her hull, Drake fell to his knees and prayed for their deliverance before helping the crew pump water out; miraculously, they escaped from the reef the next evening. Many a book on the stalls at St Paul's Cross will tell you that it was the work of a benevolent providence that the *Hinde* made it back at all.

It doesn't take a wild imagination to picture just how squalid and undignified conditions were for the eighty crewmen aboard the *Hinde*, but it was a very different story above deck, as you'll see if you venture into Drake's cabin – still in acceptable condition in 1603. While most of the crew ate rotting meat and rancid peas squatting down with a wooden spoon, Drake feasted upon freshly bludgeoned penguin, dining 'in state to the sound of trumpets and viols, from silver plates rimmed with gold' – he had brought several musicians along to score the voyage. In fact, in 1603 the cabin of the *Hinde* is still rented out as a banqueting house for those who get a thrill from dining on the ship that has compassed the world. While some of his men suffered the effects of scurvy – the lethargy, loss of teeth, jaundice and eventually death, and others were ducked in the sea and had salt rubbed into whip wounds for alleged disobedience – Drake turned his hand to painting.

Drake's voyage continues to be of epochal significance to Londoners at the start of the seventeenth century, not so much for the bounty he brought back – jaw-dropping though that was – nor even as a brilliant victory over the Spanish, but more as proof that man could, God willing, master even the most hazardous of natural environments and settle the bounds of the known world. His circumnavigation brought about a mental picture of the world that is much better informed and more clearly defined than that of his medieval forebears. As with the Berlin Wall after 1989 there is the same sense that the *Hinde* is palpable history – so help yourself to a chunk like everyone else. In five years' time there will only be fragments left; in 1618, a visitor will liken her battered hull to the bleached skeleton of a horse. It's likely that Sir Francis Drake's round-the-world trip partly inspired the name of London's most famous playhouse, which is our next stop.

You alight at St Saviour's Stairs and follow the path south. To your right, through the gaps in the houses, you can see the white flags of the playhouses in the distance, but it is an unseasonably hot day, without a breeze, so they are motionless. Your eye is drawn to something sinister attached to the wooden beam above the door of one of the houses on your left: a painted cross, vivid and blood-red. Above it, the words: 'Lord have mercy upon us'.

Get away from this house.

You'll see other people are avoiding it like the plague; fittingly. The memory of the 1592–3 outbreak, in which at least 10,000 Londoners perished, is still fresh in people's minds. Now, the tempo of plague deaths is on the rise once more, and people fear another calamitous outbreak. Get to the playhouse while you can; it's bound to be shut down before long as a potential breeding ground for the pestilence.

Turn right at the end of the street and make your way towards the Globe playhouse.

'This wooden O': the Globe

Londoners are mad for the theatre. The playhouses tend to show a different play each day (except the Sabbath), sustaining their popularity. One in three adult Londoners goes to see a play every month and this afternoon, like any other afternoon, more than three thousand of them can be found staring at a stage – double when the playhouses are full to the brim.

Follow the throngs of people pouring through the streets and alleys of Southwark for the two o'clock performance. Soon the Globe will come into view. It sits at the liminal point where the streets melt into fields, farms and ponds, and though it appears enchantingly spherical amidst the rows of sprawling tenements, as you draw nearer you'll see that it's in fact polygonal – twenty sides (in all likelihood), three storeys, a hundred feet in outside diameter and with a thatched roof. Its timber beams are invisible, utterly submerged in wattle-and-daub and plaster painted in a silver-grey tint. From a distance, you'd be forgiven for thinking it's cast out of stone like a Roman amphitheatre, which is exactly what the owners want you to think. The playhouse is open for business now that the official mourning period for the late queen, a great fan of the theatre herself, is over.

Proceed.

At the entrance, you'll be obliged to drop a penny or more into a bright-green piggy bank looked after by a 'gatherer', who, when it's full, takes it into the 'box office' to smash it open; the ensuing waterfall of coins into the chest is music to the ears of the Lord Chamberlain's Men, the company who own and manage the playhouse. For a standing place in the covered galleries, pay 2d; for a cushioned seat, drop in 3d; for a box above the stage (getting extravagant now), 6d. In fact, the most authentic playgoing experience is yours for a mere penny. This will allow you access to the open-air pit or 'yard' (an echo of the days when plays were performed in the galleried yards of inns).

If you're expecting a calm audience sitting in neat rows,

forget it. You'll be making your way through an ebullient mass of playgoers either yapping, piping, burping, cracking nuts, spitting out pips, yelling for ale, throwing their caps in the air, singing half-remembered ballads about Protestant martyrs, or kissing. These are the groundlings or 'stinkards'. Most time travellers would find the atmosphere more redolent of a twenty-first-century music festival or football stadium rather than a place to soak up some of the greatest drama known to humanity, but such is life. The pit is crawling with hawkers selling the era's answer to popcorn and Coca-Cola – pippins, oranges, pears (all of which double up as excellent missiles), grapes, figs, plums, cherries, periwinkle flowers, mussels, oysters and even the odd cuttlefish in case your ink supplies are running low. For 3d you can buy yourself a small pipeful of tobacco; virtually everyone in the galleries is smoking, some stinkards too.

Look up. Come wind, rain, hail, snow or a plague of locusts (as the Puritans hope will indeed one day come – to devour this ungodly arena and everyone in it) you're at the mercy of the elements so you will be grateful for your hat and jacket. Still, at least a little prevailing wind will relieve your nostrils of the stinkards' stench.

Over the stage is a large canopy supported by two pillars gaudily decorated with gilded crowns; the underside of the stage roof is festooned with the sun, moon and stars against a celestial blue, a 'brave o'erhanging firmament, [a] majestical roof fretted with golden fire', as Hamlet describes it (he's talking about the night-time sky but pointing to the canopy in a sort of visual simile).

The large timber stage itself is rectangular with two doors leading into a 'tiring house' (from 'retiring', so backstage), whence the actors appear and disappear head-on to the audience; no one walks on from the side. Directly above the tiring house are half a dozen boxes, the most ostentatious seats in the house hired by gentlemen, nobles and young blades and their ladies, happy to exchange a view of the back of the actors' heads for the thrill of being seen, of becoming part of the theatre themselves. The three layers of galleries, split into square units, spiral right the way around the theatre. One satire lambasts the selfish 'plumed dandebrats' in the boxes who, with their heads 'dressed up in white feathers like a shuttle cock' block everyone else's view (very broadly speaking, the higher one's social status, the higher one's hat).

The capacity of the Globe is an impressive 3,000 or so, making it the biggest playhouse in London. In the twenty-first century, we tend to think of Shakespeare's plays as graspable only after hours of hard study. But with a huge capacity and low entrance price, the Globe truly provides entertainment for the masses and you can expect to rub shoulders with butchers, porters, ale-wives and journeymen. There are legions of apprentices who have flocked here in wanton defiance of their master's wishes (unless they're accompanying their master's wife, which does happen) and the Statute of Artificers, which attempts to fix the working day from 5 a.m. to 7 p.m. between March and September, with two and a half hours for eating and drinking.

It is an indubitably commercial enterprise, competing with two other playhouses in Southwark, the Rose and the Swan; the Curtain in Shoreditch; the Fortune, famed for its flying machinery, in Islington; the Red Lion near Clerkenwell; and the Boar's Head in labouring-class Whitechapel, as well as the more reputable private indoor theatres at St Paul's and Blackfriars. Beyond the Drakeian association, the name 'Globe' speaks eloquently to the notion that the theatre is a microcosm of the world, a stage for all God's creatures, watched by the entire gamut of humanity.

Even when it's only two-thirds full, which generally tends to be the case unless there's a blockbuster like *Hamlet* or *Volpone* playing, the Globe hosts the biggest regular concentration of the public (rather than, say, merchants at the Royal Exchange) anywhere in the metropolis, the odd public execution at Tyburn and rabble-rousing sermon at Paul's Cross aside. No wonder the Privy Council eyes the playhouses with suspicion, issuing periodic proclamations for them to be shut down; they are the perfect breeding ground for the twin scourges of London, pestilence and conflagration, and a hotbed of flirtation to boot. 'In the playhouses at London,' writes one disgusted Puritan, 'it is the fashion of youths to go first into the yard, and to carry their eye through every gallery, then like unto ravens where they spy the carrion thither they fly, and press as near to the fairest as they can.'

A trumpet blasts. As the playgoers clamber to their places, see if you can make out the Globe's timbers behind the galleries. These once propped up a completely different playhouse called, simply, the Theatre, 'a gorgeous playing-place erected in the fields' half a mile north of Bishopsgate in Shoreditch. The Theatre was opened in 1576 as a partnership between joiner-turned-actor James Burbage and his father-in-law, the wealthy grocer and financier John Brayne. Following Guildhall's increasingly aggressive policy towards the City's popular inn-theatres, Burbage decided to erect a purpose-built theatre outside the city walls. The Theatre flourished, hosting some of the era's best loved plays, including Christopher Marlowe's *Dr Faustus* and Shakespeare's *Romeo and Juliet*, and establishing sinful Shoreditch as London's leading theatre district. The Lord Chamberlain's Men, including Shakespeare and, ultimately, James Burbage's actor son Richard, who had inherited the business, and who would play the title roles in many of Shakespeare's tragedies, were the resident acting company for much of the 1590s.

But a protracted quarrel between the company and their ground landlord Giles Allen left the Theatre languishing 'in dark silence and vast solitude'. One icy morning, a few days after Christmas in 1598, Allen went to the Theatre after hearing some alarming reports. He discovered flattened grass, humps of plaster, and smashed tiles. But no theatre. Its timbers had been spirited away in the dead of night by Burbage and a team of armed carpenters and builders, quite possibly including Shakespeare himself, to a warehouse near Bridewell Steps on the north bank of the Thames.

Burbage had acquired a new plot, essentially a rubbish-strewn wasteland a couple of minutes' walk from the Rose playhouse across the Thames in Southwark. This was the primordial ooze from which the Globe would rise. But first, piles had to be driven into the marshy Southwark ground and skilled labour hired to build the structure. Burbage sought investors who would co-fund the risky and expensive enterprise in return for a 10 per cent stake of future profits.

One of those shareholders was Shakespeare. In 1599, he lived within spitting distance of the building site, on a street near the Clink prison where the air hangs heavy with the noxious fumes from Southwark's tanneries, soapmakers and dyers and where wanton women ply their trade. You may even have walked past his house on your way to the Globe.

It was a joyous day when the Globe finally opened in 1599 at an astrologically germane moment; the inaugural production was probably *Julius Caesar*, which Thomas Platter, in September, thought quite the superb piece of drama. The business arrangements of the Globe were unprecedented; never before had one playwright been so invested, emotionally and financially, in a single playhouse – the greatest work of his career followed, brilliant play after brilliant play: *Hamlet*, *King Lear*, *Othello*, *Macbeth*. Unlike his fellow playwright Ben Jonson,

Shakespeare showed little interest in immortalizing his works in print; any printed version was just a spectral echo of the real thing. It was all about the performance at the Globe. A performance you are about to witness.

'That's my thunder, by God!'

The trumpet blasts a third time. The play is imminent. The playgoers even quieten down – a little. For the time traveller who can recall their English literature classes, the plot and characters of what's to follow may well be familiar – particularly if it's one of Shakespeare's classics – but the experience of watching it will be exhilaratingly alien. It will be strange to see a lithe, pretty boy in his late teens or early twenties caked in make-up and squeezed into a tight corset playing Lady Macbeth or Queen Cleopatra; strange to see actors appearing above the tiring house in the galleries intermixed with the spectators. Expect an intense experience too – no intervals, no acts, and toilet facilities in their infancy (a bucket or a trip to the Thames). If it's a fine day you'll spend much of the performance half blinded by sunshine; the Globe is positioned so that actors remain shaded unless they come right to the front of the stage, where their faces are brilliantly illuminated by the afternoon sun. Since plays begin at around two in the afternoon, the daylight begins to fade towards the end of midwinter performances, evoking moods that can be exploited for dramatic effect – as Romeo and Juliet lie dying, for instance – so the stage is shrouded in darkness.

There are no red curtains. When the play begins, the actors just emerge from the two doors in the tiring house and walk straight towards the audience. Props are used economically, if at all, but the costumes are lavish. There is scant regard for realism. Nothing hides the machinery of the play from view. Get ready to see hirelings in their blue liveries casually walk onto stage mid-speech, plonking down some furniture, perhaps shooting a quick glance into the galleries and sizing up the ladies; sometimes even great actors like Richard Burbage and Edward Alleyn will double up as stage hands. Anachronisms are rife and there are constant knowing references.

Hollywood's obsession with graphic violence is, apparently, nothing new. If you're watching a revenge tragedy, expect to see bladders brimming with pig's blood tossed onto the stage, bespattering some of the groundlings. To pull off the scene in which Gloucester is blinded in *King Lear* to the memorable words 'Out, vile jelly!', a lychee soaked in pig's blood is required. Fire and smoke are used to good effect in an age unencumbered by health-and-safety regulations. Note the trapdoor on the stage. This represents the mouth of hell. Should an evil or potentially evil spirit make an appearance this afternoon – the ghost of Hamlet's father, let's say – expect to see smoke wafting up and even sparks from firecrackers dancing onto the stage.

The sound effects will impress and startle you. Pebbles rolling in a drum simulate the sound of waves crashing onto a shore (useful for *The Tempest*), dry peas falling onto a metal sheet conjures rain and frenzied backstage cries of 'Kill! Kill! Kill!' add more than a tincture of menace to battle scenes. At climactic moments, canons are fired from the roof. But it's the clapping of thunder, more than anything else, that playhouses compete to perfect. Sometimes a sheet of metal is shaken vigorously and squibs let off; sometimes hirelings roll cannonballs around the gallery roof; on other occasions a drum is rolled across a sheet of metal. In a later period, at the Theatre Royal in Covent Garden, a playwright called John Dennis would invent an ingenious new method of feigning thunder for one of his plays which, to his great dismay, flopped. Attending a performance of *Macbeth* in the same theatre soon afterwards, his ears pricked up at the sound of his new effect. 'That's my thunder, by God!' he is reported to have shouted. 'How these rascals use me! They will not let my play run, but steal my thunder'. Few idioms in any language can have been forged in such high fulmination.

Don't expect the groundlings to maintain a sedate silence as we rather boringly do in the twenty-first century. They'll give a boisterous running commentary, casting judgements at every turn. They'll jibe and hiss and heckle. Clap in inappropriate places. Throw rotten apple cores and the bones of their lunches at the players to speed up the performance of a play – or hasten its conclusion. Sometimes audiences demand a different play altogether. Some playgoers are even known to bring their own stool and sit on the stage.

One final note. You might be surprised by the playgoers' reactions to key revelations and developments in the plot. If you're watching *Hamlet*, for instance, you might expect a sharper intake of breath when the Ghost appears at the beginning or when Queen Gertrude drinks from the poisoned chalice at the end – rather than the knowing murmurs and looks that are forthcoming. Many members of the audience are, in fact, already very familiar – intimate, even – with the story. In the twenty-first century, we tend to equate literary genius with the ability to think up character and plots from scratch and bring them to life. Not so for Shakespeare. Take *Hamlet*. Shakespeare lifted the entire story from a now lost revenge tragedy popular in the 1580s called – of all things – *Hamlet*, and this earlier play was itself based on a thirteenth-century Norse saga about a man called *Amleth*. Shakespeare and Burbage actually performed this earlier *Hamlet* at a theatre in Newington Butts to the south of Southwark in the 1580s. Londoners realize that

Shakespeare's renown lies not in dreaming up original stories but rendering familiar plots and characters in startlingly novel and vivid ways using magniloquent and inventive language – he introduces 600 new words in *Hamlet* alone. As a twenty-first-century biographer of Shakespeare points out, what the Lord Chamberlain's Men did to the wooden frame of the Theatre, so Shakespeare did to *Hamlet*. The only new character he actually introduces is Fortinbras, who is onstage for approximately three minutes. If Shakespeare had been writing in the twenty-first century he'd probably be dismissed as a wanton plagiarist.

If you're reaching the end of a dark revenge tragedy like *Hamlet* or *Macbeth*, as the corpses come crashing down upon the stage, the last thing you'll be expecting, probably, is for any of them to spring back to life and dance a jig. But that's precisely what's going to happen. If you've been watching a tragedy, they can provide a cathartic release from all the death and destruction onstage; if a comedy, then an extension of the gaiety and fun.

(In 1613 the firing of a cannon during a performance of *Henry VIII* quite literally brought down the house. The thatched roof went up in flames and the whole playhouse was reduced to a smouldering shell within an hour. One man's breeches caught fire but 'by the benefit of a provident wit' he extinguished them with a bottle of ale.)

As you shove your way out, you expect to join the crowd of people pouring through the streets to London Bridge or one of the watermen's stairs. But instead you find yourself in somewhere called Anchor Terrace, a gated complex of cream apartments. Looking down at the cobbles in the courtyard, you see a rainbow-shaped ribbon of black-and-grey tiles spelling the words 'The Globe'. You are standing above the foundations of the original theatre, now anchored firmly in the twenty-first century, not a grizzly bear or a stinkard in sight.

Epilogue: echoes of Shakespearean London

Very little of Tudor and Jacobean London remains, the rest swept away in the Great Fire of 1666 or by the building frenzies of later centuries.

Although much remodelled, the timber-framed shop façades of Staple Inn in Holborn give the closest indication of what a Tudor street would have looked like, even if the blacks and whites are too crisp and pronounced. Elsewhere, most of the Tudor buildings that have survived are palaces or portions of palaces – for instance St James's Palace, Lambeth Palace, Fulham Palace and, outside London, Hampton Court Palace. The church of St Andrew Undershaft in the shadow of the Gherkin is a rare example of a surviving Tudor church, serendipitously since it contains a statue of John Stow, who so tirelessly mapped and chronicled Shakespearean London in his *Survey of London*, first published in 1598. Not many Tudor mansions remain but the misnamed Sutton House in Hackney and the half-brick, half-stone Hall Place in Bexleyheath are both stunning.

But the intrepid twenty-first-century explorer can still find echoes, traces and even resurrections of the features of Shakespeare's London visited on our whirlwind tour. Although the *Golden Hinde* rotted away in the seventeenth century and the Puritans had their wicked way with the second, sturdier, tile roofed Globe playhouse in the 1640s, both have been painstakingly reconstructed and are prime tourist attractions on the regenerated South Bank (still, as in Shakespeare's time, a promenade of entertainment and leisure, albeit of a less violent and sordid nature).

The rebuilt Globe was opened by Queen Elizabeth II in 1997 after a relentless forty-year campaign by the American actor and director Sam Wanamaker; it stands a few hundred yards north-east of its original site near the intersection of historic Park Street and what is now Southwark Bridge Road. It runs a full programme of plays with a heavy orientation towards Shakespeare, but also stages works by new and other playwrights. The reconstruction is as faithful as modern scholarship and present-day craftsmanship allow but, as its website candidly admits, the reconstructed Globe is only a 'best guess' reproduction of Shakespeare's theatre. The full-size reconstruction of the *Golden Hinde* on Clink Street, which has also circumnavigated the world, sits in a purpose-built dock off Pickfords Wharf, its visitor attractions including actors in period dress. Bookings can even be made to spend the night below decks – though in unauthentically salubrious conditions. The golden deer sculpted on the prow must be a piece of artistic licence, since it is doubtful that Drake, resourceful though he was, could have made a new sign for the rechristened *Pelican* until he arrived back home.

The inconspicuous Bear Gardens marks the locale of the Hope, a multi-purpose arena opened in 1614 by Philip Henslowe for bear baiting, sword fighting and drama. If it weren't for the name you wouldn't, in a million years, know that bull and bear baiting had once taken place here. Bear Lane, off Southwark Street, is to the south of the early-seventeenth-century Bear Garden as marked on Claes Visscher's 1616 map of London. Tucked away in the north-eastern corner of St Paul's Churchyard, there is a plaque marking Paul's Cross carved into the pavement near a column surmounted with a gilded statue of St Paul commemorating outdoor preaching, but there is no trace of all the booksellers' shops and stalls (and Pissing Alley has been subsumed into the respectable Queen's Head Passage). However, a stylish plaque to Wynkyn de Worde, incorporating his sun emblem, is affixed to the rebuilt Stationers' Hall in Stationers' Hall Court near Fleet Street. Tobacco houses have vanished and the only gardens remaining at Drapers' Hall were once minor adjuncts to the Great Garden, divided off by a wall. They do still contain mulberry trees, albeit planted by members of the royal family in the twentieth century. Drapers' Hall and gardens can be viewed by request or on Open House Weekend each September. There are no surviving Tudor or Stuart mazes and labyrinths in London but you can try your luck in modern versions at Hall Place in Bexleyheath, Chiswick House, Fen Court off Fenchurch Street, Crystal Palace Park and, fittingly, a garish painting of an impossible maze at Warren Street Underground station.

The Dutch Church was destroyed in the Blitz but arose once more in 1954 clad in Portland Stone; it still functions as a place of (much reduced) worship and is a centre for the promotion of Dutch culture and heritage in London. As for Old London Bridge, a model survives inside the church of St Magnus the Martyr (rebuilt after the Great Fire), and although the current concrete-and-steel version, which opened in 1973, is a little to the west of its predecessor, a much-ignored concrete spike marks the relative spot where, on the old bridge, the heads of traitors were impaled. A blue plaque on Park Street marks the site of the Rose Theatre and two rather ugly and awkwardly worded plaques in Shoreditch mark the sites of the Theatre and Curtain playhouses, the latter on Curtain Road. Finally, Middle Temple Hall, a barristers' dining hall in the middle of London's legal quarter where Shakespeare is though to have performed, survives in all its leisure and grace.

1390
A Descent into Medieval London

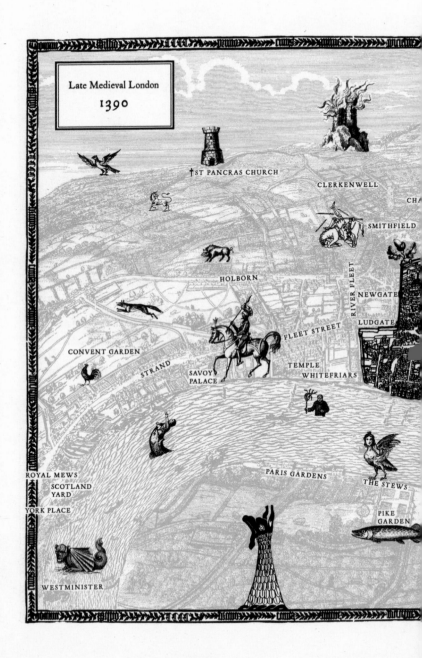

Late Medieval London
1390

†ST PANCRAS CHURCH

CLERKENWELL

CHA

SMITHFIELD

HOLBORN

RIVER FLEET

NEWGATE

LUDGATE

FLEET STREET

CONVENT GARDEN

STRAND

SAVOY
PALACE

TEMPLE
WHITEFRIARS

ROYAL MEWS

SCOTLAND
YARD

YORK PLACE

PARIS GARDENS

THE STEWS

PIKE
GARDEN

WESTMINISTER

FINSBURY FIELD

SHOREDITCH

OUSE

CRIPPLEGATE

MOORFIELDS

THE SPITAL FIELD

MOORGATE

GATE

BISHOPSGATE

WHITECHAPEL

ALDGATE

MINORIES

QUEENHITHE

LONDON BRIDGE

THE TOWER

GREAT STONE GATE

IKSIDE

WINCHESTER
HOUSE

CLINK STREET

†ST MARY OVERIE

SOUTHWARK

A cold autumn night in the city. London Wall is cloaked in drizzle. The odd taxi swings around the chocolate-coloured roundabout that is the outer wall of the Museum of London, bearing silver-haired bankers back to suburbia. An empty foot-bridge shoots across London Wall, mirroring the laser-blue stripe of Pizza Express ahead. On your right, through the glass exterior of One London Wall, you see ghostly elevators suspended in the chambers of a skyscraper.

If you walk east down London Wall, there's a point where the buildings on your left give way, revealing a lone tower, part of the Barbican complex. With its slitted windows and concrete fins, it squints down at you like a silent cyborg guard, dwarfing the church of St Giles-without-Cripplegate in front of it, painstakingly reconstructed after the Blitz.

At the entrance to a small road leading to Plaisterers Hall are eight metal bollards rising to stomach-height. The tip of every other one contains a lamp that gives out a hard-white electric glare.

Walk over to the third light on the right. It stands on the path of the north-western boundary of Londinium, though few will discern this ancient threshold, this lamp post of an urban Narnia. Londinium was, of course, a remote outpost on a rain-spattered island populated by savage tribes for whom the city was an irresistible target, as Queen Boudica underlined in AD 60 when her forces razed it to the ground. The Romans would need to build a defensive barrier. And some 140 odd years later, they did – you can see a relic of it on your right: a wall. Or at least, a fragment of one, rising from the grass like a series of shards.

Turn right, down Noble Street, and walk to the viewing platform, near the site of what was once a Roman sentry walk and subsequently a medieval watchman's walk.

This stretch of wall, which abruptly resurfaced in 1940 after a German bombing raid, is a thickened version of what was once the western edge of a Roman fort complex. Around AD 200, it was assimilated into the emergent defensive wall which eventually circled the whole city, the Thames lapping against its southern range, interspersed with bastions, towers and gates. Around a million blocks of white ragstone, used to mask a core of rubble and mortar, were shipped in from Kent for the task.

The wall fragment is impressive, rising in places to thirty-five feet, but much of what you see is medieval and Tudor repairs and fortifications – the Roman wall was only around twenty feet high.

For almost a millennia and a half, the wall was London's defensive shell, restricting its sprawl well into the sixteenth century. The surviving chunks are so palpable and *real* yet also forlorn, lost in a landscape of high-rise, high-octane finance. They mark the extent to which the historic heart of the metropolis has been submerged in urban sprawl, its old boundaries now largely imperceptible, a city within a city.

At moments like this – in the quiet of night, when the traffic on London Wall has reduced to a trickle – these forlorn chunks of ragstone and tile evoke the mystery and menace of the medieval city, hermetically sealed and dead to the world in the hours of darkness.

Return to the metal bollards. You are close enough to crouch down and touch the wall through the grey railings. On top it's scaly and cold. Firm. But if you put your finger underneath the chin of the wall you'll find it's oddly supple, flaky. Brush your fingers against the shell of the medieval city.

Go on, brush it.

Everything is black. A glacial wind chills you to the bone. You open your eyes to find yourself in a meadow under a moonless, star-speckled sky. Were it not for your flickering horn-sided lanthorn, you'd be able to see very little. You walk past trees and what sound like whirring mills. As you draw nearer, you can just about make out the contours of gables and bulging half-timbered buildings dotted about a wide, straight road receding into the blackness.

Every so often, in the distance, you see a tiny pinprick of light flashing from a great height, appearing in a slightly different place each time. You surmise that you are somewhere outside the city walls, and that a watchman is skulking behind the battlements. Perhaps if you go any nearer he will shoot an arrow at you. You blow out your lantern before the wind does it for you and begin walking towards what you hope is the gate. You check your dagger is at your side. It is.

After a couple of minutes, you realize that you were correct. In front of you, the medieval city broods, silent and black, rising sheer from a stinking ditch, and girdled by its thick walls. Not for the love of God will you, an alien, or anyone, be allowed in. At eight o'clock each night a curfew is sounded by the churches of St Mary-le-Bow in Cheapside, All Hallows Barking in Tower Ward, St Bride in Fleet Street and St Giles-without-Cripplegate, which you saw earlier, in front of the Barbican. At that point, everything grinds to a halt, people retire to their houses to put out their fires, boats on the Thames come bankside to moor, the wicket gates are bolted shut (the main gates having been shut at sundown), the nightwatchmen begin their shift. And the city falls into a deep slumber.

The best way to kill time between now and sunrise, when the gates are opened, is to circumnavigate the city walls. This will give you a feel for both the unfamiliar compactness of London and the extent of the monastic belt – the grounds of the monasteries, nunneries and hospitals surrounding much of the city, an apt visual metaphor for how in thrall the city is to the Church. The whole circuit is around two miles; the original Roman southern wall bordering the Thames has long since been knocked through, extending London to the riverfront. Watch out for the moat – it's wide and deep and, as the place name Houndsditch to the east commemorates, sometimes has dead dogs floating in it. As you shiver in the cold, try to take some comfort from the knowledge that you're the only person alive who knows that this small, walled city, which seems so shut off from the world, is the seed of something that will eventually grow into 'a human awful wonder of God', bursting out of its shell and blossoming into the biggest city in the world by the nineteenth century.

'If you do not wish to live with the shameful, you will not dwell in London'

The sun rises over the Spital Field behind you. You are glad to have passed through the oak doors of Bishopsgate without incident. The gate itself looks ancient, a three-storey Roman structure with two entranceways flanked by square, battle-mented towers with unglazed windows and loopholes dotted about the frontage. You find yourself amidst a stream of men and women bringing bread from Stratford-le-Bow and fruit from Stepney, dray carts bearing hogsheads of beer, and some sheep and hens to be slaughtered and sold later in the week. It is cold but not perishingly so, early October. The year is 1390.

By modern standards, it will feel tiny. The devastating plague epidemic of 1348–9 (what later centuries would refer to as the Black Death) halved the population of London from 80,000 to 40,000, leaving houses empty, shops dark, dogs without masters and demand for labour high. There are fewer people alive in late-fourteenth-century London than in the original Roman settlement of Londinium; the population won't resurge to pre-plague levels for another 150 years. At the moment, it's comparable in population to medieval Florence. Still, that's huge by the standards of the day – the next biggest city in England is York with around 12,000 inhabitants.

There is a straight road ahead, lined with two- and three-storey timbered houses with wattle-and-daub walls and tiled roofs: they are smaller than what you saw in Shakespearean London but at similarly eccentric angles to the street and pitch forwards, with little concern for harmony or elegance. It's curious to see little moats of cobbles and freestone outside some of the larger houses, which abruptly give way to trampled earth; paving is haphazard. Look up. The sky is a forest of timbers and towers. One hundred parish churches punch into the morning sky. But all this, you register in a matter of seconds. It is the *smell* that commands your attention. Nothing can prepare you for the miasma of medieval London, its richly layered and intricately woven tapestry of putrid, aching stenches: rotting offal, human excrement, stagnant water, cows' and pigs' skins being tanned, foul fish, the burning of tallow candles, and an icing of animal dung on the streets. Immersing the body in water is an alien and impossible concept; by your standards, people will reek of sweat and dirt, like a malodorous force field.

The futility of all the regulations concerning street hygiene, of not leaving detritus outside one's house, and so on, is underlined by their regularity of passage: they are roundly ignored or impossible to enforce properly. There are raykers, for example, but a favourite trick of theirs is simply to dump one ward's rubbish into next door's, when no one is looking. The smell of the city will remain with you, then, like a headache you cannot shake.

Walk down Bishopsgate Street. Stop when you see Leadenhall Market on your left and the Church of St Peter on your right. Sadly no literary panoramas of London that would be of any use survive from the fourteenth century but in the interests of priming you for your journey ahead, and to pass the time to Leadenhall, we do have some from the earlier Middle Ages. Unless society has quite radically changed – which, aside from the population drop, it hasn't – you're in for some excitement.

'Behold! I warn you,' writes the Winchester monk Richard of Devizes in the twelfth century, 'whatever of evil or perversity there is in all parts of the world, you will find in that city alone.' He presents us with a diabolical cast of 'buffoons, those that have no hair on their bodies ... pick-thanks, catamites, effeminate sodomites, lewd musical girls, druggists, lustful persons, fortune-tellers, extortioners, nightly strollers, magicians, mimics, common beggars, tatterdemalions'. 'So if you do not wish to live with the shameful,' he concludes, 'you will not dwell in London.' As a foil to the venerable father's city of abject vice, we have cleric and biographer William Fitzstephen's land of milk and honey, written in the late twelfth century. 'Amongst the noble and celebrated cities of the world,' he tells us, 'that of London, the capital of the kingdom of England, is one of the most renowned, possessing above all others abundant wealth, extensive commerce, great grandeur and magnificence.' His is a *noble* city brimming with riches, exploding with life and surrounded by Arcadian suburbs. In reality, the one is as wantonly caustic as the other is unashamedly eulogistic. You can make your own judgements.

Some final words of warning. First, if you venture beyond the walls into the suburbs, should you see someone in a long cloak jingling with bells and trying to disguise their disfigured face, perhaps with missing fingers and limbs too, you need to give them a very wide berth indeed. For they are, as Edward III put it, 'smitten with the blemish of leprosy'.

Second, the clichés are true: medieval London is a dangerous place. In 1321, an esquire careering through Thames Street on his way to the Tower nearly knocked down a mother and child with his horse. When someone had the temerity to ask him to mind where he was going, the squire simply drew his sword and murdered the man, and that was that. It's not a good idea to disturb people's sleep, either. One winter's night in 1322, a shopkeeper on Bread Street reproached some boisterous youths for singing and shouting outside his house in wanton defiance of the curfew. In retaliation, they taunted and teased him so he stormed out of his house and killed one of them with his staff. While not commonplace, such incidents are far from unusual in a hot-headed world where most men carry weapons, as true in the late fourteenth century as in the 1320s. Watch your step.

The anchorhold: a living death

The junction of Bishopsgate Street, Cornhill and Gracechurch Street (dead ahead), is teeming with cacophony and life. Esquires gallop past, butchers' stalls swarm with customers, and minstrels with expressive eyes bubble lute music into the air. On the opposite side of the street, the lead roof of the

Neville family's mansion, from which Leadenhall Market takes its name, shelters cheesemongers and poulterers who have travelled in from nearby towns and villages, and who are clamouring for your attention. Stinking entrails litter the street, attracting the interest of stray cats, who toss them about as though they were balls of string. Opposite the market, to your right, is an inconspicuous alleyway that squirrels into St Peter's churchyard. Take it. Like many in medieval London, it's no more than six feet wide, with the houses almost kissing overhead, plunging you into near-darkness. But you soon emerge into St Peter's Churchyard. Go in further, and peer over the stone wall.

Attached to the side of the church, sunk low into the ground, is a bulbous wooden growth – a shack of some sort. It has a tiny grille, covered with a black curtain on the inside. Curled up outside it, like a cat in front of a fire, is an old woman jabbing the cloth with her cane. Hunched into her hood, her eyes are conspiratorial. She glances over her shoulder, but you are of little concern to her.

As you draw nearer and can overhear her, you realize that she's dribbling all sorts of lurid slander and sexual scandal into the cell. More seriously, since it involves a tacit criticism of King Richard, she is airing the grievances of the Cornhill shopkeepers, who are apparently deeply unhappy about the court's preparations for some great event at Smithfield. The king's purveyors have been buying up stock of the finest cloth, saddles and trumpets at risible rates (as is their right according to the hated practice of purveyance) and there are rumours that the thoroughfare of Cornhill will be closed off entirely to the detriment of their businesses.

A heavy church door creaks open. Low-pitched chants spill into the churchyard. A priest appears, decked out in his dark robes, his bald pate surrounded by a moat of trimmed hair. He marches over to the shed and shoos off the hag, whose raucous revelations had been disturbing his devotions. Doubled over her cane, she shuffles off, muttering. Holding up the seams of his gown, the priest, down on his knees, pulls back the curtain and gives a barely perceptible nod, then rises and retreats into the church.

Kneel down in front of the grille, poke away the cloth, and peer in. A chilling sight awaits.

You are looking into a tiny, suffocating cell, no more than eight feet by six. The grille admits hardly any light but it's still enough to dazzle its sole, bleary-eyed occupant, who is slumped against the wall, muttering a prayer to himself. There is no door. He is walled in. He is barefooted, gaunt and wears a filthy, grease-smeared tunic. He makes weary, distracted eye contact. His eyes are sunk deep into his sockets, twitchy, with a tincture of madness.

He is virtually bald, but what few greasy locks he has – grey through and through – straggle down to his waist and inter-weave with a woolly rufous beard that clings to his face like ginger fur. His bed is a wooden board; his pillow, a log. Other than that, there's a tiny table on which rest a pile of books, a small, workmanlike crucifix and not much else. The cell is dank and reeks of sweat and suffering. How long has he been walled up in here? Time doesn't mean very much to him any more. Hours, days, weeks, decades – they all dissolve into one vast desert in which he bakes and shivers in the love of God.

He often harks back to the day he was walled in, he tells you, once you've earned his trust. He'd been expecting the whole parish to turn up: whispering girls, sneering apprentices, livery-men, the innkeeper, perhaps even the Alderman for Cornhill ward and his wife – all craning their necks and sliding their eyes to get a glimpse of the man who was about to spend the rest of his life immured in a minuscule cell, who would never again see the waters of the Thames, the spire of St Paul's, the bustle of the London markets or the sun setting over London Bridge. But hardly anyone came – a few old women, some beggars, a parchminer, and some drunken fishmongers, and he wasn't even sure they had come to see him.

He pictures himself, barefoot as he is today, prostrate on the cold church floor as the priest blesses him with holy water and incense; being led by his sponsors to the high altar, reciting *Suscipe me, Domine* (Receive me, O Lord) and placing two candles on the altar; taking the Eucharist and vowing to serve the rest of his life in the order of the anchorite; then being taken by the hand to his anchorhold, accompanied by the chants and psalms from the Office of the Dead. He remembers the priest, outside, administering the sacrament of Extreme Unction (usually reserved for the dying), smearing oil on his forehead, and then he walked into his new habitat.

He remembers the heavy eyebrows of the priest rising and falling, framed by the final aperture in the wall, as he dispersed some final advice; remembers the order to immure him, and the stones clunked one upon the other. And the priest's faint, barely perceptible nod as the final stone is wedged in place and the anchorite's new life, a living death, begins.

For the spectators gathered there that day, he has remained an unnerving presence in the parish church; he has a small, unglazed window through which he can witness the elevation of the host and thus share in the redemption of mankind. The anchorite's groans, cries, chants, whimpers and rhapsodic ejaculations will be the constant backdrop to their worship, though most will never see him again.

'Anchorite' is derived from the Greek word *anakhorein*, meaning to retire or retreat, and the man beneath you has certainly done that, sequestering himself from the world and devoting himself to a life of contemplation. An anchorite is not the same thing as a hermit – you will come across several hermitages too in medieval London, many in city gate towers – since hermits, though reclusive, are free to work and even socialize in the real world so long as they return to their cells each night. Anchorites, on the other hand, must vow never to leave their cells until the day they die and sometimes not even then. There is evidence that some are buried underneath their cells. The *Ancrene Wisse*, a thirteenth-century handbook for anchoresses advises them to 'scrape up earth every day out of the grave in which they shall rot', ostensibly so their hands don't become too soft and supple. It's possible this is meant metaphorically but if not, what better memento mori than to stare into your very own open grave?

As the text reveals, becoming an anchorite appeals to both men and women. There are around a dozen anchorholds dotted around London – they can be found bolted onto the churches of St Lawrence Jewry off Cheapside (the former neighbourhood of the Jews before their expulsion in 1290), St Boltoph in Bishopsgate, the Church of All Hallows by London Wall, and St Benet Fink on the other side of Cornhill, to cite four nearby examples.

Cells vary. For every anchorhold that resembles a six feet by four feet solitary-confinement cell in a modern US penitentiary, there is a more spacious one; some even have mini-libraries or a tiny garden. It would be wrong to claim that anchorites are *completely* cut off from the world; if they are to live in a cell for up to fifty years – as some do – then they have to rely on friends and family members for food and drink and to empty their chamber pots, and as we have heard, they usually have a window onto the high altar. But there should be no physical contact with other humans, and for an anchoress to touch male skin is so abominable a sin that hanging from a gibbet would be far preferable (according to the *Ancrene Wisse*).

Since these people are not prisoners, by now you must be wondering why anyone would willingly embrace such a life. Why does the lure of the anchorite's cell wrench craftsmen from their guilds, priests from their churches, mothers from their children, even husbands from their wives?

By embracing the solitary life, anchorites are hoping to sublimate their emotional impulses and carnal urges into a perpetual contemplation of God, thereby achieving their own salvation and, through their prayers, the salvation of others.

Anchorites are not shunned by the local community – far from it, most are highly respected, even revered figures. Since they are so immersed in the holy way of life, so spiritually pure, parishioners believe that anchorites' prayers are peculiarly efficacious, so they often gather outside the grille to beg the occupant to pray for their souls. Anchorites are also thought to be excellent arbiters of disputes, secret confessors and, as we have seen in the case of the garrulous old woman earlier, receptacles of gossip (though this is not to be encouraged since it can 'dissolve' the anchoress into fits of laughter 'like a drug that has the sweetness of drink' with the result that 'she staggers during psalms, is dazed during readings, and sways during prayers'). They have other uses too. If you have any valuables that you are nervous about carrying around medieval London, why not drop them through the grille; anchorholds make excellent safety deposit boxes in this pre-banking era.

Given their closeness to God, people take them to be prophets, too, or at least adept at concocting suitably oblique answers to give that impression. If you were to peel back the black curtain and ask the anchorite how your journey through medieval London will end, he might tell you: 'In icy, rolling waters.'

On that chilling note, it's time to take your leave.

Follow St Peter's Alley round to Cornhill and walk east, onto Cheapside, the first street of medieval London.

Gropecunt Lane

The medieval city is locked into an infinite cycle of trade and commerce; that's what keeps it afloat, setting it apart from political Westminster and seedy Southwark. Wholesale merchants are a major and growing force – the size and splendour of their palaces dotted about the streets are testament to that – but essentially London is a city of small shopkeepers and stall-holders, many of whom cluster in the same districts, giving neighbourhoods a distinctive sound, smell and appearance.

Take a walk down Cheapside and pay attention to the roads branching off from the main thoroughfare. You'll find bakers in Bread Street, milkmaids in Milk Street, beekeepers and wax vendors in Honey Lane, carpenters in Wood Street and iron-mongers in Ironmonger Lane – all feeding into Cheapside, which is itself named after *chepe*, the Old English word for market. Similarly, Candlewick Street, a little further south, is the abode of chandlers churning out candles – both cheap, smelly tallow ones made from hardened animal fat and classier wax ones. It's forbidden to eat meat on a Friday so where better for the fishmongers to congregate than Friday Street? In Soper Lane you'll find impoverished soap makers kipping under their shacks at night and towards Walbrook, Budge Row – from 'budge' meaning lambskin – the turf of furriers. Skinners, for their part, live and work in the Peltry, running south from the church of St John Walbrook. The city is an index of the very trade that is its raison d'être.

Free as they are from the control of the City Fathers, the Bishop of Winchester's grounds in Southwark are a favourite haunt of prostitutes, as we will see tonight (innocently), but a few streets within the city are reserved for sexual commerce, too, to which the city authorities at Guildhall turn a blind eye.

Their names are gratifyingly vivid and evocative. Love Lane, towards Cripplegate, is innocuous enough but off Smithfield you will find Cock Lane, referring unambiguously to the penis, unlike the animal-themed street names nearby (Cowcross Street, Chick Lane), which are conduits for livestock passing to Smithfield market.

In a couple of years, the authorities will try to restrict prostitution north of the Thames to Cock Lane. But for the moment, a triumvirate of seedy, narrow streets off Cheapside comprise a whoremonger's paradise. One is called Bordhaw (or Brothel) Lane; another, Popkirtle Lane (as in to yank off a woman's gown or petticoat); and, most magnificently of all, everyone's favourite medieval street name, Gropecunt Lane, a dark, narrow alley leading south from Cheapside. 'By the love of God, man, show me the way to Gropecunt Lane!' is not a phrase you get to utter in the modern world very often. So relish the saying of it in medieval London, if the fancy takes you. Some of these names – although not the raciest ones – are destined to survive into the twenty-first century long after their associated trades have vanished – traces of a colourful and buoyant economy and a teeming residential population in a ghostly commuter world monopolized by financial services.

Out of the corner of your eye you see a flash of pink, and hear a cry of rage from a fruit seller, whose basket of apples is streaming down the street towards you. In medieval London pigs pop up when you least expect it, scurrying around, rootling for food and snuffling at shit in the middle of the street, and sometimes doing worse. In 1332 a pig snuck into a shop and bit a newborn baby to death. No wonder swine killers are common sights on the streets of London. They get 4d for every pig they exterminate.

Our next stop is at the end of Cheapside, towards Ludgate. You can see it on the horizon, soaring into the skies. Veer left down Friday Street with its aroma of fish, then turn right down Watling Street, and enter the churchyard from the south, via Carter Lane.

St Erkenwald's Cathedral

From the brow of a gentle hill, the Cathedral of St Paul looms over the spill of buildings below like a giant snoozing shepherd. Medieval St Paul's, with its flying buttresses and tall spire, is sterner than Wren's neoclassical successor, more remorseless and uncompromising in its Gothic vernacular. Your eyes will be drawn to its monumental timber-and-lead spire, ribbed with small arched windows and culminating in a gilded pommel and cross, the tip of which is 489 feet above the ground, significantly higher than the tip of Wren's famous dome (365 feet). On the minutely detailed 'Copperplate Map' of London, engraved some time in the 1550s, the spire cuts through no fewer than eight rows of houses in the imperfect perspective of the time. Not until 1964, the first age of the skyscraper, would another building soar so high in the capital.

The cathedral is merely the nucleus of a virtual city within a city, owned and governed exclusively by the Catholic Church (or just *the* Church since we are almost 150 years off the revolt of Martin Luther and the birth of Protestantism), consisting of palaces, prisons, graveyards, colleges and stationers' booths, girdled by a stone wall to keep out the murderers, fornicators and n'er-do-wells who always seem to want to loiter in medieval churchyards.

Walk through St Paul's Chain into the churchyard.

You find yourself by the mighty southern entrance to the cathedral amidst traders and gossipmongers. Along the nave, to your left, are a series of rounded, Norman-style windows separated by pilasters while the 'New Work' on your right accommodates the choir, built in the later Early English Gothic style with more sharply pointed windows, protruding walls and flying buttresses. People are clustered in conversation or creeping round the corner like ants towards the parish church of St Gregory, so incongruously dwarfed by its titanic host. Follow them round to your left.

A square door reveals itself, flanked by two stone bell towers. The one on the right will shortly double up as a prison for Lollard heretics – that is, those who criticize the doctrine, riches and ceremonies of the Church as unwarranted by scripture. Go in. Plumes of incense fill the air, scouring away your thoughts and transporting you to another place.

Look up. Carved pillars shoot to the ceiling vaults, connected by arches forming a towering colonnade with a series of wide bays around the perimeter. Higher up is a clerestory with pointed arches and small windows. The pillars cast long shadows across the cold stone floor. As you move forwards you are cast into the darkness then the light – now the darkness, now the light – like a soul caught in the tumult of religious doubt. There is something tranquil about the atmosphere but the capaciousness of the nave and mysterious motions of the singing priests slicing their hands through the air makes you feel estranged, too, an infinitesimal spark against the unseen forces that govern the medieval universe.

But it's hard to train your thoughts upon the spiritual plane for too long. You have noticed something watching you from the other side of the aisle, a hawk. It scans you, resting on the wrist of a man in a jewel-studded doublet, red-and-black hose and ridiculously pointy and floppy shoes. Suddenly the hawk is distracted by the cooing of a pigeon from high above. It is about to spring into action when its foppish owner slides an embroidered silk hood over its head, and the bird becomes docile – or hoodwinked.

86

Further down the nave, a wrestling match is in progress.

And that's not the half of it. On your left, men are clustered around the font, locked in tense negotiations. Every so often you hear a tinkle of coins and a rummaging noise. The baptismal font might be where people first enter into a spiritual contract with their Maker but it's also where they forge commercial covenants with each other. A debt has just been repaid. Nearby, twelve scriveners sit at small tables, ready to write out letters, legal contracts, wills, or anything else you might like – for the right price.

You are just beginning to wonder where all the pews are when you are barged out of the way by a porter emerging through the Little North Door with a precarious pile of timbers, wilfully ignoring the penny toll. From the Little South Door opposite, farmers' wives waddle in from the villages of Camberwell and Hackney with baskets of bread and apples. Lawyers swirl around their allotted pillars, hungry for business, quills in hand. By the door in the northern aisle, people crane their necks to scan a board where employment notices are pinned up. Elsewhere, fruit sellers, stationers, butchers, mercers, milliners and quack doctors stand behind ramshackle wooden stalls in the northern and southern aisles, jockeying for people's attention, hawking their wares, crying out for business. To ease the facility of commerce, one pillar is marked with measurements so that cloth and timber might be cut to length. Beer and ale are freely available.

It feels more like a bazaar than a cathedral, and it's easy to forget that behind the archways of the colonnade, there are myriad tombs, chapels and altars in various bays and niches, glittering with candles. Beware of venturing into these dimly lit crevices; they are the haunts of cutpurses and bawds.

Although there are four 'virgers', who are meant to keep out whores, minstrels, carts and the like, the sheer size of the cathedral makes it difficult to police. The canons periodically issue high fulminations against people who 'expose their wares as it were in a public market ... without reverence for the holy place'. It might seem incongruous to time-travelling eyes to see so many commercial activities and transactions taking place within the sacred space of St Paul's. But medieval Londoners don't see it that way. After all, where else are they meant to go? Some thoroughfares, like Cheapside, are noticeably broader than other streets and there are some outdoor markets dotted about, but, as you'll discover on the course of your wanderings through the medieval city, there is a conspicuous lack of wide-open spaces, no city squares, public gardens or parks. As the biggest public space in London – and, moreover, one that is closed off to the elements – it is only natural that St Paul's should evolve into a major commercial hub, foreshadowing the success of the Royal Exchange in the sixteenth century and Covent Garden in the seventeenth. Paul's Walk, as the nave will come to be known, is the ideal place to idle, gossip, stroll, shop, people-watch, play games and present oneself to the world. Never mind religion, all the bustle inside the cathedral is a powerful metaphor for how ingrained the Church is into every aspect of Londoners' lives.

Make your way to the end of the nave. In front of you, beggars and minstrels are slumped on the stairs leading up to the choir, respectively croaking and singing. Now the colonnade on either side of you falls away, revealing the transept, as the cathedral spreads its wings towards the grand northern and southern entrances.

You realize just how much of a thoroughfare the edifice is. Porters are transporting goods on wagons and dray-carts piled high with merchandise. Boys are playing football with pigs' bladders stuffed with peas (though such is the violence of the game, you might not recognize it). If you stay long enough, you may even see folk merrily firing arrows and throwing stones at the pigeons and jackdaws high up in the crevices; an ordinance issued at some point in the late fourteenth century rails against the smashing of 'the beautiful and costly windows' on that very account.

The stained glass Rose Window rides high in the eastern wall like a magnesium moon, bathing the altar in shafts of kaleidoscopic light. You won't see much glass in the rest of the city – marvel while you can.

Behind the high altar, in the chapel of St Mary, something catches your eye. It's an elaborate Gothic shrine, carved from stone and alabaster in a pyramid shape, twinkling to the light of many candles with an altar table in front for offerings. Have a closer look. Cocooned within the ornamental carvings is one of the most magnificent tombs you will ever see: a coffin of gold and silver encrusted with gleaming jewels; in 1339, three goldsmiths were contracted to beautify the tomb for an entire year. The coffin contains the bones of Erkenwald, who you might be surprised to learn is the patron saint of London. (His name is familiar today only to historians.) As befits its beauty, this is a miracle-working shrine, and if you linger here for long enough you might see the odd infirm pilgrim hobble over, prostrate themselves in front of the shrine, then kiss the cold metal of the coffin.

Probably the son of Kentish royalty, Erkenwald lived in the first century of organized English Christianity, following St Augustine's successful proselytizing mission in 597. A pious, precocious boy who 'preferred to seek out the solitude of caves than mingle with the throngs in the courts of men', as the later *Life of Saint Erkenwald* (*c.*1000) put it, he embraced the monastic life, establishing Benedictine monasteries in Chertsey and Barking, to the west and east of London respectively. Just before he was born, Aethelbert, King of Kent, was converted to Christianity and made arrangements for whatever heathenish monstrosity then stood on what is now Ludgate Hill to be ripped down and replaced with a church in honour of St Paul. In 675 Erkenwald was consecrated Bishop of the East Saxons, who controlled London at the time, making him one of the earliest bishops of London, tasked with eradicating paganism after a series of relapses under recalcitrant East Saxon kings.

For the next eighteen years he was a holy and conscientious bishop, living into robust old age in which he took to travelling from village to village in a horse-drawn litter, promoting the Creed. After his death, his bones were housed in a reliquary in the first St Paul's Cathedral along with the litter, which became an object of great reverence; people believed that by touching or kissing it they could be cured of whatever ghastly disease they might be suffering from. Those too infirm to make the pilgrimage could simply kiss splinters that had been removed and brought to them.

A cult of St Erkenwald flourished for over eight and a half centuries. His fame received a boost when, after a great fire in 1087, one of London's many catastrophic conflagrations, his bones 'miraculously' survived. (His wooden litter, the survival of which would have been much more miraculous, didn't.) After the cathedral had been rebuilt, the canons, hankering after an inspiring patron saint, built a lavish silver shrine to the east of the high altar, spurred on perhaps by plans afoot at Westminster Abbey to canonize Edward the Confessor. The remains of St Erkenwald were translated to this new shrine in 1148. To help to raise funds, a canon penned the *Miracula sancti*

Erkenwaldi, a detailed collection of St Erkenwald's miracles to be recounted at feast days and during matins prayers.

Erkenwald cuts an inoffensive enough figure in the image above his shrine with his beard, staff and vestments. But this belies his highly vengeful nature, as concocted and recounted in the *Miracula*. The punishments meted out by Erkenwald tend to fit the crime perfectly; he is the Lord of Poetic Justice. In one miracle, a silly silversmith called Eustace plays the fool in the workshop where St Erkenwald's jewel-encrusted sepulchre is under construction. Worse, 'the others present lent a ready ear to his garrulity instead of ignoring his drunken yapping'. While not ideal behaviour, this in itself need not damn his soul. What he does next, however, does. He climbs inside the half-constructed tomb and cries out, 'I am the most holy Erkenwald: bring me figs; ask for my help; make me a sepulchre of silver!' At this, he is struck 'deep inside' with agonizing pains. His workmates scoop him out of the coffin and take him home where, 'by the stroke of divine judgement' he ends up in a far less opulent coffin: his own.

In medieval London, saints' cults are mutable and stage-managed to reinforce particular facets of belief and dogma. Around the time of your visit, a clergyman is composing an alliterative poem about St Erkenwald in the English vernacular, perhaps to be read aloud for entertainment to the Cathedral Guild at their annual feast. It addresses the conundrum of whether there could ever be a place in heaven for the virtuous pagan. It tells the story of how, in the late seventh century, some merry masons are digging the foundations for St Paul's Cathedral when they stumble across a stone coffin. Wrenching it open, they discover a gilded interior with a perfectly preserved body of a man dressed like a king. He shows not the slightest sign of decay, as though he'd been embalmed – but he hasn't. The Bishop of London – Erkenwald – is fetched from his monastery in Barking. After a night of convulsive prayer, he conducts a High Mass the next day then visits the site, which is thronged with people who believe they have witnessed a miracle. Erkenwald implores the entombed man to tell his story, and he speaks 'as though with borrowed life', as though communicating from hell.

The man in the tomb is an unidentified judge from New Troy (i.e. Londinium) who lived in the wilderness of paganism when the light of Christianity was unknown. It seems that, unlike most judges, he was renowned for his honesty and probity since the citizens regaled his corpse with regal dress and tokens when he died, presumably as a mark of gratitude. Erkenwald is keen to inquire after the location of the judge's soul – is he in a state of grace or languishing in the darkness of hell? Since he lived in a pre-Christian world, hell is the answer; shut out of the 'banquet of the redeemed', he is the 'unhappiest mortal in the world'. The crowd is moved to tears, and no one more so than Erkenwald. 'If only I could say, I baptize thee in the name of the Father, Son, and Holy Ghost', laments Erkenwald. That way, the poor judge could be cleansed of his original sin and saved. In a cartoonish twist some tears spill on to the judge's head, performing a surprise surrogate baptism. Suddenly, the judge's body crumples into jet-black stinking carrion but it's no matter because his soul soars into heaven and everyone processes through the cathedral intoxicated with elegiac euphoria.

Whether or not Londoners actually believe this story is a moot point. On one level, it is great 'deathbed literature' – and so is of 'pressing existential interest for every man and woman in late medieval England', in the words of the historian Eamon Duffy. It also illustrates, albeit rather preposterously, the absolute necessity of sacramental channels of grace (baptism, in this case) for human salvation, reinforcing the Church's hold over people's lives and deaths.

But most importantly – and this cuts right to the heart of the medieval mindset – it hammers home the Church's monopoly on the truth. The Church has a near-tyrannical control over intellectual inquiry. In a telling passage, Erkenwald berates the dean of the cathedral for resorting to something as puny and fallible as man's intellectual faculties to try to solve the mystery of the judge's identity (he had ordered an archival investigation). 'We receive no benefit seeking the truth by ourselves,' explains Erkenwald, 'but we all openly rejoice in God and ask His grace, who is generous to send counsel.' It would be another three centuries before anyone would dare to remove God from human inquiry, and this new, more rational mindset would brew to fruition in the coffeehouses and scientific academies of seventeenth- and eighteenth-century London, both of which are on our itinerary you'll be pleased to hear.

Turn left into the transept and walk towards the crucifix – or rood – above the Great North Door to the cathedral. It stands in a commanding position on a wooden platform, flanked by the chapels of St John the Baptist and the Virgin Mary. The canons will tell you this is the crucifix that Joseph of Arimathea set up in Caerleon, South Wales, when he brought Christianity to Britain in the immediate aftermath of his great-nephew's crucifixion, having travelled around the West Country with the teenage Jesus years earlier. None of this is true but still it is an object of great veneration. If you keep your eyes peeled, you'll find other relics dotted around the cathedral – the knife of Our Lord, a hand of St John the Evangelist, some hair of Mary Magdalene, a fragment of Thomas à Becket's skull, some bones of the 11,000 virgins of Cologne, even a stone from the spot of the Ascension – all preserved in beautiful, jewel-studded, pilgrim-seducing reliquaries. Perhaps they are just pigs' bones, like the Pardoner in the *Canterbury Tales* has.

As you move through the transept, you'll encounter a number of small chapels tucked away behind the columns. Mysterious cadences emanate from within. By the Great North Door, there are a cluster of chapels devoted to various saints and the holy ghost. Find the one dedicated to John the Baptist; it will be decorated with paintings and images from the saint's life, so look for a head on a silver platter. Once you've found it, peer through the grille.

Inside, a priest kneels in front of a tomb singing a requiem Mass. Beside him is the Eucharist – the body and blood of Christ in the form of bread and wine. This is one of over seventy chantry chapels in the cathedral, this one founded by Sir John Poultney, a former Lord Mayor of London, in 1349.

Chantry chapels exist to speed the souls of the dead from the flames of purgatory into the kingdom of heaven. The single biggest concern of late-medieval religion is what happens to you after you die; how you live this life is only really of interest insofar as it bears upon the next. With death so terrifyingly close at hand, it could hardly be any other way. Life expectancy is pitifully low and infant mortality pitifully high by twenty-first-century standards. The collective horror of the plague of 1348, which wiped out getting on for a third of the English population in a matter of months, remains fresh in people's minds. If you pose existential questions to medieval Londoners, you'll soon uncover a belief that life is merely an antechamber for eternal paradise or eternal damnation; a 'vale of tears' as the Life of St Erkenwald puts it, echoing the Vulgate.

That the crucifixion of Jesus Christ cleanses humankind of its original sin, which gushed from the saliva of Adam as he sank his teeth into the forbidden fruit at the behest of frail

Eve, everyone is convinced. The church is a spiritual life-support machine, funnelling grace into sinners via sacramental 'tubes', such as baptism, the Eucharist and the last rites. If any of these tubes become disconnected, then the 'essence' of the worshipper – his or her soul – shrivels up and dies.

Unfortunately, though, everyone has their own spiritual meter that clocks up 'venial' and 'minor' sin in addition to their innate original sin. There are certain things you can do to work these off – prayers, fasting, giving alms to charity. But ultimately, most Christians will end up with a negative balance sheet when they come to face their Maker at their day of judgement. Purgatory, a sad and shadowy world between heaven and hell, is where your soul is sent to burn off its sin. It must be purified before it can be admitted to heaven. The length of time you spend in purgatory, and the intensity of your torment, are conditional upon the extent and grievousness of venial sins committed upon earth (if you commit a mortal sin like murder or homosexual intercourse, by the way, you'll be going straight to hell for ever).

Some people can expect to spend thousands of years languishing in the agonizing flames of purgatory. But there are ways and means of reducing your stay. This is where the chantry priests come in.

The chapels around the Great North Door are devoted to a wide range of saints – St James, St Thomas, St Margaret, John the Baptist, even the Holy Ghost – and it's believed that priests can summon these benevolent spirits and get them to intercede with God on behalf of the bequeather's soul. The most effective way, it is believed, is for the chantry priests to sing specially tailored requiem Masses. Spiritual credit can be obtained whether the benefactor is living or dead. Purgatory was 'revealed' to the Church in the eleventh or twelfth century, and during the last 125 years, chantries have become a dominant feature of Catholicism. The fourteenth century has witnessed a boom in chantry bequests.

But it's not cheap. If you want someone to sing Masses for your soul ad infinitum you need to supply the funding. But people do, sometimes selling entire estates for the good of their soul. Roger Holme, a Londoner who must have been supremely anxious about the state of his, has recently hired no fewer than seven chantry priests to sing Masses in St Paul's. Essentially, then, you can buy your way out of purgatory; as a later German couplet puts it, 'As soon as the coin in the coffer rings / the soul from purgatory springs'.

As the Lollard followers of John Wyclif are keen to point out, there isn't the faintest shred of biblical evidence for the existence of purgatory, a claim that will come back to haunt the Church 130 years later when Martin Luther launches his revolt against the unwarranted impositions of the Papacy. Yet for most medieval Londoners, it is profoundly reassuring to know that you can *do* something to mitigate the inevitability of death and the misery of a nasty, brutish and short tenure on earth; without such beliefs, what would be the point of enduring all life's hardships and miseries? Only the wealthy can afford chantries in the cathedral itself, but many ordinary Londoners are members of religious fraternities, which club together to pray for the souls of their members after their deaths.

Leave the cathedral via the great northern entrance and curve around to the north-eastern corner of the churchyard precinct, to the al-fresco pulpit at Paul's Cross. It is full of stationers' stalls, the forerunners of the bookshops you saw in the same place in Shakespeare's London. Don't expect to see manuscript books shelved by category. Books are luxury objects, expensive to produce and the preserve mainly of the clergy, aristocracy, gentry and wealthy tradesmen; here, such people bring pieces of writing for scriveners to copy onto beautiful paper supplied by a parchminer, limners to illustrate it, and bookbinders to bind the leaves together with leather or board covers. It's a slow and laborious process, which is why booksellers, unlike other tradesmen, always remained stationary, whence the name of their eventual guild, the Stationers. For those lower down the social pyramid, the exchange of information, ideas and stories takes place orally.

This corner of the churchyard has a deeper political significance. The city of London is so small and compact (by modern standards) that an open-air parliament – or *folkmoot* – of all its citizens (who form one-quarter of the wider London population, so around 10,000 people) is not just some ancient Athenian fantasy but a reality playing a part, albeit quite limited these days, in the government of the city. The bells ringing from the timbered, freestanding Jesus Belfry on the eastern cusp of the churchyard summon the citizens together; until the ascension of Edward II in 1307, the *folkmoot* met three times a year and was compulsory for all citizens. At these meetings, the Lord Mayor and aldermen might be removed from power by the citizenry, though in practice this seems to have happened about as frequently as the queen exercises her right of veto in the twenty-first century.

Sanctuary

Follow Paternoster Row to Cheapside then head north, to St Martin's Le Grand, another precinct within the confines of a monastery, this one containing streets, alleys, shops, houses, colleges and alehouses. You'll find it on your left. It should be easy enough to get in, but you might want to think twice before doing so, for St Martin's Le Grand, along with Westminster Abbey to the west, is emerging as one of London's leading sanctuaries, sheltering fugitives from the law, increasingly for the best part of their lives. Inside, the king's writ runs dry. On the other hand, should anyone give you grief for being an alien yourself, whether the Lord Mayor or a blood-baying mob, this is the place to be, a mini city of refuge.

If Julian Assange had been living in fourteenth-century London, he wouldn't have had to seek out a foreign embassy – he could have just headed for a church. The practice of seeking sanctuary in a holy place stretches back to antiquity, and fed into Anglo-Saxon law codes. Since virtually every crime during the Anglo-Saxon period (*c.*450–1066) was redeemable for money, a sanctuary was the best place to seek compensation and, perhaps abetted by the intermediary services of a priest, to seek forgiveness and reconciliation. It has lost none of its appeal. About a decade ago, a monk at Westminster Abbey composed a set of arguments 'for and against the privileges of sanctuary at Westminster', arguing that sanctuary was a force for good, protecting the poor and the weak against arbitrary punishment in a way that was consistent with the miraculous protective power of holy relics.

But there is a darker side to sanctuary, and many members of the merchant oligarchy find it maddening to have enclaves of lawlessness right under their noses. Go to Guildhall and the aldermen will tell you how St Martin's Le Grand is becoming a haven for crooks, murderers, rapists, robbers, runaway servants, and potentially even practitioners of high treason. One petition, from 1402, complains that apprentices and servants had been robbing their masters' goods and transporting them to St Martin's, where they lived at the king's pleasure on the proceeds. To make matters worse, the precinct of St Martin's, and indeed all sanctuaries, are free from the draconian economic regulation of the city guilds, on which more later, beckoning a swarm of counterfeit traders and alien shopkeepers – mainly goldsmiths, drapers and beer-brewers forbidden from openly displaying their goods elsewhere.

They have a point. Sometimes sanctuaries – the one in front of you in particular – look more like bolt-holes for criminals than legitimate social institutions. In 1332, for example, John Frowe of Lincoln, fired by an old grudge, stalked a mason called Robert Dodmerton through the streets of London with a dagger in his hand. He bided his time and waited until his enemy was near the gate of St Martin's. Then he stabbed him in the neck and hopped into the sanctuary, safe and untouchable, while his victim died a bloody death on the street outside.

It is the dream of every prisoner carted anywhere even vaguely near the southern gate to St Martin's Le Grand, whether to the Guildhall Sessions or even execution at Tower Hill, to bolt into the sanctuary and savour the sweet taste of freedom. (The situation would persist for many years. In 1430, a soldier called Knight was languishing in Newgate prison. A group of cunning friends fabricated debt charges against him, requiring him to be frogmarched to Guildhall – St Martin's lay on the route. Lying in ambush in Panyer Alley, they waited until he was taken past the south side of St Martin's, then leaped out, and dragged him into the precinct. Violating the ancient laws of sanctuary, the sheriffs, aldermen and the City Chamberlain along with a crowd of people stormed St Martin's and wrenched Knight and his rescuers out, slamming them all in Newgate. Ultimately the case was bounced up to Star Chamber, the highest legal court in the land, which, on the king's instruction, freed the five and returned Knight to his sanctuary, underlining its inviolable nature in the eyes of the law. Given all the escapes and near-misses, you'd think someone might have suggested that carting prisoners past St Martin's was not such a great idea. But no.)

By this point, you may be wondering why on earth medieval kings, as fountainheads of justice, would tolerate places like St Martin's Le Grand, where their laws are thrown out of the window with impunity. But from the king's perspective, such a royally chartered enclave, within the city but free from the autonomy of Guildhall, is a useful check upon the overweening ambitions of the city Fathers, just like the Tower of London. But more than that, whenever a king makes a show of defending the rights of sanctuary, he is making a powerful assertion of his own power, since only the king is above the law; a similar process is at work whenever American presidents pardon prisoners in the twenty-first century.

Double back, go down Newgate Street, past the enormous monastic foundation of Christ's Hospital, through the gate itself then turn right onto Giltspur Street.

'A sport they call a tournament'

Walk up Giltspur Street (where you can buy some of the finest spurs in town, to goad your horse into action), veering left at Pie Corner. This leads into 'a smooth Field, both in Name and Deed; where every Friday, unless it be a solemn bidden Holy day, is a notable show of Horses to be sold' along with 'swine with their long sides, cows with distended udders, oxen of bulk immense, and woolly flocks'. What the chronicler William Fitzstephen called a 'smooth field' in the late twelfth century, people in the 1390s call 'Schmyt Fyeld' or, to translate into modern parlance, Smithfield. It is a suburb immediately to the north-west of the city, not yet much built up. But, aside from the odd hawk and hound, the only animals you're going to see here today are horses. And not just any horses – magnificent caparisoned steeds, some of the finest in the land. But they're not for sale. They are coming to compete in an international three-day jousting tournament organized by King Richard to amplify his chivalric credentials across the length and breadth of Christendom. It's going to be quite a spectacle.

You will be familiar with jousts from films and television. Two knights charging at each other to win the affection of their swooning damsel is ingrained into most people's mental picture of the Middle Ages. But they grew out of a more violent and chaotic eleventh-century tradition: the mêlée – in which hundreds, sometimes thousands of knights intermingled in a mock battle.

To many commentators, there wasn't much that was 'mock' about it. 'A sport they call a tournament,' wrote one hostile clerical commentator, 'but the better name would be a torment.' Still, in a martial society, it was the ideal training ground for warriors. 'A youth must have seen his blood flow and felt his cheek crack under the blow of his adversary,' wrote the chronicler and courtier Roger of Hoveden in the twelfth century, 'and have been thrown to the ground twenty times. Thus will he be able to face real war with the hope of victory.' No ivory towers or diplomatic training needed for a youthful member of the political elite then: just cold, blunt, bloody, cheek-cracking warfare.

Inherited from the ancient custom of single combat between the champions of rival armies – like Achilles and Hector, say – jousting was originally a minor part of the mêlée tournament, but eventually grew to eclipse it; by 1350 most tournaments had evolved into organized jousts. After all, it was more contained, less disruptive, and less bloody. It didn't imperil the defence of

Christendom by killing off 'those who fought' in their great numbers, and so was sanctioned (grudgingly) by the Church. King Edward I, who strove to conquer Wales and Scotland, liked to model himself on the legendary King Arthur, King of the Britons, and so encouraged non-lethal tournaments as portrayed in Arthurian romances; his 'Round Table' jousts grew popular, with the combatants often adopting names like Lancelot and Galahad.

The presence of women as spectators at tournaments from at least 1279 also encouraged the intensification of the theatrical element, with knights jousting to win the love of ladies, who played the parts of damsels in distress, mistresses and martial muses; it would not have been appropriate for women to attend the maelstrom of the mêlée.

At first, jousts were performed in London's grandest street, Cheapside, from the church of St Michael le Querne at the west to the Stocks Market in the east, though the location was never ideal owing to economic disruption and the lack of space for spectators. So from the mid-fourteenth century, tournaments commuted north to Smithfield, where the grass could be rolled, flattened, scoured of stones, and covered with sand and gravel so the horses didn't slide into the mud mid-tournament.

With the bells of the surrounding churches chiming for none prayers ('none' here meaning the ninth hour of the religious day, so – confusingly – 3 p.m., and – even more confusingly – pronounced 'noon'), make your way past the sprawling complex of St Bartholomew Hospital on your right into Smithfield proper.

A festival atmosphere awaits you. The royal standard flies. Elevated wooden stalls have been erected in the fields, forming a large square. In the centre is the king's box. The stalls are crawling with people. Apprentices yell, washerwomen cackle and old men tell tales of chivalric lore. Behind the stalls are chequered pavilions, flapping gently in the breeze, emblazoned with the heraldic arms of the contenders (though they are not here yet, their heralds and servants have come on ahead). There is music. There is verse. There are pie sellers, who have left their eponymous Corner, and are attending to their charcoal braziers. You can buy pies of goose, duck, mutton, lark, finch or hen. Skins of wine are passed around: for a penny you can gurgle down all you can. Space on the scaffolding is at a premium and many people are sitting on the ground. Some of the wealthier citizens, in their skin-tight hose, pointy shoes and dandyish black hats, are reclining on coarse skin cushions stuffed with moss or hair.

Since rich and poor have turned out to watch the games, you now have an excellent view of the social panorama of medieval London. Especially their clothes.

In medieval London, how you dress is a powerful statement of who you are. Doublets, petticoats, stockings, hats, fur-trimmed gowns, pointy shoes, corsets, jewels, hats – all are immediate and involving signifiers not just of fashion trends and taste but *rank*, and hence, in the medieval mindset, identity. Nowhere in the history of London is the relationship between clothes and social status so pronounced as in the late medieval city. Consider. In the last five minutes, you've passed a wrinkled woman in a yellow hood beaming at you and now a pie seller is tugging at your cuffs, enticing you in the direction of a warm beef pie. Both have reached various conclusions, specifically whether there's any point in talking to you, based on your appearance, and especially your clothes.

The drapers, tailors, stainers, chaucers (shoemakers), skinners and haberdashers, as well as a whole host of specialist traders in the clothing trade, are enjoying a sales boom.

Following the broadening of prosperity after the plague epidemic and the upsurge in trade following the development of chartered trading guilds, demand for fine clothes is high amongst the prosperous citizens of London. Moreover, by the 1390s you'll find a wider range of clothes available than ever before due to some mid-century quantum leaps in tailoring – namely the arrival of the button and new ways to tailor clothes to hug the body rather than having them hang more loosely, as togas did. Fashion filters down; the city bourgeois are highly aspirational creatures, mimicking the dress of their social superiors wherever possible.

All of which unsettles the ruling elite. The problem is that fashion-fuelled judgements are inevitably based upon fleeting perceptions. And perceptions are very easily manipulated if people dress 'above their station', as they are wont to do. This is less of a problem in tight-knit rural communities where it's generally pretty obvious who is a villein (surf), who a yeoman and who a lord. But a city with a resident population of around 40,000 and a daily headcount of many more is in danger of becoming a catwalk of deceit, giving people ample opportunities to reinvent themselves. 'I thought I was queen here, but now I see there are thousands of them!' shouted Joan of Navarre on entering Bruges in 1301, at the sight of reams of bourgeois women bedizened in silk, furs and jewels. Likewise, the English elites are keen to draw clear boundaries against these social encroachments to protect their perch at the top of the tree.

To this end – and this is virtually inconceivable to modern sensibilities unless you are of a theocratic persuasion, perhaps – the government tries to regulate what people wear in London, at least at certain points throughout the fourteenth century. In 1363, building on earlier legislation, Edward III acted against what Parliament rather histrionically described as 'the outrageous and excessive apparel of divers people above their estate, to the great destruction and impoverishment of the land'. These are the first comprehensive Sumptuary Laws, a Europe-wide phenomenon which seeks to limit what you can wear according to your social status, and to prevent grooms dressing like craftsmen, craftsmen like gentlemen, gentlemen like esquires, esquires like knights and so on.

Regarding what you can wear, they are detailed and unequivocal. Knights with an annual income of 200 marks may wear cloth up to a value of 6 marks but *not* cloth of gold, nor a cloak or mantle lined with pure miniver or sleeves of ermine. They should stick to other types of fur. Esquires with land yielding £200 per year and merchants with goods worth over £1,000 (who are coupled together) can't wear anything made with cloth exceeding £3 6s in price, nor jewels, unless in their hair. Cloth of silk and silver, though, is fine. Craftsmen and yeomen must stick to native rabbit, fox, cat or lamb fur. Those lucky enough to have lands worth £1,000 per year can wear whatever they damn well like, though swineherds, dairymaids, oxherds and the like, who don't have 40s to their name, must settle for blanket and russet – and rope girdles. The leg-flaunting doublets and vividly coloured hose that have caught your eye around town are meant to be restricted to men of noble rank but in practice any young fop will do their best to get hold of them.

The laws may still be in force (if force is the right word, since they're widely flouted and virtually impossible to apply) – a chronicler claims that Richard II renewed them in 1388 (but the parliamentary roll for that year has not survived into the twenty-first century). But even if not, there's no shortage of moralists, poets and chroniclers to lambast the extravagance of fashion in the reign of arch-fop Richard II. The Monk of

Evesham singles out waiters whose hanging sleeves were so fashionably long that they sloshed into the banqueters' broth; 'it [is] scarce possible to distinguish the poor from the rich, the servant from the master, or a priest from another man', writes another eyewitness who was probably exaggerating somewhat.

Ultimately, in spite of all the regulations, fine clothes seem to have the power to *confer* status, overriding one's background, hoodwinking observers and fashioning 'a social body from cloth'. It is here, in late medieval London, and particularly at great spectacles such as the joust, that England's fashion industry bursts into colourful life.

Set your stool down behind the rows of cross-legged spectators. Or did you forget to bring one? Don't worry – see in the distance, just beyond the horse pond, the cluster of elm trees? Head over. They'll provide you with an excellent vantage point.

Harken! You're treading on blood-rich soil, so tread softly, out of respect. Although Smithfield is a site of pageantry and colour – not least for the annual Bartholomew Fair at the end of each summer with its dwarves, dancing bears and fire-eaters – it's a site of slaughter and suffering too, not just of the cattle herded to the meat market each week but also humans, especially those found guilty of treason and who must endure the unimaginable horror of being hanged, drawn and quartered under the bower of these elms. What the name of the punishment conceals – and people often forget this – is that in addition to being half-strangled, hoisted down and hacked to pieces, you also have the pleasure of being castrated then having your entrails reeled out and burned on a bonfire as an eternal darkness sets in. The Scottish nobleman William Wallace, so fancifully commemorated in Mel Gibson's *Braveheart*, was the first to suffer this ignominious fate almost ninety years ago; soon others will follow in his footsteps. Thankfully, you won't be witnessing any of this; you'll see plenty of bloodshed elsewhere.

Pick an elm, clamber up it, and find yourself a sturdy branch. I hope you've already eaten; even up here you won't be able to escape the waft of sizzling meat, which could be torturous on an empty stomach. Go reasonably high for a fine view of the peaking gables and multitudinous towers of the metropolis. See too all the people standing on tiptoes on the inner ledge of the city walls, gazing down through the gaps in the battlements at the combat field below.

Now you can give it your full attention. In the centre of the field are the lists – a rectangular combat area about sixty feet long and forty feet wide marked off by a palisade – a fence of tightly packed pointed wooden stakes set in a ditch. Sleek, vivid shields hang from it, glistening in the sunlight; from a distance they look like baubles on a Christmas tree. Bolt upright, set back from the lists, stand lances – long wooden spears with deathly steel points – awaiting their masters. In the middle of the lists is a wooden barrier, around the height of a horse, stretched with a luminous canvas. This is designed to stop the horses from crashing into one another mid-combat – a practical measure, but one that has diminished the excitement of the all-out carnage of bygone tournaments.

Trumpets blast. A wave of anticipation undulates through the crowd. The young King Richard has appeared in his box, his brown locks spilling down from his crown; next to him, his twenty-four-year-old queen, the slender figure of Anne of Bohemia. One person whose stomach must be churning right now is Geoffrey Chaucer, who, aside from being an esteemed poet, is also in the employ of the court, and responsible for erecting the spectators' scaffolding safely. He will not want a repeat of 1329 when, at a Cheapside joust, the scaffolding collapsed just as Queen Philippa and some of her ladies were climbing the steps, grievously injuring ladies and knights. If it hadn't been for the intercession of the queen, the carpenters responsible would have met their end on another scaffold.

Soon, you get a glimpse of what very few other people can yet see, a vanguard of jugglers, minstrels and tumblers pouring through Giltspur Street, St Sepulchre's Alley, Cock Lane and Hosier Lane like an incoming wave and converging at the southern end of Smithfield. Behind them is a line of noble ladies on palfreys, each leading a knight, fully armed for the tilt, on a silver chain. Opposite the royal box sit London's Lord Mayor and aldermen, impeccably turned out in their ermine furs, and delighted to be hosting such a prestigious event within the liberties of the capital (though an extra-mural suburb, Smithfield is within the City ward of Farringdon, named after Sir Nicholas de Faringdon, a former Lord Mayor of London, so their pride is justified).

'Behold!' yells a member of the crowd, pointing to the cart-wheeling and summersaulting tumblers and knights sweeping towards them; '*There!*'

Silence falls. Suddenly, the area around the stalls is crawling with minstrels and heralds, leaping about with their harps, fiddles, bagpipes and flutes, singing songs of their masters' accomplishments on the tournament circuit of Europe.

The ladies on their caparisoned horses lead their knights in silver chains to the pavilion area. They dismount and their servants lead them to their boxes in the galleries. The knights' squires run off to fetch their masters' horses, which resemble walking tapestries. The contestants' padded helmets are carefully fitted. Some of the knights sport colourful wooden crests – lions, stags, unicorns, griffins, leopards, falcons and so on – and the wealthiest knights are clad in armour made from a precious metal called laton, which is a mixture of gold and brass. Now the foreign challengers, led by the Count of St Pol, trot forwards. All are ready for the tilt. All that's needed now is for the king to give his permission for the joust to begin. This is forthcoming.

It's important everyone understands the rules, so from the four corners of the field, the heralds shout them out in a medley of languages. You'd be forgiven for thinking that tilting is an elaborate and complex sport, but medieval orators have a knack for over-egging the pudding and in fact there's only really one, relatively simple goal: to knock your opponent off his horse as quickly and dramatically as possible.

Beyond that, there are just two rules to bear in mind: one, whoever 'unhorses' his opponent first is the winner (should they manage to knock each other off simultaneously then the joust must be replayed); two, 'he that smiteth his opponent's horse shall have no prize'. This is essentially a staged show of military dexterity between members of the social and political elite.

You hear an almighty scream of '*Laissez Aller!*', at which the crowd goes silent. A horn is blown and two horses accelerate down the run.

For the next three hours or so, the air is filled with the sounds of lances shattering against breastplates, horses rearing in terror, and knights tumbling and thundering to the ground, all set to gasps, swoons, tears and applause under a cream autumn sky. It will become obvious to you fairly early on in the proceedings that, however violent the tournament's history, the aim of the game is unequivocally *not* to kill your opponent.

That's not to say jousts aren't dangerous – of course, when your whole suit of armour, not including helmet, lance or shield can weigh as much as sixty pounds and there's every chance, should you be hurled down, that your warhorse will come crashing down on top of you and you will suffocate (this is how most unlucky combatants die). Also, if your opponent is galloping towards you at speeds of up to forty miles per hour, lance outstretched, you will be praying to the saints that there's no fault in your armour, or you could be meeting them much sooner than hoped. Nonetheless, the whole performance feels like just that, a performance, a theatrical re-enactment of mortal combat, a vestige of a more chivalric age rather than the real thing. You'd be right in thinking so. At the time of your visit, England is moving towards a post-feudal society in which aristocratic status will no longer necessarily be commensurate with military acumen and achievement on the battlefield.

Night at the inn

The tilting continues for a number of hours until the spectators decamp to the Bishop of London's palace in St Paul's Churchyard for a lavish, bacchanalian feast, during which oceans of Malmsey wine will be consumed. You are now feeling chilly up in the tree, and the light is beginning to die. The City at night is closely guarded – a watch of 200 men patrol the wards, four boats of archers prowl the Thames, and twenty-four men are meant to keep a vigil on each gate. Anyone (especially those of lower social status) found wandering the streets late at night without good reason and a lit lantern is liable to be hurled into one of the lock-up gaols, to appear before the Lord Mayor in the morning: not an enticing prospect. This is because the authorities are terrified of crime in a city which, on moonless nights, can be pitch-black.

Wandering about the City is not an option. So why not instruct a wherryman to sail you to Southwark, where you can find somewhere to spend the night.

Retrace your footsteps to Ludgate and head south, down St Andrew's Hill, with the precinct of Blackfriars on your right, and skirt its eastern bank (which stands in for the south-westernmost stretch of the city wall), walking towards the Thames with the precinct of Blackfriars' monastery to your left.

Before long you will find yourself on Puddle Wharf, a shallow, semi-circular beach overlooked by timbered houses and trees. This is a favourite spot for watering horses. As they rear their snouts from the muddy river and trot out, they dig puddles in the earth, whence (so one theory goes) its name. It's also the main quay for Blackfriars' monastery, so you shouldn't have to wait too long for a vacant wherry to come along. When it appears, tell the wherryman you'd like to go to the dock of St Mary over the water. As you make the crossing, note the colourful signs painted onto the whitewashed walls of the houses on the opposite bank – a cardinal's hat, gun, castle, boar's head, crane and swan.

Climb up the river stairs. The Gothic church and priory of St Mary Overie are on your left and the impressive stone palace of the Bishop of Winchester stands guard to your right, next to the inn of the Prior of St Swithun. Beyond that, where the ribbon of houses had overlooked the riverfront in Shakespearean Southwark, there's very little development. But if you walk a little further forwards and look to your right, you should just be able to make out in the dying light a cluster of detached timbered houses standing in their own gardens in the distance, set back from the riverfront, opposite Baynard's Castle and the Temple on the north bank. This is London's pre-eminent red-light district – or rather, striped-cloak district, since that is the assignation of a prostitute. Technically, the Church disapproves of prostitution, hauling dozens of men and women into its ecclesiastical courts each year to answer allegations of fornication, adultery and prostitution, and subjecting them to humiliating, musical punishments. But this doesn't unduly worry the Bishop of Winchester, upon whose seventy-acre manor within the Liberty of the Clink these brothels – or stews (from the Old French *estuve*, 'stove', since they were originally bathhouses) – lie, beyond the reach of the City authorities, and rented out to eighteen or so stewmongers, many of whom are shrewd Flemish businesswomen. Because they ply their trade on the Bishop of Winchester's land, prostitutes are nicknamed Winchester Geese.

Unpaved and fouled by the rotting intestines of animals and human excrement, the streets and alleys around here are physically dirty but their moral impurity is underlined by some of their names – Codpiece Lane, Sluts' Hole, Cuckold Court, Whores' Nest, Maiden Lane – which give more than a hint of the kind of activity that goes on here. Many of the stews were burned down in the Peasants' Revolt but were quickly rebuilt and you can find the Rose, the Unicorn, the Bell and the Bull's Head. The nuns of Stratford even have their own brothel, the Barge, channelling the income into charitable works. Brothels are tightly regulated. Prostitutes 'that would leave her sin' should not be made to work, nor should they be anyone's wife or a nun. They should await custom meekly, not grab potential customers by their gowns or sleeves. No stewholder may keep any woman 'that has any sickness of burning' and on holy days, the stews must only open from noon to 2 p.m. Bawds mustn't attempt to solicit custom from across the river (though the painted signs you saw earlier might well do the job). Customers should get their money's worth – at night 'no single woman to take money to lie with any man, but she may lie with him all night, till the morrow'. Given how frequently these are reiterated, you can assume that all this and more *did* happen, though if anyone is caught breaking the rules they are liable to a large fine (and sometimes imprisonment), further swelling the coffers (and prison) of the Bishop of Winchester. As for the 'women who live by their bodies' themselves, some are Dutch or Flemish, some from other parts of the country ('a strumpet from York' appears in the records), and some even commute from the City each night.

Turn left and make your way to the high street. It's getting later and blacker. Unless you want to spend the night in a stew, you need to find an inn (not the Tabard or Walnut Tree though – they're out of your price bracket).

You are standing outside a likely looking inn. In the courtyard, a pair of lanterns give out a meagre glow. The well-trodden soil is smeared with fresh horse dung. You can make out galleries on three sides of the courtyard, reached by an external staircase. Ahead of you, some servant boys help a pair of travellers dismount, leading their horses towards stables ahead. Eying you suspiciously are some talbots – a type of guard dog extinct in the twenty-first century, with a light coat, big ears and hefty jaws.

You walk into the stone building to find yourself in a smoky, shadowy chamber. There is the faint aroma of horse manure and dog piss, mashed into the rushes by travellers' boots, and the pungent smell of burning tallow candles. A log fire crackles away in the middle of the chamber.

Though the hall is very sparsely furnished, it's a fug of conviviality with men and women sitting on benches around a shaky trestle table eating a murky-looking soup, slurping ale, and sharing travellers' tales, some far-fetched. Some of these wayfarers are pilgrims, ready to ride to the shrine of Thomas à Becket in Canterbury on the morrow, others are merchants returning to the city having overseen shipments elsewhere; others still have business in Westminster.

You hear the click of bone dice against the table – a game

of hazard is in progress. Nearer you, two guests are taking turns to throw pebbles at a black-and-white chequered board, closely watched by some others, who have obviously placed bets on whether the stone will land on the black or the white. This game is known as queek, and is popular. You'd be advised not to join in: it might be rigged. Eight years ago, an embroiderer from the Ropery district was indicted for corrupting a queek board in which all the white squares were imperceptibly sunken 'so that all those who played with the said board . . . were maliciously and deceitfully deprived of their property'.

It shouldn't take you long to find the portly innkeeper and request board and lodging. You'll have to convince him that you're respectable first, though, and here you may well run into difficulties if you're a woman travelling solo. In this eventuality, you'd do better to seek accommodation in a monastic guest-house nearby – you could try the Bermondsey Monastery, to the east of London Bridge – whose principles of Christian hospitality will hopefully see you off the streets for the night.

Assuming for the moment you *are* allowed to stay, head over to the communal table, find a space and greet the other travellers. There are a number of ways of doing this. First, doff your hood. If they follow suit, put yours back on and say one of the following: 'Sire, God you keep!', 'What do ye? How is it with you?' or, if you like the look of someone in particular, 'Where have ye been so long?' Now share some stories of your travels, but be careful what you say – if you're taken for a sorcerer or witch, the night could end badly.

It won't be long before your food arrives. In all honesty, it won't be particularly appetizing. It's possible some of your neighbours might have forked out for meat or fish but most are tucking into something called pottage, best described as a stew with a foundation of meat or vegetable stock and layered with peas (white or green), oats, aggressively boiled cabbage and perhaps, if you're lucky, more strongly tasting additions like onion, garlic, leek, a concoction of spices, even chopped-up bacon. There definitely won't be any tomatoes or potatoes in it – they are yet to be discovered by Europeans. You might also get some white bread and cheese to mop it up.

So, keeping your mug of ale on standby, pick up your wooden spoon and shovel some into your mouth – don't worry, it will taste bland rather than repugnant.

After the meal, it's time to bid your fellow travellers good-night. Again, there are a number of ways of doing this: 'To God I you command. I take leave of you!', 'God you have in his holy keeping!' or even 'Go ye to God!' As you can see, in such a hazardous city humans like to devolve as much respon-sibility for their wellbeing to their Maker as possible. As you leave the room, note how the queek pebbles have been cleared away and replaced with giant chess pieces, carved of wood and painted in green and red. Everyone loves chess.

Don't expect a room of your own – not in an establishment such as this – and you may have to share with up to twelve other guests. Don't presume you'll get a *bed* of your own for that matter. Privacy, as you will gather, is a scarce commodity, even in the grandest of abodes. An inventory from 1384 reveals that one fine riverside mansion between the Tower of London and Billingsgate has a vast hall (forty feet long, twenty-four feet wide), a parlour, kitchen, buttery, cellars, garden and large wharf – yet only one bedroom, and that very much a site of ostentatious display.

Medieval people are much less prudish about exposing their bodies than we are in the twenty-first century. You may have to share a rough straw mattress with one, two, even three stran-gers. And you will be sleeping in the pitch black. It's unlikely you'll be sharing with someone of the opposite sex though – married couples tend to pay to secure a 'private' bed. So don't be too surprised if, later tonight, you feel your neck fanned by someone's rancid beer breath or are awoken by the stench of armpit sweat, vomiting, barking talbots, or worse.

Sleep tight.

The Tower

After a good's night sleep (no surprise encounters with your bedfellow), battle your way across London Bridge and walk towards the Tower via Thames Street. More timber-framed houses pitch into the rubbish-strewn street, as if clamouring for your attention. At the end, the street spills into a stretch of boot-mulched soil, rising into a green hill to your left, which has recently been christened as an aristocratic execution site. As the sounds of the city recede, you feel the invigorating river breeze on your face. Your eyes will be drawn to the most magnificent and muscular fortress in Christendom: the Tower of London. From a twenty-first century perspective, it is tempting to think of medieval castles as an assertion of strength and power, trumpeting the war-like credentials of whoever built them – William the Conqueror, in this instance. But in fact most fortresses are born out of a sense of acute insecurity in a politically turbulent age. And the Tower is no exception.

Aside from the moat lapping against the outer stone curtain wall, the basic structure of the fortress may well be broadly familiar to you. It came together as a series of fortified concentric circles during the reign of the ruthless warrior king and 'Hammer of the Scots', Edward I (1272–1307), following the blueprint of the vast Crusader castles in the Holy Land. The White Tower, stage centre, presides over a plethora of towers, barbicans, gates and gardens, hemmed in by a moat on three sides and, on its southern side, by the Thames. But its relationship with its surroundings is different from what you're used to. It acts as a bookend to the city rather than being adrift in a never-ending urban sprawl, as in the twenty-first century. After the winding streets choked with timbered houses, their beams held together by crude beige daub-and-wattle infill, the White Tower, wrought in stone and soaring some ninety feet into the air, lords it over the metropolis with arch-*majesté* and menace. It is as though the rest of London lies in its shadow.

Which is precisely what its founder intended. When he arrived triumphant in 1066, William felt gravely imperilled by what one of his chroniclers described as a 'vast and fierce populace'; said fierce populace amounted to only around 10,000 people, but by the standards of early medieval cities, that was a mega-city. The Normans were horribly outnumbered. Arguably, it was only because the strength of King Harold's Anglo-Saxon army had been sapped fighting off the Vikings at the Battle of Stamford Bridge that the Normans managed to win the Battle of Hastings. So William wasted no time at all in building a defensive bulwark in the south-eastern corner of the old Roman city, on the site of a fort called Arx Palatina, rumoured to have been built by Julius Caesar to command the river. But the first Tower was quite unlike the impressive structure in front of you now. Rudimentary, and of wood, it was plonked on top of a man-made mound, encircled by a ditch and a fence of spiky wooden stakes. It was one of eighty-four so-called motte-and-bailey castles that the Normans rapidly built around their freshly conquered kingdom as nodes of military and political control. But after a tiring decade of crushing rebellions in the north and west, William coveted something much more impressive, made from stone to petrify his power and cow the citizens of London.

He chose his principal building material carefully – Caen Stone from Normandy (though, like the Romans, he also mined Kentish ragstone, for the interior structure). With its pale, marble-like lustre and Norman provenance, Caen stone was a fitting token of alien occupation, a hurtful affront to a city so proud of its traditions of independence and self-government. It was evil and menacing. One chronicler, William Fitzstephen, believed that the mortar of the White Tower had been strengthened with dragons' blood; the less lyrical truth is that it contained a rusty powder made from pounding Roman bricks and tiles. Although William wouldn't live to see his vision realized, by the early twelfth century the Tower loomed large over the conquered city. There was nothing else like it in the country, *the* Tower it was, and so it remains.

Directly in front of you, a drawbridge shoots towards two sturdy, spherical towers rising from the murky waters of the moat. These are part of the Byward Tower barbican, leading to the outer ward of the fortress. Curve round towards the wharf. Here you will see cranes for loading ships tipping in the wind and, on the Thames, wherries cutting breezily through the water. Be careful: the embankment is very narrow and slippery – the river washes over it at high tide. Walk round until you are level with the Lanthorn Tower, where a lamp burns to guide ships through the mist and the darkness. It will take you past St Thomas's Tower, underneath which you can see Traitors' Gate. This is where the barges of political prisoners are received.

Look out for the narrow cross-slits bored into the curtain wall. If you see or hear any movement from behind the loopholes, drop anything you might be carrying, fall on your knees, and cry out that you come in peace, hands raised high in the air. You don't want to end up with an arrow through your neck. Once you reach the Lanthorn Tower, you should be able to see right into the heart of the fortress.

Iced in whitewash, the White Tower really *gleams*. It has a dreamlike, otherworldly quality. In a bewitching manuscript illustration depicting the lengthy incarceration of the Duke of Orléans in the fifteenth century, the Tower is clad in a fairytale magnesium white, brought into sharp relief by the grey and dreary hue of its acolyte fortifications. Looking at it now, you see that it has the same kind of characteristic rounded Norman windows as you saw in the nave of St Paul's Cathedral, and tulip-bulb cupolas atop its four turreted towers, one of which is rounded to allow for a spiral staircase (where you can climb up safely with your sword on your right-hand side). Four flags clip in the wind triumphantly – not the St George's Cross but the Royal Standard, displaying golden lions (symbol of the Plantagenet dynasty) and blue fleurs-de-lis (voicing England's claims to the dominion of France), arranged in a criss-cross formation.

The Tower is many things – fortress, garrison, prison, palace, mint – but tourist attraction it is not. So you can forget going in. It is built to keep people *out*, not so much to protect London from invaders as to protect the king from his own subjects. At its base, the walls of the White Tower are fifteen feet thick – walkways and tunnels are bored between them – and the entrance is five feet off the ground, accessible only by wooden steps which can be reeled in during sieges (while the defenders boiled up some oil, no doubt). Edward III's Garden Tower has a portcullis so heavy that it takes the brawn of thirty men to raise it (this would ultimately be known as the Bloody Tower, since it is where the two boy princes were thought to have been murdered during the reign of Richard III). To get into the Tower, you have to walk over a drawbridge, through three barbican towers – with three portcullises each – and over a moat. And this only takes you to the outer ward; you must then pass through another heavily guarded gate, behind which are springalds – machines for hurling large stones – to enter the inner ward where the White Tower dominates.

To have such layered and lavish defences says something about the nature of the society in which you find yourself. Medieval England is not quite the nihilistically violent, cut-throat realm of *Game of Thrones* but it is, or can be, a world where over-mighty subjects run amok with their private armies, and where swarms of marauding, bloodthirsty peasants actually hack off the heads of 'evil counsellors'; where sometimes the king's life can seem as cheap and expendable as everyone else's, all in stark contrast to Shakespeare's London.

The facts speak for themselves. In the four centuries following the Norman Conquest, at least three kings were murdered, and many reigns were beset by ruinous civil war or rebellion. Edward I distinguished himself by being unchallenged for the duration of his thirty-five year reign, but no monarch between William II in the eleventh century and Henry V in the early fifteenth could say the same. It's no coincidence that it was on Edward's watch that the Tower became the Fort Knox of medieval London.

We will have to settle for an imaginary whirlwind tour of the White Tower. The steps take you to the middle floor, used mainly as living quarters for the Tower garrison, with dormitories. It is dimly lit; the windows are tiny, but roaring fires crackle away in stone fireplaces as the soldiers share stories of combat, sing songs, play board games and munch their meals around long, communal tables. Seated latrines – a real luxury – are set into the wall, firing shit into underground cesspits. And there's another luxury – hot tubs.

The most memorable sight, though, is surely the beautifully simple stone chapel wrought in the Romanesque architectural vernacular (dominant in Europe from *c.*900 to 1200, drawing its inspiration from ancient Rome), devoid of the lavish colours and clutter characteristic of Catholicism. If you could venture in, you'd find a colonnade and above, a clerestory, each opening seemingly a portal to the celestial sphere. It was here, in one of the most shocking events of the Peasants' Revolt of 1381, that a drunken mob found the Archbishop of Canterbury with two of the king's most hated ministers, and the physician to the equally despised John of Gaunt. They smashed the door down, stormed the altar and wrenched the communion cup from the archbishop's quivering hand as he was administering the last rites to his companions. He managed to stammer out a brief prayer, beginning 'All the Holy Saints protect us', but help was not forthcoming: the doomed four were dragged to Tower Hill and clumsily beheaded on a log. There can hardly have been a more sacrilegious act in the Tower's history.

A vice, or tightly wound spiral staircase, delivers you to the upper floor, comprising the Great Hall, used for melodious state banquets, surrounded by a minstrels' gallery. Since the thirteenth century the king has had his own palace complex to the south of the White Tower. But initially this is where the Norman kings received visitors, passed judgement, sang, slept, feasted, admired the skyline of London and nervously scanned the eastern countryside for any menacing spots on the horizon. These days, the upper floor is occupied by the Constable of the Tower, high-status political prisoners and important guests.

The lower floor is a dark undercroft. Stored in the cellar vaults you'll find food and weaponry to withstand a siege and an armoury, churning out England's first experimental gunpowder munitions. You'll also find what an inventory of 1295 concisely referred to as 'the well with the drowned rats'. It would make an ideal dungeon, but what you won't find – not yet, anyway – is a torture chamber. This might strike you as odd. Many time travellers think of the Middle Ages as an era of savagery and brutality. No doubt in the deep, dark, rat-infested pits of the White Tower, where human screams are swallowed up by the cold sods of earth, much went on behind closed doors. But the fact remains that the first documented case of torture at the Tower is still some fifty years off, and will not occur until the reign of the mentally ill King Henry VI in the mid-fifteenth century, the twilight of the Middle Ages. The rack will not be introduced to England from the Continent before the 1420s; until then, torture remains technically illegal under Common Law.

As you leave the muddy wharf, why not take a moment to feast your eyes on the panorama upriver?

London Bridge is more thinly decked out (and the houses on it less lofty) than in Shakespeare's London, particularly at its southern end. In place of Nonsuch House is a drawbridge, which can be raised to admit masted trading and fishing vessels to London's busiest quay at Queenhithe, off Lower Thames Street, and also to barricade the city from any marauding rebels and invaders who might try their luck. In the middle, on a much longer starling, you get a chance to see the octagonal chapel dedicated to St Thomas à Becket (if you remember, this graceful building had been reduced to an unremarkable ware-house in Shakespeare's London, having been stripped and converted during the Protestant Reformation).

Beyond the bridge, the spires and timbers of the city melt into open fields and meadows swiftly after St Paul's. On the south side of the river at Bankside, the church of St Saviour dominates, along with its western neighbour, the imposing Winchester Palace. But beyond that there is only a thin crust of development before the houses give way to gardens and fields – though the Pilgrim's Way, shooting south to Canterbury, is strung out with coaching inns. It's low tide, and ugly mudflaps protrude into the Thames to the south-east.

On your right, the masts of ships bob in front of Customs

House, where all incoming ships must dock and pay their import duty. Meticulous records are kept. No fewer than 350,960 squirrel skins were imported last year to make fur coats and ermine-trimmed cloaks and gowns for judges and aristocrats to swish around in. But there's only a trickle of ships – nothing like what you saw in Shakespeare's London – since the medieval state is too weak to promote the expansion of an overseas trading network. The king only has a handful of his own warships, docked outside the Tower; if he needs any more, he will simply press merchant vessels.

'It eats and drinks with a trunk'

As you wind your way back around the triple-barbican entrance, a roar stops you in your tracks. There is silence. Then a low, rumbling growl, followed by slobbering and gobbling. You realize now why the entrance is called the Lions' Gate.

Walk through the crenellated archway so that you are between the tenements of Petty Wales and the kink in the walled moat, straddled by the Lion Bridge. Look to your right, and you'll see a mini Noah's Ark beached in the south-west corner of the Tower. It contains all manner of exotic beasts cooped up in two rows of filthy cages bored into the walls of the Lion Tower. Since the thirteenth century, successive kings have built up a royal menagerie to impress visitors and, if worst should ever come to worst, set upon invaders.

The Tower menagerie, the forerunner of London Zoo, was born in 1235, when King Henry III was touched to receive a trio of leopards from his sister's husband, the Holy Roman Emperor Frederick II, in a likeness of his heraldic Plantagenet lions. Where better to display them than in his luminous, freshly whitewashed Tower? They established a tradition of exotic animal keeping at the Tower. In 1240 the leopards were joined by a lion; in 1251 there arrived a camel, a new leopard and some frisky lynxes. But the most exciting arrival of all was in 1252, when King Haakon I of Norway gifted Henry III a white polar bear, along with a Norwegian keeper. The sheriffs of London granted the creature 2d per day from the city's funds for food. But this allowance proved inadequate, prompting a personal intervention from Henry III:

> Greetings. We command you that for the keeper of our white bear, lately arrived from Norway . . . ye cause to be had one muzzle and one iron chain to hold that bear without the water, one long, strong cord, to hold the same bear fishing or washing himself in the river Thames.
> – the King at Windsor.

Each day, the horses, wagons and carts on London Bridge came to a halt as Londoners gathered to watch the snow-white beast bounding to the river, dragging his keeper along after him, almost into the very water. Eventually they'd see the beast plunge into the Thames, emerge (if he was lucky) with a sturgeon or salmon between his jaws, then clamber out onto the bank, shaking off his fur. The keeper would then have to put his leash back on without giving the impression that he was trying to steal the bear's food, then, after the beast had wolfed down his meal, replace the muzzle. For the citizens of London it was a wondrous spectacle that leavened the grind of the working day, and which would be commemorated in endless White Bear tavern signs. You saw one back in Shakespeare's London.

It must have been a jittery boatman indeed, three years later, who was ordered to sail to the Tower with a ten-year-old elephant on board. The beast with 'small eyes at the top of his head' and which 'eats and drinks with a trunk', as one astonished monk charmingly put it, was a gift from Louis IX of France, and had galumphed up the Pilgrim's Way from Canterbury, to the delight of screaming crowds. At great expense – or rather, at his subjects' great expense – Henry III built an elephant house in the Tower, but two years later the beast was dead. Eventually, some of the elephant's bones were carved into smart reliquary cases for saints' hair, teeth, bones, and so on, in Westminster Abbey, though some suspected they were palmed off as relics themselves. In 1288 Edward I topped up the menagerie with a lion and lynx and appointed a live-in Keeper of the King's Lions and Leopards; his grandson, Edward III, added more big cats and a bear and took the animals on tour to York to strike awe into the hearts of his northern subjects. Richard II's wife, Anne of Bohemia, will soon throw a pelican into the fray.

It's not a zoo in the modern sense since it's only really the courtly elite and people acquainted with Tower officials who may marvel at the exotic animals; to admit the public would rather negate the purpose of maintaining such lavish defences. Still, news from the menagerie frequently leaks out, particularly of the star attraction: the lions. The lions in the menagerie are sometimes named after kings; when one dies, it is widely interpreted as a portent of a looming royal death. But since imagining or foretelling the king's death counts as high treason, and so incurs a very painful execution, the death of 'royal lions' is problematic. Whenever one of these creatures dies, it is kept a secret, and the royal name is surreptitiously transferred to a younger, boundingly fit beast. Conditions, too, leave a lot to be desired by twenty-first-century standards. Since Edward I moved the animals to the Lion Tower in the 1270s, they rarely leave their prison.

As you leave behind the moans and wails and screeches of the animals, you realize these are the very same noises the prisoners dragged to the Tower Hill scaffold must hear. Perhaps in their final moments of suffering, they make common cause with these poor, caged animals in a catharsis of the condemned.

Savour your freedom as you walk back into the city, towards Cheapside.

The blood of the guilds

Make your way down Friday Street. Across the road, a fishmonger glowers at a goldsmith. The goldsmith feels for his dagger and stares him out. The tension in the area is palpable. Along with the saddlers, fishmongers are the most violent of London's guildsmen, prone to bouts of homicidal fury in response to the slightest provocation; 'Billingsgate' will remain a byword for blind rage right into the twentieth century. Steer clear.

The city, believe it or not, is heavily regulated. If you set up business as a tradesman, you will find yourself ensnared in a dense web of stultifying rules and regulations: bakers alone are subject to twenty; fishermen, hundreds, all specifying what they may catch, where, when and, crucially, with what sort of net. It's a world apart from the free-market capitalism that reigns in twenty-first-century London. Medieval tradesmen don't so much compete as club together, having coalesced during the fourteenth century into spiritually charged trading associations called guilds. Unlike later trade unions, they represent the whole social spectrum of a particular vocation rather than the interests of a labouring minority against an employing majority. Legitimized by royal charter in the thirteenth century, there are around eighty guilds, and they exist to police, dignify and protect particular 'mysteries' (from the Latin *misterium*, meaning ministry or vocation), enforcing monopolistic control and ensuring a decent burial for their members and prayers for their souls after death. (Would your boss be so kind?)

It's not all good, though. If you fancy joining the fishmongers, goldsmiths, tailors, skinners, chandlers, vintners, stationers or any other of the city mysteries, you must first serve at least a seven-year apprenticeship, often under miserably strict and chaste conditions in the bud of your youth. This is to filter out the dross and ensure a continuity of craft methods. Once you are a freeman of the guild (acceding to the ranks of the 25 per cent or so of the city's population who can call themselves citizens), you have the choice of becoming a journeyman (an employee), or setting up independently as a master tradesman, but you will be subject to your guild's regulatory and punitive powers. Disobedient or slovenly apprentices might find themselves stripped naked and flogged by hooded and vizored men wielding birching rods. Sadly, most of these opportunities are shut off to you if you are a woman. Women can only trade independently if they've inherited their husband's craft, which makes some kind of sense in a world where only widows and spinsters can have money and own property in their own right.

Guild members look forward to lavish banquets each year, often on the feast day of their patron saint, ostensibly to elect a new warden and masters but equally to impress new members and guests with an ostentatious display of hospitality, at which members wear a distinctive colourful livery. Traditionally, guilds hired venues for these occasions, but now some companies are beginning to find they have the means of purchasing or building their own banqueting halls – on Broad Street (the future Threadneedle Street) can be found the fine stone hall of the Tailors and Linen Armourers and on Foster Street, Goldsmiths' Hall, to the north of the goldsmithing area on Cheapside, which you visited in Shakespeare's London. There will be a spurt of livery-hall building in the next hundred years, which will dignify face of the city for many centuries to come.

Given the tribal mentality of guilds, it's not surprising that social and economic tensions between different guilds often spill over into street violence. In 1327 the saddlers tried to force the loriners (makers of spurs and stirrups and other small iron objects), painters and joiners, whom they regarded as inferior, to work exclusively for them. This bid for economic domination soon turned violent, prompting six influential members from either side to arrange a 'love day' at St Paul's to seek forgiveness and reconciliation. To no avail. The loriners, painters and joiners turned up armed to the teeth and proceeded to attack the saddlers in full view of the saints. The assault spiralled into a pitched battle around West Chepe and Cripplegate the next day, during which time the streets' other traders had to go about their business amidst volleys of stones, the crash of swords and the groans of the wounded and dying. Only the appearance of the mayor and aldermen could stop the bloodshed and a resolution was eventually negotiated at Guildhall.

Not all disputes ended in amicable resolution. Far from it. In 1340, the Lord Mayor himself and his sheriffs became ensnared in a clash between the pelterers and fishmongers, with one fishmonger trying to chop off His Worship's head. In the event, it was the fishmonger's head that ended up being lopped off in Cheapside after a hasty trial at Guildhall. Thankfully, in the twenty-first century cut-throat competition is interpreted less literally.

The riverside palaces of the Strand

Time now to take our leave of the violent and claustrophobic walled city and embark upon something more leisurely. Head to the nearest river stairs and ask the boatman to take you to New Palace Stairs at Westminster. Say that you're a visitor to town and would like to linger by some of the bishops' riverside palaces along the Strand, take in the sights. He may well chip in with some stories of his own.

Known as *strondway* in the eleventh century, the street is so-called because it runs close to the *strond* or shore of the Thames; you need walk for only a couple of minutes down a gentle decline before you slop into the river. A gilded hinterland between the commercial powerhouse of the City and the cock-pit of power at Westminster, the Strand has emerged in the last two centuries as one of the most important and ostentatious parts of London. All along its southern stretch, from the Temple to the Palace of Westminster, it is lined with bishops' mansions with grounds rolling down to the Thames. What could be better than to have a place of your own away from the noxious city with rooftop panoramas, breezy gardens where you can lounge around in the sunshine listening to poetry and musicians, and a plenteous, in-house supply of fish? This is the Kensington and Chelsea of medieval London.

The Strand itself, though, is horrible. One royal proclamation laments (in Latin) its 'deep and muddy' condition thanks to endless carts and horses and a pavement 'so deteriorated and broken that . . . great danger is likely to ensue for both men and carriages'. Which is why we're taking the river instead.

We're coming up to our first mansion, to the left of the River Fleet and the Holy Well of St Bride (the site of the future Bridewell Palace). You see leafy grounds rolling down to the Thames and then, set back, a complex of timber-framed buildings arranged around a quadrangle, bound by a crenel-lated wall, which makes you wonder whether 'fortress' may be a more fitting descriptor than palace. No stranger to hosting royalty, this is the London inn of the bishops of Salisbury, who stay here when they have business at court, Parliament or in the city.

Moving on, try to glance up Water Lane towards Fleet Street. One day this will be cheek-by-jowl with newspaper printing houses, but for the moment there is just some ribbon development.

Now you find yourself drifting past the precinct of the White Friars, where the monks are busy brewing ale, saying prayers for the dead and collecting the rents from their extensive property portfolio; now you are sailing past a clump of tall bushy trees shrouding the legal chambers of the Middle Temple.

Next we have Exeter House, built earlier in the century by the doomed Lord Treasurer of England, Walter de Stapleton, who, after incurring the wrath of the citizens at the time of Queen Isabella's invasion of her husband Edward II's realm in 1326, was someone else who ended up beheaded in Cheapside and buried in a pile of sand and rubbish near the burned-down gates of the palace, a rather undignified end for an officer of high state. Never the most gainly or magnificent of the riverside palaces, in the seventeenth century Samuel Pepys would call it, in its new incarnation as Essex House, 'large but ugly', though as a home from home it probably won't look that unsatisfactory to you.

Barges flock to Wood Wharf like so many wasps to a sweetmeat left out in the sun, and your ferryman might shout some friendly words of abuse to his mates. If the situation of the next two inns – the first, large and set back from the river for the bishops of Chester and Coventry; the second, fronting the river for the bishops of Worcester – feels uncannily familiar then congratulations, you've just intuited the site of the future Somerset House, which the so-called Protector Somerset amalgamated out of the inns he found dotted around the site in the mid-sixteenth century.

Next is the Savoy Palace, the Strand's only secular palace, and a vast and overbearing one at that. It was granted by Henry III to his rapacious queen Eleanor's uncle, Peter of Savoy, in 1246 for an annual rent of three barbed arrows. Almost thirty years ago, it was inherited by John of Gaunt, the Duke of Lancaster and uncle of the boy-king Richard II, and virtual ruler in his name. Of all the riverside palaces you have seen, this looks most like a fortress with battlemented walls and defensive turrets. Set around two quadrangles with an entrance gate with a portcullis onto the Strand, it was rebuilt between 1345 and 1370 for £35,000 – an unimaginable sum for most people alive in the fourteenth century (the most a mason could expect to earn was £7 per year; a thatcher's mate, £2 10s) – and, not surprisingly, it was said to be the finest mansion in England, 'unto the which there was none in the realm to be compared in beauty and stateliness' (in the authoritative words of Elizabethan antiquarian John Stow), the constant retreat of kings, knights, nobles, prelates, and even captured French kings who arrived on white steeds and lived here more as guests than prisoners. There was a library, treasure chamber, vegetable garden, chapel (where Chaucer married John of Gaunt's sister-in-law), cloister for strolling and scheming, fish ponds and orchards containing pear trees with treasure buried underneath, according to one account.

Now, however, the building, as you must have noticed, is a charred timber skeleton. As a symbol of disgustingly lavish ostentation and the residence of the despised John of Gaunt, the Savoy was a prime target for the followers of Wat Tyler in the Peasants' Revolt. After murdering his guards at the entrance tower, they stormed the courtyard, broke into his treasury, crushed his precious gems and threw his gold and silver coins into the Thames. They consigned furs, velvets, cushions, fine tapestries and silk from the ducal wardrobe to a vast bonfire of vanities in the middle of the Great Hall. At one point three unopened barrels, which the rebels assumed to contain gold and silver, were hurled onto the fire, only for them to discover – as the roof caved in above them – that they had held a terrifying new substance called gunpowder. The resultant inferno consumed much of the rest of the hall and the connected buildings.

Tyler and his men were serious rebels intent on making serious points rather than plundering for plundering's sake – one peasant caught stealing was cast into the flames like all the other tokens of gluttony. The reviled duke was away fighting a campaign in Scotland but the ingenious peasants evoked him in effigy by erecting one of his jewel-encrusted doublets on a pole and lacerating it with arrows. But not all the rebels were able to meet the high standards of parsimony demanded of them by their leaders. A breakaway platoon of peasants headed for the Savoy's cellars. The aim, ostensibly, was to take an axe to the duke's barrels of fine wines but instead they themselves got drunk. When the roof collapsed, trapping them in the cellars, they did what any reasonable person would have done: drank the rest of the wine. Seven days later, they were dead.

Next is the more modest Carlisle Place and then, across Ivy Bridge Lane, the thirteenth-century Durham House, its buildings huddled into a tight quadrangle set back a little from the Thames, shaded by an arbour to its right. With three high crenellated towers, it is a stately presence on the riverfront. In 1258 the overweening nobleman Simon de Montfort offered the weak Henry III temporary shelter here in a storm. 'Thunder and lightning I fear much,' the king is said to have replied, 'but by the head of God I fear thee more,' before continuing on his way. In future centuries, Catherine of Aragon will stay here before her short-lived marriage to Arthur Tudor in 1502 and Lady Jane Grey will leave from here to be paraded to the Tower, where she was crowned Queen of England in an even more short-lived reign (ten days) in 1553.

Your river tour is drawing to a close. Norwich Place slides past, as does the Hermitage of St Katherine, Scotland Yard (where the kings of Scotland traditionally reside when they come to pay grudging homage to the kings of England) and York Place.

As the boat draws in to New Palace Stairs, you see a large rectangular hall parallel to the river with smoke rising from an aperture in the roof, a harmoniously proportioned chapel behind it, and a foliage of riverfront houses with steps sinking into the water. An enormous Gothic structure – about three times taller than it is wide – looms behind, an abbey.

Thorney Island

Clambering ashore, tossing the wherryman a coin, you pass through a stone gate into New Palace Yard, a wide open space sheltered from the wind, much of its perimeter lined with shops, houses and inns. A pair of tonsured monks in black robes brush past you, smiling and laughing, making their way towards a building site ahead. Outside the hall on the left, you see a pair of guards in the king's livery striding forth with spears. Were it not for the snippets of foreign conversations you can hear – French and Flemish in particular – and the two grand structures that dominate the landscape, one might say that the area, located a safe distance from the city, has something of a villagey air. Except the air isn't salubrious, it's swampy.

Welcome to Thorney Island – named for its brambles – an ancient flood-prone eyot which evolved from a sand bar in the River Thames over 4,000 years ago. It might not be immediately obvious but you are surrounded by water – the Thames behind you and two branches of the Tyburn ahead, though they more resemble ditches these days. To the west, there are marshlands. The whole vicinity is thus thorny, sometimes slippery and richly laden with the stench of decay and stagnation; what better birthplace, then, for Parliament?

Welcome, time traveller, to Westminster.

At some point after the Romans retreated from Britain in the mid-fifth century, the city slunk out of its walls into the western suburbs in the form of *Lundenvic,* an Anglo-Saxon trading community stretching from present-day Charing Cross to the banks of the River Fleet. By the late eighth century, the Anglo-Saxons had founded a modest wooden church on the western outskirts of *Lundenvic,* here on Thorney Island. Around two centuries later the abbot of Glastonbury and monastic enthusiast, Dunstan, founded a Benedictine abbey on or near the site of the old church. It was called the West Minster; *mynster* being the Old English word for monastery or important church. Thus the Abbey of St Peter – or what would come to be known as Westminster Abbey – was born.

When he was rebuilding the abbey on a monumental scale to manifest his equally towering piety, Edward the Confessor, the penultimate Anglo-Saxon king of England who ruled from 1042 to 1066, moved his royal palace from Aldermanbury in the city (London had snuck back within its walls by the late ninth century) to a riverside spot – near where you are standing now – to the south-west of what had become a vast building site swarming with masons, carpenters and blacksmiths. It was a decision that would prove epochal for the future of London, conclusively divorcing the political and administrative hub of the kingdom – Westminster – from the walled city, which went on to develop the inexorable commercial character it would retain into the twenty-first century.

After St Paul's – London's *East* minster, if you will – we don't need to go on another ecclesiastical tour. But know this: St Peter's Abbey, lavishly rebuilt in an uncompromising Gothic style by Henry III over a century ago to the tune of £45,000, boasts the highest Gothic vault in medieval England, a golden, gem-studded shrine to St Edward the Confessor (canonized in 1161), and is where kings of England like to be coronated and buried. It also has a big sanctuary, more infamous than St Martin's Le Grand's, very well stocked with murderers, thieves and crooks over the years.

Take a look instead at the stone building on your left with Norman-style pointed windows and wooden tiles on the roof. It is set into a crust of buildings lining New Palace Yard, but it was built in the eleventh century as a free-standing feasting hall for William Rufus, the son of William the Conqueror, who wished to assert his authority over his restless English subjects. Originally, there was no floor, just compacted earth. By the time of your visit it has evolved into the very nerve-centre of English power, the centrepiece of a sprawling palace complex, where the core and enduring machinery of state – the central law courts, Exchequer and Privy Council – whirr into life and are busy financing wars, codifying laws, dishing out justice and projecting a powerful image of royal authority.

This is Westminster Hall.

Inside, it is cavernous – *too* cavernous, thought some of the king's retinue, when it was first opened in the 1090s, to which William Rufus reportedly shot back that it was a 'mere bedchamber'.

Light streams through the windows, showing the walls to be plastered, richly painted and hung with tapestries. Wooden pillars shoot to the rafters forming arcades, dividing the hall into three aisles and smoke spirals from a central hearth into the rafters and into your mind also, evoking wintry scenes of hooves punching into frosty earth, the bugle's cry, and slaughtered deer strung up by their hind legs after the hunt. A wide gallery runs around the upper part of the hall, affording the king and his advisors privileged views of his magnates tucking into their suckling pig, meatballs in jelly, or fruit pottage and other such delights; an ideal spot for scheming. Today, the Hall is alive with a sound that would have been alien in William Rufus's time – hubbub from the law courts.

A man with a wand stands in the middle of the room, near the hearth, summoning those involved in a forthcoming case. On your right is the Court of Common Pleas; at the south-western end of the hall beneath some wizard-like statues of kings recently commissioned by Richard II, the Court of Chancery, and you'll find the Court of King's Bench in the south-eastern corner. The hall is thick with lawyers, consulting their clients, riffling through papers, pleading their cases and driving hard bargains. Elsewhere dogs root about for food and salesmen pace the floor, bearing toys, cherries and pies, trying to catch the attention of successful litigants. There are some shifty looking characters too, with stalks of straw sticking out of their shoes, skulking under the arcades.

Take a walk to the other end of the hall, to the Court of King's Bench, effectively the supreme court of royal justice. On a raised bench – whence the court takes its name – judges sit in scarlet robes, beneath shields bearing the royal arms. In front, clerks in multicoloured gowns (vertically split, half-green, half-grey or half-blue, half-white) are gathered around a green table strewn with rolls of paper, on which they scribble details of the case. Two ushers stand on the table itself and to the left is a jury. Opposite the judges stand a row of pitiful-looking men, shackled to each other's ankles, throwing the odd sideways glances at the legal proceedings trepidatiously, and stinking. They have long straggly beards; one is naked from the waist up. There are some mean-looking guards with white poles – tipstaffs – keeping watch over them.

The prospect of so many courts sitting simultaneously within the same bazaar-like space might strike you as makeshift and improper. But these brightly coloured clusters of judges, clerks, lawyers and litigants amount to a legal revolution. Traditionally, the distribution of royal justice trailed in the wake of the king, requiring his physical presence. But in the late twelfth century Henry II ordered five judges to sit in perpetuity in Westminster Palace while he was away on tour. This set a precedent for an autonomous justice system, drawing its authority from the monarch but nonetheless operating independently of him, in which cumulative judgements could coalesce into English 'common law'. From here, King's Bench judges travel the country's legal circuits applying the law; in centuries to come, these ripples of royal justice will reach the shores of America, India, Australia and others of Britain's colonies.

The idea that any subject of the Crown, no matter how humble, can seek legal redress at Westminster – and 3,000 of them do, each year – reflects well upon medieval England. But that's not to say corruption isn't rife. If the disgruntled narrator of the early-fifteenth-century poem 'London Lickpenny' is anything to go on, it is. Very.

Written very much in the tradition of a country mouse come to town, the narrator, a victim of fraud, arrives at Westminster Hall with high hopes of legal redress. He goes to all three courts, kneels before the judges in their robes, pleads his case and begs for justice to be done – but they won't even consider his case, meritorious though it is, until he hands over cash. Each verse ends with some minor variation upon the words 'but for lack of money I might not speed' (speed meaning *succeed*) – the weary, chant-like repetition giving a sense that this is how the system is destined to be for ever: grasping and corrupt.

Adjoining Westminster Hall you'll find other key institutions of government. A staircase in the north-west corner will take you to the Exchequer, with windows overlooking New Palace Yard. According to a thirteenth-century manuscript, this takes its name from a large cloth, chequered like a chess (or *échecs* in the language of the Anglo-Norman ruling class) board – which serves as an abacus, on which counters representing various sums of money are slid about as clerks calculate the nation's accounts. (Historians are unsure whether this method was still in use in 1390, but if you poke your head around the door you can find out.) The Privy Council, too, which is destined to emerge as the cockpit of power under the Tudors, meets in the Privy Palace to the south of the hall.

Of all the notable institutions found in the Palace of Westminster, the only one that will remain there in the twenty-first century is Parliament. Since, in medieval England, it is the body that votes the king cash to fight the French, thanks in large part to the Hundred Years War, it is emerging as an indispensable feature of the political landscape. At the opening of Parliament, both houses are summoned to the Painted Chamber, which is actually the king's bedchamber, exquisitely decorated in brilliant ultramarine blues and vermilions with biblical scenes and containing the large state bed enclosed by green curtains and with posts speckled with golden stars, a powerful symbol of the king's political virility. After the parliamentarians have discovered why they have been summoned, the Lords filter off to the Lesser Hall (also known as the White Chamber) and the Commons to the refectory of the Abbey, having earlier damaged the monks' chapter house.

This is one of many hints that the Commons are a hedonistic rabble, unencumbered by any notion of the solemnity and gravity of Parliament, let alone the importance future generations would attach to their constitutional duty. In the evocation of one hostile impression, composed around 1400, the members are portrayed as worthless dimwits, 'like a nought in arithmetic, that marks a place but has no value in itself ... some members slumbered and slept and said very little ... some were so pompous and dull-witted that they got hopelessly muddled before they reached the close of their speeches'. That the Southwark stews are meant to shut down whenever Parliament meets says something about their libertinism, though the wild, unregulated brothels of the village of Charing up the road are fair game. Elsewhere in the palace, you will find the new Jewel Tower, the royal kitchens and the Queen's Chamber.

On occasion, the legal benches and stalls are swept aside for grand political set pieces. Treason trials are the most exciting. Traitors to the realm sometimes arrive in true style. Sir Thomas Turbeville, accused of spying for the French, appeared in October 1295 tied to the back of a horse, surrounded by six tormentors in devil costumes. Sentenced to death by the chief justice of the King's Bench, he was placed on an ox hide and dragged to the gallows by six horses as the devils pranced about, taunting and beating him. He was then hanged and left to rot. Richard of Pudlicot, a thief who raided the king's treasure trove, arrived in a less spectacular conveyance: a wheelbarrow.

Some of the most dramatic trials in English history will take place within these walls. Thomas More who himself presided over many cases here as Lord Chancellor, will himself be sentenced to death here one midsummer's day in 1535 while Anne Boleyn will be doomed by her own uncle, a tearful Duke of Norfolk, a year later. Here, too, the fate of Guy Fawkes will be rubber-stamped in 1606 – he won't have far to walk to his scaffold in Old Palace Yard, opposite the very White Chamber he had conspired to blow sky high at the opening of

Parliament in 1605. And of course, the fate of Charles I will be sealed in 1649.

On your way out, note how the dividing arcades seem to get in the way of all the business going on in the hall. The idea of building an unsupported hammerbeam roof is currently just a twinkle in Richard II's eye, but in three years' time he will commission his chief mason Henry Yevele and carpenter Hugh Herland to construct such a structure out of oak. It will ultimately emerge as one of the wonders of European architecture, rising to almost a hundred feet in the centre, and something still to be marvelled at in the twenty-first century. Richard's reward for rebuilding Westminster Hall with such éclat, and giving the country a stupendous hammerbeam roof, will be dethronement by his magnates the first time he appears underneath it in 1399 after he had surrendered to Henry Bolingbroke in Wales.

As soon as you emerge into New Palace Yard, beware of predatory Flemish salesmen. They will be over you like a rash, poking fine felt hats and spectacles under your nose and laying down cloths on outside tables, promising 'good bread, ale and wine' and 'ribs of beef, both fat and fine'. This is the experience of the crestfallen narrator of 'London Lickpenny', to whom the salesmen try to sell 'gay gear' as the judges had justice. But since he's destitute, all this is Tartarean: 'but for lack of money, I might not speed'.

A bell inside a handsome clock tower with a pyramid-shaped roof chimes the hour – not Big Ben but its forerunner, Great Tom of Westminster. This is one of the few public clocks you will see in the city. Medieval Londoners are not oblivious to the hours of the day – they can attune themselves to the position of the sun in the sky, the nature of the shadows cast by buildings and trees, consult a sundial or astrolabe, or listen out for the conducting of liturgical services at certain points in the day (terce at nine o'clock in the morning; vespers in the evening).

But the sense of time they have is much less regimented and ubiquitous than ours and you may well find it liberating, not being enslaved to a digital clock or watch.

Walk out of the gate at the end of New Palace Yard and turn right onto King Street. It's a reasonably substantial, paved street of mainly three-storey timber-framed houses with buttresses supporting overhanging solars. There are tailors, armourers, limners, stationers and jewel makers all catering for the high-end demands of court and abbey. But near by, in places like Thieving Lane, you'll find slums; London's perennial rich–poor divide is acutely visible in Westminster – 'gorgeous garments and so much wretchedness'; 'so much portly pride with purses penniless', according to the later poet John Skelton.

In the twilight, you can make out some kind of monument surmounted by a cross in the distance. Make your way towards it. On your right you'll pass York Place, riverside palace of the northern primates, and the seed of the future Whitehall Palace. Without the extensions made by Cardinal Wolsey during the early reign of Henry VIII, it will seem smaller than when you saw it from a wherry in Shakespeare's London. But although the centre of political gravity is destined to shift from Westminster Palace to Whitehall Palace in 140 years, the law courts you have seen will remain at Westminster until 1882 and Parliament into the twenty-first century, and presumably beyond.

The Hawk House on the edge of the city

Ahead of you is the hamlet of Charing, known in the twenty-first century as Charing Cross. It takes its name from the Anglo-Saxon word *cierring*, bend – though whether this refers to the twist in the road or kink in the river towards Westminster, no one is quite sure.

Looming ahead, on the site occupied by an equestrian statue of Charles I in the twenty-first century, is a marble monument surmounted by a tall wooden cross. This is the last and most lavish of the twelve crosses erected by Edward I in memory of his queen, Eleanor of Castile, marking the nightly resting places of her funeral cortège from Lincoln to Westminster Abbey in 1290. Beggars are slumped against the stone steps leading up to the plinth.

Make your way towards the large walled complex in the distance, on the site of the future Trafalgar Square. On your left is an expanse of open fields broken only by the leper hospital of St James's; it will be another 150 years before it is converted into a royal palace (best not get too close for the moment).

In front of you is a crude wall made from earth and thatched with reeds. From what you can make out, it shields a large complex of half-timbered, two-storeyed buildings and a yard. You hear the distinctive growl of a mastiff, none too happy about your being here.

Take a step back.

At this point you notice a subtler sound: the jangle of bells, along with a sloshing, splashing, squawking, whirring then, 'Hek ek ek ek ekkkkkk!'

A hawk erupts onto the wall in a whirl of wings. It watches you as it shuffles about making little bobbing movements of the head. There is a bell on its right leg, a leather thong around its talons and a finely enamelled tag around its neck, decorated in heraldic colours. Its feet are disconcertingly large, its talons sharp. The standoff is broken by four notes of a melody, clear and calm, sung by a male voice. The hawk tosses its head one last time then sinks beneath the wall, seduced by the falconer's lure.

Welcome to the Royal Mews, home to some of the finest hawks and falcons in the land. Though it has since come to be associated with horses and carriages, the word 'mews' in its original sense derives from the Anglo-Norman word *mue*, meaning both the act of shedding feathers and a cage for moulting birds, which became its dominant meaning. In Chaucer's *Squire's Tale* a young princess, Canacee, stumbles across an injured hawk and takes it home to her mother. 'And by her bead she made a mew,' we read, which she goes on to cover in blue velvet and paint green.

Such ostentatious nursing gives us a sense of the social cachet of owning a bird of prey. Since Anglo-Saxon times, a love of hawking has coursed through the blue-blooded veins of royalty: 'As a sign of our true love and devoted friendship,' gushed St Boniface to King Ethelbald of Mercia around 745, 'we have sent you a hawk and two falcons, two shields and two lances,' – one of the earliest surviving references to English falconry.

The craze soon swept the nobility. 'It becomes the sons of gentlemen to blow the hunting-horn well, to hunt skilfully, and elegantly to carry and train the hawk,' declared one nobleman. In a warmongering age, it was a visually spectacular way for a warrior to prove his military prowess away from the battlefield in rare moments of peace. But the sport is open to women, too – noblewomen, nuns and abbesses are amongst the most avid hawkers and authorities on falconry. When Philippa of Hainault arrived in England to be Edward III's queen in 1328, she brought with her a magnificent collection of birds, for which she maintained personal responsibility.

Built by the arch-hawker Edward I on his return from crusade almost a century ago, the mews in front of you is much more than just a series of large cages. It accommodates around two dozen professional falconers along with their horses and hounds, and some chaplains. It plays a pivotal role in facilitating the sport of kings. For a hawk or falcon to hunt effectively, their plumage must be perfectly formed. So each moulting season (between late August and late October) the royal raptors, scattered in forests and woods all over the country, are recalled here to shed their feathers; it's also where newly born birds, freshly poached from their eyries, are nurtured and trained to hunt, and where injured birds recuperate. Think of it as a cross between a nursery, school and luxury health spa; more a gilded cage than a prison.

Find the entrance and shout for the porter. Because the birds are so valuable – a good bird can fetch up to £5, a quarter of a knight's annual wage – getting in might be something of a challenge. But bear in mind how sickly the birds are – surviving medieval treatises on falconry mention 111 separate diseases and distempers afflicting the birds, ranging from fevers and parasites to arthritis and digestive disorders. Why not say you've come to make an offering at the chapel of St Eustace for the speedy recovery of one of the king's sick falcons? Failing that, you could say you're here to clean out the dovecote – or simply bribe the caretaker. That tends to work in medieval London.

You find yourself in a turfed, walled garden. In the middle is a large lead bath in which various birds are sloshing about playfully. The birds are watched and occasionally prodded by a couple of falconers, who pace around the perimeter. The odd feather falls onto the water, and scuds across the ripples. Surrounding the garden, in addition to the mews themselves, you'll find a stables and kennels for the horses and hounds that chase prey across land and water, and frighten it into the air for the hawk's ambush. To provide a ready supply of meat for the birds, and to keep them well trained, you'll also find a crane house and a dovecot, establishing what would prove to be Charing Cross's long-standing association with pigeons.

There is a dining hall for the falconers but their living quarters are in the solars that pitch over the garden and street. Since they frequently rub shoulders with kings and aristocrats, their profession is a highly respectable, even prestigious one. Adelard of Bath, writing in the twelfth century, demanded virtue and cleanliness from falconers – whoring would 'transmit parasites to birds when they are touched', having bad breath would make the birds 'haters of men', and falconers' moods, moreover, could affect the weather conditions the falcons would have to face on the hunt.

Head to the chapel to make your offering. You don't want your cover to be blown. Inside, above the high altar, you will see an image of the martyr St Eustace, a germane choice of patron for the Royal Mews since St Eustace, the Church reliably informs us, was a Roman general who, while out hunting, had a vision of a white stag with a crucifix jammed between its antlers. He swiftly converted to Christianity and never wavered from his newfound faith in spite of a series of thoroughly unpleasant 'tests' sent by God (one of which included him and his entire family being incinerated inside a bronze bull). By putting a penny or two into the offering dish, which will be used for wax candles and the chaplains' salary, you are participating in a long-standing tradition of votive offerings.

Now that the chaplain can vouch for your piety and generosity, you should have access to all areas. Head for the mews proper, the chamber where the birds are caged. In here you'll see a variety of hawks and falcons in various stages of moult. Don't disturb or coo-coo the birds; they are very sensitive. (Richard II ordered a small lunatic asylum at nearby Stone House to be shut down because the wailing of the moon-sick men and women were disturbing his falcons.) A late-fourteenth-century poem called 'The Parliament of the Three Ages' captures the thrill and spectacle of a falcon hunt, describing how the falconers 'snatch off their hoods and cast them up by hand' and watch as 'the mettlesome hawks . . . ring and hurl on high' with their 'bright bells' sparkling and tinkling – 'like heavenly angels!' It is a quasi-religious experience.

You see a range of breeds in the cages. With its snow white plumage, a Greenland gyrfalcon is just about the best present you could send a king but darker Scandinavian gyrfalcons are highly esteemed too. The next best thing is the peregrine, commonly known as the 'falcon gentle', connoting its genteel status rather than any mild-manneredness in its nature, which is ferocious. The meanest falcon is the kestrel – used by ordinary people for hunting. It's doubtful you'll see any in here. On the hawk side (falcons flap their wings constantly whereas hawks glide) you'll see some goshawks, known as the cook's bird for the diligence with which they kill pheasants, rabbits, moorhens, ducks and partridges. You'll also see some grumpy sparrowhawks, which are harder to tame. The kind of bird you fly says something about who you are. Falcons enjoy a much higher social cachet than hawks, presumably because hunting with a falcon is more of a spectacle with its steep vertiginous swoops. They're not just for flying, of course – as you saw back in St Paul's, wealthy men and women like to parade through the city with a peregrine or a goshawk perched on their wrist like some kind of daemon or familiar, projecting their status to all who see them; as several inventories make clear, they kept the birds at home.

The birds enjoy a standard of living that would send most malnourished Londoners green with envy. They have a bath every three days – not something human Londoners would get to do until the mid-twentieth century. Their diet is lavish. They are fed on the best fresh meat: pieces of chicken, kid, young swan and eel are tied to pieces of string and pushed into their cages – sometimes goat and kitten too. One thirteenth-century poem includes a line in which an embittered peasant vents his spleen against a well-fed bird: 'The dog-like villain sits before his door on feast days and when he sees a gentleman carrying a sparrowhawk on his wrist says, "Ha! That kite will eat a chicken tonight which would fill my child."' When they are sick, they are nursed and doted upon by their keepers – though, like humans, they are subject to gruesome and unhelpful remedies: the flesh of a blind puppy for a weak hawk, a bat stuffed with pepper for a noisy hawk, baked lizard dust to accelerate moulting, and so on. It's no wonder that birds of prey are sometimes victims of class envy; an attack on a falcon was a surrogate attack on a nobleman. When the villeins of Preston in Sussex rebelled against their lord in the late thirteenth century, they razed his house, injured his horse and pointedly slaughtered his unfortunate falcon.

Dinner time. Make your way out of the mews and walk back towards Westminster. It doesn't take you long to find a tavern, though before you know it a bedraggled old man crashes out clutching a tankard. Falling on his arse, he is a picture of misery. His wife has been imprisoned in the Fleet prison for a gambling debt and, having just squandered the last money he has to his name on *this* – (he takes a sip) – he'd like to take a good look under God's sleeves. You extend a hand, trying to help, but he takes great offence, draws his sword, and brandishes it around wildly. Whether he is trying to smite you or not, you do not know.

But you don't want to take the risk. You reach for your dagger. Meanwhile he stumbles, trips and falls, somehow slashing his neck. As he thuds to the ground, writhing in pain, a bunch of men stumble out of the tavern, see his bloodied body, and raise the hue and cry! If the man dies and they conclude you killed him, they have every legal right to behead you. They may even try to behead you anyway.

Time to bid your leave. Run!

Can you make it to Westminster Abbey? You'll be sure of a warm welcome there amidst all the murderers, robbers and rapists.

Abjuring the realm

Around a thousand people seek sanctuary each year.

Technically you can enter any church in London and you are safe for forty days, though in practice the bigger the better, and if you can make it into St Martin's or Westminster Abbey (as you have done), which enjoy a whole string of royal privileges, you'll be doing very well indeed. You should only have problems getting in if you are deemed a traitor to the Crown or a heretic. Once inside, you must find the canon or priest and confess your crimes, or at least explain *why* you are there, and surrender any weapons you might be carrying. You will then have to swear to honour the sanctuary's rules, which means no fighting, threatening the congregants or disrespecting your host (i.e. God). You will be expected to make yourself useful – ringing the bells, helping to prepare services, that kind of thing. For the duration of your stay, a daily and nightly watch will be stationed outside the church to prevent you from escaping. The watchmen are obliged to provide you with enough food for forty days, and they will kindly allow you outside to empty your stomach and bladder. After forty days it becomes an offence for anyone to provide you with food, and you can look forward to 'rott[ing] away piecemeal', as Thomas More would put it.

If this doesn't appeal, you have three options. You can evade the guards and make a run for it. But this isn't recommended, since if someone recognizes you and raises the hue and cry, you can be beheaded on sight. Secondly – and this is the option the authorities are keen for you to pick – you can confess to your crimes in front of the king's representative, the coroner, who should appear after a couple of days (allowing you plenty of time for reflection), and hand yourself over to the temporal authorities for trial. This will land you in a disgusting cell in nearby Newgate prison, and if you've committed a felony, even stealing a couple of silver coins, hanging is by far the most likely outcome. If you aren't willing to confess, your chattels (personal possessions) will be confiscated by the Crown and your lands – if you have any – forfeited to the local squire.

Which leaves the most extreme option – abjuring the realm. Like transportation in the eighteenth and nineteenth centuries, this is a way of ridding the country of its irredeemable criminal scum. This time, you have to take the oath at the door to the church, one foot in, one foot out, in front of the coroner. You have to lay your right hand upon the Bible, make your confession, then swear to abjure and forswear the lands of the kings of England, never to return without royal permission. You will then be assigned a port, and a certain amount of time to reach it; usually this is reasonable enough, and your age, health and the state of the weather might all be taken into account, although sometimes coroners can be sadistic: there are records of abjurers assigning husbands and wives to ports on different sides of the country, and of felons being given mere days to walk hundreds of miles. You must promise not to stray from the king's highway nor dally at the assigned port, on pain of death.

Do not assume that your passage to the coast will be easy. You will be escorted, of course, probably handed from constable to constable as you traipse through the various parishes en route to the port, but you might find the constables guarding you get bored and wander back, leaving you to fend for yourself at the mercy of roving criminal gangs. Worse, you might find a mob trailing you menacingly until you 'stray' from the main road, at which point they might well raise the hue and cry and slice your head off.

When the time comes, you must get undressed, swapping your clothes for a simple white tunic daubed with a red cross, suggestive of a penitent pilgrim or even, as the historian Gervase Rosser has pointed out, a shrouded corpse – for you are now legally dead. You will walk the streets of London and then into the open countryside, barefoot and bareheaded, carrying a wooden cross and a proclamation swearing to keep the king's peace, commanding everyone to let you pass unmolested, on the penalty of forfeiting their goods. According to the *Fleta*, a treatise on the common law of England written around 1290, an abjuring felon should 'carry himself sombrely, as if on his way to be hanged on the gallows'.

Finally, the sea. Obviously, it might not be straightforward securing passage – there may be a dearth of ships, and those that are disembarking can't have much incentive to transport penniless criminals. But the law has its own unique solution. As a token of your intent to abjure the realm, you must every day paddle into the sea, either up to your knees or, as some sources would have it, neck, and scream out three times, 'Passage! For the love of God and King!' until you *are* successful.

The prospect of trying to survive in a hostile alien land is terrifying. As a contemporary Italian visitor observed, 'it is not unamusing to hear, how the women and children lament over the misfortune of these exiles, asking "how they can live so destitute out of England"'; adding moreover, that 'they had better have died than go out of the world'. So it's not surprising that many abjurers slipped away into woodlands or forests and tried to start afresh in a completely different part of the country. There was always the remote prospect of a royal pardon, too, and sometimes people confess to crimes they didn't actually commit as a means of escaping from their enemies and securing safe passage abroad, in the hope that they will one day return with the king's permission.

But perhaps, after all that you've seen, you'll be glad to abjure this medieval realm, this 'vale of tears', and return, at least for a short while, to the relative comfort of the twenty-first century. As you await the coroner, make yourself at home in the Little Sanctuary. If you want someone to talk to, or to pray for your safe passage, why not visit the abbey's anchorite John Murymouth, who took confession from Richard II during the Peasants' Revolt? He can be found by St Benedict's Chapel, with a window onto the altar.

And when you reach the sea, yell it – yell it good and loud: *'Passage! For the love of God and King!'*

Epilogue: echoes of medieval London

Very little remains of the medieval city but there are a few fragments, incongruously woven into the skein of the modern city.

The most visible, iconic remnant of medieval London is, of course, the Tower of London. The White Tower, dating from the eleventh century, is still there in all its glory but most of what you see – the various towers, bastions, bridges and battlements – were added in the later medieval period. The royal palace has all but vanished but Traitor's Gate is still in evidence, the Thames slopping against the slippery steps which have borne the trepidatious footsteps of many a former statesman turned traitor. These days the Tower, with its riverside location, is a curiously peaceful place to visit, a sensation at odds with the darkest chapters of its history. The best way to experience something of that history is to join one of the beefeater's tours.

The most visually striking survivals of London's wall can be found near Tower Hill Underground station and at St Alphage Garden off Wood Street by the Barbican (where a fragment of a bastion remains). On the Museum of London's website, you can find a two-mile London Wall Walk, beating the bounds of the walled medieval city from the Tower back to the Museum, pointing out survivals en route. The six principal medieval gates – Ludgate, Newgate, Aldersgate, Cripplegate, Bishopsgate and Aldgate – live on as place names.

The museum also contains a pair of long, pointy shoes from the 1380s and loaded dice, as well as children's toys and leatherwork from the broader medieval period. In the Victoria & Albert Museum in Kensington you can find medieval brooches, priestly vestments, a liturgical comb and a Thomas à Becket-themed casket.

Unsurprisingly, there are no anchorholds left in London – the closest thing would be a solitary confinement facility in one of London's prisons – nor can you expect to claim sanctuary from the law in a church if you've just robbed or murdered someone. That said, London has a diplomatic nexus around Kensington, Knightsbridge and Belgravia where many foreign countries have creamy stuccoed embassies which, in exceptional circumstances, can serve a similar function to medieval sanctuaries, albeit without the option to abjure the realm.

Like most saints' cults, that of St Erkenwald did not survive the Tudor Reformation, though it's interesting to note that Catherine of Aragon, the day before her marriage to Arthur Tudor (the future Henry VIII's younger brother), popped into Old St Paul's to make an offering to Erkenwald. In the light of later events, the chilly saint can't have made much of an effort to intercede with God on her behalf. There is only one London church dedicated to St Erkenwald. It's near Barking Abbey, the Benedictine nunnery that he founded for his sister Ethelburga around 666, of which only the fifteenth-century Curfew Tower remains amidst the ruins in Abbey Green. The area's baton of economic dominance has passed from the destroyed abbey to a nearby retail park. But there is an Erconwald Street in west London, near Wormwood Scrubs Park, and home to

East Acton Underground Station. Unlike its saint, it feels sedate and suburban.

In common with most other monasteries, St Martin Le Grand was suppressed during the Dissolution of the Monasteries in the 1540s though, in a strange historical quirk, the area continued to enjoy rights of sanctuary as late as 1697. It therefore became a Mecca for counterfeit jewellers who, by setting up shop in the vicinity, could laugh in the face of the City's draconian economic regulations and break the law with impunity. Today all that remains is the street name. Thus the area around St Martin's Le Grand continued to be notorious for the production of counterfeit jewellery, long after its sanctuary was swept away.

You won't find any jousts in Smithfield today but there *is* still a wholesale meat market (now covered), very rare for central London, supplying inner-city restaurants and shops with fresh meat, and trading from the ungodly hour of 2 a.m. each weekday; if you arrive at 7 a.m., you'll miss out on the best produce. Anyone is welcome to barter and buy first-rate produce on Buyers' Walk. The trees growing in Smithfield today are not the same as the elm trees that you climbed in medieval London, since the topographer John Stow reports in 1598 that 'now remaineth not one Tree growing'. He also suggests that nearby Knightrider Street takes its name from the armed knights who would canter through on their way to Smithfield jousts, but this is perhaps fanciful.

None of the bishops' palaces survive on the Strand. Only Somerset House gives a sense of the riverfront grandeur of these old mansions, though it was built not for a bishop but for Lord Protector Somerset in 1547–50 and then rebuilt in an austere neoclassical style from the 1770s. The unembanked river used to lap against the south terrace. The area's street names reflect the shift in ownership from ecclesiastical prelates to secular peers after the reformation – Essex Street, Arundel Street, Surrey Street, Villiers Street, Northumberland Street and so on. Fittingly, the site of the lavish Savoy Palace is now occupied by the equally lavish Savoy Hotel, opened in 1889 and then as now a Mecca for stars and tycoons. It's easy to assume that the Savoy Chapel just south of the Victorian hotel, reached via a seedy tunnel from the Strand, is a relic from John of Gaunt's razed medieval palace. In fact it was built in 1510 as part of Henry VII's Savoy Hospital and has been much renovated and repaired over the centuries.

Although most of the prelates' palaces were situated on the Strand, there is one remarkable semi-survival elsewhere, on gorge-like Clink Street in Southwark. On its southern side, near the site of the reconstructed *Golden Hinde*, you can find some archaeological remains of Winchester Palace, the London pad of the bishops of Winchester. Built in the early eleventh century, it remained in their possession for over 500 years, free from shrieval or mayoral authority in the Liberty of the Clink. The excavations give a sense of how sunken medieval London was, relative to the modern city, and the most striking part is the western wall of the Great Hall which rises sheer from the excavation pit in white stone, with space and carvings for a rose window, similar to the one in Gothic St Paul's. The Clink – a small, particularly unsavoury prison whose name entered the English language as a general slang term for gaol – was for those who ran amok in the brothels and beerhouses of Bankside. First mentioned in 1509, it may have been in existence in 1390; today, it is a family friendly museum celebrating hundreds of years of torture and torment.

The memory of the Royal Mews has been effaced by the bravado of Trafalgar Square. An equestrian statue of Charles I, erected in 1675, occupies the spot of the final Eleanor cross. A reconstructed cross, more elaborate than its medieval forebear, sits outside Charing Cross railway station.

None of the medieval coaching inns that once lined the approach to London Bridge in Southwark have survived – though a blue plaque commemorates the site of the Tabard Inn, immortalized in Chaucer's *Canterbury Tales*, in Talbot Yard. The nearby George Inn on Borough High Street dates from 1676 but, as London's sole surviving galleried coaching inn, is evocative of the medieval inns that were characteristic of Southwark.

After a lion in the Tower menagerie attacked some members of the garrison in 1835, the beasts were moved to the Zoological Gardens in Regent's Park, where they swelled the ranks of *another* set of exotic animals which had, since 1828, belonged to the fellows of the recently formed London Zoological Society. When the gardens were opened to the public in 1847 in an effort to raise funds, London Zoo was born, its pedigree stretching back to the early Middle Ages. You can still find echoes of the original menagerie: until 2021 you'll be able to see life-size sculptures of some lions and baboons, an elephant and a polar bear dotted about the Tower, sculpted by artist Kendra Haste from galvanized wire, giving them a fitting ghostly quality.

The City of London is full of livery halls but the vast majority date from the fifteenth and sixteenth centuries. The exceptional Merchant Taylors' Hall still stands where it has been since 1347, on what is now Threadneedle Street, though it was much rebuilt after both the Great Fire and the Blitz.

Guildhall, which has something of a fairytale castle appearance about it when viewed from the southern end of King Street, remains the administrative nerve centre of the City of London Corporation and a site of colourful pageantry. The walls of the Great Hall are medieval in origin, though dating from the early fifteenth century following a major rebuild between 1411 and 1440; the present-day hall's west crypt, however, may date from the thirteenth century. And finally, note that some of the narrow streets south of Cheapside, gently inclining down to the river, still somehow feel medieval in spite of all their grey office blocks. This can be said of Cloak Lane, College Street and Dowgate Hill and many other alleys dotted about the City.

1665
A Mournful Walk through
Plague-struck London

Plague Pits & Pest Houses
1665

† ST PANCRAS CHURCH

CLERKENWELL

GOSW
ROAI

OL
CHA

SMITHFIELD

BLOOMSBURY
SQUARE

HOLBORN

FARRINGDON

NEWGATE

DRURY LANE

ST-GILES-IN-THE-FIELDS

COVENT
GARDEN

Soho Fields

STRAND

FLEET STREET

RIVER FLEET

LUDGATE

TEMPLE

WHITEFRIARS

BLACKFRIAR

St Bride

CHARING CROSS

SCOTLAND
YARD

PARIS GARDENS STAIRS

BANKSIDE

Christchurch
Gardens

Westminster
Pest House
& Tothill Fields

WESTMINISTER

PIKE
GARDEN

HACKNEY

✵ Finsbury Field

FINSBURY FIELD

SHOREDITCH

Mount
Mill
ET

🏠 City Pest House

OUSE   CRIPPLEGATE

✵ Holywell Mount

MOORFIELDS

SPITALFIELDS

MOORGATE

BETHLEM
BURIAL
GROUND

✵ Hand Alley

Stepney
Pest House 🏠

LONDON WALL

Stepney ✵
Mount

GUILDHALL

CHEAPSIDE

WHITECHAPEL

ROYAL EXCHANGE
CORNHILL

LEADENHALL STREET

ALDGATE ✵ Aldgate

S
RAL

KNIGHTRIDER STREET

FENCHURCH STREET

MINORIES

Gower's ✵
Walk

THAMES STREET

TOWER STREET

TOWER HILL

THE TOWER

LONDON BRIDGE

GREAT STONE GATE

WINCHESTER
HOUSE
CLINK STREET   ✝ ST SAVIOUR'S
CHURCH

✵ Cross Bones Graveyard

SOUTHWARK

MAP SYMBOLS	
✵	Plague Pit
🏠	Pest House

Much of London's history lies dormant, tucked away in back-streets. Goswell Road, sloping gently from Islington to Clerkenwell, is pleasant enough, if a little transient feeling. If you ever find yourself there on a listless afternoon, look out for the Old Ivy House pub and, beyond it, in the direction of the Barbican towers that guard the horizon, a left turning into Seward Street.

Almost immediately, the city feels still. In front of you is a garish five-storey, orange-and-beige newbuild, softened a little by a row of feeble, wispy trees. Another street, Mount Mills, squirrels off to the left, passing the back of the pub and the goods entrance to a plumbers' merchants. It leads into a car park that is strangely spacious for such a densely populated part of Central London. To the left is the back of a dreary warehouse. Slender jet-black lamp posts stand in a row. It feels mournful and dead, forgotten.

At thigh-level, a gleaming horizontal pole spews from a shabby looking shed to bar your way. It is decorated in white and red, like the poles outside barbers' shops, evoking surgery and bloodletting. Private car park.

Put your hands on the cold bar.

Now close your eyes.

The wind is blowing in your face. You hear a shovel slicing into the earth. Torches hiss. People sob gently. There is the occasional whiff of garlic and tobacco. Behind you, a voice recites a prayer and from somewhere a horse snorts, straining on its leashes.

You open your eyes.

In front of you, where the car park was, is a vast, wide hole gouged into open fields. It is framed by horn lanterns. You are amongst dim figures, muffled in long black cloaks and broad-brimmed steeple hats. Some appear to be digging. Others just stand. The air is laden with the stink of death.

You take a few steps forwards and peer into the pit. It is a mass grave. There is a fresh layer of corpses about ten feet down – some wrapped in linen, others in grubby blankets, others still semi- or stark naked. Many wear strange charms and amulets tied about their necks: hares' feet, elaborate wooden crosses, signs of the zodiac, and in some instances a large paper sign scrawled with lines of 'ABRACADABRA' in the formation of a diminishing triangle, smeared in dirt, as though testament to its uselessness.

To the side of the pit stands an open wooden cart to which a weary horse is attached. It is stacked high with around twenty bodies. There are two men with lit links (cone-shaped torches made from tar or pitch). One detaches the cart from the horse while the other man pulls it towards the cliff of the pit. You move in to take a closer look. If anyone throws you a suspicious glance or questions you, pretend you are one of the mourners who has travelled here clandestinely, under cover of night, to watch your loved one's funeral.

Both men have now moved to the back of the cart. They wheel it to the very edge of the precipice. Then in a swift movement they hoist it up and the bodies come tumbling out – 'shot into the pit' as a later writer puts it – and thud into the cold earth. The cartmen seem inured to the horror. One of them clambers back onto his horse, the other lighting his way, then they trundle off into the night. They have cart-loads more dead to collect before the sun rises.

Behind you, beyond the mounds and trenches dug into the

fields by the Parliamentarian forces during the Civil War, there is a new city to explore, stirring at the first streaks of dawn.

London's year of hell

London is under a cloud of death. It is not the bustling, exuberant city you have visited in other time periods. Since May 1665, the plague has been devouring parts of the extra-mural city; now, in late August, it has begun to sweep through the walled city itself. At the beginning of the summer King Charles II and his court abandoned the capital, clergymen their flock, most physicians their patients, wealthier shopkeepers their customers and the rich their terrified servants. Some alehouses and taverns continue trading and you can find some resilient coffeehouses too, but inside, Londoners are uncharacteristically shy and suspicious of one another. Elsewhere, the schools, theatres and Inns of Court are closed and the public mood is melancholic and dejected. As people haemorrhage out, nature begins to reassert her primacy and blades of grass straggle up through the city's dry streets and even through the pebbled piazza of the Royal Exchange. In July nearly 6,000 deaths were attributed to the plague, but in reality, probably closer to 10,000 people died, since families had strong incentives to hide plague deaths, as we shall see, and the authorities were overwhelmed by the pestilence.

The scale of the slaughter is not unprecedented – the great pestilence of 1348 (the Black Death, to borrow a late Georgian term) killed a higher proportion of London's population – but no one can remember a calamity of this magnitude. In mid-September, the number of city-wide plague deaths would peak at 7,165 in a single week, though again, the true figure was probably closer to 10,000 if not more.

As you make your way down Goswell Street, a glance to your right will impress upon you how much London has grown. Its population has doubled in size from around 200,000 in 1600 to almost 400,000 in 1650 – after Paris, it is the second biggest city in Europe. Even in this dim light, you can see that the old distinctions between the walled city and Westminster have become largely obsolete since much of the hinterland has been absorbed by infill. The city walls have long since been inundated and are fast becoming an historical monument rather than a boundary. You can't see it from this vantage point, but the city is growing in the east, too, as suburbs like Whitechapel, Wapping and Shadwell swell and become conjoined to the built-up conurbation stretching from Westminster to Limehouse.

Make your way down Goswell Street, turning left at Jewen Street and enter the city at Cripplegate, by the Church of St Giles.

It is eerily silent and still. Every so often, you get a whiff of bonfire smoke – strange to smell it in the heat of summer. Tread carefully through the labyrinth of streets, courts, alleys and churchyards; a single misstep could spell your untimely death: 'so many of the fair sex and their offspring [have] perished by mischance', laments the diarist John Evelyn, 'from the ruggedness of the unequal streets'. Technically, each householder is responsible for paving the street outside their house, but this is far from people's minds as the plague sweeps through the city (it's always pretty far from people's minds in fact). People usually walk as close to the wall as possible, so the cascading upper storeys shield them from the flying muck of chamber pots and rainwater – but no one wants to get too close to anyone else at the moment, so you should walk in the middle of the street, near the central drain or kennel, swerving to avoid other pedestrians. The wooden posts marking the walkway at the edge of the street, you'll notice, are plastered in scraps of paper advertising the 'infallible' miracle cures of quack doctors.

These are dangerous times. Much of the economic life of London has ground to a halt; Samuel Pepys writes of 'the lamentable moan of the poor seamen, that lie starving in the streets for lack of money'. Living near London's eastern riverside suburbs, in Aldgate, he was well placed to observe. There is the sense that society's mores have been suspended: nurses thieve from those entrusted to their care and, if the stories can be believed, sometimes smother them too; goods are pilfered from warehouses; and the delirious dance naked in the streets, chanting. Outsiders will be treated with the utmost suspicion. You will be a sitting duck for the desperate and the destitute.

The solution? Find a white stick. Or failing that, any stick – rip one up from the side of the street if you have to – so long as it's at least two feet long. This is a sign that you live in a house that has contained the plague; you may even have had it yourself and recovered – but people will be sure to give you a very wide berth. So grasp it good and proper and swish it through the air like a denizen of Bedlam, howling, screaming and dancing, as though still delirious with infection – people will run a mile.

A few more things to bear in mind. Whenever you hear the bells tolling for the death of the latest plague victim, you'll notice old women in rags scurrying towards a cross-marked house carrying a red wand. These are the Searchers of the Dead. Do not, whatever you do, go anywhere near them; it is their job to investigate each new death and report back to the parish clerk. They are paid up to 4d per plague victim they discover, but are eminently bribeable, turning a blind eye, then perhaps further spreading the plague themselves. And of course do not touch anyone, kiss anyone, linger for too long in the rat-infested slums, or share a meal with anyone. Drink only coffee, chocolate or tea, never water.

Try to stay calm. If you are unlucky enough to catch bubonic plague, it is usually a good three days before buboes (painful black and blue swellings that typically appear in the groin and armpits) sprout and you start to feel unwell – by which point you'll be safely back in the twenty-first century where the plague can be treated with antibiotics. Unless, that is, the bacteria infects your lungs or blood vessels instead of the lymph nodes, as it does in rarer cases of pneumonic and septicemic plague. In which case, you'll be burning with fever and coughing up blood or watching your limbs turn gangrenous in no time at all, dropping down dead perhaps within twenty-four hours (try not to sneeze too much in your hinterland of agony – that's how the pneumonic plague is spread). No one said time travelling was for the faint-hearted.

'Oh! Death, Death, Death!'

After seeing a corpse lying in an open coffin, tossed into the fields between Woolwich and Greenwich, Samuel Pepys deplores how 'this disease [is] making us more cruel to one another than we are to dogs'. According to the heroic apothecary William Boghurst, it makes everyone 'uncharitable, superstitious and cruel'. He belies the trend himself, happily visiting up to forty plague victims a day from his base at the White Hart in St Giles-in-the-Fields and living to tell the tale in his account of the Great Plague, *Loimographia* – a curious word, referring to a now-obsolete branch of science seeking to describe and better understand plagues; unlike many in the medical establishment, Boghurst does not believe that it has to be a death sentence. One eighteenth-century history of the

Great Plague would echo these sentiments, claiming it 'razed out [the] hearts' of Londoners, alienating one from another in their darkest hour.

This week, 2,010 people will die of plague in London; in the parish of St Alphage Cripplegate, where you are now, the toll will be just five (but compare with 356 on the other side of the wall, in the admittedly much bigger but horribly crowded parish of St Giles-without-Cripplegate). At least, these are the recorded figures returned by the parish clerk in his weekly return for the city-wide Bills of Mortality, as conveyed by the Searchers. Published weekly from 1603 (in response to the plague epidemic whose early stages you witnessed in Shake-spearean London) in part to tip off the wealthy about whether or not to stay in town, these tabulate the number of deaths for each parish in London and her extra-mural suburbs. The largely illiterate, sometimes drunken Searchers have some odd ideas about what kills people in mid-seventeenth-century London, citing as cause 'suddenly', 'teeth', 'affrighted', 'winde', 'blasted', 'sore mouth', 'planet', 'wolf', 'grief', 'lunatique' and the enigmatic-sounding 'rising of the lights' (a choking sensa-tion in children arising from various pulmonary causes; lights being a colloquial term for lungs).

As you wind through the streets of a mournful city, prepare to see neighbours going through the motions of chatting and gossiping but secretly eyeing each other for tokens of the disease – if they see the faintest spot or speckle, they will smile, end the conversation, and send for the Examiners. Brace your-self too for the hopeful faces of famished children bobbing up and down at windows as people in the street pass by, pretend-ing not to have seen; the pained faces of mothers and fathers peering out through the crack in their doors as their houses are shut up for the obligatory forty-day period, by the end of which it's doubtful that they will still be alive; people holding up their fingers to ward off the devil as they walk past houses daubed with the red cross; swirls of thick smoke as householders fumigate their rooms with brimstone, pitch and charcoal; a dead woman lying on her side between mounds of festering vomit as her baby tries to suckle his mother's breast while a watchman keeps guard in the street, chewing tobacco.

But these are just impressions from the street. Even to begin to fathom the true horror of living in a plague-struck city, you have to put yourself in the shoes of the poor souls inside. Picture yourself as a father of six, shut up inside your plague-infested house. You have watched all your children perish – one, two, three, four, five, six – and now you must contemplate the prospect of dumping the frame of your wife onto the dead cart since buboes swelled beneath her armpits two hours ago. She has been weeping and banging the wall ever since. It will be silent, so silent once she's gone. There's no food left in the house, no relying upon the watchman to relieve you if you can't pay him, the parish relief fund is depleted and there is every chance that you will starve to death – if the plague doesn't get you first.

Even for those whose houses are as yet uninfected, the experience of living through 1665 is a form of mental torture, as 'the familiar stage sets masked by habit' which imbue people's lives with meaning, come crashing down, leaving Londoners cast adrift in a harrowing world seemingly devoid of any sense of providence. Samuel Pepys captures this feeling vividly when he laments, in his entry for 14 September 1665, 'that poor Payne, my waiter, hath buried a child, and is dying himself; to hear that a labourer I sent but the other day to Dagenhams, to know how they did there is dead of the plague; and that one of my own watermen, that carried me daily, fell sick as soon as he had landed me on Friday morning last . . . and is now dead of the plague'. The previous month he mourned the death of 'poor Will, that used to sell us ale at the Hall-door, his wife and three children died, all, I think, in a day'.

Chaos reigns. The physician Nathaniel Hodges, who distinguished himself by remaining in London, unlike the bulk of his medical compatriots, gives a vivid account of 'persons in their last agonies: in one room might be heard dying groans . . . and not far off . . . infants passed immediately from the womb to the grave . . . [T]he infected run about staggering like drunken men, and fall and expire in the streets; while others lie half-dead and comatose, but never to be waked but by the last trumpet.' At one point in Daniel Defoe's *A Journal of the Plague Year*, a casement window opens suddenly above the narrator's head and a woman screams, '*Oh! Death, Death, Death!*' Whether a summons, straight lament or plea for mercy is not clear, though no one shows much interest.

The folly of confinement

Many of these scenes of despair flow from the government's strictly enforced and ill-advised policy of confinement. Under the terms of this ordinance, inherited from earlier plague epidemics, if the Examiners discover anyone exhibiting symptoms of the plague, their house is automatically shut up – along with everyone else in it – for a forty-day period. Armed watchmen, usually wielding halberds (a cross between a spear and an axe), are placed outside to prevent anyone escaping – one in the daytime and another at night. Watchmen are also issued with padlocks and bolts. Anyone found harbouring children from condemned households could be committed for trial. And a stay in Newgate prison can be tantamount to a death sentence in many cases, as we shall see.

The policy is consonant with the idea that the plague is contagious rather than spread in miasmic air – proceeding from a 'cosmic fart', in the witty words of historian Liza Picard – but many people see no contradiction between the two, thinking that infected bodies and vapours can pollute the air. 'I am sure it is in the air,' exclaim characters in *A Journal of the Plague Year* on discovering tokens of the plague – at one point, a family becomes infected via the stench of rotting corpses next door – but equally the idea that it is spread by 'fatal breath', sweat or clothes runs through the narrative.

Most people you overhear in the streets will be just as convinced there is a *metaphysical* cause. Hardly anyone disputes it is the awful manifestation of a divine tirade, as presaged by a comet the year before. Quite what God is angry about – the licentiousness of court, restoration of the Stuart dynasty (London's last two major plague epidemics, in 1603 and 1625, had coincided with the accession of James I and Charles I), the general sinfulness of mankind or a harbinger of something even worse to come (next year has '666' in it) is very much up to the individual. In his *Account of the Great Plague of London*, apothecary William Boghurst includes a short section on preventative measures. It begins, 'First. All sins in general . . . lust, pride, whoredom, wantonness, and prophaneness; for the Plague hath been a common judgement upon these exorbitances' – irrefutable proof, if any were needed, that the worlds of science and religion were inextricably intertwined in the seventeenth century (it is only later that he moves on to practical, medical advice).

London is alive with mournful news and rumour: 'so many sad stories overheard as I walk', recalls Pepys, 'everybody talking of this dead, and that man sick, and so many in this place, and so many in that'. In the marketplaces and taverns, customers like to entertain themselves with stories – many of them, surely, apocryphal – of daring escapes, some of which, passed down by oral tradition, end up in Defoe's *Journal*. Expect to hear tales of confined families boring through the flimsy wattle walls into side alleys and escaping; of cunning householders appearing in top-floor windows and lowering a noosed rope onto the watchman's neck, pulling tight and threatening to hang him in mid-air unless he unlocks the door. Defoe tells a story of one family who went so far as to blow up their watchman with gunpowder, leaving him writhing in agony on the street as the family fled into the night.

The less imaginative – or more scrupulous – find themselves barricaded inside their own houses. Defoe provides some harrowing tales of what could become of them. We read of the wife of an East Smithfield tradesman who had the dire misfortune of going into labour infected with the plague, which must have been common enough. Her husband, not being allowed out, was unable to get a midwife or nurse – two of his servants, who might have been able to help, had fled. His only option was to shout his plight in the streets – but the only person who took any notice of him was a watchman, who made a vague promise to send a nurse in the morning. So the husband returned to his wife 'with his heart broke' and attempted to deliver the child himself. But 'he brought the child dead into the world; and his wife in about an hour died in his arms, where he held her dead body fast till the morning, when the watchman came and brought the nurse as he had promised'. Within a few hours, he had departed this world too – not of plague but a broken heart, 'sunk under the weight of his grief'.

We hear of sufferers who are so suicidally delirious they have to be tied to their beds. One who managed to break free and throw himself out of a window; another who 'had no option' but to set fire to his bed with a candle. There are lurid reports too of murderous nurses – 'dirty, ugly, and unwhole-some hags' according to the author of *Shutting Up Infected Houses* (1665) – thieving searchers and fleecing watchmen, all playing their part in a Boschian landscape of nightmare.

Just about anyone who gives it much thought agrees that the policy of confinement is cruel and unjust. William Boghurst has a blunt way of describing it – 'murder'. How, he despairs, could the incarceration of up to two dozen healthy people with one plague victim be anything other? Parishes' poor relief funds are depleted and if families don't have the money to pay the watch-men to purchase essentials like bread, they may starve. The policy is further misguided, he reasons, since it compels the 'walking destroyers' to flee, further spreading the plague. Of all the plague portrayers Daniel Defoe is a lone voice in supporting the policy of confinement, conceding that it was 'a very cruel and unchris-tian method, and the poor people made bitter lamentations' but concluding that 'it was a public good that justified the private mis-chief'. In its defence, he cites many instances of plague sufferers, in their delusion, fleeing from their houses and running amok through the city, kissing passers-by to infect them, plunging into the Thames, howling and shooting themselves in a frenzy of despair.

Such is the stuff of brilliant drama – it's worth remembering that for all its aspirations to verisimilitude, and its journalistic rigour, Defoe's *Journal* is a fictional account written almost sixty years later – but the genuine eyewitness accounts don't really corroborate this part of his evocation. At the height of the plague, when 10,000 people were dying each week, Pepys mentions zombie-like victims who look like they had 'taken leave of the world' but no careering madmen.

What would perhaps help, instead of confinement, is to send infected parties to a pest house, as is more the habit in other plague-struck European cities. In these grim isolation units – often no more than timbered sheds – plague sufferers are tended to by 'expert' physicians. That might not do them much good, but at least in cases of pneumonic plague, the sick would be isolated, preventing the further spread of the disease by sneezing and coughing (the bubonic plague, twenty-first-century physicians believe, generally spreads via a rat flea; it doesn't spread from person to person, so the pest house would do little to check the spread of bubonic plague). London has only five such institutions: the City Pest House in the open fields beyond Old Street towards Islington, a pest house for Westminster in Tothill Fields to the south of the Palace and one each in Marylebone (newly built for the pestilent parish of St Giles-in-the-Fields), Stepney (for east London) and Soho Fields (for the parish of St Martin's), some with burial grounds attached – but between them they can only accommodate around 600 people and Defoe recalls how only the City and Westminster houses are in systematic use throughout the distemper. They are generally the resort of servants exhibiting tokens of the plague on returning to their master's houses after running errands in town, who are given money and packed off to the pest house.

How would you feel if you caught the bubonic plague? You must be wondering. Between three to five days after being bitten by a flea carrying the bacteria, you can expect buboes to appear in the groin, under the armpits, or in the crevices of the neck. Buboes are about the size of nutmegs or crab apples and almost as hard, full of pus and dead blood. They are usually red, purple or black-blue and it is chilling to see such a thing protruding from people's necks like a diseased testicle – even worse to feel one on your own neck. You may also experience a fever and shivers, aching joints, excruciating headaches, the decomposition of the skin while still alive, vomiting, delirium and coma. Then, usually death (while it is possible to recover from the plague, it's unclear how many people do, and most sources emphasize that people don't in general).

What kind of remedies are on offer to fight the plague and other illnesses? You can find out by walking into the nearest apothecary's, on a near-deserted Cheapside. Just look for the sign of the unicorn or the pestle and mortar.

Boiled lizard and puppy-dog water

Welcome to the apothecary's shop. In the twenty-first century, pharmacies are white and clinical but this place is colourful and cobwebby, glistening with all manner of exotic concoctions like a leisurely wizard's lair. There are broad bottles with narrow necks and cork stoppers. The labels – where there are any – are hand-scrawled. The shop is crowded and when you walk in, the apothecary is already attending to a customer. But his eyes are quickly upon you, darting backwards and forwards like baby tadpoles as he calculates what is wrong with you.

He stands behind a broad wooden counter, on top of which is a large pestle and mortar, in which an apprentice is grinding something tough – every so often you hear the crack of animal bone – without once looking up. A book of receipts (or recipes as we'd say) lies open on the counter, splotched with spillages; the handwriting is careful and precise. The apothecary is tall and wears a wide-brimmed hat from which sprays straggly hair to his shoulders. He has a wrinkled face, wispy moustache, and a face that can very quickly contort into a reassuring smile, like a mask.

He is serving a woman who must be in her mid-thirties, and so middle aged (though life expectancy is around thirty-five years for a reasonably affluent woman like her, since she has made it this far, surviving disease and perhaps multiple childbirths, she can reasonably expect to live until sixty; for newborns, though, the prognosis is grimmer – around a quarter of all babies die before they turn ten).

'My lady,' he says, 'you are young and beautiful. But beauty is as fickle as the human heart. Allow me to recommend some of *this*. It is a lavish unguent, expensive to concoct, but infallible and true. Let me just pour some upon your face, here.' (He smears some yellowy water from a glass vial onto her face.) 'It is in high demand, the best! Good in all cases, much above the rest, deservedly gaining the name of the best.'

She is handed a looking glass, seems happy enough, pays and leaves – but it is the apothecary who glows in satisfaction. The apprentice, still not looking up, asks whether he treated her to the first unguent or the second. 'Oh,' he replies, 'the *first*: fresh from a greyhound's cock.' They both chuckle.

Though the apothecary is watching you, he seems quite happy for the moment to let you browse all the bottled elixirs, vomit cakes, pill pouches and other medical and cosmetic wares on the counter and about the shelves. Don't, whatever you do, consume any. Some of the secrets of mid-seventeenth-century medicine are enough to make even the least squeamish time traveller queasy and sick.

That unguent, for instance, was essentially the piss of a puppy, the age's answer to anti-ageing cream. Remarkably – or not, since most people don't ask too many questions about what's actually in it – there is high demand for this amongst middle- and upper-class women, including Elizabeth Pepys. On 8 March 1664 her husband Samuel expresses 'some little discontent with my wife upon her saying that she had got and used some puppy-dog water' at the suggestion of his aunt, who had been trying to source some for her 'ugly face'. It was hardly ideal that Pepys's twenty-three-year-old wife was resorting to the same remedies as his elderly, wrinkled aunt. The idea of pouring puppy urine on your face is disgusting but consonant with the belief that urine works wonders for the complexion and a fairly blatant attempt to transfer some of the bounce and vitality of a puppy to one's own face. Also, since it's fairly easily harvested from the animal, it is innocuous enough.

However, there is a second, much more gory recipe in circulation. This is transcribed by Mary Doggett, the wife of an Irish theatre manager and actor, who kept a little leather-bound book brimming with thousands of medicinal, cosmetic and gastronomic recipes she had concocted in her still room and kitchen to maintain the health of her household. These might have been exchanged with other housewives, transcribed from a published cookery book, or jealously guarded as a family secret. The idea is to build up, through active experimentation, a repository of first-hand medical, culinary and cosmetic knowledge, thereby self-fashioning an image of oneself as a 'complete housewife' – or, as we might say in the twenty-first century, domestic goddess.

Her 'puppy water' begins: 'take one young fat puppy and put him into a flat still *quartered* – guts and all – the skin upon him, then put in a quart of new butter milk, two quarts of white wine, four lemons purely paired' [my italics]. Next, various obscure plant leaves are to be sprinkled into the puppy solution topped up with a pre-prepared pint of 'fasting spittle', an ingredient included in the first official apothecaries' pharmacopoeia in 1618, and 6d's worth of the finest turpentine oil made with rose water.

Simmer. Stew. Slice in some good pippins. Wait. Cool. Smear on face. Now sit back and relax; the next time you look in the mirror, you'll see that your youth has rebloomed. Sliced puppies are the givers of life.

Your luck has run out. You're the only person left in the shop and have just caught the apothecary's eye. He says that everything in his thirty-five years of experience is telling him that you are of a melancholic disposition, harrowed no doubt by what you have seen on the streets of London, by all the bodies that have come crashing down around you in this pestilent time. The plague, he is sure, is sent by God, and it would be foolhardy to put up a fight against that. But your sorrow, he's sure, *is* something he can cure. Have you heard of his swallow water, freshly brewed, the use of which is safe, the cure certain, and the directions easy, as he puts it. Yes, adds the apprentice, 'tis an infallible cure; in great demand, continues the apothecary, not just to scour away the cobwebs of your misery, but as a catholic prophylactic that will vanquish all feverish symptoms: the griping of the guts, the rising of the lights, the defluxion of the rheums, and the agonies in the child-bearing women.

Some of this wondrous cure is being decanted into a tiny bottle and handed your way. As a stranger to town to whom great generosity is being extended, you're in no position to refuse this gratis sample. You take the bottle. You feel the weight of the apothecary's stare. The apprentice stops mashing and finally looks up at you. 'Have no fear,' says the apothecary. 'It will make your heart boom with the happiness of a hundred baby swallows. No more sad face in your looking-glass. Drink!'

Your best course of action is to take a hearty sip but do not swallow, rather bow to the men, rush out of the shop and, once you're out of sight, spit it out all over the street (spitting in the street is entirely de rigueur in seventeenth-century London). By now you will have guessed that the swallow water contains some unsavoury ingredients – you'll discover what shortly but first you must focus on getting out of the shop.

After you eject the 'medicine', ask for directions to the nearest water conduit. Even London's polluted water supply is worth risking to wash away the taste.

You may be interested to hear that the recipe for swallow water comes not from conniving mountebanks and wise women but the quill of Viscountess Katherine Ranelagh, the brightest female intellectual of her generation, a close associate of the Hartlib Circle (which preceded the Royal Society), sister of the eminent scientist Robert Boyle, with whom she shared a laboratory in her Pall Mall townhouse, and keen experimenter herself. If she believed in this stuff – and if she didn't, why copy it into her recipe books so meticulously? – then so did most of the rest of society.

It is billed as the perfect remedy for melancholy and other mental disturbances like the falling sickness (epilepsy), love-sickness and slurred speech perhaps stemming from a cerebral haemorrhage. The recipe instructs apothecaries, physicians and female domestic practitioners to go into the woods, pref-erably in midsummer, and find forty or fifty baby swallows yet to take their first flight – the recipe is very clear on this point – they must *not* have taken their first flight.

After this you must watch them. Check they don't fly. Tum-ble them into a sack. Carry them back to the still-room. Pour them into a mortar then 'bruise them to a pulp with feathers and all'. Avian holocaust complete, distil the birds' remains with two ounces of castor (a pungent reddish-brown oily gunk extracted from the groinal sacs of beavers, naturally) along with three pints of vinegar. Once everything's ready, give the patient two or three spoonfuls of the swallow water sweetened with sugar. Watch their eyes gleam with happiness and their colour return. The idea here seems to be to 'thieve' the immi-nent first flight of the baby swallows, transfer its essence into a potion, and feed it to the patient – to lift their spirits, as it were, like the joyous first flight of fledgling birds.

Other remedies are equally carnivorous. In the *Queen's Closet Opened* (1655), the exiled Queen Dowager Henrietta Maria

(Charles I's Catholic widow, who returned to London in 1660) records a 'proved' recipe for alleviating teething pains. All you have to do is mix honey and butter with the boiled brains of a hare. All that seems to be missing is eye of newt and toe of frog.

Can't this, the first age of empirical science, do any better than these effusions of folkloric gore? In the apothecaries' defence, there is some method to their madness. It is because of their characteristically large ears – and their name, perhaps – that a recipe recommends trickling a baby hare's urine down a deaf person's ear tube to restore their hearing; because of their sharp and virile fangs that another proposes holding a wolf's bones sautéed in their excrement against your sore teeth to 'appeaseth your anguish immediately'; and because of its nurturing, life-giving connotations that breast milk is again and again hailed as the infallible cure for sore eyes and encroaching blindness. According to other recipes, boiled-alive lizards strengthen the nerves and a bull's penis boosts fertility.

In fact, a number of different and incompatible medical theories have been left to stew in the tincture bottle of mid-seventeenth-century medicine. The bedrock of all medical inquiry remains the fallacious Four Humours Theory, inherited from the ancient world and revived in the Middle Ages (historians usually view the rediscovery and reverence of classical civilizations as a 'good' thing but here surely is one instance in which it severely impeded progress). Propounded most powerfully by the Greek physician Galen in the second century, it insists that good health derives from the correct equilibrium of the four humours: blood, phlegm, black bile and yellow bile. But Galenic medicine is coming to be challenged by iatrochemistry, derived from the ideas of the sixteenth-century Swiss physician Paracelsus, which maintain that diseases are pathological entities in their own right (as opposed to symptoms of humoral imbalance) and should be fought head-on with power-ful chemical remedies including sulphur and mercury.

The third dominant strand of medical science was of course folkloric and quasi-superstitious tradition, including spells, charms and amulets. If you think these sorts of remedies are the preserve of the incredulous masses, think again. The straight-talking, practical civil servant Samuel Pepys wore a hare's foot around his neck to ward off colic. In Pepys's world, the boundaries between magic, religion and science are porous and academic. If there's the faintest chance something will work, people will be game to give it a go – what's to lose?

Well might you wonder, as you see apothecaries through shop windows dishing out their spurious potions and pills to anxious customers, how the medical establishment can get away with selling remedies that, in most cases, won't make the blindest bit of difference and in many will actually exacerbate ill-health.

The plague is a case in point. We now know that it is caused by the Yersinia pestis bacterium, identified in 1894 and spread by fleas who feed on rodents susceptible to infection – particularly *Rattus rattus*, the European black rat. When their host dies, the infected fleas need to find another warm-blooded mammal. Usually this is another rodent but sometimes, par-ticularly in squalid, overcrowded environments, this might be an unlucky human; the plague fleas have especially elastic hind legs, allowing them to leap great distances. The bacteria block the flea's digestive system, so when they bite a human arm or leg, they vomit up infected blood, swiftly infecting your lymph nodes, which regulate your immune system, triggering inflam-mation in the form of buboes. In other, less frequent instances the bacteria can invade the pulmonary blood vessels bringing on the more lethal and infectious pneumonic plague which, unlike its bubonic partner-in-arms, can be spread by airborne particles via coughing and sneezing.

What effect would a myriad of fragrant perfumes, pomander balls, pouncet boxes, acidic salves, curative powders, Venice Treacle, Dragon Waters and tobacco chews have upon the progress of the plague? None whatsoever. Ultimately, the elaborate and exotic tinctures on sale in the apothecary's and cooked at home – some containing as many as twenty different ingredients – only hit home just how powerless physicians, quacks and apothecaries are to treat people effectively, let alone cure them, when they are at the mercy of a viral and bacterial environment they are several centuries off understanding. And not just for the plague; for a whole host of killer diseases such as consumption and smallpox too.

Leave the apothecary's, walk down Bread Street, and head to Queenhithe. Once a thriving medieval port, today you'll find it deserted. Hail a water ferry and ask to be taken to Milford Stairs upriver. It's time to take our leave of the city and see how the metropolis is beginning to eat into the western suburbs.

River of refugees

Looking upriver, you notice far fewer wherries riding the Thames than in Shakespeare and Chaucer's time but, as you can see if you gaze to your left, it's a very different story downriver. Towards the shipping suburbs of Wapping and Ratcliffe, you can make out hundreds of ships lying in rows of two or three spanning the river, across the twists and turns of the Thames, and receding into the distance at Greenwich. There are wherries and lighters; single-masted hoys and smacks, and much bigger seafaring vessels. These extend, your waterman tells you, virtually all the way to the coast. Tens of thousands of families are camping out on the river in an effort to avoid the violence of the contagion, furnishing their boats with straw and making tents from their sails. But even here, they can't hide from the plague. He tells sad stories of watermen becoming infected ashore and dying alone, their boats their coffins as they drift aimlessly from bank to bank; of members of dead families thrown overboard from the bigger ships – sometimes in coffins, but sometimes not, washing up on the muddy banks of the Thames.

The Thames has always been the economic lifeblood of the city; the sight of it clogged up and at a standstill – strict quarantine measures are in place for foreign trading vessels, most of which, in any case, are giving London a wide berth – only serves to hammer home the extent to which commerce in the metropolis has come to a halt.

Your waterman tells you that he won't forsake his oars even if he's the last man alive in London and he certainly hasn't given up the long-standing tradition of yelling out to any other wherryman he passes, sending kites and gulls soaring into the air in fright. As he's busy shredding his throat calling out to his mates, steal a glance towards the Bankside. It is virtually one long ribbon of timber-framed, plaster-infilled houses running from Dead Man's Place to the west of Southwark High Street to the final cluster of houses opposite Somerset House across the river. Beyond is an expanse of meadows, marshes and pastures rolling down to the far-off hamlets of Kennington and Camberwell; it is uncanny to think that one day all this will be swallowed up by a grey conurbation sprawling all the way to the Thames: the future south London. The boat is drawing near to Milford Stairs. Give the boatman his coins and wish him well.

As you clamber onto the bank, the church of St Clement

Danes tolls its bells for the latest victim of the plague and in the faces of those you pass you see eyes drifting with despair, first this way, then that.

Make your way up Milford Lane with the sprawling mansion complex of Arundel House on your left. Cross the Strand, walk through the churchyard of St Clement Danes, and turn left up Wych Street. This will take you onto Drury Lane, which sweeps up to Holborn and the fetid slums of St Giles's beyond. Unless you've got a death wish, don't follow it all the way; it's the second most infected part of London after St Giles-without-Cripplegate – clearly St Giles, the hermit saint, isn't much good in a crisis. Instead, turn left at Long Acre, once a winding rural path between St Martin's Field and Holborn but now built up and London's best place to get your coach repaired – not that there are many coaches left in the city since most of the aristocrats and gentry have fled, and many of the drivers have swapped their gilded conveyances for creaking deadcarts. After about ten minutes you should see the stately James Street. Take it. You are drawing near to a wide open space; the hoarse cries of market traders reverberate up and down the street.

An epochal piazza

It is bigger and there are more people, but apart from a handful of spectacular new stone buildings that have popped up – the Banqueting Hall at Whitehall, for instance, and the Queen's Palace at Greenwich – there's not that much aesthetic difference between the London you find yourself in now and that of William Shakespeare sixty-two years back. Generally speaking, it's a topographic hotchpotch with back alleys that seem to fork endlessly; sooty churches and cathedrals crawling with tatty stalls; and cattle holding up the traffic. Inigo Jones's masterpieces notwithstanding, London is a far cry from the pomp and prestige of places like Rome, Turin and Vienna (and what baroque Lisbon and Berlin would become), with their elegant piazzas, arrow-straight thoroughfares, grid-like streets, obelisks, grand boulevards and wide-open spaces imposed by – and manifesting – despotic authority. In general, London is a seething, chaotic, vital mess. And all the better for it.

But Covent Garden – London's first public square, in which you now find yourself – is different; revolutionary even. If the prospect of discovering a square in London seems unremarkable in the twenty-first century, that is testament to the success of the experimental Grand Piazza in which you are now standing. Less than thirty years since it was laid out, it still feels new and will ultimately prove epochal to the future of the western and central metropolis, which would no longer be a continuation of the ancient and labyrinthine city but instead elegant, harmonious, and chic.

Look around you. Lining the northern and eastern sides of the square are three uniform terraces of fine colonnaded townhouses – brick, four storeys high and with generous casement windows on the upper two floors. Dormer windows rise from the sloping roofs. Beneath the arcades, the walkways are twenty-one feet wide and paved in luxurious freestone (luxurious compared to London's many rough-pebbled, fenced-off walkways, at least), imported at great expense from the extremities of the kingdom. The façades of the houses are coated in beige stucco, an architectural marzipan that shrouds the building material and gives the illusion of timelessness. Depending on the density of the traffic at Drury Lane, you might just be able to glimpse the south-western corner of Lincoln's Inn Fields down Russell Street, but other than that you'll be hemmed in by buildings, with the sturdy garden wall of Bedford House on the south side. Perched on their hilltops, the twin villages of Hampstead and Highgate twinkle in the distance, beckoning Londoners to a game of shuffle board and a bracing swim away from the miasmic city.

Watching over the piazza is the new and austere church of St Paul – the first place of worship to be built for over one hundred years – in the style of a classical temple with Ionic columns and a clock, set in its own churchyard fronting onto Bedford Street. The eighteenth-century aesthete Horace Walpole would later view it as pretty humble fare – in his *Anecdotes of Painting in England* (1762) is an exchange between the Earl of Bedford and Inigo Jones regarding the church: 'I would not have it much better than a barn,' says the parsimonious earl. 'Well then,' replies Jones, 'you shall have the handsomest barn in England.' (Horace Walpole of course lived in one of the country's handsomest follies, Strawberry Hill, a blinding-white, kitsch-Gothic castle in Twickenham.)

Flanking the church are two imposing stone entrances to the churchyard and, beyond that, two matching four-storey houses without any arcades, guarding the entrances to King Street and Henrietta Street. On the south side, you can see into the back garden of Bedford House, which fronts onto the Strand, though 'back garden' hardly does it justice – it's a vast enclosure, about two-thirds the size of the piazza, with a thick grove of trees, a well-manicured garden with a fountain, and viewing terrace overlooking the square. To the west is Russell Street, on the southern side of which lies a more intimate Little Piazza with similarly arcaded houses and small gardens.

Without the permanently thronged market buildings that are such a dominant feature of tourist-trap Covent Garden in the twenty-first century, the square space in front of you is wide and impressive. There are flimsy-looking wooden poles which have, for the last decade or so, demarcated the central space reserved for a market. Market traders stand amongst wooden stalls and wicker baskets brimming with fruit, vegetables and flowers; some women are balancing baskets of fruit on their heads. The market is less busy than usual because of the plague but life must go on – most of the traders can't afford for it not to, they lack the means to flee for the hills as many of the owners of the surrounding fashionable residences have done.

Little spaniels bounce around, biding their time to pounce upon a watermelon or dart beneath the wheels of an apple-laden barrow; unsprung coaches rattle and screech on the cobbles of the piazza; a scrum of boys kick a ball about; widows with white sticks walk arm-in-arm, lamenting their lost husbands; a mountebank swishes around in his scarlet cloak, revealing inside pockets stuffed with amulets and potions for sale. He is one of a dying breed. In the first few months of the epidemic, London was flooded with quack-doctors, astrologers, nativity calculators, cunning men and wise women preying on the incredulity and fears of the superstitious masses – their 'cures' made even apothecaries' remedies seem sophisticated. But once the plague found its awful stride, most of these 'wizards' found it politic to vanish, scurrying back to their hovels, 'not able to foretell their own fate, or to calculate their own nativities', as Defoe wryly puts it.

There is much to take in. An urban square is a point of social convergence, encouraging people to savour the infinite possibilities and serendipity of inner-city life – to look, lope, linger or luxuriate in the lustre of metropolitan sophistication. The success of Covent Garden shows that Londoners are not averse to a mode of sociability more usually equated with the sun-drenched piazzas of Italy and the fine squares of France.

Take a walk beneath the arcades: the residents have no right to have you moved on unless you make a racket – which you won't – and besides you're still brandishing your white stick, so it's the perfect place to soak up the area's unique charm.

As you saunter along, know that you're strolling across the site of a much starker Anglo-Saxon settlement, *Lundenwic*, which we mentioned in medieval Westminster. It was in existence by the seventh century about a mile away from the ghost city of Londinium, abandoned by the Romans in AD 470. In Old English, *wic* or *wich* can mean both a settlement or dwelling place and, deriving from the Old Norse *vik*, 'bay' or 'port', and archaeological discoveries in the twentieth century have suggested that *Lundenwic* stretched all the way from the kink in the river at the village of Charing in the west to the banks of the River Fleet in the east. This sheds light on a tantalizing reference in the Venerable Bede's *Ecclesiastical History of the English People*, written in the eighth century, in which he mentions 'a metropolis ... a mart of many peoples coming by land and sea'. No archaeological evidence suggests any such thing still existed within the walls of Londinium but it was probably the port settlement further west. *Lundenwic*, it seems, was presided over by a small citadel on what eventually became Covent Garden, an idea corroborated by the street name Aldwych – 'old port' – which first appears in 1211 and, by 1665, is called Wych Street, bleeding into Drury Lane. Together these two streets may have lain to the east of the citadel.

It's easy to forget that Covent Garden is perched on fairly high ground; if you were to walk south, cutting across the Strand, you'd descend a steep incline of about 200 feet towards the muddy bank of the Thames. Nonetheless, *Lundenwic* would have been horribly vulnerable to Viking attack and after these intensified in the late ninth century (the Vikings occupied the shell of Londinium in 871, provoking Alfred the Great to re-conquer it in 886), *Lundenwic* was no longer a viable prospect and, as it was abandoned, it came to be called *Ealdwic* (old port) then, in 1211, Aldewich.

As you wander past some of the most fashionable houses in London, imagine a cluster of warships docking by the Fleet and Vikings pouring out, clutching axes. They storm towards *Lundenwic* sending women and children screaming through the fields and men cowering inside their thatched wooden houses soon to be burned to a crisp by their persistent invaders.

In the tenth century, *Ealdwic* came into the possession of the Abbey – or Convent – of St Peter, Westminster. The monks used it as an orchard, arable and pasture land, as we have seen (for some reason, the area retained the antiquated 'Covent' over the modern 'Convent', confusing the likes of Samuel Pepys, who often just calls it 'Common Garden'). After the Dissolution of the Monasteries, the land passed to the Crown, then in 1552 to John Russell, the 1st Earl of Bedford, whose successor the 3rd Earl built a magnificent timber-framed mansion with turrets and stables on the northern side of the Strand. By 1613 he had built a wall around his house and gardens, encompassing twenty acres of the former abbey's land, marking out the site of what would become London's first carefully orchestrated suburb (as opposed to the infill that occurred organically and piecemeal between Westminster and the city).

As the advantages of housing an elite population away from the insanitary and overcrowded city came into focus, the enterprising 4th Earl of Bedford forked out £2,000 for a licence to build residences 'fit for the habitations of gentlemen and men of ability' (officially contrary to Crown policy but a nice money-spinner for the depleted Treasury). The scale of the plans necessitated the involvement, with Charles I's approval, of the brilliant royal surveyor Inigo Jones, who, having travelled extensively in Italy, was seduced by Renaissance ideals of harmony, proportion and symmetry as epitomized by the work of the Paduan architect Andrea Palladio in Venice. Covent Garden was to be laid out according to these Palladian ideals. In a city whose streets are generally lined with pairs of clumsy, creaking timber-framed houses hunching over the street, the idea of building uniform terraces around a central piazza with wide peripheral streets on a grid-like layout was positively avant-garde.

Just as the earl had hoped, the beau monde were sucked out of the Strand and the City and flocked to Covent Garden Piazza and her tributary streets whose names – Henrietta Street, King Street, James Street, Chandos Street – reflect the aristocratic connection. In relation to their vast and splendid countryside estates, moving into one of Inigo's terraced houses was tantamount to slumming it – but in what style! The properties have four main storeys and a basement underneath the arcade walk as well as coach-houses, stables and two kitchens round the back and use of a sewer that cuts across the Strand into the Thames. Another novelty began to appear in some of the fashionable nearby streets – balconies, covered in crawling plants allowing the quality to wave to one another as they passed in their coaches. The earliest residents included three earls and by the 1670s King Street will be able to count amongst its residents seven members of the aristocracy and a clutch of wealthy tradesmen. No wonder: the seventeen colonnaded houses cost £150 per annum to rent (you could buy six carriage horses for the same price – or three coaches) and since the area is not 'pestered with mean courts and alleys', the poor aren't able to blot the pasteurized Italianate landscape.

The three streets flanking the churchyard constitute an elite shopping district with purveyors of silk, velvet, lace and linen making sure that the aristocracy and gentry cut a fine figure at court or in the ballroom, for Covent Garden is the acme of sophistication, a district easily as rich and superior as twenty-first-century Mayfair, Belgravia and Kensington would become.

Already, though, just thirty years after it was built, there are signs that Covent Garden is struggling to remain the fulcrum of fashion. For a start, it is incomplete – the original plan was to have colonnaded houses stretching right the way around the square, broken only by the church, in accordance with ideals of Italianate harmony. But only seventeen luxury terraced houses were ever completed along its northern and eastern stretches, frustrating what would surely have been, according to one excitable eighteenth-century historian, 'beyond dispute, one of the finest squares in the universe'.

The 5th Earl of Bedford's decision to situate a cacophonous fruit, flower and vegetable market in the middle of the square in the 1650s to maximize his income from the plot was perhaps, in retrospect, misguided and counterproductive. For when the royalist members of the nobility and gentry streamed back to London after the Civil War and Cromwellian Protectorate era, Covent Garden faced stiff competition in the form of copycat squares to the east, north and, most spectacularly, to the west. Some of these had a more exclusive and less commercial air. By 1641, much of Lincoln's Inn Fields was lined with brick terraced houses (though the vast fields themselves harboured characters of ill repute – and cattle); the first leases in Bloomsbury Square, described by John Evelyn as 'a noble square, or piazza, a little town', were signed in 1661; and in 1663 Samuel Pepys mentions 'the building of St James's . . . which is now about', referring to the super-elite St James's Square, future home of the crème de la crème of English society, on the doorstop of the king's favourite palace.

Some squares are yet to come. If you were to walk away from the Great Piazza down King Street towards St Martin's Lane, in about twelve minutes you'd find yourself amidst windmills, cowpats and flies in open fields. Directly ahead would be Leicester House, soon to be incorporated into Leicester Square in the 1670s, and to your right, a couple of miles yonder, a patch of greenery that will become Soho Square in the 1680s. In the next twenty years, the West End of London will begin to take shape.

'God has given you one face, and you make yourselves another'

As you wander through Covent Garden and the wider city, you'll see a number of 'painted' faces – not just those of the well-heeled residents but fruit hawkers and shopkeepers too – and harlots and hags with a cruder daub. Some, of course, will be wearing make-up to hide the symptoms of the plague. Back in Shakespeare's London, you may recall flashes of chalk-white faces, blazing red hair and rouged cheeks in the upper galleries of the Globe and through the glass frontages of Cheapside shops. The politically adroit Queen Elizabeth was an arch-painter herself, obsessed with projecting an image of eternal youth that belied her increasing years.

But the use of cosmetics – an umbrella term for anything that enhances one's appearance or scent, so powder, perfume, paint, facial patches and hair dye – was highly controversial until quite recently. 'God has given you one face, and you make your-selves another,' snarls the Prince of Denmark to Ophelia in *Hamlet*, voicing concerns that would have been shared by many of the members of the audience. A slew of pamphlets such as Thomas Tuke's *Treatise against Painting and Tincturing* (1616) heaped opprobrium upon anyone who dared to use cosmetics. Painting your face, he argued, is tantamount to tinkering with God's craftsmanship like an inferior artist painting over the opus of a Grand Master. Cosmetics prostitute their wearers as well, since they are magnets for the lustful male gaze. What's more, they are dishonest, self-deceptive and, since they contain foreign and exotic materials, decidedly unpatriotic. The pamphlets take, as a common thread, the idea that make-up is an affront to male sovereignty, whether to fathers, husbands or even God himself.

Some of this lingers on – in a characteristically blunt comment, Samuel Pepys describes his cousin as 'still very pretty but paints red on her face which makes me hate her' – but attitudes are thawing and by the 1690s the question-and-answer journal the *Athenian Mercury*, a sort of seventeenth-century Google, could describe make-up as 'practical and harmless', whatever the Bible and 'weak persons' might have to say on the matter. Much of this came about thanks to Charles II. Following his lead, his libidinous courtiers, and particularly the court ladies, freely smeared themselves in powder and paint and perfume, in stark contrast to what was acceptable under the Puritan Commonwealth, which had predictably outlawed 'the vice of painting' and 'the immodest dress of women' in 1650.

But with the rise of a more aspirational society that accompanied the accumulation of middle-class wealth from the mid-century, and the growth of 'Town' (the emerging fashionable suburbs between the city and Westminster) as a theatre of display for the nobility and gentry, conditions are now ripe for a burgeoning cosmetics trade.

Don't assume that by increasing their autonomy over their appearance, make-up is necessarily empowering for women. Men grudgingly come to accept cosmetics, but only as an aid for women to meet the male-authored ideal of feminine beauty. Traditionally, men wanted their women to look like the pale, ethereal, curvaceous beauties of Botticelli paintings, with 'eyes like stars or the sun; a mouth like coral, rubies, vermilion; cheeks or a complexion like the moon, alabaster, lily mixed with rose, silver, glistening gold, cream or milk; blue veins in the breast like azure rivers; and teeth like pearl or ivory', as the Shakespeare scholar Farah Karim-Cooper so evocatively puts it. This connoted innocence and virtue and also wealth and leisure since it suggested the wearer hadn't spent long hours toiling in the fields under a scorching sun.

By the 1660s, however, there is a slightly more permissive attitude towards overt make-up. You'll see that the current fashion prizes contrasts: full red lips, prominent eyes, darkened eyebrows. Gentlemen admire women with wholesome, moon-like faces and black or brown hair (red hair is out). You might be surprised to see that double chins are also at a premium.

If you're a female time traveller and want to get the Covent Garden look, here's what you need to do. First, find another apothecary's – in the seventeenth century, someone's outward appearance is seen as an index of their inner health (and moral virtue) so apothecaries stock all sorts of beautifying products, as pharmacies continue to do. For your white make-up base, ask for some Venetian ceruse, which has a thick and lustrous finish. Massage it onto your cheeks with your finger tips then add a touch of cherry-coloured cerise or vermilion. This will synthesize a blushing effect, reassuring men that you are sub-servient and coquettish, *and* eradicate freckles and warts. Your eyes need to look translucent and sleepy. For this, ask for some belladonna eye-drops to dilate the pupils. Your lips can be red-dened with fruit juice or cochineal made from crushed insects. (People further down the social pyramid incidentally use a rougher, starker white powder and a dry rouge or ochre red dabbed on with a greasy cloth.)

A word of warning – once you're all painted, if a man doffs his hat or bows to you under the colonnade, for example, *don't* smile back at them. You don't want the sheen of your make-up's enamel finish to crack – drawing attention to one's made-up face is a source of acute embarrassment and shame. In June

1662 the Dutch painter Willem Schellinks went to watch the royal family eat, as people do, and recalled Queen Catherine rushing out of the Banqueting House after her make-up started streaming down her face. For the same reason, be careful not to get caught in a rain shower or stand too close to one of the street bonfires (as others are doing, to ward off the plague), or you will quickly resemble a weeping clown of nightmare.

Jolly good, you might think, let's do it. But pause a moment to consider what you'd actually be doing to your face. Venetian ceruse is made from *white lead* mixed with egg and vinegar; cerise and vermilion contain *mercury sulphide*; and the name of the belladonna eye-drops belies its constituent part – deadly nightshade. The lead could cause your hair to thin and fall out, rot your teeth, make your breath stink, turn your skin a sickly yellow-green and ultimately work its way down to destroy your lungs. Mercury is equally pernicious, though the apothecary will assure you its toxic properties can be neutralized by mixing it with lemon juice, salt and bitter almonds. His reassurances will wear increasingly thin, however, as it burns through layers of your skin, poisons your gums, makes your teeth fall out and leaves your skin tough and leathery. And drip too many belladonna eye-drops onto your corneas and you'll eventually go blind, which would rather scupper the intended effect.

Ironically, make-up will ultimately ravage your natural beauty. People would have done well to heed the polemicists' warnings, though it was not the *soul* that painting destroyed but the *face*. Ultimately the price of powdered beauty is decay. But if your face does end up ravaged and pock-marked, whether by toxic make-up, syphilis or smallpox, there is a *chic* solution.

'Bespatch'd till they are bed-rid':
the secret language of patches

Standing on the east side of Covent Garden, catching the human traffic in and out of the piazza at Russell Street, is a handsome young man with long curly hair and a moon-shaped face – unnaturally white, evidently ceruse induced. He has a large open basket strapped around his neck and holds a Venetian-style mask and a fan. As you move closer, you shudder. It looks as though his face is crawling with the symptoms of some awful disease – or even gnats and leeches. But his expression is serene as he stares into people's faces and hawks his wares. As you move in closer, you realize his face is covered not by insects but by black patches of various shapes and sizes. From the way he tilts his head and paws the air in front of his cheeks, it's clear he's modelling his wares. They are an alien form of cosmetic rare in the twenty-first century except at the odd music festival, Hallowe'en and occasionally on the catwalk.

'In England, the young, old, handsome, ugly, are all bespatch'd till they are bed-rid. I have often counted fifteen patches, or more, upon the swarthy wrinkled face of an old hag three-score and ten and upwards,' observes one French visitor (in the early part of the next century, in fact, but his observations ring just as true for the 1660s). The last time patches had been worn so ubiquitously was in Roman London but in the sixteenth century, people began to wear them to ward off toothache. They have now spilled over into the sphere of women's fashion; men wear them less frequently, hawkers like this notwithstanding. Put your nose up to his face and have a good, long marvel – he won't mind.

He is wearing a star on his left cheek, a crescent moon on his right and a butterfly by his bottom lip. But it is the grinning skull in the middle of his forehead that grabs your attention. The patches are made from black taffeta or other fine black silk, velvet or thin leather (or, if you were poor, paper and mouse-skin) and stuck onto the face with gum mastic (a type of glue made from the sap of trees). Glancing down into his basket, you see that they also come shaped as diamonds, suns, worms, coaches, doves, cupids, trees and even the silhouettes of notable personages. Obviously, the more patches you wear, the greater the facial repose required to keep them in place. To guard against the risk of shooting stars and plunging planets, elite women tend to carry with them little gold or silver patch boxes, containing a stash of backup patches, and with the luxury of a small mirror on the lid.

Although you might agree with those who satirize them as scars, cat scratches, blots, sores, flies and gnats, most people think black patches beautify the face when set against the whiteness of the skin and enliven facial expressions. A series of ever-smaller moons radiating from the outer corner of the eye is very much in vogue, seemingly magnifying the eyes, and a sprinkling of stars around the mouth is meant to furnish the smile with a mischievous charm. But more than that, the positioning of women's patches can send out very specific signals, as revealed in various ladies' handbooks and pamphlets published throughout the seventeenth century.

Fashions move very quickly indeed, but according to one authority on fashion, a patch near the lip means 'I could be yours'; a heart-shaped patch on the temple, 'my intellect is formidable; think carefully before talking to me'; a heart-shaped patch on the left cheek, 'I'm engaged'; the same on the right cheek, 'I'm married'; a patch on the forehead, 'I consider myself superior'; a patch on the nose, 'I'm wild'; a patch on the lower lip, 'you can trust me'. A patch beside the mouth is meant to convey garrulousness – so people will be wary of approaching you, though why anyone would want to project that is unclear. Quite how satirical guides to patch-wearing are meant to be is difficult for the historian to assess but you can find out for yourself. Why not stick a patch on your nose and one near your lip, and see if the men come flocking over?

Don't think patches are necessarily vanity objects. Sometimes they are meant to foster intellectual reflections when viewed in a mirror. Stars, for instance, are supposed to refine your thoughts by keeping your lofty ambitions in sight; flies are reminders of the quickness of mind and transience of life; and worms, by emphasizing mortality and the inevitability of ageing, are the very antithesis of our modern conception of cosmetics, which strive to disguise such inconvenient truths. In this, they serve a similar function to memento mori.

Never mind all this: patches are also excellent for disguising the deep circular disfigurements of smallpox. In fact, it was probably the introduction of a smallpox vaccine right at the end of the eighteenth century that helped to bring down the curtain on the tradition of patch-wearing.

A meteoric orange wench

Leaving the patch seller behind you, walk up Russell Street, crossing Bow Lane, and take the next turning on the right: Bridges Street. Look out for a narrow passage, no more than ten feet wide, leading towards a large polygonal building with a glazed dome, hemmed in by houses on all sides. This is the Theatre Royal, barely two years old, but since the beginning of June silent because of the plague.

In Shakespearean London there was something of a

theatrical free market, with plays performed in over ten purpose-built playhouses. But at the Restoration, Charles II, a theatre nut himself, granted a joint monopoly on public theatre to courtier Thomas Killigrew (who would lead the King's Men troupe) and court poet William Davenant (the Duke's Men). They have a gentleman's agreement not to undercut or encroach upon one another's territory. After the suppression of the playhouses and shooting of the beasts in the bull and bear-baiting arena by the Puritans, the return of the theatre was greeted with great excitement. But it took a while to find its stride. Samuel Pepys visited the open-air Red Bull Theatre in Clerkenwell in March 1661 to watch a poorly attended, 'poorly done' *All's Lost by Lust*, in which a singer who struck the wrong notes himself was punched by his master in full view of the audience, much to their amusement. But by 1663 the Duke's Men were performing in a converted tennis court in Lincoln's Inn Fields and the King's Men here in this new, purpose-built theatre.

Charles II is a frequent visitor, and with the Theatre Royal's aristocratic management and relatively small capacity (of 700; the Globe's, remember, was around 3,000) the audience is significantly more socially exclusive than in the earlier Bankside playhouses – there are no stinkards and the pit is lined with benches for gallants, covered in the same fine green baize used on billiard tables; any servants and shopkeepers who attend are shunted into the third-tier galleries. Although a fine-looking building, its weatherproofing leaves something to be desired – on one occasion Pepys and his wife are forced to leave the theatre mid-play after a hail storm invaded the auditorium, the glass cupola having proved leaky.

If you were to visit this playhouse in happier times, you would notice three major contrasts with your experiences in Shakespearian London. First, there is a proscenium arch framing the stage, reinforcing, to some extent, the division between the orange-munching world of the playgoers and the make-believe world of the stage, narrowing the scope for interaction between the two. This new element of escapism is reinforced by the presence of movable and vividly painted scenery – very much following the lead of the elaborate Jacobean and Caroline court masques earlier in the century, transporting audiences to Sicily from the Strand. And finally, actresses. They are gradually replacing the boy actors who played female parts in Shakespeare's time.

This is revolutionary. When French actresses performed at Blackfriars Theatre during the reign of Charles I as part of a one-off performance by a visiting company, it caused outrage: 'monsters . . . shameful unwomanish and graceless', is how the Puritan William Prynne described them; 'Glad am I to say that they were hissed, hooted, and pippin-pelted from the stage,' writes another hostile observer. England lagged far behind much of Europe in this respect; the first actress had appeared in France in 1545 (though they wouldn't become ubiquitous there until 1610), Rome in 1565, and Italy in 1578. During his exile in Europe, Charles II had enjoyed watching actresses and saw no reason why he shouldn't go on enjoying them at his Restoration. It was also a brilliant counterblast to the Puritans' ascetic denunciation of the sex drive from a libidinous and indulgent court. In the charter he issued to Thomas Killigrew, he cleverly spun the legitimization of actresses as a reformation of the 'scandalous and offensive' abuse of boy actors.

The first female actress to appear on stage (paid, that is, unlike in a court masque, and in a secular rather than religious production) played Desdemona in *Othello* at the Vere Street Theatre almost five years ago; it was either Margaret Hughes or Anne Marshall – the records are ambiguous. Many more followed. One famed actress is Elizabeth Barry, trained and debauched by the erotic poet the Earl of Rochester, and who flourished in tragedy productions. Female playwrights are few and far between but male writers leaped at the opportunity to contrive ever more tenuous ways of getting female characters into men's tight-fitting clothing. These 'breeches roles', as they are known, give audiences the chance to feast upon the female form, showing off women's legs and ankles in particular. You can also expect to see divan scenes, in which a female character is discovered in a horizontal position, usually wearing very few clothes. And more alarmingly, rape scenes. These allow male audience members to be gratified by a sex scene without infringing upon the moral virtue of the female character and, by extension, the actresses who play them. So although female actresses achieved a measure of equality by intruding into the formerly male-dominated theatrical space, feminist critics have doubted whether this truly *was* empowering since the female form was often confined within the male figure, suggesting domination.

Actress Nell Gwyn's star is rising. The daughter of an alcoholic brothel keeper who grew up in low circumstances in Covent Garden, she began her theatrical career, as many women did, as an orange wench working at the Theatre Royal. Besides hawking sweet China oranges for 6d a go, orange women serve as sexual emissaries for the rakes and libertines in the audience and actresses backstage, for which they need to draw upon a ready supply of wit, innuendo and coquetry. Nell (which is short for Eleanor) has recently been incorporated into Thomas Killigrew's troupe of actors. Her first appearance was playing the Aztec emperor Montezuma's daughter and love interest to Hernán Cortés in Dryden's *The Indian Emperor* in March of this year. 'Pretty, witty Nell', as Pepys called her, will go on to make a name for herself as a magnetic and much loved comic actress in the course of a short but intense seven-year career. (Bridges Street actresses are perfect fodder for lustful aristocrats and Nell Gwyn would be no exception, eventually catching the eye of no less a womanizer than King Charles II himself. She would eclipse his old favourite Lady Castlemaine and another actress-mistress, Moll Davis – after spiking Davis's cakes with laxative before an explosive evening tryst with King Charles, according to some anonymous and quite possibly fictitious satires – and emerge as his clear favourite by the end of the decade, eventually bearing him two illegitimate sons and being royally rewarded with a splendid brick townhouse on Pall Mall after her place was taken by a new French mistress.)

The public love anything that has the whiff of a rags-to-riches fairytale about it, and in later years many juicy anecdotes will circulate about Nell's romance with the king, most of which play on her quick wit and guile. There is the story of how they met. In one version, Charles spotted her in the audience in the adjoining box and began flirting with her in the middle of a performance. Afterwards, Charles and his brother, the future James II, took Nell and her friend out to dinner at a tavern incognito. But when the bill arrived, both Stuart brothers were penniless. Nell had to pay, declaring, in a mockery of the king's speech, ''Ods fish! But this is the poorest company I ever was in!' Another story tells of Charles's first meeting with their illegitimate son. 'Come here, you little bastard, and say hello to your father,' Nell apparently said. When Charles objected, Nell shot back, 'Your Majesty has given me no other name by which to call him.' The little bastard was created the Earl of Burford and Baron of Heddington on the spot. On his deathbed, Charles told his brother, 'Let not poor Nelly starve,' and James was good to his word, paying her debts and giving her a pension. She will be robbed of the opportunity of growing old disgracefully, dying in 1687, aged thirty-seven, in her

Pall Mall townhouse following a stroke. This jade, this 'bold merry slut', as Pepys calls her, is one of London's first true celebrities; her face still adorns Covent Garden tavern signs in the twenty-first century.

When Nell died, she left a generous bequest for the relief of poor prisoners in Newgate; her sister had once been incarcerated there for theft. It's our next stop: walk up Drury Lane onto High Holborn.

'The drink of the gods'

Nell Gwyn first appeared on stage playing the daughter of the Aztec king and it was of course the Aztecs – whose empire was pulverized by Spanish conquistadors – who introduced Europeans to chocolate, a real novelty in Samuel Pepys's London, along with coffee and tea. As you make your way to Newgate, you will walk past the Vine Tavern on your left, by the sign of the falcon after King Street. It's worth pausing here for a moment, for it was near this site that chocolate was first sold to the public in 1652.

The first commercial shipment of cacao beans arrived in Europe from the New World in 1585 and by the early seventeenth century, it was all the rage in the palaces, mansions and monasteries of baroque Europe, a mark of exquisite gentility. The Aztecs had drunk their chocolate cold, flavoured with scorching-hot chillies and vanilla, and sometimes mixed with the blood of sacrificial slaves. The Spanish had originally considered it 'more a drink for pigs than humanity' but as it spread through Europe it became ever-more refined, being drunk hot, sweet, and mixed with cinnamon: 'a divine, celestial drink', according to the Spaniard Geronimo Piperni, 'the sweat of the stars, the vital seed, divine nectar, the drink of the gods'.

A handbill advertising the tract *Chocolate or an Indian Drink*, translated from the Spanish and heralding the medicinal virtues of the drink, claims that someone called John Dawkins, living near the Vine Tavern in Holborn, was offering chocolate 'at reasonable rates' as early as 1652 – the same year the 'bitter Muhammedan gruel' (coffee) was first dispensed to the public from a shed in a mass of tangled streets and alleys surrounding St Michael's churchyard, Cornhill. And eight years ago, a newspaper reported that the public could buy, drink, or learn how to make an 'excellent West India drink' called chocolate from a Frenchman, 'the first man who did sell it in England' from a chocolate house tucked away in Queen's Head Alley off Bishopsgate Street, near Gresham College. For Samuel Pepys, chocolate is the perfect cure for a hangover; finding his head 'in a sad taking' the day after Charles II's bacchanalian coronation, he enjoys a swift, soothing draft of chocolate that settles his stomach. Should Mr Dawkins still be dispensing the 'drink of the gods' from his house near the Vine Tavern, go in and ask for a dish. Expect a thick, luxuriant and exotically spiced glop. It will be bitter – no milk and sugar – and, if he's a purist and follows the sort of ideal hot chocolate recipes you can buy from the stalls in St Paul's Churchyard, laced with exotic spices and flavours including cinnamon, cloves, Indian peppers, vanilla, musk perfume, even ambergris if he's utterly gone to town. Either way, it will really put to shame the milky, powdery, watery froth that passes for hot chocolate in so many of London's cafés and restaurants in the twenty-first century.

Still, in a city with no tradition of hot non-alcoholic drinks, the public need to be persuaded to try this alien concoction. Thus a publicity campaign is underway, making the same kind of mendacious claims about chocolate's panacean virtues that accompanied the arrival of tobacco in Tudor London. But the most exciting claim – much repeated – is that it can restore youth, boost fertility and a powerful and infallible aphrodisiac. The merest lick, we are told, '''twill make old women young and fresh; create new motions of the flesh, and cause them [to] long for you know what, if they but taste of chocolate'; furthermore, it oils the testicles and will make you 'as strong in the back as a lion', 'as nimble as a squirrel', 'as brisk as a body louse' and 'as lively as an eel, only by virtue of that liquor' – basically, irresistible to the opposite sex. These very same claims, thinly corroborated by scientific evidence, are parroted by chocolate companies in the modern world, especially around Valentine's Day. Unlike in Paris and Madrid, chocolate drinking is not confined to the social elite; it's on sale in many of London's coffeehouses but since it is more expensive and less of a caffeine hit, it is never drunk as widely as coffee. Only in the purpose-built aristocratic quarter of St James's would a cluster of super-elite self-styled chocolate houses sprout and flourish in the later seventeenth century.

But we must resume our journey to a place where people can only dream of luxuries like coffee and chocolate. Continue up Holborn. When you reach Holborn Bridge over the stinking River Fleet, proceed up Snow Hill, to Newgate.

The Whit

London is a city of prisons, particularly by European standards. In *The Praise and Virtue of a Jail and Jailers*, published in 1623, the Water Poet John Taylor counts no fewer than eighteen prisons in London, including the Fleet (London's oldest, first mentioned in 1170, and now mainly a debtors' oubliette), the Bishop of Winchester's Clink prison in Southwark for drunkards, heretics and traitors to the crown, and the cramped, rat-infested Poultry Compter on Cheapside for homosexuals, vagrants and other deviants who had offended shrieval sensibilities.

Newgate, though, is the most infamous of them all. Before we go in, note on your left the church of St Sepulchre, whose linguistic connotations with death and burial are highly appropriate since it is here, on the morning of an execution, that the bells toll twelve times for doomed prisoners to be led from the 'condemned hold' into the Press Yard. As they set out to Tyburn, dragged backwards, head directly beneath the horse's rump, watched by people hanging out of their windows and outside their doors, the cart would pause at St Sepulchre's, where the sexton would proclaim a lengthy blessing on those 'for whom this great bell tolls'. By this stage the prisoners would probably be sick of the sound of the sexton's voice, he having popped up outside their cell door at midnight – ruining their last night of sleep – urging them to repent. Still, they could look forward to stopping off at two public houses en route to Tyburn for a drink to calm the nerves ('I'll buy you a pint on the way back!' it was customary to shout to the customers inside).

Looming in front of you is the gate, guarding the entrance to the city, associated for as long as anyone can remember with the Whit, a vast dungeon complex of anguish, despair and physical torment. It's the second incarnation of Newgate prison, built in the fifteenth century thanks to a generous bequest from Mayor Dick Whittington. Whittington, by now a legendary figure along with his wealth-creating cat, had been appalled by the 'fetid and corrupt atmosphere that is in the heinous gaol of Newgate', where 'many persons are now dead who would be alive'. But over 200 years later, it is more fetid than ever, variously described in the seventeenth and eighteenth centuries as 'the quintessence of disparagement', 'an abode of misery and despair', 'a bottomless pit of violence' and 'a hell such as Dante might have conceived'.

Go in, if you dare.

You shouldn't have too much trouble. Like much else in London, Newgate is a money-making enterprise; the chief gaoler – the keeper – buys his office from the Corporation of London and all the cellarmen and turnkeys, in turn, from him, so the whole hierarchy of gaolers will jump at any opportunity to make money from anyone who wishes to visit – even if they're just there out of morbid curiosity, like you. So be willing to tip generously and the keepers and their underlings will be more than happy to open up cells for you.

The most tawdry corner of Newgate is the condemned hold, where prisoners await their summons to the scaffold (metaphorically speaking; in fact, the condemned stand on a cart, which is whisked away, leaving them dangling from the tree at Tyburn). It is one of the first rooms – or dungeons, really – that you come across. It is dark and foul. A tiny slit of a window with thick iron bars lets in a miserable trickle of light. The walls are made from stone. An open kernel (or sewer) slices through the claustrophobic chamber, eventually gushing into the River Fleet. Three years ago, an inmate described the conditions in the condemned hold: 'neither bench, stool nor stick for any person there', he wrote; 'they lie like swine upon the ground, one upon another, howling and roaring – it was more terrible to me than death'. Everyone in here is in manacles, both the new prisoners and the dead men walking.

If you were a new prisoner, you could expect to have your wrists and ankles shackled and an iron collar placed around your neck – some of which might be connected to rings in the walls and iron staples in the floor. Or you might find your legs shackled with long wooden stilts, making it impossible to walk more than a few steps without falling over. First, they take your mobility; later, your dignity. Many felons will remain fettered for the duration of their stay but debtors and some others with sufficient means can pay an easement fee to have them replaced with lighter chains or removed altogether – the first of many brazen measures that allow gaolers to distil money out of prisoners' tears, according to John Hall, executed for robbery in 1708. An aching stench fills every corner of the unventilated room.

In the corner is a door surmounted with spikes, behind which is a small opening that allows the voices of friends and family to waft in. Perhaps, on their last night on earth, the condemned prisoners sought to tranquillize their nerves by enveloping themselves in soothing dreams. No such luck. In the black of midnight, the sexton of St Sepulchre's would appear behind the spiked door to rattle a bell and recite the following verse:

> All you that in the condemned hold do lie
> Prepare you, for tomorrow you shall die
> Watch all and pray: the hour is drawing near
> That you before the Almighty must appear
> Examine well yourselves; in time repent
> That you may not to eternal flames be sent.
> And when St Sepulchre's bell tomorrow tolls,
> The Lord above have mercy on your souls.

One of the most sinister places to visit is known informally as Jack Ketch's Kitchen, a little closet leading off from the condemned hold. Remember the traitors' heads on London Bridge, back in Shakespeare's London? It is here, in a dark, dank, low room that they are brought – along with quartered limbs – to be parboiled then skewered on various spikes all over the city. When Charles II was restored to the throne in 1660, he sought terrible vengeance on those regicides instrumental in plotting the execution of his father during 1648. There has been, in recent years, a steady flow of raw bloody meat into Jack Ketch's Kitchen.

Thomas Ellwood, a dissenter and friend of Milton who was incarcerated here in 1662 for refusing to swear the oaths of allegiance to the restored king, got an uncomfortably close look at what had become of some of the leading lights of English republicanism. 'When we first came into Newgate,' he begins, 'there lay . . . the quartered bodies of three men, who had been executed some days before, for a real or pretended plot.' He goes on to describe how

> I saw the heads when they were brought up to be boiled. The hangman fetched them in a dirty dust-basket out of some by-place; and, setting them down among the felons, he and they made sport with them. [He] took them by the hair, flouting, jeering and laughing at them; and then, giving them so ill names, boxed them on the ears and cheeks. Which done, the hangman put them into his kettle, and parboiled them with bay-salt and cummin-seed; *that* to keep from putrefaction, and *this* to keep off the fowls from seizing on them.

'Frightful and loathsome,' is how he judges the whole sorry spectacle.

Not all prisoners languish in complete squalor and horror. The rest of the prison is divided into 'masters' and 'commons' sections with further subdivisions for men and women (although complaints that the men sneak into the women's quarters and even vice versa are rife – pregnancy, or 'pleading one's belly', is a way to delay and sometimes escape execution). By the eighteenth century it cost 6s 6d (something in the region of £70 today) to do your time in the masters ward – cleaner and more dignified than the commons ward, although you could still find yourself in a shared bed wedged between a man coughing up blood on the one side and a rapist on the other. The commons side, though, is hell on earth. One early-eighteenth-century observer (writing about the next incarnation of Newgate) describes it as 'the quintessence of disparagement' and contemporary and near-contemporary accounts of prisons testify to 'foul sweaty toes, dirty shirts, the shit tub, stinking breaths, and uncleanly carcasses', layers of crunchy lice on the floor and 'a troop of *Hell Cats* [the female inmates] lying head and tail together in a dismal, nasty, dark room, having no place to divert themselves but at the *grate*'. John Hall also recalls a Buggering Hold; no prison would be complete without one.

Prisoners sleep on mouldy boards, and even in the masters wards bedspace can be scarce. In 1626, murderer Sir Nicholas Poyntz complained that he'd had to sleep in a coffin. The next incarnation of Newgate would have a windmill, but this one has virtually no ventilation, turning the prison into an inferno in hot months and a maggots' nest of disease all year round (physicians didn't have much incentive to operate in Newgate, not that it would have done the inmates much good). Trails of excrement thread through a dismal labyrinth of holds and cells, ricocheting with screams and the groans of the dying. Insects spread gaol fever (typhus). By the start of the eighteenth century, for every prisoner hanged at Tyburn, four die of disease in Newgate, frequently translating pre-trial detention or internment for debt or illegal religious worship into the worst kind of death sentence.

New inmates (known in prison slang as 'fags' or 'constables') have to pay 'garnish' to the longest serving inmate (the 'steward') in return for a supply of coals and candles. Those unable to pay it can expect to be taunted, thrashed and sometimes raped.

A prisoner's daily routine is monotonous – there is as yet no notion that these should be correctional institutions – alleviated only by heavy drinking, a spot of badger baiting and, for those able to afford it, an hour with a prostitute (easier if you are unshackled). Brandy and ale are cheap; wine less so. Chamber pots are emptied at around seven o'clock, the main meal is in the early afternoon – roast meat for the masters side; bread and water with meagre and vile meat once a week if you're lucky for the commons (aside from felons awaiting execution, there is no legal obligation for keepers to feed the inmates, many of whom starve) then candles out by ten o'clock.

Make your way to the Press Yard, a square exercise yard surrounded by three storeys of the only vaguely salubrious accommodation in the whole gaol. Here you will see prisoners punch the air in joy when they learn they've received an eleventh-hour reprieve from the merciful king or, more commonly, crumple up against the cold wall as their manacles are removed and they are bound with the very 'fatal Hempen string' from which they will dangle, dance and die later that day at Tyburn; this grim spectacle can be viewed over devilled kidneys at one of the keeper's popular execution breakfasts.

Those prisoners who can afford it – gentlemen, usually – can be imprisoned in moderate comfort with their families and pets, even hiring the services of a cleaner, in the apartments flanking the Press Yard. There is something of a jolly, clubbable atmosphere in these buildings, a ray of light in the otherwise perpetual gloom of Newgate, with the keeper dining with prisoners of quality, then gathering together in the exercise yard for a round of badger baiting with the prisoners' pet dogs. Bulls and bears would be impractical.

By now you might be wondering about the name 'Press Yard', and well you might. It's here that prisoners who 'stand mute' at their trial at the Old Bailey – that is, refuse to enter a plea, potentially an heroic move for married felons since it could prevent the Crown requisitioning their property and goods at death, rescuing their wife and children from a life of hopeless destitution – are subjected to *peine fort et dur* (literally, 'pressing hard and long'). It's a cruelly imaginative way, if I may say, of pressing someone for an answer.

A luridly nostalgic illustration from the nineteenth-century *Newgate Calendar* (by which point pressing had been abolished) shows a dandyish fellow surveying his victim as a more brutish-looking man creeps towards the prisoner, splayed out on the cold stone floor beneath a large plank with iron weights on his chest. Naked except for breeches, his wrists and feet are tied to stakes. He stares at the ceiling with the martyr's blank and disappointed eyes. This is a fairly accurate depiction of pressing. Believe it or not, this is more humane than the Tudor practice, which had been to wedge non-pleaders between two tables, the upper loaded with stone and lead, the lower with a sharp block to snap the spine. These days, however, the back-breaking is out of fashion and more weights are simply added every four hours. The accused is allowed some morsels of food and drink but, should they choose to endure their burden stoically, a slow and agonizing death is the most likely outcome.

Your next stop is the high-up prisoners' chapel, where the condemned have the unique privilege of attending their own funerals. Double back on yourself and head for the tower over the entrance gate – the chapel is on the top floor.

Newgate has had its own chaplain – or 'ordinary' – since 1544. It can be a pretty thankless job. When the prisoners bother to turn up they are known to spit and shout at the chaplain, scoff down food and drink ale from the communion table, canoodle in the pews and sometimes urinate in the corner. But there is one particular service where a high turnout is guaranteed – not just inmates but ghoulish members of the public who happily pay a substantial entrance fee to feast on the misery before them – the condemned sermon, held the Sunday before a Tyburn fair (as public execution days are called).

You'll see a mounted pulpit with a tethered Bible, oak panelling and large semi-circular windows affording views down Holborn Hill towards the River Fleet and the multitudinous spires beyond, a tantalizing glimpse of freedom. The room is divided up into a number of seating areas for prisoners, ringed by vicious spikes, though there are also galleries for the public. In the middle of the room is the condemned pew, a boat-shaped enclosure where men and women on death row cower like so many cattle at Smithfield.

During the condemned sermon they have to sit, cold as the corpses they are shortly to become (no fires burn in this chapel), on either side of a raised black coffin with yellow nails, which one of them will shortly fill. For some this is simply too much to bear as they faint, vomit, weep; for others, it is a chance to display courage in the face of their imminent demise. For the fee-paying audience this all makes quite excellent drama. Why would anyone bother going to watch contrived anguish at the playhouse when at the condemned sermon they can 'witness real agony – may see the scalding tears of hopeless remorse – may behold a real murderer, dyed from crown to sole in human blood, writhing in all the hell of horror and despair?'

On that macabre note, to a city inn for some supper, and sleep. It's been a harrowing day. Technically, innkeepers are not supposed to accept outsiders at the moment, but in practice you can bribe your way in (though hide your white stick).

The howling hour

The night is hot and sticky. You open the window. You can barely make anything out. In the warmer months, there is no street lighting. Only on moonless winter nights are householders obliged to light a candle in a horn lantern by their front door between twilight and the tolling of the curfew bells at 9 p.m., supposedly lighting people home from the alehouses, taverns and workshops.

But tonight, apart from the grudging gleam of a faint crescent moon, it is almost pitch black. You lie down, close your eyes and try to block out all the horror that you have seen today.

That's when the noises begin.

Not just the odd groan but 'loud and lamentable cries' in the face of an invisible invading force (as Albert Camus would portray a later pestilence attacking an Algerian city in *La Peste* (1947)). These cries recalls the narrator in Defoe's *Journal*, 'pierce the very heart to think of, especially when it was to be considered, that the same dreadful scourge might be expected every moment to seize upon ourselves'.

Eventually, though, the cacophony dies down and despite the odd wail, most of the inhabitants of nearby houses finally succumb to a night's – or eternity's – sleep. You are just beginning to drift off when a new note insinuates itself into the soundscape of despair. It's barely perceptible at first – four syllables separated by a brief caesura – like the horn of a ship as it pulls into harbour. Now it sounds fainter, now louder, now fainter again, now accompanied by a low rumbling – wheels on cobbles, perhaps. It's only when it reaches the bottom of your street that you hear the four words clearly:

'Bring out your dead!'

Ding, ding.
'Bring out your dead!'
Put your clothes on quick. The deadcart is here.

About half-way down the street, you can just make out what seems to be a small ball of fire suspended in the air. It illuminates the eyes and snout of a beast. Cross the road discreetly, and hunch into your cloak. It's after curfew. If you're caught wandering the streets, you could spend the night in a lock-up. With plenty of black rats. Follow at a safe distance.

As you draw nearer, you'll see a man, link in hand to light the way, driving a large, open four-wheeled cart. Another man follows, ringing a bell and shouting his morbid summons in jaded tones. It is piled high with bodies. Some are all-but naked.

A banging comes from one of the upper-storey windows of a house. The casement windows fling open and a figure appears. 'Here!' he shouts. 'My poor wife.'

The deadcart rumbles to a grudging halt. The figure in the window pushes out a shrouded lump tied to a rope. It dangles in the air for a moment, then lurches downwards as the man in the window lowers it incrementally, in silence. The bell man moves to receive the dead woman. 'May God have mercy on your soul,' he shouts to the bereaved husband, then stacks her up on the cart, not wanting to handle her for any longer than is absolutely necessary. There is to be no decent burial; the deadcart men don't even both to inquire after the identity of their latest passenger. It is too much for the man in the window to bear. He slams shut the casements and vanishes. The bellman waits a few moments and then, after shooting a shifty glance towards the window, rifles through the corpse's shroud to see if there any nice clothes or valuables to strip away.

The cart continues through winding streets towards the

great plague pit at Finsbury fields by the flame of the link, casting long shadows against the timbered walls of houses. Only very rarely are bodies lowered down on a rope. More usually, members of a stricken household lay out their dead in the street, or prop up corpses against their front door ready for collection. You notice that sometimes the cart stops and the bellman disappears into a narrow side-street or alley. Sometimes he reappears with a corpse under his arm or in a wheelbarrow, dragging its feet on the cobbles; many of the alleys are too narrow for the deadcart to squeeze through.

In the early stages of the Great Plague, victims were afforded proper – if hasty – funerals and burials in the churchyards of the city. But by now the parish burial grounds are brimful with bodies and in the hardest-hit areas it would be impossible for funerals to keep pace with the death-rate, even if most of the clergy hadn't run for the hills at the first sign of God's wrath. So gravediggers have been employed to gouge vast holes in peripheral parts of London, to serve as mass graves or plague pits, as you have seen. To prevent further infection, both the Lord Mayor in the city and George Monck, the Duke of Albemarle, one of the very few statesmen left in Westminster, have decreed that bodies must be collected each night by the deadcart men. Many are former servants, abandoned and left to fend for themselves by their masters, and so unable to turn down this dangerous and disturbing job.

And it is disturbing. Sometimes household members all die in quick succession, meaning that no one is alerted to take away the bodies until the overwhelming stench of decay seeps through the thin wattle-and-daub walls into neighbours' nostrils. It is then down to the deadcart men to enter the death-filled premises and lug these decomposing bodies onto their carts.

Londoners delight in telling each other tales of the dead-cart. Daniel Defoe crystallizes one version of the poor piper story in his *Journal of the Plague Year*, as told by the 'honest' undersexton of the parish of St Stephen, Coleman Street, going out of his way to vouch for the credibility of the story.

The poor piper was a local celebrity who would roam the streets each night, playing music at people's doors. He would usually be invited in to some public house to sing and pipe and talk foolishly for his supper and ale. As the plague sunk its teeth into London, times were tough for the merry piper. Growing increasingly thin, whenever people asked him how he went, he always joked that the deadcart had not taken him yet – so well! – but it had promised to call for him next week. One night he overindulged in a pub in Coleman Street and was laid down, fast asleep, on top of a stall by a house in a street near London Wall towards Cripplegate. Later that night, hearing the bell signalling the approach of the deadcart, some neighbours emerged with a corpse and, assuming the piper had been laid out for burial, placed the body next to his. Both were scooped up and heaped onto the cart. It was only after the cart had reached the vast plague pit at Mount Mill, off Goswell Road towards Islington (where we began our journey) that the piper awoke from his slumber and poked his head out between the stinking limbs of the dead.

'Hey! Where am I?' he asked, chilling the cartmen to the bone.

'Who are you?' whispered one.

'I am the poor piper. Where am I?'

'Where are you?' asked the undersexton in disbelief. 'Why, you are in the deadcart, and we are going to bury you.'

'But I ain't dead though, am I?' replied the piper to a chorus of nervous laughter.

Another version of the story has the piper literally piping up as the cart is trundling along, sending the bearers flying into the backstreets, thinking the devil is in the cart. Whatever the variation, this is a cheerful story about a man defying death; a vent, perhaps, for Londoners' deepest fears.

Of course, doing the nightly deadcart run exposes the bearers to a high risk of contracting the plague and although they are renowned for their steeliness, it comes as no surprise that many die on the job, leaving the stacked-up bodies at the mercy of driverless horses, who might suddenly break into a gallop, capsizing the cart and spilling the bodies into the street. Other accounts tell of the bearers of the deadcart dropping down dead at the rim of the plague pit and being thrown in along with their charges, in a sort of macabre pantomime.

As the cart reaches the end of Chiswell Street a foul miasma curls around you like a physical presence, drawing you towards the dreadful lantern-framed pit in Finsbury Fields where dead bodies are 'piled up like faggots in a stack', as the bishop Joseph Hall put it in 1625, 'for the society of their future resurrection'. In the hellscape of Defoe's *A Journal of the Plague Year* it is into this pit that many men and women hurl themselves delirious, half-naked and frothing at the mouth, an attempt to seize back one last moment of autonomy in the face of an encroaching death. Many of the Cripplegate poor 'came and threw themselves in, and expired there, before they threw any earth upon them; and that when they came to bury others and found them there, they were quite dead, though not cold'.

No doubt you have no wish to relive the horror of the pit.

Beat a path back to your inn, and try to get some sleep. We'll have a lighter start tomorrow, I promise.

A house of experiment 'for improving natural knowledge'

London basks in sunshine as you make your way to Gresham College, in the east of the city. You've been past it before – in Shakespearean London; it's between the Drapers' Garden and Bishopsgate Street, and looks very similar.

Thomas Gresham was a leading Tudor financier and founder of the nearby Royal Exchange, which we shall visit in another age. He was also a generous and cultured philanthropist. In the spirit of the Renaissance, he left a bequest in his will for the provision of free public lectures on music, astronomy, law, physics, geometry, oratory and theology – one of the first instances of the provision of free secular education (these weekly lectures are still going strong in the twenty-first century at Barnard's Inn, Holborn). Since 1660, Gresham College has been the home to one of the most prestigious and authoritative scientific societies in the world: the Royal Society.

The Royal Society exists to further the frontiers of scientific knowledge and application by harnessing a rigorous empirical method based on experimentation. It grew out of the Gresham College meetings in the early seventeenth century and those of a club of natural philosophers (as early scientists are known) meeting at Wadham College, Oxford, between 1648 and 1659. After the disintegration of the republican regime and subsequent restoration of Charles II in 1660, the Oxford group migrated to London and merged with the Gresham College group; the two coalesced into a progressive forum for the exchange, debate and demonstration of scientific ideas. Two years later their work was dignified by a royal charter, creating the Royal Society 'for improving natural knowledge'. Charles II extended to them the privilege of licensing their own publications, freeing them from the machinery of state censorship, in which the Church played a part, and so effectively granting them intellectual freedom.

The Royal Society is a physical manifestation of the core principles of the Scientific Revolution. Thanks to the pioneering achievements of Sir Francis Bacon (1561–1626) and René Descartes (1596–1650), scientists have moved to embrace an empirical philosophy. No longer is it acceptable for natural philosophers to swallow blithely and regurgitate the received wisdom of classical civilizations or to demonstrate the truth of an idea with an Aristotelian silver tongue; now everything has to be held up to the cold light of reason, to be questioned, demonstrated and judged within a critical tribunal. As the chemist and theologian Robert Boyle puts it, the Royal Society wants to drag esoteric truths 'out of [the] dark and smoky laboratories', bring them 'into the open light, and show the weaknesses'.

As part of its mission to democratize science amongst the respectable classes, earlier this year the society has taken to printing its transactions each week for public consumption, stimulating correspondence between a Europe-wide republic of natural philosophers. The society promotes clarity of meaning and precision of language; oratorical mumbo-jumbo is associated with the fuzziness of the discredited scholastic tradition.

How does it work? As one foreign observer, Samuel Sorbière, describes it, the Royal Society 'meets every Thursday after dinner, to take cognizance of matters of natural philosophy, and for the study and examination of chemical, mechanical and mathematical subjects'. Inside the theatre, experiments are performed and lectures presented to the president of the society, who sits behind a long wooden table in front of a roaring fire. The discourse is delivered bare-headed until the president gives a signal for the speaker to put on his hat. Members watch the proceedings from two rows of wooden benches, one higher than the other, auditorium-style. According to Sorbière, the conduct is decorous: 'Differences of opinion cause no manner of resentment, nor as much as a disobliging way of speech; there is nothing seemed to me to be more civil [and] respectful.'

It's a shame that Gresham House is shut up because you might enjoy some of the colourful experiments performed there. Many an innocent creature met its end in chemist Robert Boyle and Robert Hooke's air pump. 'We put in a snake but could not kill it by exhausting the air,' records John Evelyn in his diary, ' . . . only made it extremely sick, but the chick died of convulsions outright, in a short space.' Hearing that the king was thinking of turning up to a meeting in 1663, the society was sent into a flurry of preparation with one fellow pitching to show that 'a frog will live above twenty minutes after his heart hath been taken out'. Curiosities appeal to society sensibilities, with papers presented on a miraculous varnish that would defy rust, treatises on pineapples and a report of a woman who sweated so much that a quart of ill-smelling water might be taken from the palms of her hands. The society approves patents, and one of its greatest triumphs, earlier this year, has been the publication of Robert Hooke's *Micrographia* – the first book to illustrate the natural world as seen through a microscope, exquisitely illustrated with copper plates, prompting readers to marvel at the meticulousness of the universe's design.

The natural philosophers are joined by the virtuosi – amateur gentlemen scientists, cultured professionals, civil servants (Samuel Pepys, a keen member since 1665, falls into this category; he was president from 1684 to 1686 largely for his administrative nous), members of the medical establishment (physicians, surgeons, apothecaries) and a soupçon of intellectually curious merchants and tradesmen. The fees – 10s on entrance then is a week whether you turn up or not – ensure a gentlemanly atmosphere; those bastions of unreason, women, would not be permitted as fellows until 1945.

Don't assume the Royal Society is unwaveringly progressive and utilitarian. If you were to attend Gresham House or leaf through past transactions in a coffeehouse, you will find plenty to stimulate your curiosity but probably not much of direct practical use. King Charles once derided the Royal Society for 'spending time only in weighing of air' and on another occasion, he likened the fellows to court jesters. Take their advice on the plague, for instance. At various points the society attributes it to a multitudinous range of causes, reflecting the diversity of its members' opinions. There is no consensus.

The society had hoped that Charles would fund it, but despite an initial burst of enthusiasm his involvement was limited to sending the odd haunch of venison for its annual dinners and submitting faintly preposterous scientific inquiries which its members were obliged to answer.

In the early Royal Society it is surprising how intertwined are the worlds of magic, religion and science in the minds of some – though by no means all – of its members. Many of the original founders were part of an 'invisible college' of magicians who practised both alchemy and mechanical philosophy. For Sir Isaac Newton, a future Royal Society president who will emerge as one of the most influential scientists who ever lived, the ultimate end of scientific inquiry is not so much to prove the logic of the laws of the universe for their own sake but to reveal and celebrate the genius of its divine creator. And he spent a lifetime chasing the philosopher's stone.

Society meetings aren't always well attended or scintillating but the epochal significance of their collective endeavour isn't lost on its members and there is a sense that they are at the forefront of progressive scientific thinking. The European

Enlightenment of the next century would be built upon the foundations of this century's Scientific Revolution; one of its mottos, as coined by the German philosopher Immanuel Kant, would be *sapere aude* – dare to know.

'An Arcadia beyond Moorfields'

As the city festers in the heat, it's time to take the air somewhere more salubrious. How about the idyllic village of Hackney?

You'll find it virtually unscathed by plague. At a time when the Bills of Mortality are recording over 500 plague deaths a week in the extra-mural parishes of Stepney, Whitechapel and St Giles's, the Hackney parishes never return more than eighteen – and usually fewer than ten. This week (1–8 August), Hackney will suffer just 5 plague deaths compared to 122 for its southern neighbour, St Leonard Shoreditch. Like the hilltop villages of Hampstead and Highgate, Hackney has long enjoyed a reputation as a healthy and wholesome retreat for the respectable classes.

Walk up Bishopsgate Street out of the City. Eventually, the road forks three ways: to Hoxton in the west, the Old North Road ahead (following the straight course of the Roman Ermine Street to York) and, to your right, the road to Hackney. Turn right and enjoy the ramble across meadows, farmland and ditches – a very far cry from the handbag shops, high-rise estates and bingo hall of twenty-first-century Hackney Road. You may walk past some lost souls wandering aimlessly like zombies. Avoid.

In the last couple of months, a great number of journeymen, apprentices and servants have been turned out and left to fend for themselves without any means of income. Facing a hostile reception in neighbouring villages and towns, many just wander through the fields, on the cusp of starvation, tearing up the odd turnip here and there and begging passers-by for help. But very rarely do they find any succour in their hour of darkness. They are more likely to be pelted with stones, set upon by watchdogs and left to die from starvation or plague.

Before you reach the junction with Cambridge Heath Road, it's worth taking your eye off the corpse-dotted highway and turning back to admire the view: the sea of London is on display, the square tower of St Paul's Cathedral is the crest of a distant rolling wave; the crust of houses from Shoreditch to Bishopsgate, the swell on the shore. In time, the tide will draw in, immersing the green fields ahead of you in bricks and mortar, but for the moment it is a pleasant bucolic aspect. A little further to your left you might just be able to make out the point where Whitechapel Street bleeds into open country and, further east, the hamlets of Mile End and Stepney.

Go north up Mare Street then veer left into Sheep Lane, following the course of the future Regent's Canal. This will take you to Mutton Lane running south. On your right, livestock are grazing on London Fields, ready to be herded to the metropolitan meat markets; a mainstay of the Hackney economy is ensuring that Londoners don't starve, hence the animal-themed street names.

To the west of Mutton Lane is the Shoulder of Mutton Field. Here, a straggle of villagers are huddled together in a circle, their steeple hats bobbing up and down in unison. Suddenly, you hear a primeval squeal and see a flash of pink. There is much cheering, jeering, stamping, spitting – and a man falls to the ground. Hide your white stick and move in.

You can hardly believe your eyes. The villagers are taking it in turns to grease the tail of a pig and swing it around their heads. Whoever succeeds in spinning it for longest wins some kind of prize – ale, by the looks of things – and if you can send the pig flying, so much the better. I hardly need point out to you just how hard it is to swing a swine around your head and the villagers are for the most part unsuccessful in their endeavour. What usually happens is that the pig torpedoes into one of the spectators, winding him, then there is a brief window of pandemonium before it is recaptured, re-greased, and re-swung. This game of discus with a snout is a well-established weekly tradition taking place on this corner – in later decades, outside the Cat and Shoulder of Mutton pub – and will endure for hundreds of years, though not into the twenty-first century, where it probably wouldn't go down so well with the 'bruschetta society' who congregate to buy organic cheeses and exotic olives at the farmers' market each Saturday at Broadway Market, on which the Cat and Mutton pub (as it's now called) stands, nor for that matter, with anyone.

If you fancy having a swing yourself, feel free. Otherwise, turn right and take Sylvester Path, the ancient cattle-droving route that cuts through London Fields to the tip of Mare Street by the restored medieval church. Cross the Hackney Brook onto Church Street and you'll find yourself in the heart of Hackney.

Hackney Churchyard lies at the centre of a cluster of rural hamlets – including Humberton (now Homerton), Clapton and Shacklewell – dotted around meadows, woodland and market gardens. You'll soon realize that these are much more than sleepy villages. The landscape is festooned with mansions, most at least one hundred years old – some dilapidated, some efficiently restored – with large and sumptuous gardens. The settlement of Hackney was first recorded in the twelfth century and its early history is unremarkable. But as London grew in size and importance following the advent of the Tudor monarchy in 1485, Hackney's satellite villages were pulled

further into the social orbit of the metropolis. With its reputation for healthy, restorative air and proximity to both London
and Henry VIII's hunting lodges to the west in Newington
Green, it evolved into an Elysium of bubbling brooks, gleaming mansions and hunting grounds fit for kings, courtiers and
aristocrats.

On your right is Church House, all rectangular turrets and
tall chimneys, built by one of Henry VII's principal advisors
Christopher Urswick, who once entertained the intellectual
superstar Desiderius Erasmus here; beyond the church is the
Black and White House, once home to the Queen of Bohemia
(James I's daughter) and built from timber, painted black with
a high-contrast white plaster infill, and a garden frontage
almost entirely of glass; on the northern side of Church Path
is a mansion built by diplomat Lord Zouche, a keen experimental gardener who imported exotic plants like the Byzantine
hyacinth into his physic garden.

Across the road, towards Humberton, is one of the finest
mansions of all, Bryk Place. This is a beautiful three-storey
country house with stepped gables, lattice patterning and slender chimneys. Its name is testament to the cachet of brick over
other building materials – Hackney soil is conveniently good
for brick-making. Bryk Place was built by the leading Tudor
courtier Sir Ralph Sadleir, who was for a time the right-hand
man to Thomas Cromwell, and somehow managed to survive
his fall in 1540, going on to become principal secretary to the
king. After falling in love with a laundress in Cromwell's household, he decided to feather a marital nest here in 1535. This is
the result.

A fifteen-minute walk north will take you to the biggest and
most elaborate of all the Hackney mansions: Brooke House.
Built in the late fifteenth century by a wealthy ecclesiastic who
would go on to become Dean of St Paul's, it is a quadrangular

building in the style of some of the oldest Oxford and Cambridge colleges, laid out around a central quad. It is described in the 1540s as 'a fair house, all of brick, with a fair hall and parlour, a large gallery, a proper chapel and a proper library to lay books in'. It was here that Henry VIII was reconciled with his daughter, the future Bloody Mary, after a frosty five years – he had, after all, divorced her mother and cut her out of the succession. What you can see is a shadow of its former self; visiting in 1654, John Evelyn described Brooke House as 'a despicable building'; eventually it would be used as a 'receptacle for insane persons' – one of Hackney's many madhouses.

The mansions are assertions of aristocratic power but you won't find many aristocrats riding off to the hunt or going to church today. The Hackney villages are being rapidly colonized by the wealthy mercantile class, particularly those who dissent from the Church of England, who can work in the City but worship at home unperturbed by mob or magistrate at a time when dissenters suffer under the weight of punitive legislation. The Black and White House is currently occupied by city magnate and former Lord Mayor of London Sir Thomas Vyner, who has installed stained-glass windows depicting all its past royal residents and guests to boost his own cachet. Forty years ago, Bryk House came into the hands of a wealthy silk merchant who installed garish yellow-on-green linenfold panelling (less migraine-inducing by candlelight) and ornate strapwork paintings of mythical creatures. Mostly, though, the successful middle classes prefer to build their own smart villas according to the new architectural vernacular of elegant brick houses. So the bon ton have been replaced by the bourgeoisie who have grown to wealth through trade, finance, civic service and the sheer force of aspiration; people like Samuel Pepys, who declared in the summer of 1666 that he grew 'more and more in love' with Hackney every day.

Pepys had fond childhood memories of Hackney and Kingsland, having boarded there as a child, but when he came to write his diary in the 1660s he had not visited since. His first adult visit, on 25 April 1664, was born out of a desire to overcome his addiction to the theatre. With a spare afternoon on his hands, he hailed a coach and went on a joyride. He found the experience so refreshing that it developed into a fully fledged 'Hackney habit'. When he was worn out by the remorseless pace of inner-city London, he and his wife liked nothing more than to hail a coach and zoom through the green fields of Whitechapel and Cambridge Heath, the air in their faces, and watch as the bucolic village of Hackney came into view.

'Away into the fields, to Hackney, to take the air, it being hot and stuffy in the city,' he recalled of one hot summer's day; 'there light and played at shuffle-board, ate cream and good cherries. And so with good refreshment home' of another occasion, quite probably after visiting the Mermaid Tavern by the medieval church. Returning from another visit, when he ate some pullets, Pepys concluded that it was 'the first time I have been so much at my ease'. On one clammy journey home, his coach stole through the green fields of Cambridge Heath and Bethnal Green accompanied by brilliant flashes of lightning (but oddly, no thunder), delivering him home to Seething Lane with élan.

Throughout his diary, Hackney comes across as a restorative Garden of Eden away from the noxious, traffic-choked metropolis. In the magical gardens of Brooke House, he sees oranges growing for the first time – he takes the opportunity to pull one 'by stealth' and eat it – and he visits several labyrinths and an aviary. Another time, amidst ethereal organ music in the church of St John, he is thunderstruck by the beauty of Abigail Viner, a lady 'rich in jewels but most in beauty – almost the finest woman that ever I saw'. She was the wife of Sir George Vyner, a prominent Hackney gentleman and City banker, who lived in the Black and White House bordering the churchyard. Pepys's wife was by his side but he couldn't keep his eyes off this Hackney nymph. His blood up, he took the opportunity to ogle some pretty young girls at one of Hackney's prestigious boarding schools later that afternoon.

Wealth, women, cream, shuffle-board, ale in the twilight and orange trees – truly, Pepys had found paradise on earth. And like Adam before him, he overindulged in the garden of earthly delights: 'all the way back home I did break abundance of wind', he confessed in July 1666. On another, he peed at least seven times during the return journey, 'which pleased me well'.

It is time to go back to the city via the rambling Cambridge Heath Road, leading to Whitechapel. Your holiday is over.

The great dog massacre

Passing the motionless windmill of Whitechapel facing onto a view of green fields, broken only by the eastern hamlets of Stepney and Bow, make your way back to the city. Go through Aldgate (old gate), which, though much repaired, once led to the thatched villas, lofty temples and wine-kissed gardens of Londinium. Today it leads into a far smellier and less sanitized city. On your right is the church of St Boltoph-without-Aldgate. You expect to hear, at any moment, the dread pealing of the bells, marking the demise of the latest victim of the plague. But all is quiet. The sun rides high in the sky and splinters of light cobble Old Jewry in front of you, making a spangled path towards the turrets of the Tower which looms in the distance and, beyond, the smoke-belching tanneries of Southwark.

From around the corner, you hear a terrified yelp. You pelt forwards. An emaciated dog cowers beneath the bulging storey of a timber-framed house. It catches sight of you, head shooting up. Desperation swells in its eyes.

Two men creep forwards coo-cooing the creature, promising clichéd inducements – bones, din-dins and pussy cats – in sickly sweet voices. One holds a club; the other, a noose. The mutt is having none of it. He scans the perimeter but finds himself trapped by the encroaching men. On the dog's right is his worst nightmare, a wheelbarrow piled high with the corpses of dead and dying dogs, some pawing the air limply. It strikes you as a bestial parody of the deadcart.

The man with the noose lurches forwards and, in one efficient movement, catches the dog's neck. He tightens it. The dog flips and writhes like a fish. The other man steps forwards. He produces the club, takes aim, then bludgeons the dog's skull as though hammering a tent-peg into frosty earth. Specks of blood spray onto his black gown. That done, his lackey scoops up the whimpering animal and adds him to the top of the wobbling mound of dogs. Wiping his hands on a greasy cloth, he nods to his canine-killing confrère and off they go, pushing the stinking wheelbarrow towards the Thames, whistling.

You have just witnessed one sorry episode in the Great Dog Massacre of 1665. During the course of the Great Plague, Defoe reckoned that some 40,000 dogs were slaughtered. His figure is an estimate but contemporary sources show that the City Chamberlain received invoices for the killing of over 4,000 dogs and the parish of St Margaret's, Westminster for the burial of 353 dogs, so the scale of the slaughter all over the city is not in question. One particularly nasty magistrate described the hated Quakers as 'like dogs in time of plague. They are to be killed as they go up and down the streets, that they do not infect.'

It's not a good time for cats either – around 200,000 are to be slaughtered during the plague – and rabbits, pigs and pigeons are earmarked for destruction too. In the case of dogs, though, they are hunted down and are either bludgeoned to death, as you've seen, or fed poisoned meat – sometimes, in a particularly gruesome touch, the toxic corpses of other dogs. While some dog corpses are carted off to the Thames or the Fleet to pollute it yet further, many others are simply left in the kennel in the middle of the street, where they swell in the heat and eventually burst, swarming with flies and teeming with worms. On 5 July 1665, specially designated 'rakers' are ordered to clear the streets of dead dogs. Any dog-killer found favouring a particular dog can be imprisoned (amounting to a near-certain death sentence during outbreaks of the plague).

The reasons for singling out dogs for slaughter are manifold. It is believed that dog fur is a magnet for the 'effluvia or infectious steams' of infected bodies, therefore dogs spread the plague as they scavenge about the streets. If dog and cat fur had actually been a conducive breeding ground for plague-carrying fleas then there might have been some unwitting merit to the policy but, as it stands, though they can catch the plague, dogs and cats are generally weak and ineffectual carriers. Rats, which *were* the ultimate vectors of the plague bacterium, were viewed as a nuisance – Defoe notes that people tried to poison them along with mice in their homes – and sometimes a portent of imminent catastrophe, but little more. Ironically, in fact, the slaughter of their natural predators – starving cats and dogs – merely strengthened the resilience of the plague.

Another current of thought, still alive in the Middle East today, casts dogs as greedy, idle, lustful and evil. 'Greedy as a dog' and 'idle as a dog' were sayings and a 'dog', of course, is a term of abuse for women. Thomas More, quoting the Book of Proverbs, likened Protestant heretics to 'a dog returning to his vomit' and the month of August was widely understood to be the most unhealthy time of year, attributable to the malignant influence of the Dog Star, which is prominent in August. Both Pepys and Defoe believe that up to 10,000 people are dying each week in the dog days of August, 1665. By massacring dogs in their thousands, Londoners are perhaps trying to purge themselves of their bestial side at a time when they believe they are being punished for this very vice by God, as Mark Jenner would later argue.

No doubt the massacre has a slightly different meaning for each Londoner but whatever their interpretation, one thing is clear: 1665 is not a good time to be a dog.

Your mournful tour of a plague-struck city is coming to an end. As a denouement, it is only fitting that we visit the starting point of a further cataclysm that rocked London in the 1660s. Within the walled city at least, it eviscerated much of the cramped, squalid environment which had been such an effective breeding ground for the *Rattus rattus* species and their cargo of deadly fleas – though it was not responsible for the disappearance of the plague.

Fire!

Head up Great Tower Street. At Eastcheap turn left onto Pudding Lane. This takes its name not from puddings in the modern sense but rather the intestines of a pig or sheep. Hogs' entrails are carted down Pudding Lane from the butchers' scalding houses in Eastcheap to the dung boats on the Thames. It is narrow, dark and densely packed with timber-framed houses at crazy angles to the street. Hide your white stick for a moment, and ask someone to direct you towards the house of the king's baker Thomas Farryner. It's a couple of minutes' walk towards Thames Street, on the right-hand side of the road.

Once you find it, stop. It looks unremarkable enough. But in just over a year's time, the carelessness of Mr Farryner here will be responsible for razing around four-fifths of the walled city to the ground, swallowing over 400 streets and 13,000 houses, sending 100,000 refugees pouring through the fields to shanty towns beyond the walls. There had been many fires before in the tightly packed, timbered city but this would be the Great Fire, responsible for sweeping away the face and fabric of the medieval metropolis for ever.

We now know that it began in the early hours of Sunday, 2 September 1666. On that night conditions were uniquely conducive to a large-scale conflagration: after a long, hot summer there was a gusty east wind. Alerted by the smoke, Farryner and his wife leaped across the roofs to safety (unlike their timorous maid, who burned to death) but the fire spread rapidly – devouring the Star Inn on Fish Street Hill, then, disastrously for the city, snaking down Thames Street and lodging itself in the riverside warehouses. These were chock-a-block with coal, timber, oil, brimstone, gunpowder, spirits, tallow and other highly flammable materials that made perfect tinder for the Great Fire, thrusting it westwards with an unstoppable momentum, eviscerating everything in its path. People ran in terror, loading their goods onto boats and sailing to safety; the sick were carried away on beds and boards; boys tore up the streets to puncture the wooden water pipes; others just stood and watched, marvelling at this further manifestation of God's wrath. Predictably, this was not a good time for foreigners, particularly Catholics, who eventually shouldered the blame for kindling the conflagration. 'A blacksmith, in my presence, meeting an innocent Frenchman walking along the street, felled him instantly to the ground with an iron bar,' recalled William Taswell. 'I could not help seeing the innocent blood of this exotic flowing in a plentiful stream, down to his ankles.' In Moorfields, a Frenchman was almost dismembered by the mob for purportedly carrying 'balls of fire' in a chest – tennis balls.

As the fire roared through the streets, it sucked in air so that a scorching wind announced its arrival. The sound was awesome. '*Then, then* the city did shake indeed, and the inhabitants did tremble,' writes the rhetorically gifted clergyman Thomas Vincent. '*Rattle, rattle, rattle*, was the noise which the fire struck . . . as if there had been a thousand iron chariots beating upon the stones.' The city rapidly came to resemble a giant inferno, with the flames converging at one point into a wall of fire fifty feet high; 'Oh the miserable and calamitous spectacle!' wrote John Evelyn. 'All the sky was of a fiery aspect, like the top of a burning oven'; his fellow diarist Samuel Pepys wrote lyrically of 'showers of firedrops'. Evelyn's descriptions are apocalyptic – 'mine eyes now saw above 10,000 houses all in one flame . . . the noise and crackling and thunder of the impetuous flames, the shrieking of women & children, the hurry of people, the fall of towers, houses & churches was like an hideous storm'.

Though far, far fewer people died (six, purportedly), Vincent describes the calamity in terms prescient of the Blitz: 'and then you may see the houses *tumble, tumble, tumble*, from one end of the street to the other with a great crash, leaving the foundations open to the view of the heavens'.

The response of the Lord Mayor Sir Thomas Bloodworth was dismissive. 'Pish! A woman might piss it out!' he declared on being roused from his slumber in the middle of the night. How wrong he was. The fire continued with unabated fury. It was Samuel Pepys who alerted an oblivious Whitehall to the calamity unfurling in the city. Very wisely, the king instituted Pepys's advice that buckets, hand-squirts and fire-hooks would be useless; the only way to stop its spread would be to blow up houses lying in its path. (Later on, King Charles and his brother James would roll up their sleeves and join the common people in fighting the flames, to the approval of the populace.) Rushing back to the city, Pepys conveyed the order to a hapless Lord Mayor, whom he found an exhausted wreck, a handkerchief wrapped around his neck, fretting that no one would obey his orders and that the fire was overtaking his efforts to demolish houses. (He was also mindful that ripped-down houses would have to be rebuilt – but at whose expense?) Although the strategy paid off in the eastern and western extremities of the city, saving the Tower from destruction, elsewhere the gaps between the demolished houses were too narrow and the wind too powerful and persistent for it to have the desired quelling effect. Pepys, for his part, took great pains to cart his valuables off to a colleague's house in Bethnal Green, packed his wife off to Woolwich, and buried his precious Parmesan cheese in his garden, as should be everyone's first instinct when faced with the destruction of their native city.

On Monday 3 September, the Fire swept through the Royal Exchange – totem of the capital's economic might – sending the stone statues of England's past kings and queens plummeting from their niches, their heads cracking in the rubble. The next day, Cheapside, the city's 'first street', was destroyed and now the fire encroached upon St Paul's Churchyard, devouring the livelihoods of the booksellers who saw their entire stock go up in flames and some of whom, like Samuel Pepys's bookseller Joshua Kirton, seemingly never recovered from the experience; Pepys notes how Kirton died of grief a year later. But St Paul's, St Paul's would never fall! Or so those who were encamped inside it foolishly believed. Above the roof there broke out a local thunderstorm, no less, with little forks of apocalyptic lightning radiating from the burning building. Eventually, the sheer force of the heat spat out stones, and the roof blazed and melted, pouring streams of molten lead down the pavements of Ludgate Hill towards the Fleet, 'glowing with fiery redness, so as no horse, nor man, was able to tread on them' as people ran for their lives, screaming. By this point, half the City had vanished and the flames washed through the city walls and vaulted the Fleet River, laying waste to Bridewell Palace and licking Inner Temple Hall; on Wednesday 5 September, Cripplegate and some of the Temple fell. But then the wind relented, allowing the demolition work finally to have its desired effect.

'It was the saddest sight of desolation that I ever saw . . . it made me weep to see it,' wrote Pepys; 'London was, but is no more,' concluded a doleful Evelyn.

But Evelyn's poetic lament wasn't technically true. Whereas a hundred years earlier, 75 per cent of London's population lived in the walled city, by the time of the Great Fire that proportion had fallen to 25 per cent. The growing eastern suburbs like Wapping and Stepney and the north-eastern quarter of the walled city were untouched by the conflagration and in the west, it extended no further than Holborn Bridge and St Dunstan's church on Fleet Street. Covent Garden and the emergent squares of the West End were unscathed and the displacement of the richer city population gave an impetus to further development westwards.

Some people like to connect the disappearance of the Great Plague with the ravages of its companion piece, the Great Fire. It is true that after the fire there were no more plague epidemics in London – the last recorded plague death would be in Rotherhithe in the 1670s. But the fire decimated the old walled city whereas the 1665–6 epidemic erupted, if you remember, in the squalid suburban districts further west, which remained undamaged. Also, by the time of the conflagration the disease was in full retreat. As early as the third week of November 1665, total recorded plague deaths had fallen to 900 (compared with over 7,000 in the third week of September that year); on 24 November Samuel Pepys felt merry enough to return to his old oyster shop and purchase two barrels; in December he noted how 'the town fills apace, and shops begin to open again'. What may ultimately have happened is that either Londoners developed a resistance to plague bacteria after the relentless assaults of the first half of the seventeenth century or the black rats were supplanted by brown rats who were immune to *Yersinia pestis*, meaning the fleas had no cause to jump across and infect humans, though neither of these theories are proven.

But it perhaps *felt* true that the Great Fire had been London's salvation, even if such a theory wouldn't hold to the empirical standards of the Royal Society. It deprived tens of thousands of Londoners of their homes and livelihoods, but metaphorically its flames were a cathartic release from all the pain, suffering and loss that was so fresh in people's minds, a livid purification of the death-filled city. And London would rise from the ashes.

Epilogue: echoes of plague-struck London

If you stumble across a mysterious patch of unused ground in central London, the chances are that someone, somewhere, has at some point claimed that it's the site of a plague pit. Sometimes these sites are thoughtfully identified. 'Please keep off the grass' admonishes a bright-orange Hackney Homes notice on a council estate in Pitfield Street. 'This is one of many burial grounds pertaining to the Black Plague [sic] 1665–1666', as though pestilential miasma is just waiting to ooze through the soil into people's picnics. In fact, as with so many purported plague pits, the area's link with the events of 1665–6 is questionable. Its location on the periphery of the built-up city means it is plausible as a plague pit site but the main evidence seems to be the name of the street itself, which is more likely derived from a moated mansion bought by one-time resident Charles Pitfield in 1648, a good seventeen years before the Great Plague. A similarly contentious claim has been made for Islington Green, off Upper Street.

In the end, the most credible sites for plague pits are those pinpointed by Defoe in his *Journal* and those for which there is palpable archaeological evidence. So we might mention, amongst others, Mount Mills, the site of Aldgate Underground station, Hand Alley off Bishopsgate Street, Cross Bones Graveyard in Southwark and the New Churchyard or Bethlem Burial Ground, now under Liverpool Street Station. The great pit unearthed by London Crossrail excavations beneath Charterhouse Square contains victims of the medieval Black Death (1348–50) which wiped out half of London's population.

Although it's a post-Great Fire building, Apothecaries' Hall, tucked away off Black Friars Lane in Ludgate, is richly evocative of the apothecaries' trade of Restoration London. Two golden unicorns keep watch over the pilastered entrance to a crisp beige courtyard. An 'elaboratory' beneath the Great Hall on the eastern side was the site of the first large-scale manufacture of drugs in the world. For 250 years the Royal Society prepared remedies here, selling them to London apothecaries and clients such as the Royal Navy and the East India Company. Beneath the outside clock hangs a pestle and mortar. Though the western and southern aspects of the courtyard are eighteenth-century additions, the Great Hall itself is largely unchanged since the seventeenth century. It is, in fact, the oldest surviving livery hall in the City of London. At Open House Weekend in September each year you can visit the Parlour, which contains the society's display of drug jars. The whole complex has something of a master wizard's leisurely lair about it.

Although it once more conforms to Inigo Jones's original layout (the later famous fruit and vegetable market was removed to Battersea in 1974), none of Covent Garden's original houses remain and it has become an overcrowded Mecca for tourists and street entertainers. Bedford Chambers on the north side, built in the late 1870s, gives a suggestion of the appearance of the original residential arcades, with their red bricks, quoins and stone colonnade. An Apple Store occupies a prestigious location in one of the colonnaded buildings. St Paul's Church, that handsome barn, is still a sombre and elegant presence, even as it serves as a backdrop for jugglers and acrobats.

Moving on to cosmetics, the Queen's Gallery in Buckingham Palace has in its collections a diamond-studded patch box of enamelled gold, which belonged to Queen Mary II (who ruled England with her husband, William of Orange, from 1689 to 1694, a quarter of a century after your tour). She eventually succumbed to smallpox, which perhaps explains why she owned it. The Victoria and Albert Museum has two English examples made in the eighteenth century, one in Silver Room 67 with a tortoiseshell lid depicting a squirrel, rabbit, dragonfly and sun. There is also a sumptuous French patch box closer to our period, produced around 1680, in Silver Room 69.

The Theatre Royal Drury Lane is still in operation, a stalwart of the West End theatre scene, now owned by the composer baron Andrew Lloyd Webber. It mainly shows highly commercial musicals, marking a departure from the more refined tone of the Theatre Royal of the 1660s. The current building is the fourth theatre to stand on the site, making it the oldest such establishment in England to be in continuous use (give or take a few years when it was being rebuilt), entertaining theatregoers for over 350 years.

Further east, in a maze of narrow walkways, a blue plaque on the wall of the Jamaica Wine House in St Michael's Alley, Cornhill, marks the approximate site of London's first coffeehouse, opened by Pasqua Rosée in 1652. Chocolate houses, unlike coffee shops, are something of a vanished tradition, though many high-end chocolate traders such as Artisan du Chocolat in Bayswater, Paul A. Young in Islington, Soho and elsewhere, La Maison du Chocolat in Piccadilly and Said in Soho will serve you a decadent cup of pure hot chocolate if you're willing to fork out the relatively high price.

Newgate was finally demolished at the beginning of the twentieth century, bringing down the curtain on one of the most troubling set pieces in London's history. An enlarged Session House (known as the Old Bailey) was built on the site in 1907 and continues to operate as the Central Criminal Court. The oft-repeated claim that the Viaduct Tavern, on Newgate Street opposite, has a handful of surviving prison cells in its basement is apparently fallacious.

Since 1967 the Royal Society has occupied an opulent creamy stucco building on Carlton House Terrace, overlooking St James's Park. It remains true to its purpose as enshrined in its founding charters in the 1660s: 'to recognize, promote, and support excellence in science and to encourage the development and use of science for the benefit of humanity'. It can lay a strong claim to being the oldest scientific society in continuous operation in the world. Better still, it hosts an imaginative programme of accessible public lectures. They're mainly free.

For much of the twentieth century Samuel Pepys would scarcely have recognized what he knew as the bourgeois idyll of Hackney. The coming of the railways, heavy bombing in the Blitz, and waves of immigration from the 1950s changed the tone of the area decisively. But over the last twenty years it has been subject to a process of rapid if uneven gentrification, and with its achingly cool coffee shops, wine bars, art galleries, baby masseurs, farmers' markets and skyrocketing house prices, it has, in a sense, come full circle. Sadly, there is little trace of its aristocratic past: most of the mansions have been demolished, though the Black and White House is commemorated by the street name Bohemia Place in Hackney Central. There is one exception, the misnamed Sutton House in Homerton; this is in fact Bryk Place, the mansion built in 1535 by Sir Ralph Sadleir and renovated in the Jacobean era by a wealthy wool merchant. Formerly a squat, it was saved by the National Trust, who did an amazing job of restoring it to its original splendour. Pay a visit to see its rich Jacobean panelling in emerald green, corn yellow, blood-red and gold. There is still a Cat and Mutton pub on the southern corner of Broadway Market but happily no sign of any pig swinging.

Finally, the Monument. It was designed by Christopher Wren to commemorate the site where the Great Fire was kindled in 1666. At 202 feet, it is as high as it is near Farryner's fateful Pudding Lane address. It is a freestanding Doric pillar, fashioned from Portland Stone and surmounted by a flaming urn of gilded bronze; purportedly, Charles II turned down the opportunity of a statue on the very reasonable grounds that *he* hadn't started the conflagration. That honour, of course, went to the Catholics, as a Latin inscription in 1668 made clear (it wasn't removed until 1831). After a trickle of suicides, the

gallery at the top had to be caged off. The column was renovated in 1842 and steam-cleaned in 1954 after some bomb
damage in the Second World War. It is open daily, at very reasonable prices, but you do have to climb over 300 steps in
order to feast on the sight of the sprawling cityscape at your
feet.

1884
Depravity and Wonder on a
Tour of Joseph Merrick's London

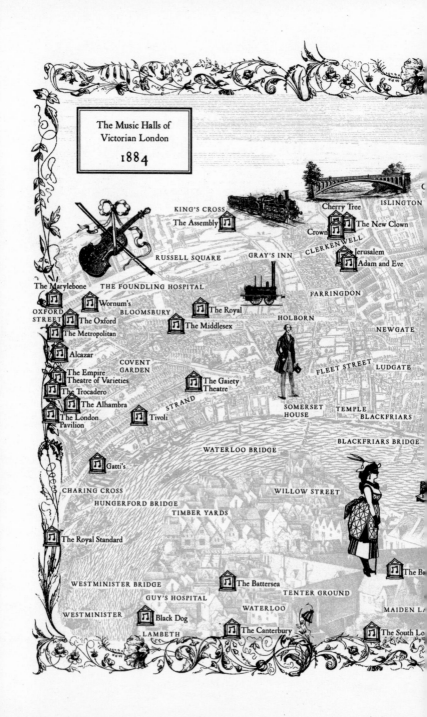

The Music Halls of
Victorian London
1884

KING'S CROSS
The Assembly

Cherry Tree   ISLINGTON
The New Clown
Crown
CLERKENWELL
Jerusalem
Adam and Eve

RUSSELL SQUARE   GRAY'S INN
FARRINGDON

The Marylebone   THE FOUNDLING HOSPITAL
Wornum's
OXFORD   BLOOMSBURY   The Royal
STREET   The Oxford   The Middlesex   HOLBORN
The Metropolitan   NEWGATE

Alcazar   COVENT
GARDEN
The Empire   FLEET STREET   LUDGATE
Theatre of Varieties   The Gaiety
The Trocadero   Theatre
The Alhambra   STRAND   SOMERSET   TEMPLE
The London   Tivoli   HOUSE   BLACKFRIARS
Pavilion

BLACKFRIARS BRIDGE

WATERLOO BRIDGE

Gatti's

CHARING CROSS   WILLOW STREET
HUNGERFORD BRIDGE
TIMBER YARDS

The Royal Standard

The B

The Battersea
WESTMINSTER BRIDGE   TENTER GROUND
GUY'S HOSPITAL
WESTMINSTER   WATERLOO   MAIDEN LA
Black Dog
LAMBETH   The Canterbury   The South Lo

DALSTON HACKNEY

NEWINGTON GREEN

The Rosemary Branch

Blockmaker's Arms

Old King John's

The Hackney Empire

The Sebright

...erland Head

The Hoxton Varieties Theatre

Medley

The Shoreditch Empire

The Morpeth Castle

Pied Horse

MOORGATE

Bald Faced Stag

The Temperance

SPITALFIELDS

The Royal Cambridge

LIVERPOOL STREET

GUILDHALL

LONDON WALL

The Seven Stars

The Laurel Tree

Lusby's

The Green Dragon

CHEAPSIDE

Wilcox's

The Temperance

WHITECHAPEL

BANK

LEADENHALL STREET

ALDGATE

CANNON STREET

FENCHURCH STREET

MONUMENT

Wilton's

...UTHWARK BRIDGE

CANNON STREET BRIDGE

TOWER OF LONDON

LONDON BRIDGE

CLINK STREET

The map shows some of the most popular and iconic music halls operating around 1884.

MAP SYMBOL
Music Hall

SOUTHWARK Pilgrim's BOROUGH

Jolly Tanners

At the eastern end of the Strand, a bronze statue of William Gladstone stands atop a plinth. Four times Queen Victoria's Prime Minister, the man who brought compulsory, state-funded elementary education to Britain was an eminent, emblematic Victorian. Behind him sparkle the cream-white turrets and spires of the Royal Courts of Justice, which opened when he was in power; their neo-Gothic style lacking the menace of the genuinely Gothic buildings you saw back in medieval London. Across the road, the multi-tiered tower of Wren's Church of St Clement Danes, now the spiritual home of the RAF, peeks above the trees like a spacecraft ready to blast off.

Facing away from the church, the Gladstone memorial has three stone steps leading up to a niche. Go and rest your back against it. He is flanked by four female effigies representing brotherhood, aspiration, courage and education. Education directs the attention of a schoolboy towards the Thames, Inspiration has her hand on a book (the Bible, one presumes) and salutes the sky, Courage raises a scythe ready to slice the head off a serpent hissing at a small child and Brotherhood nurtures two infant boys. Gladstone himself looks solemn and stately, as you might expect, but also mildly outraged, all clenched fists and frowns. Well might he: he's staring right down what was, in his day, a street of filth and shame, the very antithesis of the noble and apparently rock-solid values typified by his companions in effigy and an affront to his own Christian values, which saw him scouring the streets late at night to rescue fallen women.

Ahead of you, like a thunderous whirlpool, traffic swirls around the behemoth Australia House, so suggestive of Empire with its muscular Doric columns and lofty statues. To your left, drab modernist blocks smeared in exhaust fumes have effaced any trace of Arundel House, one of the great riverside palaces you saw back in Shakespearean London. And on your right, dreary Aldwych curves towards Kingsway.

Close your eyes. The traffic heaves and roars like an ocean. But then, some new sounds – the hoot of a steam train, the clopping of hooves and the screech of iron-shod wheels on cobbles, the click of footsteps and the short, shrill blast of a whistle.

A first-time visitor to the Victorian city doesn't so much *see* London – it's barely visible – as *hear* it, 'the grind and howl of machinery, railways shooting above houses and soon to be beneath them'. The words are Dostoevsky's, for whom London is 'always in movement night and day, wide as an ocean'. But when you do open your eyes, you think you must be dreaming; everything is wrapped in a sooty, yellowy-green mist.

The fog hangs in the air like a thick, icy pall. In this decade, the 1880s, around two days of every week are afflicted by what Dickens calls 'the London Particular' and many others a 'pea souper', after the fog's thick consistency. At this moment, elsewhere in the city, horse-buses are toppling over, steamboats crashing into piers, street robberies are being committed and children getting separated from their mothers. It's deadly, too, containing the toxic gas sulphur dioxide. Each week, the very old, the very young, and those with respiratory conditions are carried off by the fog. And if you're not careful, you're going to be its next victim.

Suddenly, a hansom cab erupts into your field of vision and swerves sharply as the driver, who is standing behind the canopy, demands to know whether 'you have *eyes*, fool? Clearly, you are smack, bang in the middle of a traffic intersection. There is a policeman stationed a few feet ahead of you – your eyes are by now beginning to attune themselves to the dismal visibility – doing his best to conduct the mayhem. Wearily, he gesticulates for you to get onto the pavement in front of the Royal Courts of Justice, a buoy of familiarity in this alien world.

Your reach the relative safety of the pavement, where you're jostled by a scrummage of people. You see that the men are all wearing dark overcoats and black top hats and that most of them are carrying umbrellas. Some of the women, the bustles of their dresses adding to the bustle of the crowd, have flowers in their hats. There are majestic black lamp posts everywhere – gas lit, naturally. They blaze merrily in the fog.

Looking back across the road, you can just make out that Australia House has vanished, as has Aldwych, to be replaced by a terrace of four-storey buildings with carts and wagons unloading in front. There is no longer a statue of Gladstone, just another ornate lamp post, and although the church of St Clement Danes *is* still there, a ghostly presence on your left, it seems somehow more austere, devoid of the softening effect of the trees, which are yet to be planted.

Welcome to one of the most exciting places in the world: Victorian London, city of parks, wharves, gin palaces, a crystal palace, museums, workhouses and dioramas (specialized theatres to view large pictures through peepholes where tricks of the light conjure changing landscapes). To explore every last corner of this illimitable city would be a limitless task in itself. So let us take wonder and depravity as our twin themes, setting out to see something of the dark underbelly of Victorian society leavened by some spectacles and joyrides.

'The most vile street in the civilized world'

If, when it comes to the pleasures of the flesh, you think of the Victorians as prudish, our first stop might surprise you. Stand with your back to the church, looking west. Take a closer look at the building across the junction. It houses the Rising Sun pub on the right and on the left a bookshop, its sooty panes stuffed with second-hand volumes. Forking into the distance are two narrow, rambling streets, one tucked away behind the Strand, the other directly behind the first. The one to your left, Holywell Street, seems to be sucking people in; swarms of men – and some women too – are hovering in front of certain shop windows to the irritation of pedestrians trying to use it as a thoroughfare. Every so often, a hatted man vanishes into a shop. They have come to sink their teeth into the forbidden fruit of Victorian London of a gloomy November afternoon.

Holywell Street is no ordinary backstreet. In spite of its connotations of sacred cleanliness, in the eyes of the press it's a 'foul sink of iniquity', a place where 'dirt and darkness meet and make mortal compact' or, in the words of *The Times*, 'the most vile street in the civilized world'. This is the home of London's booming pornography trade. You may as well leave your prudery at the junction, for no one produces smut like the pornographers of Holywell Street.

It feels as if you've gone through a portal back to Shakespeare's London: you see half-timbered houses, gables stooping over the street and bulging bay windows, incongruous in a city happy to see historic buildings sacrificed to the juggernaut of modernity. There are some Georgian-looking houses too but they appear to have had classical-style façades grafted onto earlier builds. The street has a certain picture-postcard charm, but many of the old buildings are grimy – sleazy, even. Books are everywhere: piled up in shop windows, spilling out into the street on wooden trestles and being unloaded from horse-drawn carts.

Look up. By now you will have noticed that the shop signs in Victorian London are quite boring compared to what you have seen in pre-Fire London – small, square boards protruding from buildings like flags, listing the name and address of each vendor – *H. Smith, 30, Bookseller*, generally without illustration. But coming up on your right, at number 37, is a relic of the magic of bygone days: a golden half-moon, its lips pouted into a sulky expression, peeping at you beneath bushy eyebrows with sad, lonely eyes. According to an antiquarian book from 1883, this is the last remaining old shop sign in situ, once belonging to a mercer's shop, now announcing a vendor in books and second-hand china. To the left of the moon is a tiny alley reeking of urine, Half-Moon Passage, down which you can see a thick huddle of vehicles and people on the Strand, framed in a piercingly bright aperture as though you are looking through a camera obscura.

Once the terrain of radical pamphleteers and print-makers, after a government crackdown on politically subversive materials Holywell Street (and to a lesser extent neighbouring Wych Street, which you walked down in the plague-struck city) emerged as a powerhouse of pornography from the mid-century on, with transgressive individuals like William Dugdale diverting their revolutionary impulses from radical politics into lucrative pornography. In 1857 the government legislated against obscene publications, threatening pornographers with prison sentences. Although he managed to evade custodial sentences for some time (brazenly threatening a court with a knife at one point), Porn King Dugdale was one of the first casualties, dying a miserable death in the Clerkenwell House of Corrections in 1868 after being handed a sentence of hard labour which, at his age, was tantamount to a death sentence.

But in spite of the new laws, shopkeepers are resourceful and you can still find, dotted amongst the chemists, clothes-men's stalls and the more respectable second-hand bookshops, dollops of pornography. Currently the head honcho of the porn industry is a shadowy figure known only as 'Cameron', who some say has powerful connections and so is immune to prosecution. (They are wrong – next year he'll be seized in a police raid with 'five cabloads of indecent books', 140 stereo-scopic slides (giving the illusion of depth to his explicit pictures) and 16,000 prints; his fate will be Clerkenwell for the obligatory two years' hard labour.)

The sight of customers glued to certain shop windows is testament to the resilience of the trade; 'at present the sale of [illicit books and prints] is only partially suppressed', declared the authoritative Survey of London in 1878, while a mid-century *Daily Telegraph* article laments members of the weaker sex 'furtively peeping in at these sin-crammed shop windows, timorously gloating over suggestive title-pages'. Incidentally, if you see a well-dressed man lurking outside a picture shop wag-gling his fingers underneath the tail of his coat, he may well be soliciting for gay sex. This tip comes from William Dugdale's *Yokel's Preceptor* (1855), a compendium of homosexual cruising spots in London masquerading – completely unconvincingly – as a guide for countryside bumpkins to get streetwise in town. You could probably find a copy in one of the bookshops.

Since the law has been tightened, you're unlikely to see any-thing too shocking on display in a window; more likely, the presence of explicit publications will be signposted by mildly suggestive titles and prints (or very soft porn, if you like). Find such a place and go in, keeping yourself to yourself.

Inside, it is musty. The bookseller eyes you suspiciously at first, but seems to satisfy himself that you're not an undercover policeman, the bane of his existence. There is the expected quotient of youths snout-deep in greasy books, a faint sheen of perspiration on their upper lips. Every so often a hawker comes in to buy or sell. No one is going to disturb you, so get browsing.

Staring down at you like a nonchalant pole dancer are a range of titillating titles: *The Pupil of Pleasure*, *The Seducing Cardinal* and *The Lustful Turk*. A little further into the shop you'll find *Captain Stroke-All's Pocket Book!*, *Gay Girls of New York* and *The Spirit of Flagellation* (a Victorian obsession – and essential reading if you're of a mind to visit one of the many flagellation brothels in the city). Still further down there's *The Amatory Experiences of a Surgeon* next to *Kate Handcock* and then *Memoirs of a Woman of Pleasure*. The short novel *Revelries! and Devilries!!* (first published by Dugdale in 1867) has a lascivious frontispiece with two naked women holding birches ready to lash a pair of bare buttocks.

The authority for all the titles listed above is the third volume of the *Index Librorum Prohibitorum* (List of Prohibited Books, Vatican-style) published this year by pornophile Henry Spencer Ashbee under the pseudonym of Pisanus Fraxi. Part précis, part review, part critical analysis replete with astoundingly long footnotes, which gives it an illusory academic quality belying the sheer filth of many of the titles, it is the most comprehensive erotic catalogue ever published.

To get the very latest – and riskiest – publications, you might have to have a discreet word with the bookseller, and even then it may depend on whether he's on good terms with 'Cameron' or not. Some, like *The Story of a Dildoe!*, privately printed in 1880, obscenely illustrated (you can imagine how) and limited to a print run of 150, are very rare and are passed from hand to hand much like illuminated manuscripts in medieval London.

Others, like *Randiana, or Excitable Tales; Being the Experiences of an Erotic Philosopher* (1884), are so salacious they're best kept behind the counter. If *Randiana* tickles your fancy, you'll be treated to a potpourri of sexual encounters featuring orgies, ecclesiastical buggery and lesbian sex scenes complete with gutta-percha dildoes brimming with warm oil and milk.

The remainder of Victorian society is united in hailing such books as evil incarnate, a corrosive threat to the very fabric of society. Inspector Moser of the Criminal Investigation Department thought the 'blackguard purveyors' of Holywell Street should be 'taken and nailed by the ears to the nearest gatepost', echoing a punishment sometimes meted out to Puritans in sixteenth- and seventeenth-century London. But if you actually pluck up the courage to open any of the volumes mentioned above, you'll soon see that their tone is generally comic (sometimes deliciously so) and picaresque. The realism and moralizing that you find in many Victorian novels and much journalism is often conspicuously absent in a world of sexual fantasy. For the most part, they are mild compared with what is freely available on the internet and in bookshops in the twenty-first century.

But remember – *you* have travelled from a society with more liberal and informed sexual values than Victorian London (even if you might disapprove of pornography). If you are a man, imagine thinking of your body as a physiological economy with a finite amount of resources to 'spend' (the most commonly used word for ejaculation in this era). Imagine being taught that every youthful sexual indulgence is an unmitigated evil which wastes your vital force and stunts your physical growth and mental development. Any kind of incontinence is dangerous, you believe, but none more so than masturbation, which will lead to jaundiced skin, eruptions of acne, introversion and the inability to look anyone in the face. The fate of a compulsive masturbator is to become a drivelling idiot or insufferable hypochondriac. Even within the presumed safety of marriage, you will have to walk a tightrope between abstemiousness and gratification – have no sex, and you'll be ruined, but have too much and you'll melt into a goo of despondency as the symptoms of 'spermatorrhoea' (an umbrella term for diseases caused by a loss of semen) take hold, leading to heart disease and death.

It's even worse for women. Female time travellers, imagine thinking of yourself as a sexless baby-producing machine, almost entirely devoid of any erotic desire and actually incapable of it during pregnancy when your baby will suck away your vital force from within. You will surrender to your husband's desires only occasionally. Like men, you believe that sex serves a practical purpose – the population of the earth – but beyond that is profoundly dangerous. Continence is the key. Your sexual life is likely to be a sore and bitter trial.

These ideas, so jejune and objectionable to twenty-first century eyes, are lifted – sometimes word for word – from Dr William Acton's *Functions and Disorders of the Reproductive Organs* (1857), no radical polemic but mainstream medical opinion. Anyone deviating one iota from his worthy advice (memorably described by one historian as 'part fantasy, part nightmare, part hallucination') is either indifferent to their health or just plain *low*. It is only after you get your head around Dr Acton's alien sexual precepts that you can begin to understand the hysterical tone that unites press, police and politicians in lambasting pornography. For pornography is not just a foil to Dr Acton's belief system but its antithesis, presenting as it does a world of sexual riches where women are game for anything and men are 'limitlessly endowed with that universal fluid currency which can be spent without loss', as historian Steven Marcus puts it. It is also, of course, an incentive to dreaded masturbation. *That* is why men like William Dugdale have to be destroyed in hard-labour camps.

Notwithstanding their value as escapism, the books around you expose the folly of prevailing sexual norms. 'I began to see that such things are harmless, though the world may say they are naughty,' writes 'Walter', the pseudonymic author of *My Secret Life* (privately printed from 1888), 'and saw through the absurdity of conventional views and prejudices as to the ways a cock and cunt may be pleasurably employed'. His Odyssean sexual memoir, running to eleven volumes over 4,000 pages, reveals that not everyone adhered to middle-class sexual ideals – to put it mildly. The memoir is so frank that a British printer would be sentenced to two years' imprisonment for supplying it – in 1969! With its vivid descriptions of deviant sexual behaviour, it still has the power to shock in the twenty-first century with sentences like 'while I fucked her, I hated her – she was my spunk-emptier' and 'her cunt constricted . . . and sucked round my prick from tip to root moistening both itself and occupant, and my sperm shot out and filled it'. As you can see, very little is left to the imagination.

One by one, Dr Acton's ideas are scuttled. Men can philander away their days to their hearts' content – they will suffer no adverse effects unless, of course, they catch a sexually transmitted disease, which is always a risk for men like Walter. Women are not passive and sexually submissive in the least; all you need to do, in Walter's world, is fill up her belly with wine and meat, 'let the grub work', and she's anyone's. And women *enjoy* it, as the many sex scenes ram home. Nor are men, contrary to Dr Acton, in their uninhibited state, always sex machines. *My Secret Life* addresses the taboo of impotency, with Walter on one occasion horrified to find his genitalia reduced to 'a sucked gooseberry, a mere bit of dwindling, flexible, skinny gristle'. No doubt about it, Walter is exceptional. His memoir is a violent reaction against the repressed nature of Victorian sexuality.

To get your hands on photographic pornography, you will probably have to ask. Prepare to be treated with suspicion. In 1880 a police inspector went undercover in search of a family-run mail-order enterprise that was corrupting public-school pupils by sending them unsolicited pornographic pictures in envelopes marked 'art studies', in the hope that they would order more. The trail led straight to a Holywell Street bookshop just like this one. Risqué photographs were purchased easily enough but to get his hands on some 'choice specimens', the police officer had first to earn the keeper's trust before being led upstairs into 'a dirty little place, which was part bed-room, part workshop . . . as filthy a hole as I have ever been into', where he purchased some expensive hard-core pornography (for two guineas) – and left a shilling for the 'little wretched piece of forlorn humanity' that was the shopkeeper's baby. The next day, the shop was raided, 5,000 indecent photographs were seized and the man arrested. He was sentenced to two years' imprisonment, which can only have intensified the forlornness of his wretched offspring.

Put your book back, nod at the shopkeeper, and return to the street.

Outside, a window opens. A washerwoman appears in an upper storey, hanging linen out to dry. She looks down at little dogs skipping about and costermongers balancing baskets of flowers and apples on their heads. In the distance, the spire of St Mary le Strand peaks over the lurching gables. Make your way to the end of the street. Should the pornography have put you in the mood for hedonistic excess, fork right and double back into Wych Street. In appearance, it's very similar to Holywell Street: grimy, narrow and with bulging bay windows and inelegant gables toppling over the street. Many of these are brothels. You may even find one of the aforementioned flagellation establishments, if that tickles your fancy.

For as long as anyone can remember, people have talked about demolishing the two sordid streets in order to widen the Strand, which can become horribly congested in the hinterland between St Clement Danes and St Mary le Strand, something of a drawback for the road that connects the wealth and power of the City with Westminster. But this won't happen for another fifteen years. One melancholic, end-of-the-century painting depicts the sun setting over a forlorn Wych Street, moist after the rain, as a few solitary figures totter into the encroaching twilight. A couple of years later, both Holywell and Wych Street would be gone, flattened to make way for soulless Aldwych.

Time now to seek out some more depravity in one of the most squalid parts of town, Whitechapel. Retrace your footsteps past the church of St Clement Danes, go onto the Strand and wait on the pavement. You're looking for a bus – a horse-bus, that is – heading east.

The horse-bus to Whitechapel

It will be green, bedecked in advertisements and say 'Bayswater to Whitechapel' on the side, and you shouldn't have to wait long – it runs every eight minutes, just as in the twenty-first century, from 8 a.m. to midnight. Don't worry about finding a bus stop since they don't exist, just hail one – they always keep to the left and the driver will be very keen for your custom, veering in front of other traffic to pick you up. The cad, or conductor, will stand on a little foothold by the back of the bus, blowing a whistle to indicate to the driver to stop. Don't worry about buying a ticket either – you pay on your way off:

3d in this case (though cads are known to arbitrarily double it – 'how strange it is', comments *Punch*, 'that conductors never know how to conduct themselves').

At least 200,000 people ride buses every day, mainly the middle classes. It takes around 50,000 horses to keep London's public transport system circulating, caking the city in 1,000 tonnes of dung a day. Which is one of the reasons it smells so bad, despite huge advances in hygiene and health.

Around fourteen people can squeeze into the bus's inside compartment, which has straw on the floor, small windows, and plenty of advertisements (though sadly the days when bus companies provided reading material for their customers are gone). Don't expect any riveting conversation, rather insouciant disdain – as Charles Dickens points out in his *Sketches by Boz* in the 1830s, 'it is rather remarkable, that the people already in an omnibus, always look at newcomers, as if they entertained some undefined idea that they have no business to come in at all'. Watch out for fleas and pickpockets. Men will be expected to surrender their seats to oblige female passengers, and sit on the roof if necessary.

Even if you're not a man, it will do to head upstairs, onto the top deck, for the view. You find seating for as many as ten people either on two benches facing one another or in a 'knife-board' layout whereby the passengers sit back-to-back down the middle of the roof. Since you are new to town, this is the perfect place for you as we rattle past Bank, down Leadenhall Street, through Aldgate and into Whitechapel. The buses are not speedy – they won't go much faster than three to four and a half miles per hour and they get clogged up in almighty scrummages of traffic at bottlenecks like the Strand and Bank. So you'll have plenty of time to sit back, relax and take in the sights on our journey to Whitechapel.

You rattle down what's left of the Strand, entering Fleet

Street, where a dragon monument on a tall plinth marks the threshold of the city. One of the busiest streets in London, Fleet Street is of course a turbine of news, both enlightening the world and receiving its news via telegraph connections. Since you're facing the side of the street, you have a clear view of the names of papers emblazoned onto the fronts of three-storey buildings, many with balconies: '180,000 Weekly . . . People's Journal . . . People's Friend . . . News of the World . . . Daily News . . . Musical Gazette Review . . .', a staggering array of titles for sale and hawked about the streets, far, far more than we are used to in the twenty-first century. As of 1883, 15 morning dailies, 9 evening papers and no fewer than 383 weekly publications, of which 50 are local rags catering for a dramatically expanded city and her billowing suburbs, are published in London. These figures reveal that this is the first age of a truly *mass* media; since the seventeenth century, the circulation of papers had been limited largely to the respectable classes by various taxes on paper, production and advertisements. But the mid-century lifting of the last of these 'knowledge taxes', dovetailed with the introduction of faster rotary presses, has seen an explosion in 1d and ½d papers, informing and misinforming a newly educated working class. The news has never been so vivid. The (admittedly more expensive) *Illustrated London News*, a weekly, can sell up to 75,000 copies and the *Graphic* even has two issues per year in colour. It's a giddy time to work on Fleet Street.

The advertisements painted and pasted onto buildings and the worded shop signs which have replaced the painted symbols of yesteryear betray an increasingly literate city. In 1871, 80 per cent of all grooms and 75 per cent of all brides could sign their name in the church register following marriage (rather than making a crude mark); the phasing in of compulsory elementary education will exacerbate this trend. Other advances are visible from the horse-bus too. You see more bobbies (the Metropolitan Police came into existence fifty-five years ago) and gas-lit street lamps are everywhere, as are telegraph wires ('enough to make you believe that some gigantic spider has spun a web over your head').

Streets slide by. Endless terraces recede into a heap of brick and stone. There is no sense, as there was in medieval and seventeenth-century London, that you are close to nature, that the threshold where the city melts into open fields and meadows is just round the corner. In Victorian London, a sense of liminality has been supplanted by one of *illimitability*, of 'a world without end', as the author of the *World of London* put it as early as 1844. He went on to describe a metropolis that was 'spreading its gigantic arms on every side . . . seiz[ing] upon surrounding villages, expel[ling] the rural deities from their ancient seats, and aim[ing] at an universal empire of bricks and mortar'. To other observers, the Victorian city is 'the Great Wen', 'the monster city' and even 'the human awful wonder of God'.

If you're suspicious of what sound like fawning testimonials, let the hard, unpoetic facts speak for themselves. At the time of your last visit in 1665, London's population was around 400,000; now, in 1884, it is home to around 4.5 million – more than Greece, more than Switzerland, more even than the combined total of Scotland and Wales; by 1911, it will reach over seven million and be the biggest metropolis on earth, as it already is. Part of the reason for that is coming up ahead. Look right, towards the dome of St Paul's Cathedral. On the other side of Ludgate Circus, a viaduct looms. If you crane your neck further, you'll see that it shoots across the Thames parallel to Blackfriars Bridge (opened in 1769). This is the London Chatham and Dover Railway Bridge, only twenty years old. Look up and you might be able to see passengers waiting for the train at Ludgate Hill station, on top of the viaduct. This line connects south London with the City and, via the Snow Hill Tunnel, to Metropolitan Service stations like Farringdon and King's Cross. City workers can now live a long way out, in more salubrious suburban climes.

Thanks to the coming of the railways and trams, far-flung places like Kingston upon Thames, Harrow, Hillingdon, Bromley and Bexley are now connected to the core, if not actually part of London. Slightly less far-flung but formerly independent satellite towns and villages like Putney, Wandsworth, Battersea, Poplar, Bow, Lewisham, Hackney and Greenwich however *are* existing within the thirty-year-old Metropolitan Board of Works. This evolved from the old Bills of Mortality and it's instructive to think that whereas in Shakespeare and Pepys's London, the whole city, if at all, was pictured in terms of death and dying, now people associate it with *improvement* and modernity; the purpose of the Board of Works, as the name suggests, is to provide infrastructure to accommodate the rapid growth of the city. The old, increasingly unwalled City, where you visited an anchorite's cell and strolled in the Drapers' Garden, is now just a tiny slither of the metropolis, a nut, albeit one of supreme economic importance. Since your last visit, smart middle-class enclaves have sprouted in Kensington, Chelsea, Kennington, St John's Wood, Knightsbridge and Bayswater, areas that Roy Porter would wittily label 'stuccovia', with their endless snow-white terraces, stately porches and pilasters. They don't lie on our itinerary today but they have retained their smartness and social cachet into the twenty-first century, if you fancy seeking them out.

And yet, the corollary of such rapid urbanization – the population of London will increase by 870,000 in the 1880s alone – is a transient population, the loss of community ties, atomisation, and in some places, urban ennui. Some observers find it a hideous and harrowing place. 'London has a terrifying face,' wrote the Italian novelist Edmondo de Amicis in 1878. 'You seem to be lost in the necropolis of the world, breathing its sepulchral air.' A malignant apparatus, he believed it sapped the life of all who entered, reducing them to 'a living cog in a vast machine'. When London grinds to a halt, it can be horrible; 'a wet Sunday in London: shops closed, streets empty', observed a Frenchman in the 1860s, adding that 'the few people in this desert of squares and streets, hurrying beneath their umbrellas, look like unquiet ghosts . . . after an hour's walking one . . . can understand suicide'. So ebullient by day, the City grinds to a halt at night. In 1871, the social statistician Charles Booth counted almost 119,000 clerks, accountants and bankers working in the City but in the twenty years since Booth made his calculation, its residential population has fallen by 54,000 to 75,000 and it will go on falling as tradesmen and financiers move out to the suburbs, laying the foundations for the ghostly, anonymous City familiar to anyone who has ever visited it at the weekend in the twenty-first century.

Reaching Cornhill, you glance to your left and see the Bank of England, rebuilt earlier in the century in a neoclassical style, parcelled in by a windowless wall, like an inviolable economic fortress – which, with its vast reserves of gold coin and bullion, it is. As you are pulled towards Leadenhall Street, you see soberly dressed men in black coats and black hats everywhere, as though you've stumbled into a Magritte painting.

But the city isn't all grey. Middle-class Victorians are very keen on the moral and spiritual benefits of fresh air and outdoor recreation, underpinned by the Romantic perception of nature as an articulation of divinity. In 1833 a Select Committee expressed concern that untrammelled urban growth was divorcing the working class from their natural environment and supplanting healthy exercise with illicit rat fights, boxing matches and drinking to oblivion. Parks were the answer; completed in 1844, Victoria Park, close to your destination in east London, is a fine repository of such ideas.

As you approach Aldgate (one of the original Roman gates but long since demolished), the halls, taverns and counting houses of the City give way to tattier clothes shops, many staffed by Jewish immigrants from eastern Europe and Russia. You are entering the East End, the site of harrowing poverty, of 'courts, many of which the sun never penetrates, which are never visited by a breath of fresh air . . . dens in which these thousands of beings [the poor] who belong, as much as you, to the race for whom Christ died, herd together', as *The Bitter Cry of Outcast London* laments.

The people of the abyss

A perennial problem for the intrepid London explorer – in whichever century they might find themselves, not least the twenty-first – is how to respond to the problem of acute poverty, in London so often witnessed cheek-by-jowl with extreme wealth in a juxtaposition as provocative as it is distasteful. But as you tread Whitechapel's gloomy maze of streets, signs of prosperity are few and far between. The slums you pass may not be as dark, stinking and tightly packed as in some other deprived parts of London (for that, go to Flower and Dean Street in Spitalfields or some of the meaner parts of Southwark), but this is a realm of almost pure poverty, of barefooted children shivering in doorways in patched rags, of red-faced men staggering down the street clasping window ledges with one hand and a bottle of gin in the other, of world-weary housewives in upstairs windows pushing scraps of bread into birdcages and staring into the middle distance blankly.

Everywhere, monotony and want, interspersed with the odd doss house, gin palace, chapel and penny gaff.

Most of the middle- and upper-class people further west are more acutely aware of the predicament of the poor than in earlier eras. A deeper interest was sparked by a fear of contagion following the outbreak of cholera earlier in the century, and by Edwin Chadwick's subsequent *Conditions of the Labouring Population* (1842), which demonstrated a direct link between pauper colonies and the killer disease. These days, thanks to the coming of Bazalgette's sewer system, the increased provision of clean water, and advances in science and healthcare, cholera is in retreat – in fact, the population of England's average life span will have risen by 50 per cent by 1901. Yet a keen interest in London's slums – or rookeries, as they're called, after seething colonies of rooks clumped in trees – endures. In part, this is because poverty has come to be seen as a contagious disease, infecting the bloodstream of the city, fostering immoral behaviour and epidemics of crime. But also because they have become a source of fascination and voyeurism in their own right.

Most people's perception of London's poor and their slums stems more from media portrayals than any meaningful, real-life interactions; Victorian London is, after all, a heavily stratified society. Some of these have proven landmarks in modern journalism, such as Henry Mayhew's *London Labour and the London Poor* (1851), which began as a series of articles that personalized the poor, describing their living conditions in stark forensic detail. Other depictions, though, while not necessarily exaggerating the plight of the poor, are lurid and sensationalist, designed as much to titillate and horrify as inform, even showing signs of conforming to an emergent genre of poverty literature. That's not to say there aren't some heroic individuals and their followers who genuinely want to help the poor – there most certainly are, as we shall see – more that London's fascination, even obsession, with the 'people of the abyss', as one author puts it, may well strike you as distasteful and disturbing. But now *you're* complicit too.

You hear the clatter of wheels on cobbles and a horse-bus pulls into view, incongruous in these dead-end streets. It lumbers along a while before slowing to a halt in front of a toothy man with a barrel organ, circled by a congregation of barefooted urchins, swaying to its rhythms, linking arms and leaping about. Inside the bus, you see huddled faces of men and women pressed against the window – their eyes wide and staring, relishing this spontaneous display of costermonger culture, exchanging delighted glances with one another, some even scribbling notes. The denizens of the street take no notice of these day trippers and, after a while, the driver takes up the harnesses and the bus is dragged off towards some other spectacle.

That was the Victorian equivalent of the twenty-first century's 'poverty porn', in which the lives of the (usually benefit-subsistent) poor are televised – and, depending upon your standpoint, sympathetically documented or exploited – for commercial entertainment. But in Victorian London there's no screen, the poverty is witnessed at first hand. The touring of poverty-stricken districts is called slumming and it is an intensification of a long-standing London tradition – in the eighteenth century, St James's fops and rakes enjoyed swapping their velvet jackets and periwigs for workmen's rags and going on an urban safari to the tar-caked wharves of Wapping or the slums of St Giles's to see how the other half lived, for giggles. In the 1880s the pull of the massively expanded East End is much stronger and it's currently the fashion for omnibuses to infiltrate some of the poorest neighbourhoods – like this one – for paying customers. London guide books – ever a big-selling genre – are beginning to direct visitors not only to tired and obvious sights like St Paul's Cathedral, Westminster Abbey and Crystal Palace, but to world-acclaimed philanthropic institutions in deepest, darkest Whitechapel, Spitalfields and Stepney. This reinforces the demand for slumming; Londoners want to see if things really are as bad as they have been led to believe in 'the continent beyond'.

For some, the sight of such bounteous poverty, of crumbling soot-black terraces, of children rooting through mounds of filth like rats for a scrap of food, of limp bodies, ruined by alcohol, carried in a human tunnel to the emergency department of the Royal London Hospital, solicits a profound sympathy for their fellow-humans and their charitable impulses leap into action. For others, though, it's all in an evening's entertainment, a thrill, not unlike going to see a horror movie in the twenty-first century. It won't be denied that even in the case of committed philanthropes, there is an element of morbid voyeurism to all this, and this is why slumming is a source of mockery from some quarters. The journalist Henry Wood wrote of an irresistible 'attraction of repulsion' and even the social investigator Beatrix Potter confessed to feeling 'a certain weird romance' for the slums. Others see it as a way of doing penance for the sins of their neglectful and exploitative class, the sight of poverty here becoming a form of bourgeois punishment, a strange thought.

Even royalty go slumming. Two years ago the Prince of Wales donned overalls and set off in a carriage (with police escort) to inspect the worst slums of Holborn and Clerkenwell. In one, he found 'a shivering, half-starved woman, and her three ragged, torpid children, lying on a heap of rags in a room bereft of furniture'. He'd wanted to give her a handful of gold coins but was advised against doing so for fear of retribution from her obviously feral neighbours. In *The People of the Abyss*, the American journalist Jack London (real name: John Griffith Chaney) went slumming for several months, immersing himself in the world of the East End poor, living on the streets and in workhouses, for an account that would go on to influence George Orwell's *Down and Out in Paris and London* (1933). 'The region my hansom was now penetrating was one unending slum', the American recalls. 'The streets were filled with a new and different race of people, short of status, and of wretched or beer-sodden appearance. We rolled along through miles of brick and squalor.' Elsewhere he notes how East End children tend to grow up into 'rotten adults, without virility or stamina, a weak-kneed, narrow-chested, listless breed'; the abyss, he concludes 'is literally a huge man-killing machine'.

Not many of the houses you're passing were originally intended for the proletariat – they are too big for that, with cellars, kitchens, servants' quarters and multiple bedrooms. But the coming of the railways allowed moderately well-off workers to run for the hills, to the suburbs, while the labouring classes, their ranks swelled thanks to the population explosion, began to colonize their vacated houses en masse, with up to half a dozen families jam-packed into single-family houses.

What is desperately needed is a large-scale programme of house building to ease the overcrowding but landowners and speculative builders, chasing profit, are far more concerned with middle-class housing, of which there is a glut in some areas. Five years ago, two in five of the 4,800 houses that had sprung up in East Dulwich for tradesmen and clerks lay empty; it is a similar story in desirable districts elsewhere, in Bloomsbury and Bayswater – a kick in the teeth for the Whitechapel poor, should they ever venture that far west, which is unlikely. The shortage is exacerbated by the building of the railways, which displaced over 100,000 people – most poor, since it's more costly to plough railway lines through plush districts – forcing them into ever-crowded tenements.

On the next street of anonymous terraced houses a tall man in a thick black coat and gloves raps on a door. His attire, and the way he carries himself, makes him stick out. No one heeds his call. Eventually, an upstairs window grinds open and a woman in a greasy white apron appears, glowering down. The visitor identifies himself as the Board Man and demands to be let in. She nods calmly and disappears. The next thing he knows, bottles, candle stubs, boots, perhaps worse – are raining down on his head. The man shouts up that he is going to have her banged up, at which she slams the window shut, cackling. The Board Man dusts down his jacket and moves on to the next house along while a gaggle of urchins collect around the missiles, pointing and laughing at this outwitted bogeyman.

Wind your way back to Cannon Street Road before they turn on the only other well-dressed person in the street: you. Keep walking south, across Cable Street, until you reach St George Street.

Until about thirty years ago, this was known as Ratcliffe Highway, variously described by Dickens as 'a reservoir of dirt, drunkenness and drabs' and a resort of 'the accumulated scum of humanity'. Here you'll find sea dogs whoring in brothels, ex-soldiers with wooden legs languishing in doss houses, and all elements of the criminal underworld drinking themselves silly in pubs and gin palaces. The hamlet of Ratcliffe, Saxon for red cliff, was perhaps originally named after the reddish colour of the area's soil. These days, many would say the area is red with blood. A pair of murders in December 1811 – one involving a fourteen-week-old baby having his throat slit, and both seemingly random and motiveless in nature as though an eruption of the innate savagery of the area – still cast a deathly shadow over the street, and no amount of renaming is ever going to change that; even in the twenty-first century, where it is known just as 'The Highway', the stretch is morose and overbearing.

This is one of the worst streets in London. It's not a good idea to linger. But do note in passing Jamrach's pet shop – or Animal Emporium as he grandiloquently calls it – almost directly in front of you at number 179–80, on the ground floor of a glum terrace. This is not a pet shop in the modern sense, stocked with parrots and goldfish, but a place where you can swan off with a tiger, lion, alligator or orang-utan. A family business, it has been run for the last forty years by one Charles Jamrach, a man who boasts that he can procure for his clients any beast in the world, no matter how exotic, from his extensive network of overseas agents. He has a menagerie a little further up, on Betts Street, where his ferocious wares are displayed in cages. You can pick an elephant up (metaphorically) for around £300 (roughly comparable to £30,000 today). If you do decide to go shopping, be careful. Sometimes, the beasts aren't secured very effectively. Sometimes, they escape.

In 1857 a nine-year-old boy got the fright of his life when a fully grown Bengal tiger sauntered down the street and clamped him between his jaws – foolishly, he had been gawping at it. Within seconds Mr Jamrach came rushing out of his shop and tried to prise the boy from the tiger's jaws with his bare hands, only to find himself dragged along with the child. Only after one of his men arrived with a crowbar and cracked the tiger across the eyes did it drop him (at least, this is the heroic account Jamrach himself gives in *The Boy's Own Paper*, published twenty-two years after the event). Jamrach had to pay the boy's father £300 in compensation but was at least able to sell the truant tiger to the proprietor of a rival menagerie, who, with some artistic licence, branded him 'the tiger that swallowed the child'.

Mr Jamrach buys his exotic merchandise from seafarers docking at the port. It's our next stop: we are going to see the British Empire in action.

'The trysting place of the globe': the Port of London

Leaving Jamrach's on your left, walk past the church on St George Street and turn right onto Old Gravel Lane. The air is laden with the scent of burning tobacco. Cross the bridge and make your way past all the warehouses and lodging houses that curve right onto Wapping High Street, where, through gaps in the buildings, you can make out endless wharves and stairs abutting the Thames. Almost immediately, down a little alley, you will come across the site of Execution Dock. Here, in the Middle Ages, began the practice of hanging pirates from a riverside gibbet until three tides had washed over them, a further example of that age's penchant for poetic justice. A little further down the same street you'll find the headquarters of the first organized police force in the country – the Thames Police, established in 1798.

That the river police predated the Metropolitan Police by thirty-one years is revealing – in the eighteenth century, at a time when overseas trade was expanding spectacularly, ships might languish for months on end in an almighty traffic jam in the Pool of London, waiting to unload their cargoes at the Legal Quays upriver via lighters; people liked to claim that you could walk from one bank to the other using the decks of ships as stepping stones. Pilfering was rife – not just from the ships and lighters but from Customs House upriver, in which merchandise might lie unattended for long periods; it is alleged that

£500,000 per year (almost £50 million, crudely put, in twenty-first-century terms) was lost in this way. But with around 8,000 vessels mooring or anchoring midstream at any given time, a river police could only ever be part of the solution. The other – one that would decisively transform the face of the East End – will reveal itself to you in a couple of minutes when you reach Wapping Basin, the gateway to the London Dock.

When you reach the bridge, look right. From this vantage point, you can see straight into a vast wet dock cut off from the tides by locks, surrounded by quays, cranes and warehouses, and fortified by walls thirty feet high: an impregnable fortress not unlike the Tower but economic in nature. It is brimming with ships. Alas, without written permission from the secretary of the London Dock Company at their Leadenhall headquarters, you won't be able to gain access – but we do have the sensuous account of Henry Mayhew, who came here one October morning in 1849 and wrote about it for the *Morning Chronicle*. Against a backdrop of masts, quays and sheds he saw

> tall chimneys vomiting clouds of black smoke [and] now men with their faces blue with indigo . . . then will come a group of flaxen-haired sailors, chattering German; and next a black sailor, with a cotton handkerchief twisted turban-like around his head . . . and shortly afterwards a mate with green para-keets [small parrots] in a wooden cage.

The air is pungent with the fumes of tobacco, rum and hides and fragrant with coffee and spice, intermingled with 'the peculiar fungus smell of dry-rot'. He captures a rich maritime cacophony too:

> The sailors are singing boisterous nigger songs from the Yan-kee ship just entering, the cooper is hammering at the casks on

the quay, the chains of the cranes, loosed of their weight, rattle as they fly up again; the ropes splash in the water; some captain shouts his orders through his hands; a goat bleats from some ship in the basin; and empty casks roll along the stones with a hollow drum-like sound.

According to Baedeker's *Guide to London* (1889), there is capacity for 300 large vessels, innumerable lighters and 220,000 tons of goods in the warehouses. And 70,000 pipes of wine in their cellars.

The London Dock is just one of almost a dozen artificial lakes scooped out of marshy riverside land in St Katherine's, Wapping, Rotherhithe, West and East Ham, and especially the Isle of Dogs to accommodate the explosive growth of overseas trade as Britain emerged as the world's leading imperial power and her capital, London, the fulcrum of a global trading empire. The West India Company, ever a victim of river theft, took the initiative in 1799, opening the first major enclosed dock; over the next ninety years, competing joint-stock dock companies followed suit, not always to the overall harmony of trade. Docks tend to specialize in particular imports: you'll find rum and hardwood at the West India Dock; tea and spices at the East India Dock (both on the Isle of Dogs); ivory, coffee and tobacco here at London Dock; rubber, sugar and of course live turtles – for turtle soup, a Victorian delicacy which you must try – at St Katherine's Dock by the Tower of London. All bounties of economic glucose, ready to be pumped into the bloodstream of empire.

Skim some glances across the Thames towards Pickle Herring Stairs opposite the Tower of London; to Cherry Garden Stairs, no longer the gateway to the Pepysian pleasure resort but now set amidst the rope-makers and biscuit factories of Rotherhithe; to the smoke-belching factories of the Isle of

Dogs – everywhere you look, ships, ships, ships. Unlike Paris, Vienna or Rome, ever since its inception in AD 47 London has evolved as a *port* city, rising to prominence and prosperity on a perpetual tide of commercial traffic – particularly now, in an era of free trade at the height of Britain's imperial might.

For the French critic and historian Hippolyte Taine, the Port of London was 'one of the great spectacles of our planet'. In his *Notes on England* (1872) he describes, from his vantage point at the top of Greenwich Park, 'a forest of yards, of masts, of rigging . . . a continuous heap, crowded together, massed against the chimneys of houses and the pulleys of warehouses, with all the tackle of incessant, regular, gigantic labour'. 'Golden rain' showers down upon 'the brackish, tawny, half-green, half-violet water' as the sun shines through foggy smoke and the surface reflects the 'striking and strange reflections' of slender, swan-like ships hailing from all parts of the globe. For him, London's docklands are 'the trysting place of the globe'.

For many of those who actually work in the docks, though, the reality is less romantic. Visit the gates of the docks at around 7.30 a.m. on any weekday morning and you'll come face-to-face with the very tissue of human desperation and want at the daily 'call on'. At these unedifying spectacles, you'll see thousands of men competing for a day's casual labour loading and unloading ships at the lowly wage of 4d or 5d per hour like a pack of feral dogs ravenous for a chewy piece of meat. Even working every day, which is by no means guaranteed, it is near-impossible to pay the rent on a decent house; many of these men live in doss houses. About one-third of dock labour is more skilled and more permanent jobs are available, but for these people, there is no certainty of a stable income. In Mayhew's account, the dock foremen appear, 'then begins the scuffling and scrambling, and stretching forth of countless hands high in the air, to catch the eye of him whose voice may give them work . . . some men jump upon the backs of the others . . . all are shouting'. It is not just unskilled labourers competing for the work but others who have fallen on hard times and drunks chasing their next pint and pipe. But labour supply vastly outstrips employer demand, so many leave empty handed each day, and 'to look into the face of that hungry crowd, is to see a sight that must ever be remembered'.

It's an extreme juxtaposition of wealth and want, of the bounties of the world stacked up inside the warehouses and the poverty-stricken labourers clamouring for work outside. Visiting a low lodging house later that day, Mayhew finds 'at least 20 to 30 of the most wretched objects I ever beheld': some shoeless, some shirtless, all stinking. They are eating pea soup washed down with ale out of yellow basins, the implication being that it's scarcely better than vomit. It is as though labourers' diets have not progressed since the Middle Ages.

Retracing your footsteps, plunge back into the abyss, and make your way north towards Whitechapel Road.

For some, the scenes of monotonous poverty that everywhere surround you can be epiphanic, fostering monumental acts of philanthropy. The American banker George Peabody opened his first block of dwellings for the deserving poor in Spitalfields twenty years ago; in 1885, Nathan Rothschild of the famed banking dynasty will found the Four Per Cent Industrial Dwellings Company to provide affordable housing for the increasing numbers of Jewish tenants streaming into the East End; and Angela Burdett-Coutts too, one of the wealthiest women in England, is another pioneer of social housing, masterminding the Holly Lodge Estate in Highgate.

But it is Thomas Barnardo who is the age's leading philanthropic entrepreneur. The Anglo-Irishman, enrolled at the Royal London Hospital in Whitechapel, abandoned his dreams of joining a medical mission to China after an encounter with a ten-year-old boy called Jim Jarvis, who attended a ragged school he had set up in a converted donkey stable in Stepney. After the session the boy, who had a prematurely aged face, was loathe to leave, instead warming himself by the fire. Learning that Jarvis was an orphan sleeping rough in a hay-cart, Barnardo brewed him a restorative cup of coffee (he liked coffee, Barnardo, converting a mammoth Limehouse Gin Palace into a coffee tavern in 1872 replete with biblical quotations above the 'bar') and bid the boy show him where all the other local homeless children slept. The barefooted Jim led him to a grotty shed on Petticoat Lane. Together, they clambered onto the roof, revealing a hidden colony of ragged, barefooted children, huddled up against one another, their feet in the gutter and heads resting against the crown of the roof. All in the perishing cold, with no covering.

In that moment, Barnardo decided to devote the rest of his life to helping weak, vulnerable and homeless children – 'no destitute child ever refused admission', as the sign above his hostels announced. He opened his first one – for destitute boys – at 18–26 Stepney Causeway, about a ten-minute walk east of your current position, in 1870; a girls' hostel in Barkingside, beyond Epping Forest, soon followed.

His philosophy is simple – every child deserves the best possible start in life. At a time when it is generally believed that poverty stems from an individual's inherent slothfulness and moral torpor and *not* the shortcomings of society or one's upbringing, this is radical stuff, requiring radical intervention. He rescues vulnerable children from alcoholic and neglectful parents (carrying out 'philanthropic abductions' if need be – he is repeatedly taken to court for this, but always wins), providing them with the requisite skills and training to unlock their full potential, and often even transporting the less promising ones to more salubrious homes in Canada and Australia.

Dr Barnardo, who is not actually a real doctor, produces thousands of 'before' and 'after' photo-cards, designed to highlight the transformative impact of his benevolence, with captions like 'once a little vagrant . . . now a little workman'. Sold singly for 6d or in packs of twenty for 5s, this is a key fund-raising strategy, and if he needs to doctor the photographs to flesh out the contrast – why not? It is all part of his grand plan to lift hopeless children out of the abyss.

But there are limits to philanthropic charity, however momentous. On the horizon, nestling in the right angle formed by Thomas Street and Charles Street, is an austere H-shaped block, rising to six storeys at the rear. A queue of men in flat caps are queuing outside the entrance on Thomas Street, many of them slumped against the wall, resigned. Welcome to the Whitechapel Union Workhouse. The bottom of the horizontal 'H' contains the male and female wards; the stem is a two-storey office block; and the top row consists of further wards, a dining hall and chapel, imbecile ward and relieving offices.

The workhouse is Victorian London's main 'solution' to the problem of poverty, replacing the Poor Laws of the Tudor and Stuart eras. These grim, joyless buildings are seen as a means to an end – to get the slothful but able-bodied poor back into work. As such, conditions inside are designed to be as horrible as possible, like a prison camp. You are fed, clothed and accommodated, it's true, but beyond that any last vestiges of self-worth are ground down by a dreary regime of monotonous labour, harsh discipline, stifling rules, disgusting food, patronizing sermons and very little companionship or conviviality. Wearing workhouse clothes, separated from your family, and sleeping in chilly dormitories on straw mattresses amongst strangers, it's no wonder that if there's any prospect of eking out an existence in the outside world, however meagre, you will surely leap at the opportunity, no matter how humiliating.

Joseph Merrick, the Elephant Man, and other 'freaks of nature'

Whitechapel Road is as busy as an anthill with costermongers talking their impenetrable cant, policemen moving people along, drunks and medical students standing around smoking in their white coats.

With its sickly beige bulk and a circular clock gouged into the middle of its gable, the Royal London glowers down at Whitechapel Road like a Cyclops. It's one of around twenty general hospitals dotted about the city, all palpable manifestations of the Victorians' philanthropic drive. Charitable institutions, they exist to provide medical treatment to the deserving poor. Situated in one of the poorest and most squalid parts of London at a time of rapid population growth, the need for a hospital here, in Whitechapel, has never been more urgent.

Busy at work inside, operating upon the emaciated frames of some of the poorest people in London, is an ambitious surgeon in his early thirties. His name is Frederick Treves, and he is now best remembered for his association with what he memorably described as 'the most disgusting specimen of humanity that I have ever seen', a specimen he took under his wing, promoted within the medical establishment, and whose story (or at least, a version of his story) he shared with the world: Joseph Merrick, the Elephant Man. At the time of your visit, Merrick is still being exhibited in a small shop on the other side of the Whitechapel Road. For the moment, before Treves's intervention, he is the hottest freak show in town.

The shop is between a pawnbrokers' and a greengrocer, at number 123. A group of about twenty people have gathered outside, some with white coats, others in top hats and shabby suits, as well as a sprinkling of boys and girls with their parents. The façade is shrouded by a hanging canvas announcing that the Elephant Man can be seen for the admission price of 2d. (Building labourers earn about 4s per day, so this is not expensive; for the same price, you can get a 'second class warm bath in Whitechapel'.) The canvas is decorated with an almost laughably crude picture of a man/elephant hybrid. The crowd look puzzled, as though they can't fathom how such a beast would fit into the small shop in front of them.

A boy appears at the door in a faded red waistcoat with brass buttons. Immediately, people start shouting questions at him, to which he only replies, 'I don't know, I don't know,' and opens the door. The group streams in. Join them.

Inside, it is dark and dank. A faint smell of wax hangs in the air. The far end of the shop is partitioned off by a theatre-red tablecloth hanging from a few rings. People's eyes are drawn to it. Every so often there is a faint, almost imperceptible jogging of the fabric accompanied by a fluty cackle. A young showman, one Tom Norman, wears a curly brimmed hat, white gloves with rings on the outside, and a garish waistcoat tinkling with silver coins. He inquires whether any lady in the audience might be in a delicate condition (i.e. pregnant). No? Good. He takes everyone's money, sends his juvenile assistant to mind the door and launches into his well-rehearsed spiel, highlighting the wonder of the thing, not its aberrance.

'Ladies and gentlemen, with your indulgence, I would like to introduce you to Mr Joseph Merrick, the Elephant Man. Before doing so I ask you please to prepare yourselves – brace yourselves to witness one who is probably the most remarkable human being ever to draw the breath of life.'

He whisks open the curtains and there, crouching on a podium, is a misshapen bundle, covered in a brown blanket, huddled over a brick heated by a Bunsen burner, faintly rocking. Of this apparition bathed in the ghostly blue of the gas flame, no one is quite sure what to make. Sideways glances are exchanged. Norman continues, 'Please do not despise or condemn this man on account of his unusual appearance. Remember we do not make ourselves, and were you to prick or cut Joseph he would bleed, and that blood would be red, the same as yours or mine.'

With that, he orders the Elephant Man to stand up. The blanket falls to the floor. In that moment, much air is sucked out of the room. Some people back away, as though trying to evade a snake. Some grab each other's arms. One screams. But most people just stand there gawping, as they are meant to, caressing his body with their eyes, their necks craned in wonder at how God could permit such a being to come into the world.

Physically, Joseph Merrick is grotesque. He has an astonishingly large head (thirty-six inches in circumference) with a bony, loaf-shaped growth sprouting from his forehead. The whole of the right-hand side of his face is hideously deformed, as though a child were trying to build a monster from clay but got bored half-way through. From the back of his head droops, in the words of Frederick Treves, 'a bag of spongy, fungous-looking skin' and 'from the upper jaw ... another mass of bone ... protrud[ing] from the mouth like a pink stump, turning the upper lip inside out and making the mouth a mere slobbering aperture'. Much of this pendulous skin has the texture of cauliflower and, to make matters worse, gives off a stench that is nauseous even by the standards of Victorian London, hardly a sweet-smelling city. He is naked from the waist up, barefooted, wearing only a pair of ill-fitting trousers. His neck can barely support his heavy head, so it permanently droops like a sunflower at the end of the summer. His left hand is surprisingly well-formed and slender; the other hideously swollen and about four times the size, a monster's hand.

His face is 'no more capable of expression than a block of gnarled wood'. 'At no time had I met with such a degraded or perverted version of a human being as this lone figure displayed,' wrote Treves, who in his capacity as a surgeon at the Royal Hospital had come across his fair share of arresting deformities and mutilations.

Some of the audience look bemused and Norman has done well to collect the money before unveiling the monster – the canvas outside gave an impression of a big beast rampaging through the jungle, not the shrivelled, forlorn character hunched over the Bunsen burner, 'the embodiment of loneliness'. Though his skin is grey and lumpy, if he weren't promoted as the Elephant Man it's unlikely anyone would make such a pachydermal association, though the stump of a protuberance from his upper jaw was once much longer and might conceivably have been described as a trunk. From the perspective of a twenty-first-century time traveller, he looks much more like E. T., or simply the victim of an acid attack; to frame him as an elephant man is a stroke of promotional genius, and Tom Norman has a compelling backstory to go with it.

The Elephant Man was born in Leicester, says Norman, and came about because his mother, when pregnant with him, fell under the hooves of a travelling menagerie of elephants in the crush of the crowds. Look behind you. Through the pane of glass above the door, you can just make out the pilasters and arches of the Royal London Hospital. Medical science has come on a long way since the days of swallow juice and puppy-dog water; the Four Humours Theory is moribund, the Germ Theory is now widely believed, and there have been some striking advances in anaesthetics and surgery. Yet the crowds seem satisfied with this neat explanation.

Joseph's symptoms only began to develop when he was five years old, says Norman, and when he was eleven or twelve, his mother died and his father married his evil stepmother, and he was thrown out for being a burden. Ultimately he realized that the only way he could make a decent living was to become an exhibit. Finding the local showmen to be kind and accommodating, this dream came true, and now, aged twenty-one, he is as comfortable as he was uncomfortable before. In case the audience don't believe the story, they can purchase a little three-page pamphlet, which the elephant man penned himself (with his left hand, presumably).

The crowd stand around, not quite sure what to do with themselves, some smoke, some buy the pamphlet, others go up to prod this freak of nature.

If the Elephant Man has got the juices of your voyeurism flowing, you'll be pleased to hear that he's just one of a panoply of freaks on display in Victorian London. An intensification of a long-standing tradition of exhibiting curiosities and exotic specimens, not least at Bartholomew Fair, what *Punch* branded 'Deformito-mania' took root as prosperity increased and the Saturday half-holiday became more widely observed. 'Poor Madame Tussaud's', *Punch* decried in 1847, 'with her chamber of horrors is quite thrown into the shade by the number of real enormities and deformities that are now to be seen, as the showmen say "Alive, alive!"' Freaks could be exhibited in grand halls, aquariums, galleries, or just humble shop windows. By mid-century, the Egyptian Hall in Piccadilly emerged as *the* place to see all manner of monstrous beings. There was never a better time than the mid-nineteenth century to be a professional freak or a showman.

If you'd visited London three years ago, in 1881, you could have seen the African Leopard Boy, twelve-year-old black but with splodges of white skin like an inverted Dalmatian. He was promoted as a 'hybrid between two races of people of totally different colours'. And two years ago, Londoners could visit the Westminster Aquarium and see Krao, a seven-year-old girl from the distant land of 'Indochina', whose body was covered in hair like an ape. A little further back, in 1865, the *Lancet* caused great excitement with its report of a young Portuguese man with 'two complete and well-formed penises, placed side by side'. Both worked. It seems he was attached to the lower limbs and genitalia of a partly developed twin. Even in the twenty-first century, deformito-mania hasn't quite vanished from the West End: until recently, a club in Leicester Square employed a pair of dwarves to play strobe-lit ping pong for the amusement of the crowd.

Even so, you're still likely to find the sight of so many people crammed in to gawp at the Elephant Man, and the broader commodification of Victorian freaks, somewhat distasteful, perhaps cruel. Not to defend the freakoholics too much, since so many are driven to places like this out of prurience, ghoulish curiosity, or just boredom, but there is an extra resonance that might not be immediately apparent, and which goes some way towards explaining the depth of the obsession.

In 1859, Charles Darwin's *On the Origin of Species* was published, persuasively vocalizing ideas about evolution that had been in circulation for some time. Many of the freaks on display in London – not least the Elephant Man – are interpreted as some kind of derailment of nature, retrograde examples of barely evolved beings, if not the missing link itself. The title of the pamphlet introducing Krao, the young ape-girl, is 'Krao, the Missing Link, *a living proof of Darwin's theory of the descent of man*'. She is revelatory, it explains, conclusively debunking the 'usual argument against Darwin' that man and monkey had independent origins; 'ALL SHOULD SEE HER'. Similarly, Tom Norman likes to tell people 'the Elephant Man is not here to frighten you but to enlighten you'.

As the historian Nadja Durbach has pointed out so convincingly, in an age of imperialism, Victorian freak shows say
something about British society. As the pamphlet makes clear,
Krao was discovered in Laos, some outpost of barbarism
unblessed by the benevolence and civilizing agency of the British Empire; her exhibition in London, the crucible of that
empire, holds up a mirror to the highly civilized nature of the
homeland. Similarly, if anyone had any doubts about the virtues of inter-racial marriage, the mutant Leopard Boy is your
answer. Freak shows are foils, situating Victorian men, women
and children within a rigid scheme of races, civilizations and
evolutionary development. More than anything, they put the
otherness of alien races in the spotlight.

Death, incidentally, need not be a barrier to display. The
indigenous Mexican Julia Pastrana, better known – again, particularly after the publication of Darwin in 1859 – as the
Baboon Lady, had a rare genetic disorder (hypertrichosis)
which gave her a thick beard, heavy eyebrows and hairy forehead; the disorder is sometimes called werewolf syndrome, but
people also thought she most resembled some sort of gorilla.
She was displayed at the Regent's Gallery in Piccadilly until her
death, at which point her husband, who also happened to be
her manager, determined to wring further profit, had her
embalmed (along with her dead child for good measure). She
lived on as a mounted specimen at the Burlington Gallery on
Piccadilly 'her skin . . . as fresh and her body . . . plump as if
she were alive'.

Though by 1884 public opinion, fed and amplified by the
press, is beginning to turn against the commercial exploitation
of freaks and is banned outright in the City of London, it's still
going strong in the East End. For the young surgeon John
Bland-Sutton from the Middlesex Hospital near Oxford Street,
who would go on to write a pioneering study of Siamese twins,

there was nothing better to do on a Saturday night than wander out towards Mile End 'to see dwarfs, giants, fat-women, and monstrosities at the freak shows'. It was on one such visit that he saw, exhibited opposite the Royal Hospital, 'a repulsive human being known as the Elephant Man', the apogee of deformito-mania, the creature cowering before your very eyes.

There are two Joseph Merricks known to history. One, portrayed by Sir Frederick Treves in his *The Elephant Man and Other Reminiscences* (1923), is a creature mercilessly exploited by showmen, 'shunned like a leper, housed like a wild beast . . . his sole idea of happiness [being] to creep into the dark and hide', until he is discovered by a kind surgeon (Treves), taken under the wing of the medical establishment from 1886 to 1890 and introduced into polite society – including that of women, who seemed to invest value in his personality rather than appearance as a freak. In a powerful section, he juxtaposes the happy, sociable entity Merrick has become on his watch with the 'half-dead heap of miserable humanity' he found cowering in a side room at Liverpool Street Station after he was fleeced by a different showman (not Tom Norman) on an abortive tour of Europe in 1886.

Treves's is a very neat account – too neat, one might say. It is a pacey narrative with clear, despicable villains, a hero who overcomes just about the unluckiest hand one could ever be dealt with superhuman magnanimity, and achieves friendship, fame and a measure of happiness before his poignant death one afternoon in 1890 when Merrick sets his enormous head flat on the pillow in an effort to 'be like other people', dislocating his neck in the process.

While it would be wrong to dismiss Treves's version of events as purely fictional, he does make some curious factual slips, mistaking Mile End Road for Whitechapel Road, misidentifying the shop where Merrick was exhibited, getting key biographical details wrong (though Merrick may have lied or been unclear), and even getting his name wrong, calling him John not Joseph. As for Merrick's poor crippled mother, she is accused of being 'worthless and inhuman' and 'basely desert[ing] him' when in fact she had died of bronchitis when Joseph was about to turn eleven. We are entitled to ask – to what extent was Treves's guardianship of Merrick garnering *him* kudos? He certainly had an incentive to depict Merrick's time at the hospital through a roseate haze.

Tom Norman and (if we believe he actually wrote his auto-biographical pamphlet himself) Merrick give a very different version of events. Far from being plunged into the 'Slough of Despond' as a performing freak, Merrick had embraced the exhibitionist life with open arms. He had been mocked, bullied, shunned for his deformities all his life; they had prevented him from working as a hawker of haberdashery in Leicester (people used to scream and slam the door in his face when he appeared on their doorsteps). They had made him a burden upon his family. They had seen him endure four years of hell in a work-house, with an anonymous death in a pauper's grave the only thing he had to look forward to. When he heard that the manager of the local Gaiety Theatre was looking for novelties to exhibit, he leaped at the opportunity, a move that eventually saw him arrive in Whitechapel with Tom Norman.

As for the accusations of cruelty and exploitation? Balder-dash. Victorian freaks were free agents who usually earned more than their showmen, since they split the profits 50–50, and the curiosity could make extra money through the sales of freak pamphlets whereas the showman had overheads to worry about. Spectacles like the Elephant Man weren't slaves; they were neither cheap nor expendable, so what would have been the point of tyrannizing them?

'Who really exploited poor Joseph?' asks Norman. 'I, the showman, got the abuse. Dr Treves, the eminent surgeon (who you must admit was also a showman, but on a rather higher social scale) received the publicity and praise.' A virtual prisoner in his hospital basement quarters, and with a 'neverending stream of surgeons, doctors and Dr Treeve's [sic] friends' whose curiosity he had to patiently endure without being able to make a living out of it, was the basement really anything more than a more comfortable version of the workhouse? Was Merrick ever any the wiser as to the causes of his condition, or to the possibility of a cure?

There's no doubt that Treves opened doors for Merrick which otherwise would have remained barricaded with a double portcullis. He got to attend the theatre, read books, meet famous actresses and even, on one occasion, the Duke of Cambridge, who reportedly said, 'He is less disgusting to see than might be, because he is such a gentle, kindly man, poor thing!' Norman still maintains, however, that the Elephant Man felt suicide was the only way out of this glorified-workhouse existence; his body was, after all, discovered in a position which he, more than anyone, knew would lead to asphyxiation.

Look at him now, Joseph Merrick, the man who adores lighthouses; Joseph Merrick, the man who dreams of moving into a blind asylum where people might actually see his soul rather than his humungous head; Merrick the man who, shaking a woman's hand for the first time, crashed to his knees and started weeping effusively; Merrick, the monster who props up his head at night with his knees, his arms wrapped tight around his legs as though snug in his mother's womb: and ask yourself, is he a defenceless victim or master of his own destiny? Ask *him* if you like – if you can make sense of his 'distorted fluting voice', that is, and if Tom Norman will let you near him, which is by no means guaranteed.

Whatever reservations we might have about Treves's account, his final eulogy to his old patient surely holds true: 'As a specimen of humanity, Merrick was ignoble and repulsive; but the spirit of Merrick, if it could be seen in the form of the living, would assume the figure of an upstanding and heroic man, smooth browed and clean of limb, and with eyes that flashed undaunted courage.'

Make your way out of the shop into the Whitechapel dusk.

'Lighthouses, my boy!'

On the course of your odyssey through Victorian London, have you noticed the 'big, isolated clumps of buildings rising above the slates, like brick islands in a lead-coloured sea?' Perhaps not, since they are very much a common sight in twenty-first-century London. But in the 1880s, these red-brick, three-storey buildings with soaring gables, windows protruding from sloped roofs and towers are the manifestations of a revolution in educational provision, harbingers of a future welfare state. 'Lighthouses, my boy!' says Sherlock Holmes to Watson. 'Beacons of the future! Capsules with hundreds of bright little seeds in each, out of which will spring the wiser, better England of the future.'

Elementary schools, my dear Watson. Although some are built in the fashionable neo-Gothic style that can be seen in many of London's most monumental new public buildings, St Pancras station for instance, the favoured vernacular for the new Board Schools is the revived Queen Anne style, as described above. This is stylish, stately and most importantly unencumbered by medieval associations with religious dogma; as the first Board-appointed architect put it, 'in its aim and object [the architecture of the Board Schools] should strive to express civil rather than ecclesiastical character'.

There's one round the corner in Buck's Row, a four-storey cube structure with huge graceful windows, tightly packed into – and soaring over – a snugly packed labyrinth of slum housing. Making the most of the limited space available, it has a playground on its roof. Go and have a peek.

Until the mid-nineteenth century, the idea that the state – and one so firmly wedded to laissez-faire principles of economics, at that – should or even could intervene in education was quixotic, a mere pipe dream for a tiny number of reformers. Formerly, education for the London masses – and we are talking about *primary* education here – was in the hands of the Church: the National Society for Anglicans and the British and Foreign School Society for nonconformists, though sometimes this amounted to nothing more than going to Sunday School once a week. There were also 250-odd ragged schools for the kind of children described by Charles Dickens as 'too wretched, filthy and forlorn' to enter the charity schools. The purpose wasn't education as such, more to 'show them some sympathy, and stretch a hand out, which is not the iron hand of law, for their correction'.

But in 1870, the whole system was overhauled, and the state made perhaps its biggest intervention yet in people's lives in the form of the Education Act, pioneered by the Liberal statesman William Forster, which, in London, made primary education the responsibility of the London School Board. Since that parliamentary lightning strike, primary education has been compulsory for every child up to the age of ten. Politics not philanthropy propelled this volte-face. 'Civilized communities throughout the world are massing themselves together,' Forster warned in 1870, 'each mass being measured by its force'. But here was the rub – Britain was a small country, surpassed by the likes of Germany, which was seen to have a superior education system, in industrial production. 'If we are to hold our position among men of our own race or among the nations of the world, we must make up for the smallness of our numbers by increasing the intellectual force of the individual.' How else, too, to combat the rising tide of crime and pauperism, the strikes, the riots? By the time of your visit the impact upon London society has been palpable and by the end of the decade, the Board will have provided just over 400,000 places in over twenty schools.

There have been teething problems, to put it mildly. In the early days it was not unusual to see pupils and sometimes their parents hurling stones and insults at these alien 'teachers' in the streets. Many children were unused to structure and orderly behaviour, and staff found themselves acting more as disciplinarians than educators – one London doctor even coined a new medical complaint, 'Board School laryngitis', a condition exacerbated by the enormous class sizes – seventy or eighty pupils (though this will be reduced to fifty in 1891), segregated by sex.

By far the biggest problem is non-attendance; in 1902 there will be 20,000 prosecutions for this, showing how seriously successive governments take primary education. In poor households, young children are valuable resources, helping out with the business and doing chores around the home. Non-attendance on wash days is particularly acute. It is the task of the School Board Man (or Woman) to visit working-class houses and inquire after children reported absent from school – a thankless and sometimes dangerous job, as you saw earlier.

Still, the impact of the reform is clear. Charles Booth may have noted that some of the Board Schools' early intake were 'filthy, dirty . . . sickly looking with sore eyes and unwholesome aspect' and a few 'hopelessly dull, almost vacant', but he and other reformers agreed that by end of the century, London's droves of poor were beginning to show shades of humanity – all thanks to the factories of civilization you see here before you.

Walk west, back towards the city, with the Board School behind you. The fog follows you, rubbing its back upon the window panes, to borrow an image from T. S. Eliot, yellowish but somehow obsidian too. A black cat creeps out, looks at you like you're part of the furniture, then vanishes into the smoggy swirl. After a couple of minutes you'll be passing the spot where, four years from now, the first victim of Jack the Ripper will be discovered with throat slashed and abdomen lacerated. Move on, back to Whitechapel Road.

A journey through hell: the Underground

Even immersed in daytime fog, the city is ebullient, but Victorian London really comes to life at night, with street lamps blazing through the smog and hordes of pleasure seekers streaming through the streets, desperate to shake off the monotony of the working day in whichever entertainment venue tickles their fancy. They want colour, they want excitement, they want bonhomie, even the prospect of an illicit sexual encounter. And where better to find it than the music hall? We're going to follow suit and visit London's very first purpose-built music hall: the Canterbury, in Lambeth.

Fancy hailing another horse-bus? Thought not. Chances are you'd miss the start of the performance. Perhaps you've got your eye on a nice cabriolet or brougham? Forget it – you don't have enough money in your purse. You *do* have another option, though. It's been open for twenty years. It is the first of its kind anywhere in the world. It's a feat of modern engineering. It is, of course, the nascent London Underground, running over 800 trains a day.

Relative to London's other methods of transport (with the possible exception of steamboats), the Underground is lightning fast, allowing the labour force to live further from their place of work in more salubrious suburbs, which are swelling in size as a result. Two years after the Metropolitan Railway (which would go on to become the Metropolitan Line in the twentieth century) opened in 1863, one labourer told Henry Mayhew that cheap tickets (3d return on trains departing at 5.30 a.m. or 5.40 a.m.) enabled him to live way out in the wilds of Notting Hill in a much bigger house than he'd be able to afford in central London, and saving him a six-mile walk to work each day.

Luckily for you, Whitechapel, already on the East London Railway from New Cross to Liverpool Street, got its own Underground station when it was connected to the Metropolitan District Railway (ultimately to become the District Line) via a spur. Since last month, the District Railway and its supposed partner but more frequently antagonist, the Metropolitan Railway, have been operating a circular service around the inner core of the city. One day it will be marked yellow on a tube map and called the Circle Line, and already it is the source of urban legends about passengers dying and going round and round *ad infinitum* and people using it as a cheaper alternative to the office. It will only be a matter of time before someone suggests holding an annual Circle service cocktail party.

Turn left at the main road. After about a five-minute walk, you'll find yourself outside Whitechapel and Mile End Underground station (known just as Whitechapel Underground in the twenty-first century), with two arches serving as entry and exit and a giant billboard initiating east Londoners into the mysteries of the new transport system, promising frequent trains, cheap fares and season tickets. The inner circle, as it's known, will take you as far west as Notting Hill Gate and Kensington (High Street). But this evening, we will be going no further than Westminster Bridge. Make your way through the arches and buy a second-class ticket at the booking office.

First, a word of warning. Although there will be some familiar features – not least the advertising posters – the Victorian Underground differs from its twenty-first-century successor in several key respects, which you'd be wise to take to heart if you want to re-emerge without incident. Trains run every ten minutes or so, and take around seventy minutes to do a loop of the whole inner circle. There are little bars in some of the stations, should you need a pick-me-up. Since the platforms are made from wooden planks rather than concrete, the tunnels are echo chambers for customers' footsteps. Most are lit by pendulum gas lights (though electricity is being phased in), which sway a little as the trains pull in, scattering shadows.

Once you reach the platform, you'll notice there's no yellow line to stand behind. This isn't quite as dangerous as it sounds, since electrified rails won't be introduced for another six years. It's still eminently possible to be mangled by a train though, since travellers are in the habit of trying to board or alight while the train is still in motion. And the combination of gas lights, wooden carriages, wooden platforms and people freely smoking is, of course, what we would call in the twenty-first century a health and safety nightmare.

If you ask someone for the eastbound or westbound platform, they'll probably snort in bemusement and walk away. There is no eastbound and westbound, only 'up' (towards the City and beyond) and 'down' (towards the West End and beyond). The same goes for 'the Tube', which hasn't come into use yet, so don't even think about mentioning it. The roof of the tunnels that you will go through this evening have been dug no more than a few feet beneath street surface via the 'cut-and-cover method'; the first deep-cut electric line – or tube – won't open for another six years.

Like pretty much everything else in Victorian London, the Underground is stratified by class. You'll see signs adorning the platform, 'wait here for first class', 'wait here for second class' and so on. As you might expect, the first-class carriages are sumptuous; a Jubilee carriage in 1887 has 'gilded mirrors, buttoned leather door panels and string net luggage racks and rich lettering'. The second-class carriages are less well lit and more spartan; the third-class smoking carriages are disgusting, saliva-strewn, stinking and overcrowded. In contrast, the electrified 'Tube' trains, when they are introduced in the 1890s, will be controversially egalitarian.

Maps of the Underground do exist but they tend to be large and unwieldy, though the one bound into the back of a London handbook by Leipsic Karl Baedeker in 1878 is accurate enough (though to scale, not harmonized like Harry Beck's 1931 version, which is still in use in the twenty-first century). The guard will shout out the stations at each stop and their names are displayed on square signposts on each platform, but don't expect to see the iconic red roundel logo – that won't come into play until 1908.

And what of riding the things themselves? The cars are pulled along the tracks by steam locomotives, which gives the whole thing a slightly quaint, toytown feel. But the smell is anything but, and with its smoke and fumes, writers like to conflate the Underground and the Underworld. The novelist George Gissing evoked King's Cross station as 'a cacophony of voices, banging doors and screeching wheels; and a pandemonium of advertising posters, steam, smoke and soot that swirled around the station'. To ease overcrowding in prisons, now that the policy of transportation has been abandoned and capital punishment reduced, the *Pall Mall Gazette* helpfully suggested that prisoners be condemned to round trips on the Underground.

The American journalist R. D. Blumenthal recorded his experiences of riding the Underground from Baker Street to Moorgate in June 1887. 'I had my first experience of Hades to-day,' he begins, 'and if the real thing is to be like that I shall never again do anything wrong.' He continues, 'The compartment in which I sat was filled with passengers who were smoking pipes . . . and as the smoke and sulphur from the engine fill the tunnel, all the windows have to be closed.' This noisome cocktail of sulphur, coal dust and foul fumes meant that by the time he reached Moorgate, 'I was near dead of asphyxiation and heat.' For some, there is no 'near' about it; the newspapers are full of reports of passengers expiring down in the Underground. If you haven't already, get yourself a scarf from one of the rag stalls by Whitechapel station to breathe through – we don't want you to asphyxiate. If you do feel queasy – or worse – when you emerge into daylight head to Gower Street in the West End and seek out the chemist who sells 'Metropolitan Mixture', a special cough medicine for people gasping for breath after a ride on the Underground.

Trains explode. In 1864 the *Morning Post* reported how at 'Paddington (Bishop's Road) Station' (now just Paddington), as a train was waiting at the 'up' platform, the boiler exploded, blowing off parts of the station's roof. Now, as in the future, the Underground is a prime target for terrorists. At the moment, there is a lingering threat from Irish republicans. Just over a year ago, a bomb went off on the Metropolitan Railway, near Paddington again, injuring seventy-two passengers packed into third-class carriages.

None of which is to say that the Underground is unsuccessful, despite the exploding trains and lethal fumes. It is a phenomenal success. Around 300 million journeys are made each year, more than two-thirds in third class.

One final thing: check your ticket. Is it stamped with an 'O' or an 'I'? Remember, the Circle is shared by two companies; the Metropolitan Railway runs trains clockwise on the outer rail and the District Railway anti-clockwise on the inner rail. In theory, you're meant to be issued with a ticket for the shortest route. But since the two operators are at each other's throats half the time, in practice passengers are sometimes given an 'O' or an 'I' (outer or inner) depending on whether the station is operated by the District or the Metropolitan. And you've just walked into a District station. If it says 'O', fine, you'll be there in a jiffy; if it says 'I', however, you'll be on your merry way for a good fifty minutes – the trains only run at twenty miles per hour (as opposed to sixty on the Metropolitan Line in the twenty-first century).

I just hope you're not asthmatic.

The Canterbury Music Hall

Cross Westminster Bridge and make your way to Westminster Bridge Road, in Lambeth.

You've seen Lambeth before, gazing across its desolate marshlands from a wherry in the deathly London of 1665. Back then, there was the Archbishop of Canterbury's palace Lambeth House, a few houses, and not much else. But over two hundred years later it has gone the same way as Hackney, Holloway and Camberwell, gobbled up by the octopus-metropolis, turned from green to grey, and assumed a new identity as an 'inner-city suburb' – a largely working-class one.

And now here you are on Westminster Bridge Road, amongst terraces of modest houses with bay windows and bricked-off porches, factories coated in grime and tram lines, with the neo-Gothic peaks of the Houses of Parliament visible across the river.

In front of you stands the Canterbury Music Hall, rebranded the Canterbury Theatre of Varieties when it reopened in sumptuous new premises in 1876, but generally known by its old moniker. Named after the Canterbury alehouse that once stood on the site, and was reportedly visited by pilgrims en route to Thomas à Becket's shrine, it's almost 30,000 square feet, spread over four storeys with a stone façade, curved windows and a mansard roof with carved classical figures. A white flag flies and two giant gas lamps blaze over the entrance. Above the second storey, the word 'Canterbury' appears in white capital lettering, and set into the roof are the words 'OPEN EVERY EVENING AT 7.30' in a circular backlight.

Although it's a contentious claim, most people think of the Canterbury, which opened in 1852 on the site of an old skittle alley, as the first of almost 400 venues that have come to embody the Victorian ardour for novelty, variety and performance: the music hall. It has come to define cockney culture like no other institution save perhaps the humble pub, aspects of which it distils, along with the spectacle of the pleasure garden, the audience interaction of the playhouse, the rowdy singalongs of song and supper clubs, the lung damage of Tudor tobacco houses, the conviviality of the old coffeehouses, the variety entertainment of saloon bars and the new gastronomic wonders of Victorian restaurants. You might like to think of music halls as urban circuses, ferments of the most exciting and energetic aspects of metropolitan culture. The music hall phenomenon was facilitated by the liberalization of theatre regulation in 1843, rising wages and shortened working hours, the government's heavy taxation of gin (which indirectly encouraged the expansion of saloon bars) and the entrepreneurial acumen of men with a steely eye for profit.

I hope you're in the mood for a backslapping singalong. It's half past seven. In.

It feels like you've entered a shimmering fantasy world. 'The visitor finds himself in an extensive rocky corridor,' writes the *Observer*, 'with aquaria on either side leading to a series of caverns with ferns growing among the rocks, streamlets, and waterfalls, the whole being illuminated with coloured lights'. The *Sunday Times* thinks it the most picturesque entrance ever contrived, although the calming effect of the circling fish is offset somewhat by the rumbling of Waterloo-bound trains on the viaducts overhead. Beyond the grottoes is a covered arcade with a pair of stone steps leading up to the box office.

Go and collect your refreshment ticket – you'll find it's been thoughtfully pre-ordered for you – and continue on your way through what the *Observer* describes as 'an elegant fernery, covered with a glass roof, where picturesquely drooping ferns in nooks of rock work and rippling streams line the footpath on both sides', with mirrors everywhere, creating an illusion of infinite space. The Canterbury is keen to distinguish itself from the less grandiose, more disreputable music halls of the East End, and it is hoped that these striking displays of *rus in urbe* – transposing the unspoilt natural world into the decadent and artificial city – will appeal to middle-class and even upper-class sensibilities (though, in the case of the latter, this is largely wishful thinking since they don't deign to visit such establishments as this).

Next is a vast lounge which, with its multicoloured counters of onyx (a substitute, albeit a superior one, for marble), purple-upholstered chairs and wall panels of rich amber satin, is likely to strike you as a tad gaudy and ostentatious. Go to the bar and get yourself a stiff drink – the entertainment is best not enjoyed sober. With your refreshment ticket, you can get a range of food options – baked potatoes, oysters, lamb chops, poached eggs, washed down with one free drink of wine, whisky, gin, hot brandy or stout. You can come and go as you please during the performances to buy more; sadly the days of waiter service are gone. But unlike in many of the bigger and smarter music halls, you can regale yourself in the auditorium. For 3d you could buy a fetching pale-blue programme with bright pink text and line drawings of trumpeters, elves, pixies and troupes of dancing women, but it's probably better to be surprised. When you buy your refreshment, the server is likely to say, 'Please remember the waiter.' This means he wants a tip.

Make your way into the auditorium. If a well-dressed woman, pungently perfumed, shoots a look straight at you or deliberately bumps into your legs – she's a prostitute. The management has tried to rid the new premises of the oldest profession but the historical link between theatrical arenas, dark crowded spaces and prostitution endures.

A dreamy satin curtain, amber with a tincture of purple, whispers down to the wooden stage. The whole room is opulent and capacious although it smells like a chimney. In front of you is the pit with rows of seats and space at the front for the orchestra; unlike in the Globe, these seats are relatively expensive, at 1s per person, 3s if you wish to sit in the orchestra section. The cheapest tickets are for the upper balcony, on benches a mere one foot from the floor, at 6d. To put that in perspective, the average daily wage of a building labourer at this point is around 4s, so the cheapest ticket at 6d would be approximately one-eighth of his daily wage, crudely comparable to between £10 and £12.50 in twenty-first-century money; economy tickets are more affordable for building craftsmen, on 6s 3d a day. Above this are the galleries with upholstered wooden armchairs for 5s and private boxes for as much as two guineas (£2 2s).

Vaulted arches circle the room and then, the marvel of Lambeth, an oculus – 'the Canterbury is the only place of entertainment in London where genuine stars can be seen', quipped a newspaper called *Judy* when the Canterbury reopened in 1876, 'because of the sliding roof'.

The galleries are supported by carved palm trees painted in gold with gas lights dangling like illuminated fruit; there are ferns and plaster cherubs and nymphs. There is gilding everywhere: decorating the arches, in the gallery where the chairs are upholstered with another imperial colour – purple – and on the leaves of the two palm trees that flank the proscenium. Patently, the proprietor was not desirous of a subtle look: it is an escapist aesthetic.

Strange to think that this opulent arena, like so many of London's music halls, grew out of a stuffy saloon bar attached to the Canterbury Arms, where the proprietor, a Hackney-born man called Charles Morton, held free and easies (rowdy piano singalongs). He was the first publican to launch a purpose-built music hall, in 1852, where he held supper concerts on Thursday and Saturday nights, which quickly became nightly fixtures. Soon outgrowing its premises, the ever-resourceful Morton built a much bigger hall enclosing the existing one like a Russian doll, which was seamlessly engulfed when he knocked the old walls out in 1854. The building you are in now has been once refurbished and once enlarged and is now under the management of George Villiers.

The lavishness of the setting, gaudy and kitsch though it might seem to you, is slightly at odds with the milieu of the audience – around 2,000 of them and characterized by a London County Council inspector in the 1890s as comprising mainly 'mechanics, primarily tradespeople and their wives, working men, lads and girls'. Unlike in some of the East End music halls, the lowest social stratum are absent and professionals and gentlemen are in very short supply. Still, this is a cut above the Cambridge Music Hall in Shoreditch, the East Ham Palace and certainly the Imperial Theatre in Canning Town.

The orchestra tunes up. Time to take your seat in the hall. If you look up, you'll see that the ceiling is painted to imitate the sky, like an Italian cathedral.

The curtain rises.

A man with a blacked-up face appears in a red-and-white striped suit and proceeds to stand on his head and sing a ridiculous song, the plumes of his moustache pouring into the stage dust. The audience are absolutely delighted by this, hooting and cheering. Before you know it, the topsy-turvy balladeer has disappeared into the wings, replaced by a top-hatted man with a troupe of dancing dogs, who get onto their hind legs and yelp to the crashes of the orchestra's drum, before the stage is invaded by seven cyclists who collectively play around fifty instruments between them in a chaotic cacophony. Eventually they too vanish and the orchestra plays some cheery, spirited music while a stagehand with a blank expression comes on with a ladder to tie a rope between the two palm trees that make up the proscenium. When the music stops, a 'dentalist' – a very particular breed of acrobat with which you will not be familiar – appears. He ascends the ladder facing the audience as the orchestra play low, menacing music.

He leaps from the ladder and catches the rope in his teeth, dangling with a skeleton-like grin. There he hangs for minutes on end, his feet twitching and dancing in mid-air like a prisoner dying at Tyburn, while the orchestra breaks into searing violin crescendos. Eventually, the acrobat jumps down, at which point the orchestra screeches to a halt and the audience give a round of applause. He takes a bow, and spirits himself away (a carriage is waiting for him outside – he has to perform this another six times tonight in music halls dotted all over London). Next up is Victorina Troupe, a remarkable woman who will swallow a sword fired from a rifle.

You're beginning to get a sense of how sacrosanct *variety* is to music hall. Over the next three hours you can expect to see a potpourri of entertainment: twelve, possibly as many as twenty acts. You might see ventriloquists, 'dancing Quakers', memory men, dioramas in which famous battle scenes are reconstructed with painted scenery, models and taxidermy, ballet acts, on one occasion 'Felix the talking duck', frog imitators and sorcerers.

Acrobats are always well received, sometimes flying (sans safety net) from rope to rope above the heads of the audience as they dine. The French acrobat Charles Blondin triggered something of a tightrope mania after he crossed the Niagara Falls seventeen times in the 1850s and 60s replete with mid-crossing somersaults, a blindfold, a man on his back and, on one occasion, on stilts. He appeared in the Canterbury in 1861, crossing between the balconies to your left and right; at the Moorish Alhambra music hall in Leicester Square, one of the finest, you could pay £5 to be carried on his back. But this was nothing compared to what he did in Liverpool, pushing a lion cub in a barrow across a tightrope. At Crystal Palace in the same year, he delighted audiences (but not Charles Dickens) by lugging a stove onto the tightrope and cooking an omelette in mid-air while playing the violin, giving whole new meaning to the term *haute cuisine*. But it wasn't his first choice of act. He'd wanted to repeat his earlier performance, pushing his own five-year-old daughter in a wheelbarrow across a tightrope as she scattered rose petals on the crowds below but the Home

Secretary, fearing she might come to resemble something of an omelette herself should she fall 180 feet to the concrete floor, intervened and ordered him to revise his performance.

'Nigger' or 'burned-cork' minstrels are popular with the audience, whose belief in the racial inferiority of black people is yet to be corrected. These are highly popular acts imported from America, with over 150 such performers by the 1870s. They consist of blacked-up white performers playing 'tambos' (naïve young women), zip coons (impecunious dandies) and straight-talking 'interlocutors', all perpetrating appalling racial stereotypes with such subtle lines as: 'I is a bad nigger. I allus carries a razor an' a gun.'

The relentless pace of technological change is one of the defining features of the Victorian era and music hall shines a spotlight on this. Eight years ago, audiences were intrigued to hear muffled tunes radiating from a mysterious drum-like apparatus dangling from the proscenium. This was a demonstration of an early telephone system called the Cromwell Varley, the Canterbury having been connected to the Queen's Theatre in Long Acre via an overhead wire. London's first street to be lit by electricity – the aptly named Electric Avenue in Brixton – is just a couple of years around the corner, and electrical conjurors like the Wizard of the North abound. Many unsuspecting volunteers shriek in horror as bolts of electricity flash between them, and audience members crane their necks in wonder as performers set fire to handkerchiefs by conducting static electricity through their fingertips.

Magnetism is, of course, excellent music hall fare. The French illusionist Jean-Eugène Robert-Houdin toured Britain in 1848 with a fun trick whereby he'd place a magnetized box weighing only a few pounds onto a fixed metal plate and then invite burly members of the audience to pick it up – which they couldn't. After demagnetizing it, he'd emasculate them by picking it up with his little finger. A man called Erich Weiss was so inspired by this performer that he changed his name to Houdini and made his debut in 1900, with the first of many dramatic life-or-death feats of escapology that have passed into legend.

Time now for some songs. As much as audiences love the eccentric and exotic variety acts it is *music* that really fires them up, casting their inhibitions aside, uniting them in carousal. Like David Bowie when he appeared as Ziggy Stardust and the Thin White Duke in the 1970s, music hall performers as a rule appear in the guise of the character they're singing about, or the narrator of the song, so these are inherently theatrical renditions. The audience are in high spirits but generally well behaved; music halls in the 1880s are a far cry from their forerunners, the song and supper clubs of the 1830s and 40s, in which waiters had to chain bottles to their trays to prevent the chop-munching bohemians from hurling them at hapless performers on stage.

Perhaps you have a cursory knowledge of music hall and are looking forward to cracking into some classic numbers that can still raise the odd goose pimple in the digital age; to boom out 'Daisy, Daisy, give me your answer do . . .', to observe the melancholic major-to-minor key shift between the first and second 'Let's all go down the Strand!' (followed by the lazy 'have a banana'), to trot out the staccato 'He's the man who broke the bank at Monte Carlo'. If so, you are going to be disappointed. None of those songs have been written yet; some are decades off – 'Let's All Go Down the Strand' won't be performed until 1909, long after the heyday of the music hall. The only 'famous' ones to have been written are 'Champagne Charlie' (1866) and 'The Boy I Love is up in the Gallery', which

Marie Lloyd pilfered from Nelly Power in 1885. But though their form might be unfamiliar, the essence of the songs is not.

A dandily dressed man struts onto the stage in black-and-white striped trousers, a gauche bright-yellow jacket and fancy slippers. He wears a necktie and has a cane, which he's very proud of, tapping it against a bottle of champagne. These are all tell-tale signs that here is a *lion comique*, a caricature of a swell (or toff, as we'd say), essentially a harmless twit. Think of him as a forerunner to Harry Enfield's Tim Nice-But-Dim character if you like. He begins:

> I'm sure I can't think what the world's coming to,
> The times are so wretchedly slow,
> 'tis hard to make out what a fel-ah should do,
> Or yet where a fel-lah should go.
> I've buzzled by bwain and I've scratched at my wig,
> Till I've almost torn out every hair,
> But I cannot produce an idea worth a fig,
> It's wea-ly a dweadful affair.

By singing their hearts out, the *lions comiques* allow the working and lower-middle classes to share in an idle and indulgent life they will never know, a short, sweet taste of the exotic. But the popularity of most music hall songs stems from the way they hold up a mirror to the audience's lives. Music hall is all the toil, heartbreak, humour and misery of their own lives writ large, framed in a proscenium, and illuminated in a blaze of gas. Sometimes, mind, there is just urban ennui. Jenny Hill, the daughter of a Marylebone cab minder, thrived on playing waifs and strays, suffusing her performances with a nobility quite at odds with the lowly social station of her characters. In the song 'City Waif' (1889) she sings:

And what does this big, cold world care
For a poor little chap like me.
Out of my bed in a doorway,
Bobbies all hunt me down,
And no home have I beneath the sky
But the streets of London town.

In a couple of years, Charles Booth will estimate that one-third of all Londoners are living in or on the cusp of poverty; many of the people in the audience tonight could easily find themselves in the City Waif's unenviable situation.

Since music hall is such a popular medium – quite possibly the most inclusive form of theatre ever seen in London, with fourteen million tickets sold each year by the 1890s – you might wonder why it's not more radical and risqué. They are certainly a far cry from the kind of songs that were belted out at song and supper clubs like Evans's Late Joys in King Street and the Cyder Cellars in Maiden Lane during the 1840s, with their relentless focus on 'grinding' women and 'cracking their notches' (suggesting that Covent Garden had lost none of its libido). It's true that proprietors, especially in the more respectable halls like the Canterbury, are aiming to provide family friendly entertainment (suitable for women), and to stay on the right side of the licensing authorities. But don't discount the possibility that some of these songs *are* in fact cunningly risqué. They may sound saccharine to you, but have a good look at your fellow audience members and you'll see that some of them are extracting an altogether different meaning. Take the Vesta Victoria song 'Our Lodger's Such a Nice Young Man', which on the surface sounds innocent enough until you reconsider lines like 'He kisses mama and all of us, cos Papa was away' and 'at night he makes the beds and does the other little jobs'. A consummate performer like Vesta Victoria or Marie

Lloyd could speak volumes merely by raising an eyebrow or pursing her lips.

Politically, though, there's no doubt about it: unlike broad-side ballads and aspects of the pauper press, the songs are generally unwaveringly conservative and patriotic, even though this is not always in tune with the more radical and liberal lean-ings of parts of the audience. Though social ills and one's place at the bottom of the pile are often a source of lament, songs are *rueful* not *radical*. They're accepting of the status quo and find reasons to be cheerful not in Marxism or Chartism but in a mythical, rose-tinted past. 'My brother's in the gas trade too, you know,' Little Titch, one of music hall's biggest stars, once said, 'in fact he travels on gas. He's a socialist orator.' Music halls, which are becoming increasingly commodified at this time, are owned and run by capitalist bourgeois who are hardly likely to encourage left-wing songs. And the government – the ultimate regulatory force, who could in theory wipe the the-atres off the map – has seen purpose-built music halls as a threat ever since their incarnation in 1852, only four years after a wave of revolutionary fervour swept through Europe. The Establishment is keen to purge the music halls of any kind of critical engagement with politics, and encourage the entertain-ment as a kind of political anaesthetic, bursts of jingoism aside. They want to mollify the music halls.

One of the most famous music hall tunes is Charles Mac-Dermott's 'We Don't Want to Fight (but by jingo if we do . . .)', written to sweeten British public opinion towards fighting Rus-sia in the Russo-Turkish War of 1887–8. Audiences took to it with gusto, shouting the lyrics out in the street; the govern-ment even sent recruiting officers into the halls to sign up the most passionate nationalists. But there was also the highly popular 'I Don't Want to Fight, I'll be Slaughtered if I Do', which trod a very different path, lamenting how soldiers are just pawns in politicians' and generals' games, and blaming Fleet Street for drumming up anti-Russian sentiment. But even this was not wholly unsatisfactory to the government since it channelled critical and potentially rebellious impulses into the drunken haze of a harmless half hour.

Scraps of grainy, black-and-white footage of fin-de-siècle Victorian music halls have survived into the twenty-first century, though they are frequently of dismal quality. Eleven years from now, in a darkened room in Paris, audiences will be gripped with panic and filled with wonder at the sight of a steam locomotive zooming directly towards them in a fifty-second film by the Lumière brothers. (The cinematograph had made its debut the year before but still, some spectators allegedly ran to the back of the room to avoid being flattened by the train). Many music halls such as the Empire in Leicester Square incorporated films into their repertoire of variety from the 1890s onwards, but ultimately moving images brought about the slow death of the music hall, first in the form of cinema then television.

As you leave the hall, you see the *lion comique* who performed 'It's wea-ly a dweadful affair' clambering into his brougham, swigging from another bottle of champagne. He is driven off nto the night, alone. Artistes are hugely in demand; some are handsomely paid. But so often their fame masks an inner loneliness, the bottle their boon companion. George Leybourne, who sang 'Champagne Charlie', was encouraged to stay in character offstage. His manager arranged for him to be driven through town each day in a brougham, dressed as a tawdry swell and guzzling champagne provided free by the vintners. Once the star performer at the Canterbury, as work dried up later on in his life, he sant into depression and died aged forty-four, of alcohol poisoning, penniless.

Even Marie Lloyd, perhaps the most famous artiste of her

day, 'tasty, trippy, twiggy, timely, telling, tender, tempting, toothsome, transcendent, trim, tactical, twinkling, tricksy, triumphal and tantalizing', who burst onto the scene at the Eagle in 1885 and dominated it for the next thirty-two years, sometimes darting between four music halls a night – she too ended her days in heavy drink, her infectious smile and onstage exuberance hiding years of domestic woe (she suffered abuse from more than one husband). Before Lloyd's death, Virginia Woolf described her as 'scarcely able to walk, waddling, aged, unblushing'. At least 50,000 people attended her funeral and T. S. Eliot would say that 'no other comedian succeeded so well in giving expression to the life of an audience'. She was fifty-two.

Our time here, too, has ended. Make your way to Westminster Bridge, and have one last look at the Victorian megalopolis splayed out before you, blazing in the misty night. It will be another seventy-three years before you see it again. And when you do, much of it will lie in ruins.

Epilogue: echoes of Victorian London

So much of Victorian London is solidly present in the cityscape we see today, though of Holywell Street and Wych Street there is no trace. They were wiped off the map at the beginning of the twentieth century to make way for the building of Aldwych, a one-way street that runs up what is thought to be the eastern border of the Anglo-Saxon settlement of *Lundenwic*. The golden crescent moon that hung for several centuries outside number 37 Wych Street is now in the Museum of London.

In the East End, the drab building where Joseph Merrick was exhibited still stands on Whitechapel Road, renumbered 259, almost directly opposite the Royal London Hospital, behind a granite drinking fountain. Today, it is the UKAY international Saree Centre, testament to the continued multiculturalism of Whitechapel, now home to many Bangladeshi families.

According to one of Frederick Treves's medical students, Merrick used to speculate on how he would look after his death, embalmed in a giant bottle. We can't answer his question since his bones are no longer on public display (nor was his head ever pickled). They are currently housed in the private pathology collection at Barts and the London School of Medicine and Dentistry, Queen Mary, University of London. But there *is* a replica skeleton on display at the Royal London Museum, located in the former crypt of St Philip's Church behind the old hospital on Newark Street, along with some photos and an elaborate model of a church Merrick made while living at the hospital. In his memoirs, Sir Frederick Treves recalls Merrick's disguise, 'a giant cap, black like the cloak, with a wide peak . . . from the attachment [of which], a grey flannel curtain hung in front of the face. In this mask was cut a wide horizontal slit through which the wearer could look out'. This disguise is in the museum too and helps the visitor imagine the Elephant Man shuffling through the streets of Whitechapel trying not to be noticed. The museum is open Tuesdays to Fridays.

Around 630 elementary schools were built by the School Board for London between 1870 and 1904 and latterly by the London County Council. Many have a distinctive Queen Anne-style aesthetic and they can be found dotted around the twelve Inner London boroughs as well as Wandsworth and Lewisham. The Victorian Schools in London (VSIL) website has a comprehensive illustrated database of schools in South-wark, Lewisham and Greenwich. Many others are mentioned in the Survey of London (accessible via British History Online) and in the volumes of Nikolaus Pevsner's *Buildings of England* that explore the capital.

By the time of his death in 1905, Dr Barnardo's institutions cared for over 8,500 children in almost a hundred different locations – he personally having supervised the welfare and training of 60,000 boys and girls in the course of his life. According to fellow philanthropist Charles Booth, not one for histrionics, Barnardo had created 'beyond question, the greatest charitable institution in London, or, I suppose in the world'. It remains the UK's leading children's charity.

Whitechapel Underground station is, of course, still there; peculiarly, the Overground actually dives beneath the Underground at that station. The Metropolitan and District Lines are still going strong, marked in maroon and green on Harry Beck's iconic map. The Circle Line, though, isn't a complete circle any more, meaning it's harder to die on it inconspicuously than in the good old days. The best way to bring the history of the Victorian Underground to life is to visit the London Transport Museum in Covent Garden, where you'll find locomotives that used to run on the Metropolitan Railway and a wooden carriage built in 1900. There is also a green horse-bus from around 1875, designed to carry up to twenty-six passengers, owned and run by Thomas Tilling.

Towards the docklands, at Tobacco Dock, there is a bronze statue of Mr Jamrach's tiger raising his paw to the boy he nearly had for his lunch very near the site of Jamrach's pet shop. Tobacco Dock is a vast warehouse, built in 1811 to store tobacco and wine. In spite of a multimillion-pound renovation in the 1990s and quixotic visions to bring into existence the 'Covent Garden of the East', the Grade I listed warehouse, although a conference venue and events space, lies empty most of the time and there is something morose and deadening about the whole Docklands district.

In Lambeth, nothing remains of the Canterbury Music Hall. By 1914 the venue had incorporated film into its variety programme and in the 1920s, it became a cinema. The German bombing campaign of 1942 left it a shell and it was finally demolished in 1955. The British Library Sound Archive has fascinating recordings of some music hall artistes performing at the beginning of the twentieth century, including Marie Lloyd.

Wilton's Music Hall by Cable Street in Shadwell is a surviving example of a classic mid-Victorian music hall. Originally a pub with a concert saloon, it emerged as a bona fide music hall in 1859 and flourished until a Methodist takeover in 1888. It was threatened with destruction in the 1960s but saved after a high-profile campaign and is now back in use as a pub, theatre and concert hall.

One final thing. There is a project afoot to narrate and score all eleven volumes of *My Secret Life*, the mammoth, anonymously written erotic memoir. Volume One is available at: mysecretlife.org replete with soft-focus slideshows of Victorian pornography. Enjoy.

1957
London Rising:
A Tour of the Blitzed City

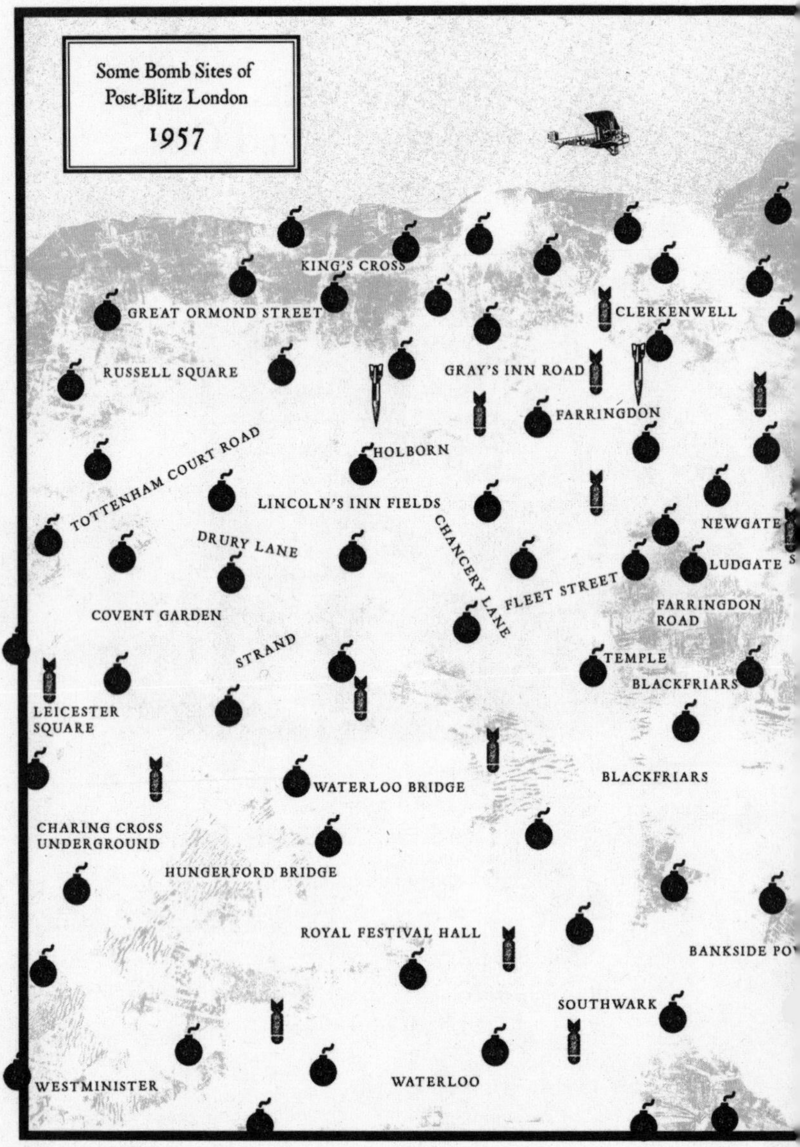

Some Bomb Sites of
Post-Blitz London
1957

KING'S CROSS

GREAT ORMOND STREET

CLERKENWELL

RUSSELL SQUARE

GRAY'S INN ROAD

FARRINGDON

TOTTENHAM COURT ROAD

HOLBORN

LINCOLN'S INN FIELDS

NEWGATE

DRURY LANE

CHANCERY LANE

LUDGATE S

COVENT GARDEN

FLEET STREET

FARRINGDON
ROAD

STRAND

TEMPLE

BLACKFRIARS

LEICESTER
SQUARE

BLACKFRIARS

CHARING CROSS
UNDERGROUND

WATERLOO BRIDGE

HUNGERFORD BRIDGE

ROYAL FESTIVAL HALL

BANKSIDE PO

SOUTHWARK

WESTMINSTER

WATERLOO

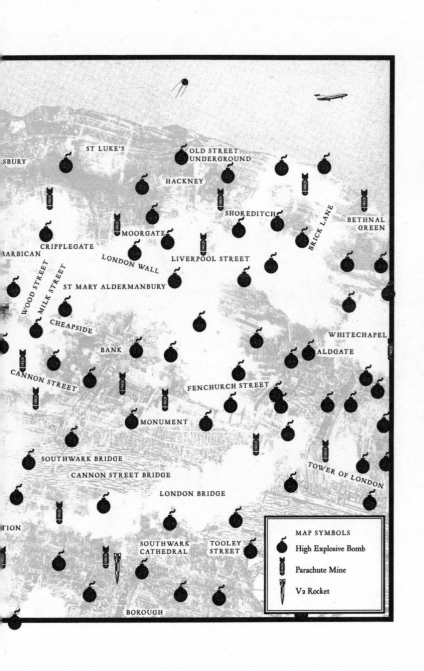

If you take a walk from Cheapside to London Wall via Wood Street, Milk Street or Gutter Lane, you can't fail to notice a conspicuous lack of historic buildings. There are exceptions, of course – the much-rebuilt medieval Guildhall on Gresham Street and the lone St Alban's Tower, formerly part of a rare Gothic Wren church near Love Lane – but these are mere flotsam in a sea of concrete, steel and glass.

At the east end of Love Lane, where, in creaky chambers, medieval prostitutes plied their trade, you'll find St Mary Aldermanbury Garden. It's a rare tranquil spot, a few feet below street level, between the City of London Police Headquarters, tasteful and unthreatening in silvery Portland stone, and a green glass fountain erected in 1969. Two trees burst through the grass like sprawling crucifixes.

Up a few concrete steps you find a knot garden with honeycombed chambers and a pyramid-shaped hedge in the centre, a delightful and unexpected echo of Tudor London. Beyond that is a memorial garden to parish denizens John Heminges and Henry Condell, the actors who preserved many of Shakespeare's plays for posterity by compiling the first folio. Naturally, there's also a bust of the Bard whom they helped to make famous.

Sit down on the stone wall and enjoy the contemplative atmosphere. Aside from the occasional whinny of one of the horses stabled in the police headquarters behind you, there is hardly any sound.

Suddenly a screeching siren destroys the calm. You swivel around but there is no police headquarters – only a bombsite.

You find yourself on what's left of Love Lane, a little before its junction with Aldermanbury running south. The nondescript office blocks have been replaced by a large car park brimming with colourful vehicles: two-door Ford Populars with their distinctive bullnose bonnets and raised headlights; simple, tractor-like Austin Sevens; and Morris Minors, cramped but pleasingly curvaceous. You may see some flasher cars too: Humbers, Wolseleys and Triumphs, some decked out in bright two-tone colours or with open tops; it is a sunny summer's day.

A church now stands where the garden was; though 'stands' is perhaps not quite the right word since only the walls are in place. At first, you think it's in the process of being built but on closer inspection you see it has been utterly disembowelled. There is no roof to the nave and the whole thing looks as if it might topple over at any moment. Behind the church-shell, a cluster of beige and grey office blocks have survived. But much of everything else is a wasteland, sad and unending.

Imagine you were a time traveller with no knowledge of twentieth-century European history. Given the advancements you have seen in medicine, technology, education and politics over the centuries, it wouldn't be unreasonable to expect that, the further forwards you go, the more refined and civilized societies would become. If so, then the scars of London from the Second World War will stop your naïve optimism dead in its tracks. If you were to take a walk through the East End or Bermondsey – or indeed, here – you would see buildings wrecked, streets churned up and huge craters gouged into the earth by parachuting missiles, incendiary bombs and pernicious, pilotless V-1 and V-2 rockets. 'There are shades of barbarism in twentieth-century Europe,' writes the historian

Norman Davies, 'which would once have amazed the most barbarous of barbarians'.

True, the city was not, in the end, bombed to oblivion like Hamburg and Dresden; in fact, most of the iconic sights of London – the Tower, the Houses of Parliament, Southwark Cathedral and so on – survived. According to official figures, almost 30,000 civilians were killed in London by bombs and rockets between 1940 and 1945 (in contrast to over 40,000 fatalities in a single week in 1943 during the Allied bombing of Hamburg). But people at the time fully expected it to be obliterated. 'London will be one vast raving bedlam,' predicted the military strategist and yoga expert Major General J. F. C. Fuller; 'the hospitals will be stormed, traffic will cease, the homeless will shriek for help, the city will be a pandemonium' one that would meekly capitulate to Hitler after the government had been 'swept away by an avalanche of terror'. The anxious government made provision for millions of cardboard coffins and quicklime for expeditious burials, as though they were expecting another Great Plague to descend; one official report calculated that over half a million people would be killed in London in the first six months of a bombing campaign. All this took its toll. Just look into the hardened faces of those you walk past. Many of those with grey hair and lined faces have lived through two wars – and the Pathé newsreels warn them another might be on its way, against a nuclear-armed USSR, that could make the Blitz look like a children's picnic. As for the young – anyone under twenty-five – a grey and bomb-ravaged city is all they've ever known, though things seem to be improving a little of late. Nonetheless, these are deeply uncertain times, where the physical existence of the city is not something to be taken for granted.

But it's only when you walk through the area between Cheapside and the Barbican (which took its name from an old

Roman fortress) and witness a scene of pure destruction that the Blitz sheds its abstract form in your mind and becomes a harrowing reality, even a dozen years after the final rockets fell on London.

Make your way to Gresham Street, near the bomb-damaged Guildhall.

'You could actually feel your eyeballs being sucked out'

You might well have seen the photos of the smoke-swirled dome of St Paul's Cathedral soaring unscathed above a smouldering wasteland below, a majestic totem of the resilience of London and Londoners in one of their darkest hours. But that night, 29 December 1940, a thirty-five-acre area to the south of the Barbican was turned into a blitzed wasteland by incendiary bombs in what is sometimes described as the Second Great Fire of London. Every street from Moorgate to Aldersgate Street (due north of St Martin's Le Grand, which we visited in medieval London) was practically destroyed. By 1945 the destruction reached as far as Gresham Street, and you could walk for minutes on end without seeing a single erect structure. Twelve years on, while bold and imaginative plans for the regeneration of these areas are being concocted and considered by the London County Council, the area still lies mainly in ruins.

The travel writer H. V. Morton paints a grim and elegiac picture of the district in his *In Search of London*, published in 1951. Looking towards Moorgate from Milk Street, he laments a landscape of sunlit cellars, rubble and weeds. 'Here and there the side of a building rises gauntly from the rubble, a detached gateway stands by itself in the undergrowth, the towers of a few churches, or a spire, lift themselves mournfully, like tomb-stones in a forgotten cemetery.' Brick walls enclose the ruins. Had not the Corporation of London put up signs commemorating fallen buildings and streets, the area's medieval topography would already be fading from memory. 'There is a savagery, a fury and a hideous wickedness about the ruins of London – and of Berlin also – that chills the heart,' wrote Morton. The church of St Giles-without-Cripplegate is 'a ghastly ruin'; the halls of the haberdashers, wax chandlers, coachmakers and bar-ber surgeons, no more. A familiar landscape, one that endured over centuries, has been rendered unrecognizable. He asks a postman who happens to be passing, 'Do you ever get letters addressed to *this*?' pointing at the ruins. 'Every blinkin' day', the postman replies, 'and from all parts of the world.'

Along the bombed part of Gresham Street some new build-ings are very slowly replacing the wrecks, but beyond that there has been very little progress at rebuilding, and the site appears to you as a series of walled-off ruins, as it had to Morton.

As you continue this mournful walk, try to imagine the hor-ror. Entire streets going up in flames; houses collapsing burying their occupants alive; rubble spilling out onto the streets. People cowering in corrugated-iron Anderson shelters in their back yards; the rapping of the ack-ack units trying to shoot down German planes in the dead of night. Small houses with their fronts ripped off like cans of sardines; staircases leading to floors that no longer exist while families drink their morning cups of tea with the walls blown away. People pulling rings from dead bodies while 'blitz-trippers' gawk at the damage. Giant chomp-marks on the edges of buildings as though Godzilla had gone on a rampage.

But amidst the mayhem, some lighter moments. Hitler and Mussolini's effigies undamaged when a bomb ripped through Madame Tussaud's in Baker Street. The command that flashed up on cinema screens in the middle of air raids: 'Walk, not run, to the exits. Do not panic. Remember, you are British'. 'Open as usual, close shaves a speciality' in the window of a barber's shop in Shepperton which had narrowly missed being flattened like its neighbour. The swimming baths at the Ladies Carlton Club in Pall Mall turned into a giant pigsty.

The London *Blitzkrieg* began in earnest on 7 September 1940 – Black Saturday – targeting Woolwich Arsenal, the docks and the East End. 'Blitzkrieg has come to London in all its fury and brutality and filth,' reported the *Evening Standard*, adding that 'the dogs of war are off the leash, and they roam in search of indiscriminate plunder'. It would last for 57 consecutive nights. Len Jones was an eighteen-year-old living in King Street, Poplar, one of the worst-hit areas. He recalls the impact of the blasts, for which he was entirely unprepared. 'You could actually feel your eyeballs being sucked out,' he writes of the turbulence following nearby explosion. 'I was holding my eyes to try and stop them going.' Later, he saw two heads protruding from a mound of rubble that had, until very recently, been his father's workshop; 'I recognized one head in particular; it was a Chinese man, Mr Say, he had one eye closed.' Quivering like a jelly, he tried to burn his own finger with a match to check that he wasn't a ghost. That day 430 East Enders perished and 1,600 were seriously wounded in a scene of carnage that saw corpses lying in the roads, pepper-, rum- and rubber-scented plumes of smoke poisoning the atmosphere, and hordes of rats scurrying from burning warehouses.

Though parts of south London were decimated, in the early days – and in the latter, terrible V-2 stages too – it was the densely populated, slum-infested East End – 'the squalid, miserable, dirty, magnificent East End', as the journalist Walter Boon puts it, 'a land of docks, and warehouses and factories, of canals and railway tracks and gas works', that was the hardest hit. 'Finally we can look the East End in the face,' the queen was reported to have said after Buckingham Palace was bombed.

Boon, who was driven by a compulsive desire to reach for his typewriter and record his experiences of blitzed London, transcribed a conversation between regulars in a draughty East End pub, in which all the windows had been blown out, in his *Hell Came to London* (1941).

Lamenting the bloodshed but demonstrating stoicism too, it begins, 'A man bangs his mug down on the scarred oaken bar. "Wot Hi s'ys lads, if Hi 'ad my 'ands on this 'ere bleedin' 'Itler Hi'd tear 'im limb from limb." Another answers, "We'll git the barstard, never you worry, myte." And there is a chorus, "Yes – we'll get 'im ... 'E'll wish 'e'd never been born, 'e will" ... "Thinks 'e'll get us darn, 'e does, killin' our women and children. 'E's got another think comin'!"' After this, the six o'clock news begins to filter in from the wireless 'like a voice from another world'.

If you question people in the street about how effectively the authorities coped with the Blitz, the chances are they will not get a particularly good press; Londoners had to seize the initiative for themselves, storming the Underground for shelter when this had been specifically prohibited (in case Londoners turned into troglodytes). The mere mention of some local authorities will make people roll their eyes or hang their heads in shame. In the first week of the Blitz, West Ham Council instructed several hundred people – including many mothers and children whose homes had been destroyed – to take cover in the basement of South Hallsville Road School in Canning Town, despite the fact it had no air-raid shelter. They would send buses to evacuate them from there. But the buses were misdirected to Camden Town, and when they eventually arrived in Canning Town they found that the school had been turned into a mountain of rubble by a parachute bomb that left a twenty-feet-deep crater; the main school building had collapsed into the basement. Virtually everyone inside was killed – Seventy-seven the government said, though to many eyewitnesses this smacked of face-saving Ministry of Information propaganda (we will be visiting the site of this mendacious ministry later). To add insult to injury, the site had in fact been flagged as high-risk on account of its location near factories.

Other councils, chief amongst them Stepney, one of the most devastated areas, proved exasperatingly reluctant to rehouse displaced families even though they had the power to requisition empty properties; two months into the bombing, the borough still had no billeting or rehousing department. Not even perpetual bombing could overcome the inviolable sanctity of private property, it seemed. Other local authorities fared better: Lambeth and Bermondsey nurtured little nascent welfare states within their boundaries, though these were castigated by other authorities – Labour- and Tory-dominated alike – as sinister communist initiatives.

Many of the overgrown craters you see weren't made on impact but were caused by large steel-coated naval mines carefully parachuted from German planes, that fell slowly and silently to meet their targets. These had the power to propel a man a quarter of a mile and fling buses and railway carriages into the air like children's toys. They didn't always explode at once. Sometimes they insinuated themselves into existing bomb craters or basements and lay unnoticed; on other occasions they were time-delayed, a lurking menace ready to blow buildings sky high. Had such a bomb that embedded itself thirty feet into the pavement of Dean's Yard, perilously close to the south-west tower of St Paul's Cathedral, not been masterfully dug up and defused by the Royal Engineers over the course of three days in September 1940, it may well have obliterated Wren's masterpiece, which could have had an appalling impact on morale. When it *was* eventually detonated, far out in Hackney Marshes, it left a crater a hundred feet wide. One John Lindsay Thomas was munching sandwiches on a sunny bench in the churchyard on his lunch hour: 'I suddenly noticed an approaching figure in the shape of a London "bobby",' he recalls.

'"What are you doing here, sir?" he said. "Didn't you see the barrier tapes?"

'"Yes," I admitted, "but nothing seemed to be happening and so I thought it was just some kind of leftover."

'"Well," he said, "you could call it that. Actually it's a 2,000-pound unexploded bomb and you are almost sitting on top of it. If it goes up, it'll take most of the Cathedral with it – as well as you!"

'Needless to say,' he concludes, 'I thanked him roundly, apologized, and left.' Very British.

Clearing mines could be a terrifying experience, and soldiers would draw lots to see who would go into the bomb hole first. 'The most found of anybody was a piece of leg in a Wellington boot,' writes Bert Woolhouse, a Royal Engineer responsible for clearing mines, of one attempt that went disastrously wrong; for his part, he was thrown many yards, covered in rubble and conked on the head by a falling chimney.

While this area was being turned into a wasteland over the Christmas of 1940, Londoners scampered for cover in the nearby Underground stations: St Paul's, Moorgate, Bank and Liverpool Street. Picture the scene. The platforms are strewn with sleeping figures like rushes on a Tudor floor. People have slung hammocks over the rails and are trying to get a good night's sleep (the rails are unelectrified after 10.30 p.m., though late risers are in for a nasty shock). People using the tunnels as toilets. Swarms of mosquitoes feeding on sweaty bodies. The cries of newborn infants ricocheting off the walls.

But there was a community spirit too: huddling together, singing songs and drinking tea. It was a lot worse for the West Indians, Jews, prostitutes and other 'outsiders' who were assigned the Tilbury Shelter in Stepney, where they had to sleep in foul parts of a massive undergrounds goods yard amidst mouldy margarine and trodden excrement. A witness from the Mass Observation Society likened this sleeping arrangement to the Black Hole of Calcutta.

Simmering class antagonisms between east and west London sometimes rose to the surface: on one occasion, a hundred East Enders marched to the Savoy Hotel, demanding to use its luxury underground shelter; luckily for the hotel, the all-clear sounded shortly afterwards.

Stand on tiptoes and look over the walls into the bombsites – they're not very high, and you might even see the odd street urchin scramble over to scavenge for valuables in the bombed-out houses. Here and there the odd remnant of a wall stands, forlorn, but most of the rubble has been removed. Look closely and you might be able to make out some flashes of pink in the vegetation. This is the rosebay willowherb, a tall plant with pink flowers which, as a pioneering species, is often the first to colonize burned, barren areas like the sites of forest fires, flowering and spreading its seed rapidly. During the summers of 1941 and 1944, Londoners marvelled at how quickly this plant bloomed on bombsites, coating the devastation in a layer of misty pink, healing – as some interpreted it – the gaping wounds of the city. If cities are manifestations of man's dominion over nature then the sight of grass, flowers and weeds returning to the heart of the metropolis suggests that that victory was only temporary in the first place.

Sometimes the city embraces this reversal – if you walk back to Gresham Street, opposite the Goldsmiths' Hall, you'll find a sunken garden, laid out by fire-watchers in 1941 on a bomb-site where the Church of St John Zachary stood before the Great Fire.

Heartless missiles

Some of the biggest craters you see were made not by parachute mines or incendiary bombs but by a new weapon: doodlebugs.

By mid- June 1944 London had not been bombed for three years, and the tide seemed to be turning against Hitler in Europe after the successful D-Day landings on 6 June. Londoners were quietly confident. But a final, horrifying double-whammy of terror was to come. These were the *Vergeltungswaffen*, vengeance weapons, launched in response to Allied bombings and incursions but with targets of minimal military significance, though hugely demoralizing to the people of London.

Launched from across the Channel, the V-1 was a pilotless plane – or drone, as we now might say – carrying high explosives whose engine was timed to cut out after a certain period, at which point it would go into a steep dive and explode on impact. By the end of the month around a hundred of these were raining down on London each day; over 2,000 would fall in total. You might be making the bed, taking your children to school, huddling around the wireless, doing the grocery shopping then ... a far-off hum and a penetrating, ever-louder rattle. At which point, you'd hope against hope that the noise would continue and recede into the distance. If it didn't – if it suddenly stopped – the engine had cut out and you were about to be blown up. Numb with terror, you'd dive for cover and hope for the best. By the end of the summer almost 5,000 people had been killed by V-1s. These indiscriminating missiles seemed to have a propensity for blowing up sick people and babies in hospitals – over a hundred hospitals were hit. What a chilling sight, living in the suburbs, to see a V-1 flying overhead to make its kill in central London.

Still, at least you *could* see them, and they could be shot down by ack-ack fire or otherwise disrupted. The same could not be said for their successors, the V-2 rockets, which carried one ton of high explosive and travelled at speeds of up to 2,000 mph, rendering them invisible, swooping down from altitudes of sixty miles. Defence was impossible. Londoners were sitting ducks. Goebbels waxed lyrical about the new missiles 'screaming down onto London'. Although the details were desperately censored at first by the Ministry of Information, people soon realized they were facing an even deadlier threat when entire suburban streets were disembowelled, taking on the appearance of wastelands. The first you knew of it was a double bang, a blood-coloured flash and a mountainous halo of jet-black smoke rising into the sky.

On 25 November 1944 a V-2 screamed down upon a Woolworth's in New Cross thronged with Saturday shoppers; 160 died. A thirteen-year-old eyewitness was forever haunted by 'a blind[ing] flash of light, and a roaring, rushing sound . . . and a little baby's hand still in its woolly sleeve in a twisted and bent pram'. Where the Woolworth's had been, 'there was just an enormous gap covered by a cloud of dust'.

Just over 500 V-2s dived into London, killing around 2,500. V-2s could leave craters up to fifty feet wide and ten feet deep, making parts of the East End, south-east London and Deptford look like the surface of the moon. Overall, the V-1 and V-2 doodlebugs damaged almost 1.25 million London houses – nearly half the capital's entire housing stock – around

116,000 irreparably and almost 288,000 seriously. This would be the bedrock for the great housing experiments of the 1950s and 1960s, perhaps the most impressive of which, the brutalist Barbican, would rise from these very ashes.

It all began in a street in Bloomsbury, our next stop. You've ridden the Victorian Underground and made it out in one piece. So the 1950s successor will be an absolute doddle; Harry Beck's iconic Tube map, familiar to twenty-first-century eyes, is now available in the stations. Walk to Aldersgate Street, named after the original Roman gate to the City, and find the Underground station there. You want to take the Metropolitan Line westbound (no one says 'up' or 'down' any more), change at King's Cross, then take the Piccadilly Line south to Russell Square.

The dream of the high-rise

When you emerge from Russell Square station, turn right and make your way past streets of dilapidated terraces, past Brunswick Square Gardens and on to Guilford Street, with Coram's Fields on your left. They are named after the Foundling Hospital opened by the philanthropic mariner Thomas Coram here, in 1745, amidst green fields and clean air – he had been appalled by the sight of abandoned infants starving in the city streets and dying on dunghills. After the hospital moved to Berkhamsted, the site became London's first public children's playground a decade later.

Turn right onto Lamb's Conduit Street. If you're imagining flocks of lambs on their way to the slaughterhouses of Smithfield, oblivious to their fate, I have to tell you that the street is in fact named after the philanthropic William Lambe, who, in 1577, put up an enormous sum of money to rebuild the Holborn Conduit, siphoning off water from the River Fleet. As you can see from some of the patched-up houses, it suffered a little in the war but remains, in essence, a leisurely, even peaceful Georgian Street, lined with bars and boutiques on the lower levels of reasonably smart four-storey townhouses. In the distance, sleek red Routemasters shimmy down Theobald's Road towards Oxford Circus and anxious parents cart their sick children into the new NHS hospital at Great Ormond Street.

When you reach the house at number 29, turn right onto Dombey Street. It's a graceful street of early-eighteenth-century houses with white marble porticoes, dark-maroon brick and black railings. Coming as you do from the twenty-first century, it's entirely possible that you won't even notice what lies mid-way down the street, though for contemporaries in their pencil skirts, suits and sunglasses, it's astonishing – depending on your point of view, a totem of London's post-war resurgence, the height of futuristic wonder, the brawn of socialism or just a stark, deadening monstrosity. To you, though, it will look like the kind of thing you find round virtually every street corner nowadays: a council estate.

As you draw nearer, you see that it's a wide stack of concrete-framed, brick-fronted units with rectangular, five-paned windows and divided by a balcony with black iron railings. With its façade perfectly in line with the terraces, it feels careful and appropriate, congruous with its Georgian neighbours. This is the Blemundsbury block, one of the first – if not *the* first – of the high-rise estates to be built in central London after the Second World War, certainly the first to rise to ten storeys. It opened in 1949 as part of the socialist government's hyperdrive to build hundreds of thousands of new homes for a population in dire need.

By now, the building boom is well underway: 2.5 million new houses and flats have been built in London since the war and of these, the high-rises are by far the most conspicuous.

Almost 69,000 flats in blocks of ten storeys or more will be built before the high-rise mania cools and then collapses in the early seventies. So buildings like the one in front of you would prove epochal for the future of the London skyline, as revolutionary as schools and hospitals in Victorian London. The building boom now underway – involving commercial skyscrapers as well as residential ones – will transform the skyline as much as the temples of Londinium, the spires and domes of Sir Christopher Wren in the seventeenth century and the sleek furnaces of modern capitalism in the form of gherkins, cheese graters, walkie-talkies and shards that will appear from the 1980s onwards.

And what exactly *is* a skyscraper in 1950s terms? Originally, the term applied to vessels with triangular sails pointing up to the sky, but by the Victorian period it could mean an unusually tall man – 'I say old sky-scraper, is it cold up there?' is one rather fetching usage from 1847. Tellingly, an American-authored *Short Guide to Britain*, written for troops stationed here during the war, reported that 'London has no skyscrapers'. Though that's debatable since there's a ten-storey art deco building at 55 Broadway, above St James's Park Tube station, and other commercial and academic high builds at 80 Strand (the Shell building) and the colossal Senate House (the headquarters of University College London) in Bloomsbury, which we'll be visiting later. But the general point rings true – London does not seem like a natural home for the high-rise, they are too brash and flash, out of keeping with English traditions and more consonant with American cities. And then there's the ground. Manhattan is perched on hard granite; London on clay, stretched out across the flood plain of the Thames on loose soil known as alluvium, deposited by clay, silt and sand. In the first half of the twentieth century, people worried that tall buildings would be swallowed up. And yet, solutions were found. It is the policy of Mr Macmillan's government that state-funded architects should reach for the stars; the higher local authorities build, the more money they receive.

What lay behind this architectural volte-face? First, bombs. Thanks to the carnage wrought by Luftwaffe raids and pernicious V-1 and V-2 rockets, 116,000 houses in the capital were obliterated; ten times that number needed repairs. And besides, many of London's slums, even those untouched by bombs, had been virtually uninhabitable for as long as anyone could remember. Inner London councils had built around 67,000 flats for a quarter of a million people by 1939. The war merely exacerbated both the problem and the scale of its solution; in 1951 the Conservative government led by Winston Churchill came into power on a ticket of building over 300,000 houses per year. The changing face of London manifests a radical shift in the scope and priorities of the state. You might be pleased to see that the government, finally, has heeded *The Bitter Cry of Outcast London* (1883) and now the state considers it its duty to provide decent housing for the population. This idea was given a fillip by the 'homes for heroes' policy of the Liberal prime minister Lloyd George after the First World War (he didn't want those returning heroes to become Bolshevik revolutionaries after all), and by the eve of the next world war, 10 per cent of Britain's housing stock was council-owned. But it was under Clement Atlee's visionary post-war Labour administration that people began to think of public housing as a right not a privilege. Aneurin Bevan, architect of the NHS and minister for housing, was a passionate, idealistic socialist who saw no reason why workers shouldn't live in the same comforts as doctors and politicians or the Labour Cabinet, for that matter. The house-building programme was an essential part of the fledgling welfare state.

In 1947 the government handed responsibility for London's planning to London County Council, whose architecture department became one of the world's largest and most innovative architectural practices, passionate about the revolutionary social impact domestic architecture could have. Initially led by Robert Matthew, it was in thrall to modernist architectural ideals. Behind many of these schemes loomed the extraordinary influence of Charles-Édouard Jeanneret-Gris, the Swiss–French architect and writer better known as Le Corbusier, the titan of modernism. Le Corbusier thought of his designs as machines. By housing people in identical collective dwellings – or 'machine-homes' as he called them – he wanted to remove the need for neighbours to 'keep up with the Joneses', to free them from status anxiety. Egalitarianism from without, he hoped, would foster moral improvement from *within*, sublimating a concern with oneself into a desire for collective improvement, which would ultimately destroy a bourgeois society founded on egotism and self-interest. And indeed, blocks like the one in front of you are vivid manifestations of socialist ideals; there is nothing remotely individual about them.

Which makes it all the more surprising, perhaps, that the Conservative governments, returned to power by the electorate in 1951 and 1955, acquiesced in the policy of building behemoth high-rise estates (as Macmillan's would continue to do when re-elected in 1959). But it made sense. Prefabricated off-site, concrete estates were quick to build, and didn't require too much skilled labour. Clearly, they could accommodate a much higher population density than low-rises: good for meeting that 300,000 per year target. For the councils, too, they offered a quick, effective and prestigious solution. The stock of Finsbury Council soared immeasurably when Bevan himself came to lay the foundation stone for the ground-breaking, stylish Spa Green Estate off Rosebery Avenue, designed by Berthold Lubetkin, in 1946. For the architects, too, it was an opportunity to demonstrate their prowess, to change the world one concrete slab at a time.

As the high-rises float in the air, so too does a sense of excitement, that the architects' and politicians' dreams are coming true. One of the most regrettable differences between council estates in the 1950s compared to the twenty-first century is one of perception. As Lynsey Hanley laments in her impassioned *Estates: An Intimate History* (2007), all too often, in the media or in conversation, the word 'estate' is loaded with pejorative epithets like 'tough', 'rough', 'mean', 'edgy', 'crime-blighted' and 'drug-ridden' – and not always undeservingly, by any means. But, back in the 1950s there is very little prejudice towards places like Blemundsbury. On the contrary, to move into a pristine new block, escaping the rat-infested write-offs that we walked past in Victorian London, is, for most, a dream come true. Moving into one of the towers on the Woodberry Downs Estate, far out in Manor House, one new resident was euphoric: 'The excitement of opening the front door, our own, finding a nice living room, large bedroom with fitted wardrobe and fitted chest of drawers ... separate toilet, a lovely kitchenette full of cupboards and shining stainless steel sink and draining board. What more could we want? We felt like King and Queen.'

But in time, the high-rise dream soured. What went wrong?

In their mania to build a high quantity of homes at lightning-fast speed, the quality of the housing – so sacrosanct to Bevan – suffered, and speculative builders rose to the fore. Corners were cut. There was already criticism of the gargantuan high-rise estates by the mid-1960s, but people's worst fears seemed to be realised by another tragedy at Canning Town in 1968. Impoverished East Enders had been waiting for up to twenty years to move into a brand-new estate. And now one was ready, the Ronan Point Estate on Clever Road: twenty-two storeys high but with a footprint of only eighty feet by sixty feet – just the kind of efficient, high-density housing that appealed to governments and local authorities.

One of the bright-eyed new residents was a fifty-six-year-old cake decorator called Ivy Hodge. Her enjoyment of her new home was abruptly cut short when, one morning, she arose at 5.45 a.m. to make herself an early morning cup of tea, as the sun peeked over the factories and marshes of Waltham. As she lit a match beneath her stove-top kettle, there was an explosion. The two south-east facing walls of her flat were blown clean out, and she was thrown across the room (not, luckily, out). Tragically, the force of the explosion knocked out every load-bearing panel on that side of the building; one by one, people's living rooms fell in like a gruesome parody of vertical dominoes, all the way to the ground floor. Four died; luckily, most occupants were still in bed so avoided being crushed. Disconcertingly, when the block was restored residents were warned not to light their kettles with matches – as though there were a chance it might happen again. (When it was demolished in 1986, workmen discovered an inherent flaw in its design.)

But the sun may have set on the high-rise experiment even without a Ronan Point. By that point, high-rises were becoming magnets for social problems, blighted by crime and drugs. Many residents felt sequestered from the local community, prisoners in their own homes. Many complained that the blocks felt like dehumanizing ghettoes and slums in the sky, devoid of the vibrant street life of old working-class tenements, rather than utopian urban idylls.

But that's for the future. For the moment, take a left onto Harpur Street. There's an early Georgian house on the corner. Pause there for a moment and turn round for one last look at the Blemundsbury block. Feel how it rears over you like an immense wave, ready to obliterate you in a spume of concrete.

Time to recharge. Jump on the Tube at Holborn. It's two stops to Leicester Square on the Piccadilly Line. You will emerge into the bright lights of the West End. Make the short journey to Shaftesbury Avenue and walk left. At Frith Street, take a right and throw yourself into the whirl of Soho.

Laid out from the 1670s as part of the burgeoning West End, Soho, which in all likelihood takes its name from the old hunting cry 'So-Ho!' from the days when these streets were hoof-harrowed fields – part of a royal hunting ground – never reached the same dizzy heights of fashionability and exclusiveness as neighbouring St James's, Mayfair or Marylebone. With its winding alleys of cheek-by-jowl townhouses, taverns and brothels, it instead grew into an 'upmarket but never august district' known for its cosmopolitan and bohemian feel. Perhaps the flow of immigrants from France after an eruption of religious intolerance there in 1685 contributed a certain *je ne sais quoi*; the Huguenot Church survives in a maroon, Victorian–Gothic building at 9 Soho Square. But even in its bomb-churned, crater-pocked state, the *energy* of the place is somehow undented. It's emerging as one of London's prize post-war blooms, a shimmer of colour in a drab, austere world. People are beginning to let their hair down here, to bask in the wonder of being alive with impunity and panache. And it's all being fuelled by a certain bitter black infusion brought not by the French, but by the Italians who flocked here in between the wars, many working as chefs and waiters, as a decline in domestic servants built up more of an appetite for eating out.

Rock 'n' roll espresso bars

Coming up on your right, next to a guitar shop, is a sun-kissed glass shopfront. Above is a brash white sign, emblazoned in a chunky, gold-tinted, handwriting-style font with the words *Moka Bar*. The door is propped open. Skiffle music streams from a jukebox and wafts into the street. In the brightly lit interior, customers lean over a curvaceous Formica-covered bar on a neat row of metal stools. In the centre of the bar broods a sleek metal presence that will be familiar to you from the contemporary world, but which is exotic here: 'a great burbling, wheezing, spluttering monster [which] would grudgingly excrete some bitter caffeinated essence'. It is marked with the word GAGGIA. A barman calmly steps aside from a volcanic eruption of steam and lays down a small glass of steaming black liquid in front of a girl with flowers in her hair. She takes a sip, strikes a pose and lights up a cigarette, then scans the room for a Teddy boy. Welcome to London's first espresso bar, opened in 1953 by an itinerant dental salesman from Italy called Pino Riservato.

Pino Riservato had a dream. He wanted to improve the abysmal quality of England's coffee. Travelling up and down the country selling his wares, Mr Riservato was mortified by what passed for coffee, especially in London. He wasn't the only one. In *Down and Out in Paris and London*, written in the 1930s, George Orwell had depicted 'an ordinary London coffee-shop' as a 'little stuffy room with high-backed pews' serving meagre snacks from a menu scrawled in soap on a mirror and dismal-tasting coffee. Luckily, Riservato was related by marriage to the Gaggia family, and set about trying to sell the revolutionary high-pressure, steam-blasting espresso machine to English cafés. But they didn't take the bait. So the salesman decided to go it alone. In 1953 he renovated a bomb-damaged laundrette, decorated it in a bright, modern style, installed his Gaggia espresso machine, recruited an Italian actress for a glitzy opening and sat back to see what happened. Lured by the exoticism, sophistication and novelty of the new coffee joint on the edge of Soho, Londoners flocked in their masses – Moka Bar was soon dispensing over 1,000 servings of espresso and other coffee a day. Exactly 301 years since the city's first coffeehouse opened in St Michael's Alley in Cornhill, coffee culture had burst back onto the scene, powering the resurgence of a downhearted and bomb-blasted metropolis.

Keep walking up Frith Street until you reach Old Compton Street, the main artery of Soho. Turn left. Coming up on your left, beyond Dean Street, are two more espresso bars: Heaven & HELL and the 2i's. These are just two of the 500-strong spawn of Moka Bar – the great majority done up in an experimental, bohemian fashion with bamboos, rubber plants, outlandish artwork and murals, exposed brickwork, black ceilings and resourceful, makeshift furniture. Nothing stuffy or ornate here. Apart from the Gaggia machine, which might cost up to £400, to open a coffee bar all you really needed to do was, as a character in a TV programme put it, 'find yourself a dirty old cellar, get a couple of barrels and a long plank, candles in bottles and you're in business' (like all good satire, this contains more than a grain of truth). This makeshift, speakeasy-style aesthetic is part of what gives coffee bars their soul; they feel fresh, modern and *cool* (a term originally used by black American jazz musicians but now lodging itself in the public consciousness). From the perspective of the twenty-first century, with its sky-high rents, it's refreshing – or perhaps painful and maddening – to think that in the 1950s, it's possible for young people to rent property in central London cheaply.

You're outside Heaven & HELL Coffee Lounge, marked by a red neon light. Teenagers and advertising executives spill out onto the street, smoking and talking. Strangely (to your eyes) no one is drunk; though they're open until midnight or later, coffee bars are teetotal affairs without a liquor licence. As the name suggests, it's a concept coffee bar. The upstairs section is decked out like heaven, replete with bright lights, angels on the walls and ethereal music, whereas the downstairs, HELL, is a more diabolical affair, bathed in red light and pumping out music loud enough to burst your eardrums.

Its neighbour, the 2i's, is emerging as a crucible of rock 'n' roll. It was originally owned by three Iranian brothers, but the three soon became two – hence the name – before the establishment was taken over by a fearsome Australian wrestler called Paul Lincoln, or Dr Death as he likes to be known, in 1956. If you're young, and fancy yourself as a musician, you can go down into its inferno-like basement and join hordes of other teenage hopefuls trying to impress the court of music producers, managers and agents who flock here each night to scout new talent. You might be interested to hear that Cat Stevens and Cliff Richard all cut their teeth in the heaving basements of London's coffee bars. These rock 'n' roll joints are not for the faint-hearted: sometimes it gets so hot that sweat runs down the walls and people who have fainted have to be passed through the air vent into the street, where they are revived with fresh air and a shot of industrial-strength espresso.

And there are other coffee bars, like their eighteenth-century progenitors we shall encounter soon, all defined by their kaleidoscopic diversity. At the A&A on Charing Cross Road, you'll find taxi drivers reading poetry to each other between shifts. Beyond Soho there are skiffle enthusiasts at the Troubadour on the Old Brompton Road, jazz musicians at the Nucleus in Covent Garden, and folk singers performing at Bunjies on Litchfield Street in a haze of marijuana smoke. Music was written into the genetic code of coffee bars in the same way that news was hotwired into the identities of the seventeenth- and eighteenth-century coffeehouses. After the gleaming espresso machine, the jukebox is usually a coffee bar's pièce de résistance.

At the end of Old Compton Street, turn right, then right again, onto Meard Street. At a time when many Georgian houses are being ripped down – or earmarked for destruction – Meard Street has thankfully been left unscathed. Laid out in 1732, with a rare antique street sign to prove it (high up on your right), it is a gorgeous parade of auburn townhouses, with sash windows and white porticos above front doors that lead directly onto the street. But inside 23 Meard Street, the atmosphere couldn't be less Georgian.

You leave daylight at the doorstep and make your way in. Muffled organ music greets you. Down you go, into the basement bar where you are caught in an explosion of kitsch-Gothic, complete with a jukebox playing something that wouldn't be out of place in *The Phantom of the Opera*. Customers sit on shiny black coffins, sipping espresso, strumming their guitars and flicking ash into candlelit skulls. 'Your coffee off a coffin' is Le Macabre's slogan. (It certainly beats 'To inspire and nurture the human spirit – one person, one cup and one neighborhood at a time', which is Starbucks's mission statement).

The walls are crawling with skeletons – plastic, you hope – and painted cobwebs brought into relief by the tar-coloured walls. Your attention will also be drawn to the episodic frescoes. In one, we see a lustful skeleton waltzing into a graveyard with a naked woman on his arm. To the rhythm and groove of a skeleton band, they dance and twirl in the moonlight. The skeleton perches his glass of red wine on a coffin lid and moves in for the kill, as it were. Finally we see them, limbs entwined, resting their heads against the tombstone, her jet-black hair washing through his ribs, enjoying some 'tomb-stone talk'.

Order yourself a coffee – an espresso in a glass or cappuccino in a white cup. It won't taste a million miles away from what you're used to in the twenty-first century – and settle down on a coffin to soak up the atmosphere.

Though there are some startled-looking tourists and the odd shopper who has strayed off the beaten path, the bulk of the clientele are teenagers – boys with greased-back hair in white T-shirts and leather jackets, girls in vivid red-and-blue dresses which have something of medieval London about them, others clad from head to toe in black, some wearing sunglasses, foreshadowing the goths of the 1980s. Though they are a favoured haunt of musicians, advertising executives and single women, coffee bars, particularly at night-time, cater to teenagers – a social group who are finding they have higher levels of disposable income since the austerity of the war years loosens its grip. They're too young to drink alcohol, and are unmoved by the vast, art deco Lyons Corner Houses with their delicatessens, hairdressing salons and stolid bourgeois clientele. Coffee bars seem like the perfect solution, a place to pose, flirt, sing, smoke, play and cast artistic judgement, to forge their own identities away from the suburban parental eye. In a short film from 1958 called *It's the Age of the Teenager*, one scowling manifestation of this zeitgeist stares right down the barrel of the lens and issues a stark ultimatum: 'This is us, see, we're *today*; if you don't dig us shoot away to some square joint with the rest of the creeps.'

But as the coffin becomes unaccommodating to your buttocks, and the cat next to you croons a little too loudly as he strums his guitar, you can feel the spell of Le Macabre beginning to wear a little thin; with fashions in youth culture changing so quickly, you can see how, before long, the whole coffee bar scene could all seem a bit *démodé* and uncool. Let's leave London's premier gothic espresso bar. In fact, let's leave Soho altogether, head up Tottenham Court Road and cut through the gorgeous, leafy squares of Bloomsbury as we make our way to the eastern edge of Russell Square.

The Ministry of Truth

The trees of Russell Square look like glittering waterfalls in the sun. Picnickers lie on the grass, some smoking, others eating sandwiches, all making the most of their lunch hour on this grassy island surrounded by a moat of roaring traffic.

You cross to the western side of the square, which is vast, the second biggest in London after Lincoln's Inn Fields, not unlike the kind of thing you might find in Moscow. The street is lined with late-Georgian terraces with creamy, band-rusticated stucco on the lower floors and sash windows reflecting green leaves on the upper. On the corner of the northern side of the square, T. S. Eliot, who evoked an unreal, degenerate 1920s London so powerfully in *The Wasteland*, is busy at work in his capacity as the director of publishers Faber & Faber, dashing the dreams of hopeful poets. His late and rather disturbed wife, Vivienne, used to turn up outside the office wearing a sandwich board proclaiming 'I am the wife of T. S. Eliot abandoned', which no doubt had him raking his fingers through his immaculately Brylcreemed hair. On another occasion, she is alleged to have poured a tureen of hot chocolate through his office letter-box; they lived nearby on Bedford Place so presumably the hot chocolate was still hot – or tepid at any rate. He recently married a new, less tempestuous wife, Valerie, almost forty years his junior, who had worked as his secretary in the office ahead.

On the western side of Russell Square, almost level with the centre of the garden, the terraces part, revealing a narrow street, at the end of which is one of the most extraordinary buildings in London. Make your way over to inspect it.

A huge stepped pyramid hogs the horizon rising sheer and steep. It looks stark, new and muscular, with precise rows of rectangular windows running down the entire length of the building. Right at the top, a flag flies imperiously. You might empathize with the impressions of George Orwell, as narrated in *Nineteen Eighty-Four*: 'The sun had shifted round, and the myriad windows ... with the light no longer shining on them, looked grim as the loopholes of a fortress. His heart quailed before the enormous pyramidal shape. It was too strong, it could not be stormed. A thousand rocket bombs would not batter it down.' George Orwell is describing the terrifying, history-effacing Ministry of Truth, but this was based on what was then the tallest secular building in London, the nerve centre of the sprawling University of London: Senate House, the building in front of you. If we think of the University of London as a federal university, consisting of over thirty teaching and research institutions, then Senate House is its White House, formulating academic policy; it also contains teaching space and a vast, rebuilt library.

At 210 feet, St Paul's Cathedral is the only building in London that stands higher. Nicknamed 'the dummy skyscraper' when it first opened because London's stringent building regulations prohibited occupation of its 210-foot tower, to the amusement of passing Manhattanites, during the war it was commandeered by the government for their Ministry of Information, a power-house of publicity and censorship, drip-feeding stories to Fleet Street. Working here, amongst all the administrators and second-rate hacks, was George Orwell's first wife Eileen, who no doubt drip-fed *him* a story or two for his epic dystopia.

Taking the philosopher and exponent of utilitarianism Jeremy Bentham (1748–1832) as its 'spiritual founder', the resolutely secular University of London prides itself on its progressivism. Ever since University College London's foundation in 1828, conformity to the Church of England was not, as it was at Oxford and Cambridge, a prerequisite for admission and religion was never part of its syllabus, for which it was vilified as 'the godless institution of Gower Street' and 'the synagogue of Satan'. It wasn't long before a rival, King's College, was founded 'to immure the minds of youth with a knowledge of the doctrines and duties of Christianity' (although ultimately the two were incorporated into the federal University of London). It was the first English university to admit women on an equal footing with men.

William Beveridge, architect of the welfare state, became the vice-chancellor of the university in 1926, and was instrumental in the acquisition of the Bloomsbury site in front of you. The university's previous headquarters at the Imperial Institute in Kensington, was palatial, wrought in an ornate, neo-Renaissance style, but for its new home, Beveridge and others wanted something much more modern, something that would really make a statement. As he put it in a lecture in 1928, the University of London wasn't 'dropped as it were from heaven on two monkish medieval towns' – naming no names – but was 'a university for the nation and the world', attracting legions of overseas students. The architecture should reflect this. Senate House and its connected buildings shouldn't just mimic other universities or regurgitate outmoded architectural styles, he argued, it 'should be something that could not have been built by any earlier generation than this, and can only be at home in London': 'an academic island in the swirling tides of traffic, a world of learning in a world of affairs'. No ivory towers here.

So the architect Charles Holden, renowned for his design of the twelve-storey 55 Broadway, thitherto the highest building in London, as well as some suburban stations on the Piccadilly Line, was hired to build a spine structure with wings leading to the perimeter of the Bloomsbury site, guarded at either end by mighty towers. In the event, by the outbreak of the war, funds had only stretched to cover part of this master plan, Senate House and the Library. Holden set about his work, using brick and mortar but fronted with Portland Stone, and a steel frame – not for any structural reasons, but to bear the great weight of the books. Holden's patrons, who had wanted something 'clear-cut but not harsh, dignified but not ponderous, graceful but not florid' were delighted with the result, gushing about the building's dignity, beauty and modernity, but suffice to say wider opinion was less unequivocal in its praise. Evelyn Waugh wrote of 'that gross mass of masonry', 'the vast bulk ... insulting the autumnal sky' in his novel *Put Out More Flags* (1942); fellow novelist Graham Greene wrote of a 'high, heartless building'. The pre-eminent architectural critic Nikolaus Pevsner, usually a fan of Holden's work, had no time for its cocktail of modernist and Georgian forms, which he considered architectural bedlam.

Love it or loathe it, all agreed on its overbearing, even megalomaniacal quality – which seemed to suit perfectly its appropriation as the Ministry of Information during the War (and as the inspiration for the sinister Ministry of Truth in Orwell's novel). The location of the ministry was meant to be a state secret, but taxi drivers knew that when someone asked for Senate House, they weren't heading for a spot of study in the library. The journalist Norman Riley, who worked in the ministry during the war, described how, in smoke-wreathed Beveridge Hall, 'day and night there is a clatter of typewriters and a babel of different tongues ... on a dais extending right round the room are fifty to sixty telephone boxes, most of them with direct lines to Fleet Street offices'. At peak times, over a hundred journalists crammed into this room. In the basement were censors (like Winston Smith in *Nineteen Eighty-Four*) and on the upper floors, a repository of knowledge: 'on each side of the labyrinthine, carpeted corridors, are rooms, scores of them, occupied by experts on India, religion, broadcasting, films, public meetings, propaganda, politics or nothing in particular'.

Though Orwell portrays the Ministry of Truth as an inviolable fortress, its real-world counterpart took some hits in the Blitz – nine, to be precise, in the autumn of 1940. Duff Cooper, the parliamentary under-secretary to the Minister of Information, left a vivid account of one strike, on 7–8 November 1940, in a letter to his wife (his comic tone perhaps designed to allay her worry). Curled up on his rubber mattress, he is awoken by a 'Splaaash! Craash! Tinkle! Tinkle!' and finds himself on the floor. Getting up, he discovers the passage outside 'filled with a red fog which was just dust. There were air-raid wardens rushing about in steel helmets.' As he puts it, 'we really had been struck on the boko [nose] by the *Luftwaffe*'. The damage was significant: 'A bomb . . . had broken through one floor and exploded on the floor below. It had done in the University library. Our windows on the courtyard side had been twisted into shreds. The courtyard is full of masonry. But not a single soul even scratched. It was all great fun.'

Its library may have been blown to pieces but ultimately, Senate House came through the Blitz relatively unscathed. People have theories on why this is, none proven. Some say it's because the dummy skyscraper acted as a navigational beacon, directing the Luftwaffe towards King's Cross and St Pancras stations; others, more fancifully, claim that Hitler himself coveted the building, thinking it would make an excellent headquarters for the Nazi dominion of Britain (Oswald Mosley was another who purportedly had his eye on it in the 1930s for a future Fascist parliament).

In spite of the drabness of the post-war years and the scars London still has to show, splotches of the city are slowly turning to colour. We have seen it in Soho. And we are about to see it again, in Chelsea.

Go back to Russell Square station and make the journey west, to Sloane Square. You'll have to change twice.

Made in Chelsea

You walk out of Sloane Square Underground station into the fresh air of the King's Road. Originally Charles II's private carriage track from Hampton Court Palace to Westminster, it cut through a 'village of palaces' – Chelsea, whose Anglo-Saxon name has variously and evocatively been translated as 'chalk wharf', 'shelf of sand' or 'place of ships'. Once, this was home to such illustrious personages as Sir Thomas More and Princess Elizabeth Tudor, who relished its tranquil riverside aspect a safe distance from the slippery pathways of power at Westminster. It has been said that Chelsea bathes in the best light in London – clear, white, pure and vital – and the river-fronting Cheyne Walk has traditionally been an abode of esteemed artists like Joseph Turner, James McNeill Whistler and Dante Gabriel Rossetti. Men of letters, too, have found that the area has a fibrillating effect on their muse. The King's Road became a public highway only in 1830, by which point many of the old palaces like More's Beaufort House had been pitifully ripped down for development by the Sloane and Cadogan families; it wasn't long before the King's Road was lined with smaller but tasteful brick houses and shops. But it never lost its faintly bohemian air.

You won't feel it immediately, this countercultural pulse, but it is there, somewhere, lurking behind all the butchers, fishmongers, greengrocers, picture-framers and florists that give the King's Road something of a small-town air.

If you walk for eight minutes or so, beyond Thomas Crapper's toilet production company at number 120 advertising 'a certain flush with every pull' you'll find two wellsprings of bohemian energy: the Fantasie coffee bar, London's second, opened in 1955 by the solicitor-turned-photographer and general bohemian *homme d'affaires* Archie McNair; and the Markham Arms, a dingy boozer with a mahogany façade, gold lettering and a slightly deaf landlady. It is here, pontificating at the bar with a glass of red wine, sinking espressos and poring over freshly developed photographs, or kicking about on the street sharing puffs and gossip, that you might find some members of what newspaper gossip columnists have cheerfully christened the Chelsea Set.

It will be their outfits you notice first – brash, bright, colourful and screaming out for attention, a real foil to the drabber and more demure clothing worn by everyone else in the street. The Chelsea Set are eccentric aristocratic bohemians. Some have jobs in the media, public relations and fashion photography, but most of them are happily nurtured by never-ending trust funds. Many of the locals will speak of them pejoratively, as the idle and profligate rich, but they are coming to think of themselves as part of a self-conscious and timely movement to break away from the stifling conformity and post-war ennui of 1950s London. They intend to toss aside Establishment values and embrace a faster, loucher and more vital way of life. Their main weapon is shock; they are connoisseurs of outrage. This is mainly achieved by displays of intense hedonism. They like to hold pyjama parties in Soho nightclubs, culminating in riots, and are the initiators of something that would prove an enduring London tradition: the Circle Line cocktail party, where you dress up to the hilt, drink (heavily), dance and play music – to the horror and bewilderment of other passengers.

Their anti-Establishment leanings aside, you might think of them as a cross between the Bullingdon Club toffs and the 'rahs' from *Made in Chelsea*. Were it not for their fashion. More than anything, the Chelsea Set like to ruffle feathers with their choice of clothes, for which they are famed. If you see anyone in an unthinkably un-PC outfit – 'blacked up' as an African tribal leader, say, or a Red Indian chieftain with a vivid plume of feathers – or in ridiculously exaggerated versions of upper-class clothing from days gone by, in skinny trousers or flowing, untucked-in bright shirts or even – shock, horror – blue jeans (aping the working class), then you have stumbled across a member of the Chelsea Set. Say hello and expect to be drinking shortly (excitingly, the coffee at the Fantasie is sometimes laced with vodka). You'll find them kicking about the King's Road in the daytime and indulging in sex, drugs and partying in Soho at night; beyond that, some of them would rather be seen dead than venture east of Sloane Square.

You might find one of their number, a raffish twenty-seven-year-old called Alexander Plunket Greene (or Plunket to his friends), chatting to customers in a basement Italian restaurant called Alexander's a little further down the street. Described in his youth as 'a teenage scene unto himself', Plunket, a bohemian rich boy and industrial idler, is the living embodiment of the Chelsea Set: living in his recuperating mother's empty house, not getting up until four o'clock in the afternoon, nominally enrolled at Goldsmith's Art College in New Cross, where he perennially carried a pile of papers marked 'FILM SCRIPT' under his arm, but in effect living for the night, networking jazz bars, drinking to excess, living on a single meal a day of spaghetti and corned meatloaf, never once cleaning up, and having sex with the cleaner his mother eventually sends to tidy up. At Goldsmith's, when he was sixteen, he fell for a 'pixie-sized but blunt and strong-willed student' called Mary Quant, the daughter of two Welsh teachers desperate for their daughter to pursue a steady and sensible vocation (she couldn't think of anything worse, of course, and wanted to work in fashion).

While, unlike him, she actually turned up to college early

each morning, Quant fell under Plunket's spell and took to gadding about Chelsea and Soho with him, performing theatrical practical jokes (like pretending to be dead in the luggage compartment of a train), drinking whisky with an arty, bohemian crowd at Finch's on the Fulham Road and, whenever Plunket's funds came through, promptly blowing the lot on a criminally expensive champagne dinner. More than anything, Plunket was known for his remarkable (or to many, hideous) fashion sense, turning up to college in his mother's pyjamas which were far too short for him, to parties in gaudy dinner jackets, to restaurants in St James's in a suit but no shirt, with only a row of painted buttons on his chest. Though she had an intuitive fashion sense, some of this no doubt rubbed off on Mary, who began to take an interest in equally transgressive women's outfits. Though they didn't know it at the time, their relationship would bring about an earthquake in fashion, shower glitz on the dreary post-war city, and crown Mary Quant as queen of the miniskirt and bob cut.

The epicentre of this revolution is a little further down the road, beyond the Markham Arms and next to an estate agent's. Just look out for six white, shadowed capital letters above a glass shopfront: BAZAAR. It's our next stop.

One of the more memorable photographs taken during the Blitz shows a pair of constables carrying two semi-naked bodies through a vast mound of rubble and shattered glass. It seems to tell the familiar story of senseless destruction, until you notice that the men are smiling, and that the corpses over their shoulders aren't human, they aren't even male or female – they're androgynous white mannequins, pulled from a bombed shop window on Oxford Street. It must be one of the earliest appearances of the mannequin in photography, since they were a relatively new phenomenon at the time.

Mary Quant's Bazaar, which opened a year and a half ago, is famed for its clever curation of mannequin scenes, which change every Saturday night. They are a brilliant way of catching people's attention; luring the right sort, repelling the wrong, and providing endless fodder for chatter at Chelsea dinner parties. Expect outlandish and surreal scenes and feel free to comment, but don't imagine that any negative opinions will be taken to heart. Mary and her husband like to lurk behind a ventilation grille listening to their customers' feedback – and the more derisive the laughter, they claim, the more stock they would sell that week. There are plenty who are not enthralled and you may well spot members of the Chelsea Society, a rather staid heritage organisation founded in the 1920s to preserve Chelsea the way they liked it, shaking their fist at this degenerate upstart.

Amongst her tableaux during the 1950s and early 1960s were: a photographer-mannequin strung up by his heels, as though caught in a tree trap, pointing a camera, David Bailey style, at a woman-mannequin also suspended at a jaunty angle ('we wanted to give the impression that here was a dress so outstanding that it was worth while getting into any position to have a look at'); a woman-mannequin in heavy tweed country gear with a huge fishing rod dangling into a goldfish bowl with a live goldfish sloshing about; bright-white mannequins strumming away on snow-white instruments – guitars, saxophones, trumpets – wearing round goggle-style sunglasses; and a handsomely turned-out figure taking a giant lobster (dead this time) for a walk on a gold chain just like the nineteenth-century French Romantic poet Gerard de Nerval, who was said to walk his pet lobster, Thibault, in the Palais Royal gardens in Paris on a blue silk ribbon.

Mary Quant, who has a horror of people turning out 'like jellies from the same mould', is inspired by Nerval's refusal to do the expected thing. See for yourself: go into Bazaar. You might have to wait a while first, though – the queue in the forecourt is six deep.

It's not a big shop but it is bright and buzzy. The comforting smell of bolognese wafts up from the restaurant below. The first thing you'll notice is there isn't actually that much stock for sale – at this stage, Bazaar is a small-scale and sometimes quite precarious enterprise; Quant banks on selling the entire day's stock so she can afford to buy the cloth for the next day's outfits over the counter at Harrods early in the morning. Then she will spend the rest of the day frantically making the new batch of clothes, which tends to arrive at six o'clock – the optimum time to shop, as you can see. Expect to see bright, adventurous, sexy clothes. Polka-dot dresses. Short skirts. Simple, tight-fitting fabrics without waists. Floppy, colourful hats. The black stockings and white leather boots that would become synonymous with the 'Chelsea girl' or 'dolly bird' look. And other offbeat garments and accessories. Everything screams out youth, sex and rebellion in an explosion of vivid colour. As Quant herself put it in the mid-1960s, 'I heard my clothes described as dishy, grotty, geary, kinky, mod, poove and all the rest of it. People either loved or hated them.' The customers are generally young, usually female, either alone or with their boyfriends, and with a range of accents. Despite the high demand, the atmosphere is casual and laid-back; unlike in many clothes shops in London, you won't be pestered by officious *Are You Being Served*-style shop assistants brandishing tape measures in your face.

A small woman with short brown hair, an angular jaw and sharp cheekbones appears, fixes herself a drink from behind the counter and pours you one too. This is Mary Quant, the creative force behind Bazaar. Although it's busy, she seems more than happy to chat with the customers, many of whom she is on first-name terms with, and the shop feels a bit like a never-ending cocktail party. Fired by that energy that accompanies a lack of sleep – she was drinking till late last night, and up early to begin work on today's stock – and obviously excited by the continuing success of her enterprise, she is a fount of stories and confessions.

'We've been having some miserable weather recently,' she tells you, which is why the mannequins are clad in radiant colours. That way the customers find the clothes irresistible. She opened Bazaar in the depths of November, you glean, almost two years ago. You won't find anything else like it, not in London, not in New York, not in Paris. She'd been working for a Mayfair milliner, next door to Claridge's, when Archie McNair, a mutual friend of her and Plunket, suggested it would be fun for the three of them to work together. With the help of some seed money from the two men and a mortgage, they purchased the freehold for this building, the plan being for Plunket to run a jazz club on the ground floor and for Quant to open a boutique to sell the kinds of things she'd been designing for her bohemian circle, a *bouillabaisse* of clothes and accessories, as she puts it, brimming with sweaters, scarves, hats, jewellery, trinkets, that kind of thing. At first, she thought of herself as a buyer, supplying young women with cool and exciting clothes, but it soon became apparent that she couldn't source the looks they wanted. Her eureka moment seems to have come when an American customer purchased a pair of her mad pyjamas then, while paying, casually mentioned he intended to produce them for the mass market in the States. There was nothing else for it. She would have to design the clothes herself.

Her bedsit took on the appearance of a miniature workshop. It was mad, she says. She couldn't get into bed each night for all the cloth cuttings and paper patterns. Her two Siamese cats used to gobble up the paper patterns, impeding progress; it transpires that the tissue paper is made from a by-product of fish bones! She likes to emphasize the precariousness of the whole endeavour, how easily things could have gone wrong – but she's known since she was a child that it was her destiny to become a famous fashion designer. Take the building. Once they'd acquired it, their student-architect friend merrily removed the old iron railings and stripped out the front of the house to make a broad shop window. Only he forgot to get planning permission, and the council ordered them to restore the building to its original state – which would have ruined them. But after a rainstorm of tears in front of the architectural officer from the London County Council and some promises to strengthen the fortifications, all was fine. Still, if she hadn't been able to produce garments that sold immediately, the whole thing would have gone bust pretty pronto. But she did. It was a success – almost a *violent success*, she says – on one occasion, a woman grabbed a new dress from her in the street and paid for it *there and then* without even bothering to try it on! Now Chelsea girls pop in several times a day to see what she's concocted; each day holds something new, depending on her mood.

Some of the customers are terrifying. 'That's what *this* is for' – she pours herself another glass of Scotch – she doesn't like it much, but it takes the edge off her nerves. She recalls one particularly hair-raising moment when a man in a loud waistcoat turned up with his blonde girlfriend. 'He told her that she could have whatever she liked then stood back and smoked an expensive cigar. The girlfriend started rifling through the stock and threw whatever tickled her fancy – virtually everything – onto a mound on the floor. Just then a friend of Archie's walks into the shop, sees the man with the cigar, and goes a bit white in the face.' He took Plunket aside, whispering to him that the man was a renowned international gangster whose favourite trick was to run up an enormous bill then pay by cheque, which would later bounce, by which point he'd be out of the country. 'So we were worried,' she tells you. 'Very worried. After what felt like hours, the value of the mound was nearing £400,' (around £8,000 in 2015 money, time traveller) 'and even the boyfriend was starting to look a bit tetchy. We would have called the police but the phone line had been disconnected because we forgot to pay the bill. Come 7 p.m., we were desperately thinking up ways to refuse his cheque. For want of any better alternative, we served them drinks. Then suddenly, the man puts his hand in his pocket and pulls out – not a gun or a cheque book but an enormous wad of notes.' He simply peeled off the fivers and paid for the lot in cash. She came to be quite friendly with him after that – one of several criminals to frequent her boutique.

A regular customer marches up to the counter. Mary seems to lose interest in you, pours the newcomer a drink and starts chatting to them instead.

Bazaar is about as epochal a shop as you'll find anywhere in London, the progenitor of the wild fashion experiments that would come to define the Swinging Sixties. Before Mary Quant and Bazaar, fashion designers didn't really cater for the young; when they left school, women were expected to dress like their mothers. 'Growing up seemed terrible,' recalls Quant. 'It meant having candy-floss hair, stiletto heels, girdles and great boobs.' It meant projecting an image of chasteness and respectability, shrouding one's youthfulness in white gloves, heavy jewellery, matronly frocks, and matching bags and shoes. As the jazz player and critic George Melly put it, before the mid-1950s, 'only tarts and homosexuals wore clothes which reflected what they *were*'. What Mary Quant did was to emancipate young women from mimicking their mothers, giving them the power to express themselves through their clothes. Above all, with her short skirts (and they'd only get shorter over time), vivid colours, tight cuts and low cleavages, she made women's clothes adventurous and sexy. In her autobiography, she characterizes the aesthetic of her new clothes. They say: 'I'm very sexy. I enjoy sex, I feel provocative, but you're going to have a job to get me. You've got to excite me and you've got to be jolly marvellous to attract me. I can't be bought, but if I want you, I'll have you.'

'There was a time when clothes were a sure sign of a woman's social position and income group,' writes Quant – your experiences in medieval London, where sumptuary laws tried to dictate who could wear what, leave you in no doubt about that. 'Not now,' she continues. 'Snobbery has gone out of fashion, and in our shops [by the time she was writing, in 1966, she had opened another branch in Knightsbridge] you will find duchesses jostling with typists to buy the same dresses.'

It's a wonderful image, wonderfully exaggerated. But it conveys a general truth – no longer is it the social elite who set the fashion, as had happened for over 800 years in London. Although it would take a while to filter into the mainstream, day in, day out, from the till of Bazaar, Quant is presiding over the democratization of women's fashion, 'catch[ing] the spirit of the day and interpret[ing] it in clothes before other designers begin to twitch at the nerve ends ... The clothes I made happened to fit in exactly with the teenage trend,' she reflects, 'with pop records and espresso bars and jazz clubs.'

Time for a nosh up! Go down to Alexander's, in the basement below Bazaar. Perhaps owing to hostility from the staid Chelsea Society, Plunket's application to open a jazz club was turned down. Instead, he opened a 'camp' Italian-style restaurant; 'camp' because it was much more jaunty and laid-back than your average prim-and-proper restaurant. Expect delicious bolognese cooked by Italian chefs, a convivial atmosphere (including another drink with the owner, perhaps), and sometimes waiters in drag. This winning formula will in time attract a slew of celebrity diners including one Brigitte Bardot, who apparently had a stupefying effect on the waiters.

As you make your way out after your meal, you notice that the queue has vanished and the King's Road is full of Philipino au pairs walking yappy little poodles, and slickly suited shoppers. You swivel round and see that Bazaar has been replaced by an inconspicuous coffee shop and the Markham Arms is now a Santander Bank. What ever bohemian cachet the area enjoyed in the late 1950s has vanished without a trace, and you now find yourself within a soulless enclave for the super-rich.

Epilogue: echoes of 1950s London

Thankfully, London has not suffered an aerial bombardment since the Second World War, so many of the buildings featured in this chapter – the Blemundsbury block on Dombey Street, the Georgian houses on Meard Street, the former Faber & Faber headquarters at 24 Russell Square and nearby Senate House – are all still there for the exploring.

The website bombsight.org has a compelling interactive map of explosions during most of the Blitz. When you zoom out in the 'aggregate' view (October 1940 to June 1941), the effect is disturbing; it looks like some kind of mutant vivid-red heart girdled by the M25 (the map is modern). It doesn't paint a complete picture of the destruction, as the rocket attacks towards the end of the war are not charted. It is easy to spot likely sites of rocket explosions, though. Since V-2s could wipe entire streets off the map, an area hit by a V-2 is now frequently the site of a car park or a 1960s housing estate; the lack of mature trees is a telltale sign of rocket damage.

Occasionally, as on Leyton Marsh, small craters are still visible. On Tottenham Court Road, opposite Heal's department store, is a forlorn three-storey building with a Caffè Nero on the ground floor. Seemingly for no good reason, it's surrounded by a moat of open space. This is the site of the V-2 blast that destroyed Whitfield Tabernacle on 25 March 1945, killing nine people and damaging the surrounding buildings – in fact it was the last V-2 rocket to hit London. It was never redeveloped and remains a favourite spot for people to sit and eat their lunch, perhaps oblivious to the area's tragic history. You can see V-1 and V-2 rockets in the Imperial War Museum, which give a little bit of a face to an enemy that was, for Londoners, stealthy, invisible and inescapably deadly.

Strangely, the surviving stones of St Mary Aldermanbury that stood in the sunken garden where you landed in 1950s London were transported to Fulton, Missouri in 1966. They were rebuilt as a memorial to Winston Churchill at Westminster College, where he delivered his famous 'Iron Curtain' speech in 1946.

On the other side of London Wall, the Gothic-style church of St Giles-without-Cripplegate was painstakingly reconstructed after it was disembowelled by German bombs in August 1940. It stands in the centre of the perfectly wholesome but somehow faintly sinister in aspect Barbican complex, one of the few high-rise brutalist estates to have increased in desirability since it was completed in 1976. It was conceived as a bold experiment in utopian housing provision, and is perhaps the apex of Le Corbusier-inspired social housing in London (though from the 1980s, the flats rapidly became unaffordable for most and, by 2000, 80 per cent were privately owned). The name *barbecana*, 'fortified outpost', possibly derives from an extra-mural watchtower pulled down in the thirteenth century. With over 4,000 residents, today it is a bastion of population in a city that, in residential terms, is deserted.

Since the high-rise dream began to sour from the 1970s, far fewer social housing units were built in this manner although the brutalist Trellick Tower in North Kensington, designed by Ernő Goldfinger, was completed in 1972 and has remained iconic, overcoming the blight of crime in the 1970s.

The espresso bars of 1950s Soho, always very much of their time, were losing their edge within a decade of Moka Bar's launch in 1953. Their relevance was challenged by an expansion of nightclubs and live music venues. And the original teenage consumers who had championed them grew up, shooting away to 'some square joint' of their own, no doubt, as they swapped their leather jackets for respectable overcoats and started a family in suburbia. By the mid-1960s the old coffee bars seemed garish and démodé. None survive. The site of Moka Bar at 29 Frith Street is currently occupied by a jeweller and pawnbroker (no blue plaque), the 2i's at 59 Old Compton Street is a restaurant and cocktail bar (though it does have a plaque modestly proclaiming the birthplace of rock 'n' roll) and Le Macabre at 23 Meard Street is a nondescript office block. The oldest coffee shop in Soho is Bar Italia, opened in 1949 and still run by the same Italian family. It predated the espresso bar boom and always stood slightly aloof from it. It is open from 7 a.m. until 5 a.m. Over the last decade, there has been a resurgence of small, independent coffeehouses in Soho challenging the hegemony of the ubiquitous chains. Flat White on Berwick Street, Milk Bar on Bateman Street and Nude Espresso on Soho Square are the pinnacle of cool (and the flat whites are to die for); further afield, you might try the Espresso Room on Great Ormond Street, Towpath on Regent's Canal and the Idler Academy in Westbourne Park.

Upmarket King's Road still retains strong links with fashion and is crowded with high-end outfitters. Mary Quant is in her eighties. After the success of the Chelsea Bazaar, she went on to open a second store in Knightsbridge, over the road from Harrods. Here, according to *Fashion Design, Referenced: A Visual Guide to the History, Language and Practice of Fashion* (2013), champagne flowed, jazz was played, and models strutted through the crowds carrying copies of Marx and Engels. Latterly, she launched her own cosmetics company before selling it to a firm in Japan, where her designs continue to be highly popular. But there is also a Mary Quant London Shop at 37 Duke of York Square in Chelsea, specializing in skincare and make-up. Alexander Plunket, emblematic doyen of the Chelsea Set and Mary's partner in arms, died in 1990.

1716
Four Days in
Dudley Ryder's London

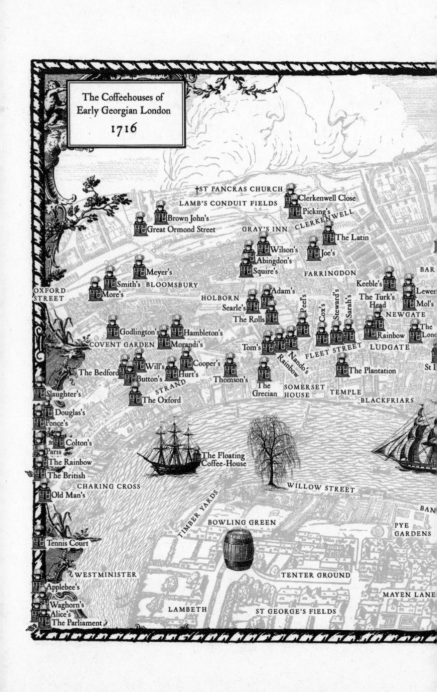

The Coffeehouses of
Early Georgian London
1716

ST PANCRAS CHURCH
LAMB'S CONDUIT FIELDS
Clerkenwell Close
Picking's
Brown John's
Great Ormond Street
CLERKENWELL
GRAY'S INN
The Latin
Wilson's
Joe's
Abingdon's
Squire's
FARRINGDON
Meyer's
BAR
Smith's BLOOMSBURY
Keeble's
More's
Adam's
Lewer
The Turk's
Mol's
OXFORD
HOLBORN
Peel's
Head
STREET
Searle's
Cox's
NEWGATE
The Rolls
Steward's
Sarah's
The
Lond
Godlington's
Hambleton's
Rainbow
Morandi's
FLEET STREET
LUDGATE
COVENT GARDEN
Tom's
St I
Will's
Cooper's
Rainbow
Nando's
The Bedford
Hurt's
The Plantation
Button's
Thomson's
Slaughter's
STRAND
The Oxford
The
SOMERSET
TEMPLE
Douglas's
Grecian
HOUSE
Ponce's
BLACKFRIARS
Colton's
Paris
The Rainbow
The British
CHARING CROSS
The Floating
Coffee-House
WILLOW STREET
Old Man's
BAN
Tennis Court
PYE
TIMBER YARDS
BOWLING GREEN
GARDENS
WESTMINSTER
Applebee's
TENTER GROUND
Waghorn's
MAYEN LANE
Alice's
The Parliament
LAMBETH
ST GEORGE'S FIELDS

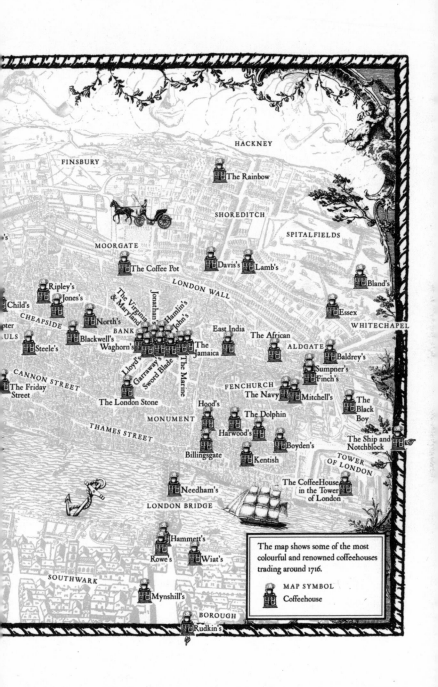

HACKNEY

FINSBURY

The Rainbow

SHOREDITCH

SPITALFIELDS

MOORGATE

The Coffee Pot   Davis's   Lamb's

Bland's

Ripley's
Jones's   LONDON WALL
Child's   Essex
The Virginia   WHITECHAPEL
& Maryland   Jonathan's   Hamlin's
North's   John's
pter   CHEAPSIDE   BANK   East India   The African
ULS   Blackwell's   The   ALDGATE   Baldrey's
Steele's   Waghorn's   Jamaica   Sumpner's
                                                                    Finch's
CANNON STREET   Lloyd's   Garraway's   FENCHURCH   Mitchell's
The Friday   Sword Blade   The Navy
Street   The Marine   The
                                                                  Black
The London Stone   Hood's   The Dolphin   Boy
            MONUMENT   The Ship and
THAMES STREET   Harwood's   Boyden's   Notchblock
                        Billingsgate   Kentish   TOWER
                                                         OF LONDON

                                                The CoffeeHouse
                    Needham's   in the Tower
            LONDON BRIDGE   of London

                Hammett's
            Rowe's   Wiat's

SOUTHWARK   Mynshill's

            BOROUGH
            Rudkin's

The map shows some of the most
colourful and renowned coffeehouses
trading around 1716.

MAP SYMBOL
Coffeehouse

Go to Fleet Street at around six o'clock on a cold winter's evening and you'll find yourself swept along in a torrent of commuters as red buses with misted-up windows inch their way towards the Strand like mastodons and waspish motor-bikes torpedo past. Just after Fleet Street melts into the Strand, marking the western extremity of the City of London, there is a dark alleyway called Devereux Court, built in the late seventeenth century. Blink and you could miss it. Before it, on the left, is the narrow-fronted headquarters of Twinings Tea surmounted by sculptures of two Chinamen and a golden lion; in the distance is an unloved statue of Dr Johnson besmirched by pigeon droppings.

Turn left down the alleyway and you enter a different world. The snarl of traffic evaporates, the sirens lose their bite, and you find yourself in a narrow walkway flanked by high and graceful Georgian buildings used today as barristers' chambers; or, in the words of a Scottish visitor to eighteenth-century London, 'you quit all the hurry and bustle of the City in Fleet Street and the Strand, and all at once find yourself in a pleasant academical retreat'. Follow the twists and turns of the cobbled alley, lit by a street lantern. Beyond are the gardens of the Middle Temple with their handsome walks, venerable trees, and whispering fountains. Only the occasional barrister or law clerk trotting by, the click of their heels echoing from the buildings, disturbs the calm.

On your right is the Devereux Arms, an unremarkable early Victorian boozer with a yellowy-beige stucco frontage, white window frames and dubiously ribbed quoins, very different from the brown and red-brick Georgian houses in the rest of the courtyard. Up high, resting on a scrolled plinth, is a maroon bust of the 3rd Earl of Essex, Robert Devereux, the one-time favourite of Queen Elizabeth who launched a deeply mis-guided coup against her councillors from his house on this spot in 1601, for which he was swiftly beheaded. Carved into the plinth – very faintly – are the words 'This is Devereux Court, 1676', one of London's oldest surviving street signs. On the ground floor is a plaque – not a turquoise one imprinted with the English Heritage logo but a quieter black one pro-claiming, in beige lettering, that here stood the Grecian coffeehouse, famed meeting place for natural philosophers from the Royal Society including Sir Isaac Newton and the astronomer Edmond Halley.

Put your hand on the plaque, and press. As you breathe out, it becomes shrouded in the icy swirl of your breath.

People are hurrying back and forth, locked in conversation and barking orders. It's hard to get a good look at them – the street lantern has vanished but before long, a nimble little urchin, his cheeky, weathered face caked in grime, scuttles through the courtyard carrying a big cone-shaped torch, lighting the way for his customers. Turn back round and have another look at what was the pub. The stucco façade and white window frames have been scoured away to reveal warm red bricks and a mod-est marble portico characteristic of late-seventeenth-century buildings. The heraldic arms of the Devereuxs that were hang-ing above the doorway have been replaced by a giant creaking wooden sign dangling from a sturdy iron branch from which freezing-cold rainwater trickles down your neck.

The first-floor windows are frosted with condensation and smoke but you can just make out dancing yellow spots from within, flickering candles in a sea of passing shadows. The Earl of Essex is still up there but he no longer looks down upon a trickle of people entering the Devereux Arms. He now guards the entrance to something much more exciting: the Grecian coffeehouse, a cauldron of learning and wit.

Prepare to go in.

Be warned, though: it's not a good idea going into a coffeehouse looking like a woman. If you are one, you might want to go to a draper's to get hold of a velvet jacket, waistcoat and pair of breeches, tie a silk cravat round your neck, and don a periwig. Otherwise you might be taken for a prostitute. Coffeehouses like to fashion themselves as enclaves of rational thought and enlightened debate and the sad truth is that even in the great age of Enlightenment it's still believed that women are essentially incapable of such things, dominated as they apparently are by their tyrannous sexual organ. Unless they are widows who have inherited their husband's business, the only place for a woman in a coffeehouse – should they be buxom and of fair complexion, that is – is ladling out steaming drink behind the bar.

Tuesday, 21 February 1716

A dish of bitter Muhammedan gruel

It is dark. You are stumbling up a crooked staircase, groping for a coarse handrail. When you reach the landing, you almost crash into a man cradling his periwig in despair. Coffeehouses are democratic theatres of judgement. They thrive on quick-wittedness and rhetorical flair; this wretched creature is the victim of what the French call *l'ésprit d'éscalier* – thinking up that perfect riposte too late (on the way downstairs from a French salon, in the metaphor) by which time you're the laughing stock of the coffeehouse, your reputation in tatters, and the next time you show your face in there people will exchange knowing looks. They will *remember*. With that in mind, go in; for a mere penny you can talk politics and philosophy with some of the finest minds in London, powered by infinite refills of disgusting coffee. (There is a particularly nasty slang phrase for *coitus interruptus* – 'to make a coffeehouse out of a woman's cunt' – to go in and out without spending anything.)

As the door creaks open, you are engulfed in a cloud of smoke, sweat and steam and smacked by a wall of heat as though you've entered a Turkish sauna. Candles flash. Timbers creak. A parrot squawks. Ned Ward, the author of the *London Spy* journal described a coffeehouse as a soot-coated den of iniquity populated by 'a parcel of muddling muck-worms ... busy as so many rats in an old cheese-loft ... and the whole room stinking of tobacco'. He exaggerated for dramatic effect of course, but London coffeehouses are a far cry from the salons of eighteenth-century Paris or the ornate coffeehouses of twentieth-century Vienna. With the exception of the majestic establishments around aristocratic St James's Square in the West End and the leading financial coffeehouses of Exchange Alley in the City, most are spartan and cobwebby, with wood shavings on the floor, mildewed notices and letters pinned to the wall, no upholstered furniture and dirty windows. You are there to be stimulated, not pampered. In front of the fire, different-sized kettles whistle and burble. After the rain-rattled alleys outside, it looks to you like a picture of warmth and welcome, a cosy fug.

You see rows of periwigged men sitting at long wooden tables drinking, thinking, writing, piping, gossiping, debating, pinching snuff and discussing science and literature late into night. There are as many as forty people in here, most smoking, their swords lying by their sides. Every so often someone hauls up the flotsam of their stomach into little silver spittoons dotted about the tables. A frustrated scholar hurls a scrunched-up bit of paper into the face of the long-suffering coffeehouse cat, in whose mind a plot seems to be forming to spend a penny of his own in the bubbling coffee cauldron – one satire suggests that would *improve* the taste of the 'bitter Muhammedan gruel', of the 'soot-coloured ninny-broth', the 'politicians' porridge' or whatever you want to call it. Through the windows you can see the moonlit gardens of the Temple and, beyond, the Thames. To the side, the ancient proprietor Mr Constantine is bent double, sorting through the various messages and letters that have arrived for his customers in the penny post. This septuagenarian is a walking advertisement for the life-giving properties of coffee; in eleven years, he will be hailed as the oldest coffee-man in Christendom (only to die the next year).

You attract the attention of some of the other patrons. One points at you with his pipe and shouts, 'Your servant, sir! What news from Tripoli?' When you don't reply, he tries again, 'What news have you?' By now, half the room has gone quiet and people are eying you expectantly. They are ravenous for a chunk of news or gossip to chew, digest and regurgitate. This can be absolutely anything in the world: 'there's nothing done in all the world, from Monarch to the Mouse,' chirps a poem, 'but every day or night 'tis hurl'd into the *Coffee-House*'. Don't worry, it's fine to make something up – that's what plenty of other customers have done.

Tell them you have it on good authority at the Royal Exchange – from a ship captain come quick passage from Gothenburg – that that rapscallion, the Regent of France

('Frog' doesn't yet exclusively apply to French people) is preparing to invade England but the fleet will, by a sweet providence, plummet to the ocean floor as soon as it leaves Calais.

Nodding in approval, the men shuffle up and clear a space for you. Their pungent lemony perfume wafts into your nostrils as you sit down. The table is showered with just about every form of media imaginable – newspapers, polemical pamphlets shot through with capitals, newsletters in beautiful calligraphy, broadside ballads with musical notes, party-political playing cards. Contemporary pamphlets and diarists and future historians, for that matter, make much of the supposed egalitarianism of eighteenth-century coffeehouses, having fishmongers outwit fops and butchers trump baronets in philosophical debate. 'Pre-eminence of place none here should mind,' proclaims the *Rules and Orders of the Coffee-House* (1674), 'but take the next fit seat that he can find.'

Take this with a grain of salt. To insulate themselves from the loneliness and anonymity of the biggest and fastest-growing city in Europe, Londoners tend to gravitate towards coffeehouses whose atmosphere and clientele they find congenial. While for socially ambitious, news-hungry individuals, this might mean spending their time drifting between five, ten or even fifteen different coffeehouses talking to strangers, discussing the news, and trying to be witty, a baker or butcher would be far more likely to stick to their own locale rather than, say, venturing into an upmarket coffeehouse in Mayfair or St James's.

The coffee is foul and the spitting alarming, but what will take the most getting used to is the way customers listen in to each other's conversations, interjecting with impunity and dishing out judgements at the drop of a hat. So if you hear something interesting, don't be shy: get stuck in. Expect to hear customers discussing a kaleidoscope of topics from politics to philosophy, science to sex, ventriloquism to vivisection, gardening to grave-digging. Conversations are fast-flowing; 'I cannot talk of Christianity in a coffee-house,' reports a Mancunian poet in 1729. '[It] is a plain calm business, and here people are, and love to be, all of a hurry'. You'll hear wide-ranging discussions twined from a single conversational thread. One diarist recalls how, last year, a coffeehouse conversation about a recent execution transmogrified into a discussion on 'the ease of death by beheading', with one participant telling the company about an experiment he'd conducted in his garden in Islington, slicing a viper in two and watching in amazement as both ends slithered off in different directions. Wasn't this, as some of the company conjectured, proof of the existence of two consciousnesses?

As is rapidly becoming apparent, London's original coffeehouse are nothing like the bland mega-chains that have invaded the streets of twenty-first-century London. Just imagine walking into a Starbucks, sitting down next to a stranger and asking for the latest *news*. You'd be taken for a freak. But that was the very raison d'être of their predecessors. No one considers it rude. In fact, it's considered polite.

The philosopher Lord Shaftesbury, who died three years ago, liked to describe how aspirational citizens could chisel away their rough edges and accrue sophistication, virtue and wit through a kind of 'amicable collision' with other refined individuals, giving a polish to the manners'. Thanks to these sociable encounters, citizens would become polished and ultimately *polite* – the word derives from the Latin *politus*, made smooth. It was coffeehouses, time and time again, that were hailed as 'academies of civility' (not least in the pages of the hugely influential *Spectator* and *Tatler* journals) as they offered infinite opportunities for social interaction and emulation. So there is a real social incentive to talk to strangers in coffee-houses; face-to-face interaction is seen as improving, a catalyst for measured debate rather than the kind of wild rants and vitriolic character assassinations that fester online in the twenty-first century, where keyboard warriors are willing to say anything from behind the mask of a computer screen. As the Scottish diarist James Boswell put it after enjoying a two-hour literary debate at Tom's coffeehouse in Covent Garden in 1762, 'The degree of distance due to a stranger restrained me from my effusions of ludicrous nonsense and intemperate mirth. I was rational and composed, yet lively and entertaining.'

It's time to yell out for a pipe, tobacco and dish of coffee. A cherubic boy in flowing periwig and silk cravat will magi-cally appear and pour your coffee *à la mode* – that is, from a great height. For your penny's worth, you can drink as much as you can bear. 'Bear' because eighteenth-century coffee is absolutely, stomach-churningly revolting, especially for the time traveller accustomed to silky-smooth flat whites brewed with mathematical precision in one of London's independent coffee shops in the twenty-first century. The grinds are rarely fresh, the coffee is horridly overboiled and usually left to stew for hours in front of an open fire, giving it a stale, prune-like quality. It's not just that our taste buds have grown more refined: the earliest samplers of coffee found it disgust-ing too, routinely comparing it to oil, ink, soot, mud and sometimes just shit. One thought it tasted like a 'syrup of soot and essence of old shoes'. But it is the effect of the gruel that keeps Londoners coming back in their droves. People love the way it stimulates the body, sparks ideas and galvanizes conversation.

The Grecian was opened in the mid-1670s by a Greek

émigré, an ex-mariner called George Constantine, who you saw earlier. Reflecting the owner's nationality and its situation in the academic bowers of the Temple, it soon attracted classical scholars who liked to loaf around discussing the finer points of Horace, Virgil, Homer and the other great luminaries of antiquity. In the fashionable *Tatler* in 1709, the editor Richard Steele reported that the 'learned Grecians' had been occupying themselves by putting the events of the *Iliad* and *Odyssey* into chronological order and recasting it in the format of a journal. But its most enduring association is with science. Particularly since the Royal Society moved its headquarters to Crane Court off Fleet Street in 1710, the Grecian has evolved into an informal meeting place and debating forum for natural philosophers who like to decamp here for a pipe of tobacco and dish of coffee after witnessing experiments at the Society including, four years ago, the dissection of a dolphin in front of Isaac Newton (the creature paid a high price for straying into the Thames).

The empirical values of the Royal Society, as we experienced in the plague year of 1665, are democratized in the Grecian. Where better to establish one's reputation than in a coffeehouse in front of an inquisitive, talkative, mainly sober audience?

In a brasher and more impetuous age, men had settled their differences with duels and dust-ups. Now, thanks to places like the Grecian, they can do so through dialogue and debate, marking a step towards a more civil society. Of course, the old ways didn't vanish overnight and some coffeehouse conversations can be quite barbarically pedantic. In the Grecian, a thankless debate between two old friends on how to accent a particular Greek word became so heated that all civilities were roundly dropped. The only way to resolve the matter, it seemed, was to disinter historical convention with a duel in Devereux

Court, which is precisely what came to pass, one of the combatants skewering the other to death in a scene worthy of the *Odyssey*.

Pick up a newspaper, the *Flying Post*. The date, you learn, is Tuesday, 21 February 1716. From what you can gather from its pages (well, page – the publication constitutes one sheet printed on both sides) and the discussions swirling around you, about two weeks ago six peers of the realm were sentenced to death at Westminster Hall. They had spearheaded a northern and Scottish rebellion against the new, German-speaking Protestant king, George of Hanover, in the Jacobite Rebellion. Jacobite is derived from the Latin *Jacobus* since the rebels pledge allegiance to the Catholic Pretender James Stuart (or James III, as he calls himself), son of the banished James II. One of the ringleaders was James Radcliffe, the twenty-six-year-old 3rd Earl of Derwentwater, whose wife recently wept on her knees at St James's Palace begging for a reprieve, but King George refused to see her.

But reports and rumours are notoriously mercurial with 'nothing certain ... one report contradicting another'. Now the Grecian is awash with speculation that the rebel lords *could* be granted a last-minute reprieve – and this being a coffeehouse, everyone has an opinion as to whether this is a good thing. Traditionally, informed political debate had been the preserve of the social elite. But in the coffeehouse it's anyone's business – that is, anyone who could afford the measly 1d entrance fee (around 35 per cent of London's male population). This culture of political debate is a distinctive feature of the times – but it doesn't mean the political system is any more democratic. The genius of the coffeehouse is that it *flatters* you into thinking your opinion matters even though, most of the time, it is roundly ignored by the ruling oligarchy.

A chameleon diarist at Freezeland Fair

A young, smartly dressed man with an affected air of confidence scuttles across to the table. He removes his hat and sword, calls for a pipe of tobacco and hovers behind the other customers. His hopeful gaze darts all about the room, as though he wishes to be seen by someone who knows him, but he isn't hailed by anyone. After he imparts a piece of news – you can't hear what – the men shuffle up and he plonks himself down with ostentatious satisfaction. He sits there, listening intently, sometimes making as though to interject into a conversation but not quite having the courage. This is Dudley Ryder, a twenty-three-year-old law student from Hackney, son of a wealthy Cheapside linen draper, religious dissenter, habitué of over a dozen coffeehouses and an avid social climber. Dudley dreams of making his father proud by flourishing at the Bar, amassing great riches and taking an intelligent and subservient wife. But, crippled by shyness and lacerated with self-doubt, he's not sure he's going to make it.

Each night, to a flickering candle, he pours his darkest thoughts, wildest dreams, primal urges and most brutal, penetrating character judgements (including upon his own personality, with which he is immensely dissatisfied) into the pages of a secret cyphered diary, which he reads back at regular intervals, in an effort to mould and improve himself in the spirit of the Enlightenment. Ryder doesn't see anything immutable or God-given about his personality. This sets him apart from the Puritan diary writers of the seventeenth century, who wrote to inspect their souls each day in an effort to bring them closer to God. Ryder, in contrast, uses his diary to bring himself closer to the person he wants to be, a social composite of all the people he's observed and admired around town, whose traits and behaviour are archived in his scribblings.

Unlike the raw and salty Samuel Pepys, Ryder doesn't see anything wrong with concealing his true nature. Walking a horse to Hackney one spring morning when his mind was sluggish and thoughts unforthcoming, he affects a 'thinking studious posture' in case he runs into someone he knows to 'give them a notion of me as a great thinker'. This is just one of the many masks he likes to wear in certain social situations – elsewhere, he feigns the wit, the gallant, the dutiful son, the big brother, the bookworm, the philosopher; he even plays the unrequited lover with gusto though he would rather not have had to. In this great age of dissemblance and guise, he is the paragon of an aspirational London bourgeois, careful not to say anything that might be deemed impolite or ungenteel, a man of many masks.

Ryder is a consummate coffeehouse politician too, using his diary to gather news, rumour and opinion. He likes to be seen to be au courant with the very latest stories. Tonight, he will write in his diary (which gives you a sense of what he's talking about on the other side of the room): 'At 6 o'clock went to the Grecian Coffee House. There is a great deal of the best company there. Stayed by some of them, heard their talk. The six condemned lords are to be executed Friday.' He also gleans, to his dismay, that Lady Derwentwater is planning to turn up at the Houses of Parliament the next day to urge the MPs to address the king in favour of the condemned lords. As a staunch Whig, and so a staunch supporter of the House of Hanover, Ryder hates nothing more than Jacobite traitors and sincerely hopes that the Earl of Derwentwater and his friends will die.

Ryder himself will be the first to admit that the law is not his passion. He prefers instead to immerse himself in wine and philosophy, and to ice-skate on the New River, take girls on spooky walks across Hackney Marshes, watch executions, read Quintilian, swim at Islington Spa and debate politics and philosophy in coffeehouses. As someone who, as far as his gauche personality will allow, throws himself into whatever the city has to offer, he is, in short, an excellent person to know as we tour a city on the cusp of the modern world. Take a seat opposite him and call for a dish of 'soot-coloured ninny-broth' and a pipe of tobacco, still as popular in the eighteenth century as in Elizabethan and Jacobean times.

Last month Ryder committed to the leaves of his diary a vivid account of a once-in-a-generation experience: walking the frozen Thames. Before the building of the Embankment from 1862, the Thames was significantly wider – only around 200 feet from the Strand, as we've seen – and so flowed more slowly. Also, the nineteen arches of London Bridge were easily clogged up, further slowing the flow upriver. So, during particularly harsh winters, the Thames was susceptible to freezing over – as it did at least twenty-three times between 1391 and 1831. Sadly the ice is now melted, robbing you of the chance to skate on the surface of the Thames yourself, but given the sense of wonder that flows through Ryder's evocations, the chances are he'll be more than happy to reminisce with you now. As most people in the coffeehouse can recall, towards the end of November 1715 a great frost descended upon London and some bulky blocks of ice got stuck in the arches of London Bridge, slowing the tide as far as the turn in the river at Charing Cross. The watermen found themselves sharing the river with shoals of ice but, stubborn creatures, they continued to ply their trade until early December, by which point the river had frozen solid and thousands of amazed people were crossing from one bank to another. 'I was extremely struck at the sight of it', recalls Ryder. 'It looked as if there had been a violent storm and it had froze the waves, just as they were jostling and beating against one another, and the billows and foam and white froth were grown stiff just as they were at the height of their hurry,' anticipating James Boswell's evocation of the 'pleasing horror' of the 'rude and terrible appearance' of a semi-frozen Thames in 1763. The atmosphere on the ice was firmly carnivalesque. 'A great many tents set up,' Ryder continues, 'in which were coffeehouses and wine and ale and other things sold. I went across the river upon the ice in a path that had been worn out, it being all rugged and uneven.'

As his story gathers pace, you can expect some of the customers around you to chip in with their own impressions, their eyes glazing over with nostalgia for 'Freezeland Fair'. Expect to hear tales of tents propped up on the ice with redundant oars; of the House of Geneva (a gin booth), in which you could get hammered; of a stall selling sumptuous hot gingerbread; of games of nine-pin bowling; of an ox being roasted in the middle of a ring of spectators near Hungerford Stairs; of an enterprising husband-and-wife duo running a poetry tent; of a roasted mutton booth at the live sign of the rat in the cage; of the leeching watermen who dug channels in the middle of the river, laid planks, then charged tolls for walking across – in addition to the entrance and exit fee they already levied.

No doubt some of the customers in the coffeehouse will have little printed mementoes of their visit with their name in a decorated box underneath the caption 'printed on ice'; these tokens, which have been a feature of Frost Fairs since Elizabethan times, are little plays on the transience of ice versus the permanence of print, celebrations of the surreality of water turning to land and all the unexpected liberty that it entails. 'Where little wherries once did use to ride, and mounting Billows dashed against their side', begins one, 'now booths and tents are built whose inward treasure, affords to many a one delight and pleasure.'

It wasn't all fun and merriment on the ice, however, and you should expect to hear sadder tales too. Of Doll the Pippin Woman, eulogized in John Gay's mock-heroic poem 'Trivia: or, the Art of Walking the Streets of London' (1716), who slipped only to be decapitated by sharp shards of 'cracking crystal' – 'her head, chopped off, from her lost shoulders flies' crying 'pip pip pip!' as it bounces along the ice; of the four young men who strayed from the beaten path and were never heard from again; of the poor people frozen to death at home, unable to afford the inflated prices of coal or meat, victims of the uncaring laws of supply and demand.

The last frost fair, as gloriously romantic and dream-laden as its predecessors, would be in 1814. After the building of the five-arch London Bridge in 1831 and the Embankment, the river became narrower, deeper, less clogged and faster-flowing, making it less susceptible to freezing even during the exceptionally harsh winters that followed. But the frost fairs bowed out with élan – at the last one, it was reported that 'a very fine elephant was led across the Thames a little below Blackfriars Bridge'. But the thaw, when it came, was sudden: the ice cracked and floated away, taking booths and printing presses and terrified people with it, pummelling any vessels lying in its path and smacking into the arches of London Bridge like a meteorite shower.

Time to leave.

If you enjoyed your time in the Grecian, you should know that it's one of at least 550 and possibly several thousand coffeehouses all over London. Unlike the cloned coffee shops of the twenty-first century, the atmosphere of each one is unique, defined by its location within the metropolis, which itself determines the kind of person you'll meet inside. 'Some coffee-houses are a resort for learned scholars and for wits,' writes the young Swiss traveller and nobleman César de Saussure, 'others are the resort of dandies or of politicians, or again of professional newsmongers; and many others are temples of Venus.'

The walls of Don Saltero's Chelsea coffeehouse are festooned with taxidermic monsters including crocodiles, turtles and rattlesnakes, for local gentlemen scientists like Sir Isaac Newton and Sir Hans Sloane to muse upon over coffee; on the other side of town, the Hoxton Square coffeehouse is renowned for its inquisitions of insanity where coffee drinkers view, prod and talk to alleged lunatics before voting on whether or not they should be incarcerated in a local madhouse; Lloyd's, Garraway's and Jonathan's, all clustered around Exchange Alley in the City, are Meccas for insurance, auctioneering and wheeler-dealing in stocks and shares; whereas the coffeehouses and chocolate houses of St James's are hotbeds of kamikaze gambling. The Chapter coffeehouse in St Paul's Churchyard is a resort of writers pitching their latest idea to publishers and cash-strapped curates ghost-writing sermons, and in the gate-house of a dissolved priory in Clerkenwell there used to be a Latin coffeehouse operated by Hogarth's father where people were encouraged to converse in Latin (it was short-lived). In a couple of decades' time there will be a coffeehouse in Covent Garden containing a 'theatrical thermometer' with gradations ranging from 'excellent' to 'execrable' for tormenting play-wrights and another, Moll King's, where libertines could sober up after a night of heavy drinking and browse a directory of whores – then be led to the requisite brothel. Elsewhere, there are coffeehouses north of the river, south of the river and, once upon a time, *on* the river. Until 1704, there was a floating coffeehouse moored near Somerset House, a glorified dancefloor for rakes and dandies to dance the night away and stare at the stars on her rain-spattered deck. It was known as the Folly of the Thames.

Places like the Grecian embody a new way of interacting in cities: they are smoky, candlelit forums for the exchange of information, debating of ideas and transaction of commerce – not to mention, as we have seen with Dudley, the stage-management of personality. *The Economist* once described them as 'the internet in a cup', though of course they thrive on real world, face-to-face interaction, and are all the better for it.

The phoenix city

Edified and refreshed, you place a penny on the counter and leave the flickering candles and bubbling cauldrons of the coffeehouse behind you and venture forth, weaving right onto Essex Street then right again onto the Strand. Welcome to Dudley Ryder's London, a phoenix risen from the ashes of the Great Fire, a city of opulent buildings, fine squares and intellectual freedom but also one of squalor, brutality and vice, of maggot-ridden offal festering in dark unswept streets, of syphilis-ridden prostitutes wolfing down exotic jellies for the titillation of their clients in the jelly houses of Covent Garden, a world of savage justice.

The population of London has almost reached 630,000, making it the biggest city in Europe; in less than a hundred years it will be the biggest on earth. It is a ravenous city. The burial rate still exceeds the birth rate and each year tens of thousands of arrivals are sucked in from the countryside and further afield – moths to a metropolitan flame. Monarchs have all but given up trying to limit the growth of London, 'this great and monstrous thing'. Only when you consider that the vast majority of England's six-million-strong population live in close-knit communities of fewer than 500 people, only when you consider that the next biggest city – a dwarf by comparison – is Bristol with around 50,000 inhabitants by 1750, do you begin to comprehend the gargantuan quality of the capital. 'I found myself in the strangest forest,' wrote one American visitor to London, 'surrounded with noise, dirt, business [and] the vast extent of the city'; for James Boswell, who would arrive in London in 1762, Fleet Street was a whirl of anonymity, 'the noise, the crowd, the glare of the shop signs ... agreeably confused me'. For outsiders and indeed, for anyone, places like the Grecian are mini-utopias within a seemingly never-ending urban sprawl.

The metropolis is now one continuous built-up stretch from Tufton Street to the south of Westminster Abbey and Hanover Square by Oxford Street in the west to the docks and wharves of Limehouse in the east; from Hoxton Square and Pitfield Street in the north to Blackman Street in Southwark in the south. But the map of London has sprawled much more in a horizontal than vertical direction; once you've crossed the Thames, you don't have to walk very far south until you hit open fields. The whole conurbation can be walked in the space of three hours if you so wish, but it won't be an easy or comfortable journey on foot.

Since concluding an eleven-year war with France and her allies in 1713, London has been in the grip of a building boom as partnerships between aristocratic landowners and speculative builders bear fruit. Bloomsbury, Soho and St James's are already flourishing, Piccadilly is coming together and, following the completion of London's newest square, Hanover Square, two years ago, more land is being parcelled out for development in Mayfair by the Grosvenor family (Marylebone, at this stage, remains a small village on the other side of the

Tyburn Road). Square by square, the West End is coalescing, a world of tall neo-classical townhouses, broad paved streets, private carriages, concert rooms, peruke makers and chocolate houses. It's only a shame that we won't have time to visit.

On her eastern boundaries too, London is spreading her tentacles and reaching into green fields and pastureland like an octopus. Daniel Defoe remembered the Spitalfields of his youth as just that, fields, but by the time he came to write his *Tour through the Whole Island of Great Britain* in the early 1720s, the whole area was 'close built, and well inhabited with an infinite number of people'; Brick Lane, once 'a deep dirty road' rutted by carts loaded with bricks from kilns in the fields to Whitechapel, had become 'a long well-paved street'. Writing about the East End more generally, Defoe computes that around 200,000 inhabitants 'dwell now in that part of London, where, within about fifty years past, there was not a house standing'.

Back to your current location; though it's well past sunset, the Strand is alive with people carousing in taverns, sauntering past Somerset House, which has seen better days, and riding carriages to the playhouses at Covent Garden and Lincoln's Inn Fields. For most, the nightly curfew is no more than a distant memory – or a positively medieval concept. Everywhere you look, you see rapeseed oil lamps attached to people's houses. To you, the glow is feeble, but to the people around you, astonishing, extending the world of commerce and sociability into the hours of darkness, and colonizing the night. The lamps have illuminated the principal thoroughfares of Westminster and the City for the last ten years on weakly moonlit nights between six and eleven o' clock. It will be another twenty years before they are lit all through the night, every night of the year, but with their oil-burning wicks and convex glass reflectors, these lamps are big improvements on the old flickering candles in fragile horn-paned lanterns. For eighteenth-century Londoners, even the semi-illumination of the streets is a truly revolutionary development, extending the world of commerce and sociability into the hours of darkness, colonizing the night. By the end of the eighteenth century most of London would be fully lit, causing an astonished Russian to marvel, 'wherever you look, you see a succession of lights which from afar appear to be one continuous fiery thread stretched across the sky'.

You need to find an inn – nothing flash or lavish, just something comfortable, reasonably clean and convivial. The inns around the Strand are a bit pricey so why not try the Black Horse on Bow Street, Covent Garden? It is featured in *A New View of London, or, An Ample Account of that City* (1708), one of the most comprehensive visitors' guide books yet published, so you can safely assume it will be decent and comfortable. It's only fifteen minutes away but it's not going to be immediately obvious how to get there. Street numbering is conspicuously absent and street signage is patchy at best, though you will see some street names carved into rectangular stone plaques high up on buildings. Maps of London exist, of course, but the most accurate ones are huge and unwieldy, intended more to be rolled down from the wainscots of drawing rooms and admired over tea than carted about outside; if you pored over one on the streets you'd look ridiculous and quite possibly come a cropper at the hands of a cutpurse.

One option is to hire the service of a link boy – a boy or youth who, for a fee, will weave a red thread through London's labyrinth of backstreets and blind alleys, lighting the way with a large torch (you saw one of these creatures earlier, outside Devereux Court). You'd be well advised not to do this. Some link boys seem to have been the forerunners of rent boys. In a poem by the Restoration debauchee Lord Rochester, a libertine and his mistress both covet their pretty young link boy – whoever gives him the best kiss is the deciding factor in, as the libertine puts it, 'whether the boy fucked you, or I the boy' – and there is unmistakably something phallic about the torch that link boys carry. They're also assumed by many to be in league with particularly unsavoury aspects of London's criminal underworld, luring newcomers straight into the hands of tricksters, footpads and women of the night.

Avoid.

So how are you to find your way around town? If you haven't already noticed them, look up and you'll have your answer – a galaxy of shop signs shimmering in the lamplight and creaking in the wind.

'Mr Richard Cushee, mapmaker, at the Globe and Sun,' and others

Huge (by twenty-first-century standards) and powerful status symbols – some reportedly cost as much as a flabbergasting £100 (you could buy a coach for less in 1748) – the signs jut out at right angles on thick iron branches from every house you pass; some sculpted out of copper and pewter, others gaudily (and sometimes gilt) painted on wood with elaborate frames, some sculpted into stone niches. What you see are the forerunners of the brand logos of later centuries, clamouring for the attention of passers-by.

There has never been – and never will be – as dense a concentration of signs as there are in the early eighteenth century. Charles I encouraged people to hang a sign from their shop or house 'for the better finding out such citizens' dwellings, shops, arts or occupations, without impediment, molestation, or interruption of his heirs or successors', a privilege technically

granted only to public houses before (though flouted, as you
saw in the bookselling quarter in Shakespearean London). They
allow Londoners to forge mental maps of their neighbourhoods, triangulating their position via memorable landmarks.
A uniform system of street numbering is still fifty years off.
For the moment, addresses are listed with a certain charm,
as follows: 'Mr Richard Cushee, mapmaker, at the Globe and
Sun between St Dunstan's Church and Chancery Lane' or
'Richard Rock, purveyor of tincture to cure the teeth, at the
Hand and Face near Blackfriars Stairs' or 'Bezaleel Creake, at
the Bible and Ink-Bottle in Germain Street [Jermyn Street]
near St James's' – this last bookseller sounds like he was a member of London's 750-strong Jewish community, which has been
growing since Oliver Cromwell permitted Jews to live freely
(if not unmolested) in England in the 1650s after a 300-year
banishment. Sensibly, signs have to be hung at least nine feet
off the ground so they don't crack the skulls of coachmen and
horseback riders, or chip the roofs of sedan chairs and
carriages.

Unless you want to make a fool of yourself, don't take the
signs too literally. It can take some lateral thinking to fathom
their meaning; any cryptic crossword skills you might have will
come in handy. Thus the sign of Adam and Eve connotes
apples (not, as some gullible travellers believe, snakes); a unicorn is usually an apothecary's – the magical nature of the beast
presumably enhancing the appeal of the potions and pills on
sale behind the counter whose medicinal benefits, it has to be
said, are generally as mythical as the fabled creature itself; the
royal bed, an upholsterer; a bugle's horn, a post office; the head
of Sir Isaac Newton, a maker of scientific instruments; the
Golden Fleece, a woollen draper's; a spotted cat, a perfumer. If
this last sign confuses you, bear in mind that one of London's

most fashionable perfumes is called the civet handkerchief scent, the main ingredient of which is musk, a pungent buttery slime scraped from the anal scent glands of African civets. In 1692 Daniel Defoe bought seventy of the creatures in an effort to build a perfume-making factory in Stoke Newington – just one of his many doomed money-making ventures (the snouted, mongoose-like creatures were carried away by his creditors).

Think you've got the hang of it? Think again. Beyond the nine-feet-high rule, there's no regulation, and many shopkeepers and households choose whatever tickles their fancy. Thus the sign of the beehive is popular with wax-chandlers, as is logical, but it can also be a more general symbol of industry shared by linen drapers, hosiers and even cricket bat makers – but bemusingly not honey merchants. Chillingly, the sign of Death's head is the preserve of undertakers *and* apothecaries. A hand and pen around Fleet Street doesn't, as elsewhere, connote a scrivener's but rather a place where you can get yourself a clandestine marriage in the Liberty of the Fleet (should you meet anyone nice on your travels) and other signs are either mind-bogglingly cryptic or just plain nonsensical. Well might you wonder why a dog in a crock is the sign of a breech maker. And why would a bon-bon seller be identified by the sign of three herrings? Many proprietors just want whatever will turn heads, and this is what inns, taverns and alehouses are up to as they vie for customers with their lions, dragons, mermaids, goats in boots, flying pigs, hogs in armour, painted boards of busty Nell Gwynn (still famous almost thirty years after her death) and the Man in the Moon with pouting lips and sad eyes, as you saw on Holywell Street in Victorian London. Others you'll find more offensive. The sign of two maids endlessly lathering and scrubbing the cheeks of a naked black man in a bathtub denotes a Labour in Vain tavern; it speaks volumes about ingrained assumptions of racial superiority in an age when much of the prosperity of the City of London comes from the slave trade.

A correspondent to the *Spectator* suggests that a house's sign reflects the temperament of the occupier with a 'surly choleric fellow' favouring bears and 'men of milder dispositions', lambs. Whether there's any truth in this is hard to tell but signs are, after all, part of how citizens present themselves to the world.

Sometimes, though, the city's topography is the formative influence. A house on the cusp of town and country is sometimes called the World's End. It might be identified by a globe floating in the inky void of space, with smoke rising from the crevices of the earth, or a horseman rearing over a dark abyss. But since London is spreading her tentacles in 1716, the sign of the World's End is sometimes beached 'inland', bringing a flash of the apocalypse to the finest of West End squares, a palimpsest of the shifting limits of the city.

Because London has such a restless population, constantly uprooted by plagues, fires and the caprices of profit-mongering landlords, people often find themselves sharing subdivided houses where surreal hybrids are born, some of which – like the fox and seven stars, the wolf and woolpack, the sheep and dolphin or the angel and punchbowl – can make visitors feel like they're drifting through the most outlandish of dreamscapes.

Be warned: some signs bite. You may encounter a live sign. Keep your eye peeled for live cats in baskets, birds in cages and squirrels in barrels – usually with bells attached to their necks to attract attention; cruel, but interesting. Elderly Londoners may recall a late wine merchant in Cornhill with a tethered vulture squawking about his shopfront. Sometimes when live signs perish they are stuffed and put straight back to ensure brand continuity.

A few final notes. When the hedgehog appears, which is very rarely, there are apples impaled on his spines, though no one really knows why. You'll see the cat and fiddle all over the place. People assume this derives from a sixteenth-century ballad but it could equally be a corruption of a celebrated knight called Caton le Fidèle, who won victories against France in the Hundred Years War in the fourteenth century and whose name it seems the English never quite mastered. The golden ball, a very simple sign to manufacture, is one of the most popular tradesmen's signs. See how beautiful it looks in the moonlight. But don't gawk beneath the signs for too long as they creak and groan in the wind. Two years from now a huge one in Bride Street near Fleet Street will come crashing down, hauling the frontage of a building with it and crushing four people to death.

Once you've found the sign of the angel (marking an inn) behind St Clement Danes Churchyard, turn left up Wych Street. You'll know once you've reached Drury Lane; a much meaner, narrower street called Little Drury Lane will intersect it on its southern side. After around a dozen left turnings you should find New Broad Court, which connects to the northern end of Bow Street (ask someone if you get lost) and there, swaying in the wind, is the sign of the black horse. Your inn awaits. Sleep tight; tomorrow will be a day of high-octane sightseeing.

Wednesday, 22 February 1716

'The Square of Venus'

When you step out of your inn after a hearty (and, by your standards, alcoholic) breakfast, you feel charged for a day of sightseeing. But there are clouds brooding in a silvery sky. If you don't fancy the prospect of huddling with other citizens under the jetty of the nearest timber-framed house – and there are many survivals – why not splash out and travel in style, by sedan chair? They are a ubiquitous and tantalizing presence – hovering about the streets like magic carpets while you battle through the sludge. You can hail them in the street like a modern taxi but the clouds are beginning to dribble so your best bet is to head to the nearest public sedan-chair rank. It's in Charing Cross. The quickest route is to cut through the Great Piazza onto the Strand. En route is Button's coffeehouse, a haunt of writers presided over by Joseph Addison, the godfather of wit. Inside is a peculiar lion's head postbox into which, during the run of the *Guardian* paper two years ago, writers fed literary submissions, the best of which would be 'roared out' in a special weekly issue called the lion's digest.

Covent Garden feels like a different world from the one you visited just fifty years earlier, seedier by far. Cutting through the marketplace, you pass vegetable hawkers, toothless prostitutes, destitute actors, hungover aristocrats and the odd stray pig on its way to rummage. Around the perimeter of the market, where men on stilts will mesmerize tourists in the twenty-first century, cockfights and boxing matches have broken out. Drunken rakes are staggering about burping, hungry for flesh and wine. For them, the night has only just begun. From the upper-storey windows of the soot-stained terraces around the northern and eastern sides of the piazza, you see furtive figures with long, free-falling hair whisking open curtains then retreating into a haze of smoke (you saw similar scenes on Bow Street and Drury Lane last night). These are some of the most expensive prostitutes in London and there are more of them in the 'Square of Venus' than anywhere else in the city. It is the very sink of vice. Blind fiddlers are in high demand as they're perfect for orgies, unable to name and shame clients. In 1776 one man would hire out a room at the Bedford Arms for a scored orgy with four prostitutes. When it was finished, he promptly shot himself in the head. From 1757 will appear an extraordinary little compendium, published annually, called *Harris's Lists of Covent Garden Ladies*, giving the name, address, age and physical attributes of all the noteworthy neighbourhood prostitutes along with concise reviews. It is described as the 'essential guide and accessory for any serious gentleman of pleasure'. One of the best places to pick up a prostitute is in a jelly house. To be sitting alone in such a place, playing with exotic jelly oozing from tall-stemmed glasses, is tantamount to wearing a striped cloak in medieval London or a starched-blue ruff in Shakespearean London.

All this social grime has accumulated as many of Covent Garden's former residents, the titled and wealthier families, transplant themselves into the gorgeous residential squares of Bloomsbury, St James's, Leicester Fields, Soho and Mayfair. The area has been invaded by coffeehouses, taverns, brothels, bagnios and gambling dens, evolving into what historian Vic Gatrell has described as 'the world's first creative bohemia'. Tempting though it may be, don't tarry. The Mohocks are about. Aside from slashing people's faces at night, this gang of aristocratic thugs like to attack old women, seal them in hogsheads, and roll them down streets. If they're capable of doing that to frail grannies just imagine what they might do to you.

'Prithee, sir, make way!': A whirl in a sedan chair

Turn right onto the Strand and walk towards Charing Cross. Note the change of tone here too; most of the glorious riverside palaces have been split up into commercial leaseholds by property developers after the westward exodus of their former titled residents (though the Duke of Northumberland, one of Charles II's illegitimate sons, still lives in Jacobean splendour in the turreted Northumberland House at the western end of the street).

The sedan-chair rank is near the equestrian statue of Charles I, which you might recognize from the twenty-first century. Private sedan chairs have fashionable sash windows and are brilliantly painted and gilded, sometimes with a coronet on the roof, and curved inwards at both ends forming an elegant waist. But such vehicles are the preserve of the *beau monde* and wealthy professionals, commissioned from luxury sedan-chair makers around Leicester Square, status symbols par excellence. When they are dressed for a night out, owners of private sedans don't have to worry about getting muddy in the street or other external nuisances; the bearers can switch to shorter poles, pick them up *inside*, carry them out into the street and deposit them in their host's dining room or mistress's bedroom, as appropriate, without their ever having to set foot in the street.

You'll be travelling in a bog-standard public chair. Unpretentious but durable, they frequently resemble boxes of soggy leather, albeit boxes with front and side windows. The leather is a uniform black, giving pubic sedans an instantly recognizable aesthetic just like the black cabs of the future. There are around 300 in London.

Don't try to stop a sedan that's already occupied or reserved or you'll be shouted at. It's easy to identify a free chair. Just look for a pair of chairmen carrying one in reverse to their rank, looking over their shoulders. Think of this reverse motion as the eighteenth-century equivalent of an illuminated yellow taxi light. You might want to take a note of the registration number on the back of the sedan. Should the chairmen refuse to carry you, demand an extortionate fee or be drunk and abusive then you can report them to the Hackney Coach Office and they can have their licences revoked, but note that *you* can be fined for incorrectly querying distances and fees. (*'Haquenée'*, incidentally, is Old French for an ambling horse or mare, often kept for hire; it took on a new meaning after the introduction of horse-drawn carriages in the seventeenth century – it has nothing to do with Hackney the place.) The bearers of sedans are generally muscular, stentorian and Irish. They pride themselves on their speed – 'I do not believe that in the whole of Europe better or more dexterous bearers are to be found', writes César de Saussure, who had the unfortunate experience of being barged out of the way by one when he first arrived in London. Announce your destination – Moorfields – and hand over your fare, which will be no greater in real terms than the cost of a taxi ride in modern-day London. Then, the chair men will unstrap their leather shoulder harnesses, lay down their ten-foot wooden carrying poles and raise up the gently domed, hinged roof. There's no need to clamber or stoop; it's all very civilized.

A brief calm. You take a breath. The chair rattles. And then you're almost shaken out of your skin as the chair men hoist you into the air with a loud, synchronized grunt.

And you're off.

It's springier than you might imagine; the poles are long and elastic, and the whole experience reminds you of being in a plane with perpetual turbulence. From the outset, it's clear that the chair men are complete maniacs, running as fast as they possibly can and stopping for no one. They definitely don't recognize the distinction between the street and the walkway and it's mildly alarming to watch pedestrians leap out of the way like rabbits in headlights as the bearers yell 'Have care!' or 'Prithee, sir, make way!' *Prithee*, from *I pray thee*, is another way of saying please but this is a command not a polite request, as newcomers to London have learned the hard way. Gliding through London may feel a bit embarrassing at first, as though you're asserting your superiority over everyone else on the street, and you are. But lower the window, sit back, and let the sights and sounds of the city flood in. Your conscience will soon be eased.

The rich cadences of broadside ballad singers mingle with the chiming of church bells and the shopkeeper's cry of 'What do ye lack? What do ye lack?' – as ubiquitous here as a flickering neon shop sign in twenty-first-century London. As you make your way down Cheapside, you see watchmen with white sticks tapping on front doors and bellowing out the time and weather on the strike of every hour, old women hunched on ponies selling crumpled newsletters, famished vagrants face down in the oozing pavement, and apprentices playing football from one side of the street to the other, to the horror of coachmen. You turn left at Threadneedle Street, passing by the back of the Royal Exchange, which emits a dull buzz from its open-air piazza, and whizz towards Pig Street.

In your haste, you realize that you haven't told them where you want to be deposited, so crane your neck out of the window (holding your periwig in place if you're a man – you don't want that to blow away) and shout round to the front chair man, 'Prithee, good man, Bedlam!' You might think it's in poor taste to spend your first morning in eighteenth-century London laughing at incarcerated lunatics. But know that viewing the 'moon-sick' is a tradition in which even the most sophisticated members of society partake with a twinkle in their eye. Writing in the previous century, the loftily cultured diarist John Evelyn admits 'stepping into Bedlam' (as the Bethlem Hospital is colloquially known) after dinner with Lord Hatton 'where I saw several poor miserable creatures in chains; one of them was mad with making verses' before resuming his daily business with renewed vigour. What better way to lift the spirits?

Unlike coaches, sedans can penetrate narrow alleys and wide thoroughfares alike. This affords you a good – if slightly blurred and fleeting – look at the buildings around you. After the Great Fire, only 9,000 new houses emerged from the ashes of the razed 13,200 but they were sturdier, more dignified, more elegant and, of course, more brick. In the wake of the calamity, sprawling, highly flammable timber-framed houses were expunged from the minds of architects and builders; in the new aesthetic order, there were to be no more lustful gables kissing above the street blocking out the light, and no more timber.

The new houses are elegant, neoclassical terraces three or four storeys high, two rooms deep, and two or three windows wide. They are set back from the street with marble porticos and pilasters, and attics set into a roofline often shielded by a parapet. Heavily influenced by the clean, straight lines and symmetrical forms of classical architecture, the whole effect bespeaks order, harmony and politesse. If you're familiar with modern London, you'll recognize this new architectural vernacular from areas where it has survived into the twenty-first century, in places like Downing Street, Spitalfields, Soho and Islington. They are likely to be rosier in colour than you expect, mind. In the twenty-first century, we tend to think of buildings from the eighteenth century as brooding browny-grey or even soot black – but it's only in the last two years that builders have begun to use grey and brown bricks. Prior to that, softer reds and pinks were in vogue.

There are still timber-framed houses clustered and dotted around the City; some 5,000 of them survived the flames. As you are carried up Broad Street, which marks the north-easterly limit of the fire's destruction, you'll see new brick frontages suddenly give way to timber-and-plaster sprawls. Not all these older houses are tumbledown wrecks and some are venerable, stretching back into pre-Tudor times, but it's clear they are a dying breed, eclipsed by a new architectural vernacular. Some have Georgian-style façades wedged onto them in order to appear modern, an architectural equivalent of the guises adopted by Dudley Ryder.

You see the crumbling Roman walls at Little Moor Gate. And you have arrived – in style. Get out and go through. When you turn round, the sedan will have vanished.

Bethlem: 'An abode for those who have fallen out of wit'

For a hundred years now, Moorfields, laid out with trees and walks, has been a retreat from the filthy confines of the City, a place for citizens 'to rejoice their spirits with the beauty . . . of sweet flowers [and] the harmony of birds'. But it being February, today it's close to a quagmire with carts and wagons and pedestrians fighting a losing battle against the mud. The streets are dotted with bookstalls and it is here that Dudley Ryder likes to buy little crisp pamphlets – a proposal to ease the nation's debt written by John Locke, for instance, or a polemic attacking the rite of baptism – to occupy his mind as he wanders through the archery fields, vinegar yards and winding lanes of Hoxton and Hackney.

The most impressive feature of the landscape, though, is what one foreigner describes as 'an enormous building with huge gates'; another 'one of the largest and handsomest buildings in London' hogging the entire southern stretch of Moorfields. According to the surveyor of London John Strype, 'it is stately and graceful to behold, and tends much to the honour of the City'. This isn't, as the naïve country bumpkin narrator of the *London Spy* assumes, the Lord Mayor's residence nor, as a French guide book suggests, yet another royal palace.

It is the Hospital of Bethlem – 'an abode for those who have fallen out of wit'. It is the most ostentatious lunatic asylum in the world.

As the name suggests, New Bedlam is the latest incarnation of an earlier lunatic asylum operating from the priory of St Mary Bethlehem in Bishopsgate from the fourteenth century until it was wiped out in the Great Fire (even before that, if you remember, there had been a small asylum near the Royal Mews in Charing). The previous Bedlam, set where Liverpool Street railway station would later stand, was a modest building with a square-towered church, gabled dwellings and some gardens. Its successor, built by Renaissance man Robert Hooke between 1675 and 1676, was on an incomparably grander scale and based on the Tuileries Palace in France (though some mistakenly thought Versailles was the model) with stately columns, a neoclassical portico, narrow cupolas, walks and a thick, 700-foot brick wall; it was, in the words of John Evelyn again, 'magnificently built and most sweetly placed in Moorfields'.

What he doesn't mention is that Bedlam is built on the boggy foundations of the ancient City ditch, which you experienced first-hand back in medieval London, giving it something of a sunken and melancholic aspect that the grandeur of the building can never quite disguise. Nonetheless, to twenty-first-century sensibilities, the building seems like a perversely ornate setting in which to house something as grim and clinical as a lunatic asylum, but the architecture is tailored to project the philanthropic excellence of the City Fathers who so magnanimously raised some £17,000 to erect it. From the outside, at least, it looks like a museum or art gallery, as befits a place where lunatics are carefully curated and displayed to the world. It's no oubliette; it's at once a monument to the destructive force of madness and an assurance that mental illness is being tamed and controlled by the authorities instead of ripping through the fabric of urban society. That's part of the reason why the public are admitted – it's not simply callous voyeurism.

As you reach the steps, look out for two large figures carved from Portland stone guarding the gates – the 'brainless brothers'. With his hands in shackles and his body and face contorted into a posture of despair, the figure on the right represents acute, raving, beyond-the-pale madness while his languid counterpart on the left sprawls more gracefully, striking a thoughtful pose. He represents melancholy. Bedlam confines what contemporaries see as distinct breeds of lunatics – the 'incurables', doomed to perpetual incarceration, and the 'curables' who might one day walk free.

Next, you go through a court and up a small flight of steps to the entrance to the building where there are two more stone maniacs – one male and one female – this time holding a money box: 'pray remember the poor lunatics, and put your charity into the box with your own hand'. The entrance fee is a mere 2d, so taking a turn in the lunatic asylum isn't so different from visiting the theatre or coffeehouse. And you are contributing to the £400 a year it costs for the upkeep and 'care' of the inmates. So don't feel too guilty as you enter Bedlam – it's in the patients' interests that as many people pour into the hospital as possible no matter how callously voyeuristic they are.

Make your way into the large room on the ground floor. On your left is a chamber where physicians and apothecaries examine the patients and on the southern side a commodious space for the governors to meet every Saturday to deliberate upon their fate and consider new applications. To get someone sectioned in the eighteenth century you need to present a petition to the committee of seven governors, and it must be countersigned by respectable people within the community such as churchwardens or lawyers.

At the end of the hall, on either side, are two foreboding iron gates leading up to the galleries. Do you want to see the mad men or the mad women?

As you approach a second iron gate at the top of the stairs, brace yourself for a harrowing cacophony, 'such a rattling of chains, drumming of doors, ranting, hallooing, singing' that it seemed as though the damned had broken free from hell, according to the *London Spy*. Then, in the words of César de Saussure, 'you find yourself in a long and wide gallery, on either side of which are a large number of little cells where lunatics of every description are shut up, and you can get a sight of these poor creatures, little windows being let into the doors'. Most inmates are enclosed in their cells like terrorists in a supermax prison in twenty-first-century America, but what César terms 'inoffensive madmen' (and in fact, women too) are also permitted to walk in the gallery and mingle with the spectators. The galleries are divided in half by an iron grille to segregate the sexes. The second floor, he notes, shares the same features as the first but is 'reserved for dangerous maniacs, most of them being chained and terrible to behold'.

Hooke's building is designed to house up to 120 patients but Bedlam sometimes holds up to 200 'standard' lunatics and 80 crazed maniacs upstairs.

What kind of people should you expect to see incarcerated in this place? Such was the impression Bedlam made on visitors – both British and foreign – that many left little pen portraits of the inmates they encountered. They strike a tragicomic note. The narrator of the *London Spy* (admittedly no stranger to histrionics) meets a 'man who wore a crown of moonshine' – someone who speaks nonsense – who was planning to wage war on the stars in the sky with his army of eagles unless the sun sends him 'a cloud laden with claret' every day since the Man in the Moon has guzzled all of his.

Just as in Shakespeare's plays it's often the jester who speaks the truth in a sea of courtly obsequiousness, so Ned Ward encounters some sagacious lunatics of refreshing lucidity. One, a firebrand republican, is spouting against the evil of monarchical government, for which he is rebuked by a crowd who tell him he deserves to hang for such sedition. 'I can tell great men such bold truths as they don't love to hear, without the danger of a whipping post,' he retorts. And he is right. In eighteenth-century London, for all its newspapers and coffee-houses and dissenting academies, there are still clear limits to the freedom of speech; the madhouse and the scaffold are the only public places where Londoners can speak their mind with impunity.

A Russian traveller encounters some of the female inmates, including a 'woman of about forty sat staring at the floor'. This poor creature wrongly believes, at the end of each day, that she is to be burned to death in the morning. 'Tomorrow, tomorrow,' she exclaims, 'they will burn me alive!' Elsewhere he encounters a man who believes he's a cannon.

And what of the audience? Expect to see a wide social spectrum – from men and women of fashion right down to the meanest artisan. Bedlam is an essential stop on any London sightseeing itinerary – on 'the rainiest day that ever dripped' in December 1710, for instance, the great Irish satirist Jonathan Swift took in the sights of the town, setting out at ten o'clock to see the lions at the Tower, then going to Bedlam, having a hearty dinner at one of the chop houses behind the Royal Exchange and topping off his day with a puppet show. If you were to come back on a public holiday you should brace yourself for a more Saturnalian atmosphere with fruit, nut, and beer hawkers, prostitutes parading up and down the galleries, and cruel crowds 'rioting up and down the wards making sport of the miserable inhabitants'. The 'wild motions', piercing screams and unhinged behaviour of the inmates inspire extreme antics and are even a turn-on for some of the spectators who feel that the laws and moral codes that usually govern society have been temporarily suspended. There are punch-ups, foul-mouthed exchanges and eruptions of lust: 'Mistresses, we found, were to be had of all ranks,' writes Ned Ward, 'there wanted not a suitable Jack to every Jill . . . every fresh comer was soon engaged in an amour; though they came in single they went out by pairs'; it was, in short, bedlam.

More than anything else, the antics of lunatics elicit laughter. 'On holidays numerous persons of both sexes . . . amuse themselves watching these unfortunate wretches, who often give them cause for laughter,' observes César de Saussure in 1725; 'I saw them in a loud laugh of triumph at the ravings they had occasioned,' writes a visitor in 1753. But looking into the eyes of the spectators as they see a straitjacketed maniac for the first time, you might come to think that this is not just a case of schadenfreude. Their laughter belies a nervousness, concealing deep angst and horror at the precariousness of life in eighteenth-century London which, for all its burgeoning modernity, is still a foreboding place to live with tragically high rates of infant mortality (by the mid-1730s, of every five babies born, one will die before its second birthday), a deathly spell in Newgate hanging over tradesmen like a sword of Damocles, press gangs stalking the streets, the injustices suffered by unhappily married women, and the dread that the plague will one day return. All that is enough to send even the sanest soul stark raving mad. Elevating the unfortunates of Bedlam into the sphere of humour, then, can be seen as a form of cathartic release.

Before you leave, you have the option of visiting, by way of grand finale, the ward for 'incurable maniacs' on the top floor. It's one of the darkest and most depraved corners of the metropolis. If you decide to follow the other excited visitors through the metal grille on the top floor, you can expect to find a series of tiny numbered cells, some empty, some containing chained lunatics on pallets of hay. There are hatches in each door. Why don't you poke your snout right through for the best view? Everyone else is. Some of the less threatening incurables may be milling about in the gallery, building their castles in the air or staring into the middle distance, lost. There will be carers and nurses about so you shouldn't be in too much danger.

The atmosphere of the incurables ward is powerfully evoked in the eighth and final episode of Hogarth's *A Rake's Progress*. We find a senseless Tom Rakewell, once so fresh-faced and cherubic, now looking every bit the brainless brother. He is languishing amidst a cast of tormented characters, his legs in manacles, a gormless smile on his face. He keeps company with a mad musician trying to play a violin with what looks like a stick and wearing his sheet music as a hat, a 'moon faced' melancholic lamenting his harlot lover, a deranged astronomer using a rolled up piece of paper as a telescope, a zealot who has mistaken the sunbeams for the presence of God, an insane tailor who's playing with his measuring tape as though it's a friendly snake, and someone who thinks he's an archbishop. In attendance are two fashionable ladies, whispering and giggling, voyeurs on the pandemonium, conspicuous in their crinoline dresses against the writhing, half-naked forms of the lunatics. One of the ladies holds up a perfectly folded fan, as though to insulate herself from the corrupting force of the madness.

Make a relieved exit, walk back into the City and hail another sedan chair. You're looking to go to Fleet Street, as far as the Devil Tavern.

The street of ink: home of the Snotty-Nosed Gazette

The ride to the Devil Tavern should take about fifteen minutes. When you see the sign of the Devil having his nose tweaked by a pincer-brandishing St Dunstan, alight. Chaos and commerce await as you set foot in the well-hooved Street of Ink. For the narrator of the *London Spy*, 'the rattling of coaches loud as the cataracts of the Nile robbed me of my hearing, and put my head into as much disorder as the [clamour] of a rural mob at a country bull-baiting'. It is the news criers who give the street its unique soundscape. You'll see them – young urchins as well as weathered old men and women – careering about the streets belting out the news with thick bricks of newspapers. 'Lament, ye heroes, who frequent the wars,' proclaims a mock-heroic poem on the death of an illiterate old hawker in 1708, 'the great proclaimer of your dreadful scars.'

You'll find London's newspaper boom is in full swing after the unanticipated and almost casual lapsing of pre-publication censorship in 1695. As the editorialist of the *Grumbler*, a short-lived moralistic essay paper, grumbled less than a year ago: 'the meanest artificer now thinks himself qualified to judge everything'. He blames this squarely on the recent 'inundation of newspapers' which has brought on a 'universal thirst for news'. For César de Saussure, nothing is funnier than seeing shoeblacks and other 'men of that class' clubbing together to buy a paper and bothering their little heads about politics; 'you often see an Englishman taking a treaty of peace more to heart than his own affairs'. He overstates his case a little – London would have to wait until the reign of Queen Victoria for a mass media worthy of the name as you have seen for yourself – but here is, nonetheless, a real glut of news: this year, no fewer than thirty-six periodical titles will be sold on the streets of London (admittedly not all newspapers in the modern sense) with a total weekly circulation of around 66,000, rising to 100,000 by the 1740s (which puts France's 1740 total to shame: 15,000 for the whole country). Some early papers, incidentally, have fantastic names: in 1679 Londoners were treated to the *Snotty-Nosed Gazette*; in 1696, *The Night-Walker: Or, Evening Rambles in Search after Lewd Women*; and later this year, *News from the Dead*. No one is interested in fair and balanced reporting. As in the twenty-first century, most papers are highly partisan, reinforcing what people already believe, assimilating events into rival world-views, and crystallizing pre-existing prejudices. Finding himself with an hour to kill in the British coffeehouse one summer's day in 1715, Dudley Ryder felt a morbid curiosity to dip into a Tory paper whose political leanings clashed violently with his own, and recorded, 'I never met with an author so very bold with truth and so impudently asserting falsehoods in my life, and yet his paper must do a great deal of harm at least in hardening the Tories against any possibility of conviction.' No doubt readers of the *Guardian* feel exactly the same when they dip into the *Daily Mail*, and vice versa.

Although clusters of newspaper printing houses can be found in the historic print districts of Ludgate and St Paul's – and some even further north and east – it is Fleet Street, as the conduit between the literary enclaves of the Inns of Court and St Paul's Churchyard, and lying in between the two most important producers of news in London – the City and Westminster – that is emerging as a metonym for the newspaper press, an association so powerful it has endured into our own time even as London has become a diaspora of newspaper headquarters.

Going east you have Mrs Salmond's Waxworks to your left, a precursor to the more famous Madame Tussaud's in Baker

Street with which you may be familiar. Mrs Salmond, an eccentric toymaker who likes to sleep in a shroud, moved here five years ago and runs the museum with her husband. It costs 6d to get in. Amongst the waxy canon is Queen Boudica, a gaunt-faced Charles I on his execution scaffold and a figure of an old woman running away from an embodiment of Time, who is annoyed by her refusal to yield to the mortal dictates of the egg-timer he wields. A little further down, before Fetter Lane, is the church of St Dunstan-in-the-West with its large gold-on-black clock – the first public clock in London to have a minute hand. The hours are kept by the legendary British warrior-giants Gog and Magog, naked except for sparkling golden thongs. They thwack the bells on the stroke of every hour with meaty clubs.

Whores, mug houses and a river of filth: the cradle of modern journalism

By now you should be passing some dark arches on your left leading into tight, winding passages. Some take you to sodden courtyards such as Hen and Chicken Court, with only two houses; one to the Cheshire Cheese Tavern; some seemingly nowhere at all. It is in discreet corners like this that sirens lurk, ready to suck the innocence of passers-by. 'As I came along Fleet Street had a mind to attack a whore,' writes Dudley Ryder of a night boozing with friends in the City, 'and did so: went along with her a good way, talked with her tolerably well and at last left her.' He rarely does any more than talk. 'Had a mind to fill a whore's commodity,' he writes on another occasion, 'and went about the streets in order to do it, but could not conveniently do it without hazarding my reputation.' On these unedifying occasions, he usually ends up back in his Temple digs 'frigging' himself, waking up the next morning full of remorse and resolutions.

Further down, on your right, is Salisbury Court where Samuel Pepys had a bladder stone removed and miraculously survived. From one of the buildings in the court, you can hear people belting out songs. Walk closer. You see people walking in – and staggering out – of what looks like a tavern, with misted-up windows. After a while, the singing stops, a beefy, backslapping cheer is raised and you hear sharp clinks and loud and hearty laughter.

This is not a tavern or alehouse but a mug house, one of only seven in London. 'Mug' is a slang word for a face and in these rowdy establishments each member has their own drinking vessel, decorated with (or shaped like) the face of King George or one of his ministers, from which they gulp copious toasts of loyalty and dance, cheer, chant, clap, sing and sometimes fight pitched street battles with besieging Tory and Jacobite mobs, which sometimes end in bloodshed. The aim is to shore up support for the Hanoverian regime not through civil conversation and rational debate, as you'd expect in a coffeehouse, but through a direct appeal to the passions, galvanized by ale. They are more egalitarian than coffeehouses, bringing together gentlemen, professionals (like him), tradesmen and apprentices, who, throats awash with ale and arms linked in dance, all but forget their social distinctions; 'We are all upon a level there and those that can entertain the company with the most songs is the most taken notice of,' writes an impressed Dudley Ryder of a visit to this mug house. He likens the effects of the singing and dancing to whipping a lethargic horse into a furious gallop. Their association with political violence means they will be a very short-lived London tradition.

Two men, the worse for wear, fall out of the mug house and proceed, arm-in-arm, towards Fleet Street, one stopping to piss against a wall as the other rants against the House of Lords. From what you can glean from their curses and mumblings, it appears that after many hours of debates and speeches, the peers today voted to address the king in favour of the condemned Jacobite lords. The mug house men are vexed, since they believe this would cast the odium of the executions, if they go ahead, upon the king. They totter off into the night, baying for the blood of the Earl of Derwentwater.

Returning to Fleet Street, you'll find on your right the spire of Wren's St Bride's church. It has four octagonal tiers of gradually diminishing size, eventually vanishing into an obelisk that thrusts into the turquoise Fleet Street sky. As the apprentices propping up the bar in the Old Bell or Sugar Loaf Tavern might tell you, some time ago (they're not quite sure when) a baker's apprentice from Ludgate Hill fell in love with his master's daughter. With his father's blessing, he plucked up the courage to propose to her. But he wanted to do something special for the wedding and pledged to bake an incomparable cake for the wedding feast, something mesmeric to prove his worth. But the muses were not generous and he found himself suffering an acute case, if I may, of baker's block. Gazing up at the spire of St Bride's one day for inspiration, he realized the answer had been in front of him all along: a multi-tiered wedding cake with layers of diminishing size, just like the spire. English weddings would never be the same again.

A foul stench rises from the River Fleet, now ahead of you. There was a time when barges plied its clear waters with cargoes of oysters and herring but these days it's a filthy, stinking sewer, a cesspit of dead dogs, suicide victims, and sometimes after mass slaughterings at Smithfield Market to the north, blood. This, time traveller, is the primeval ooze from which the newspaper industry would emerge.

And to think, it was once London's 'second river' and the

western frontier of the Roman settlement of Londinium. Rising in Hampstead as twin streams (which may be familiar to you as Hampstead and Highgate ponds), the Fleet gushes into the Thames at Blackfriars running through Kentish Town, St Pancras, Holborn and Clerkenwell en route but it is destined to be buried alive between Holborn and Ludgate Circus to make way for the Fleet Market; the southern section, from Fleet Bridge to the Thames, will become Fleet Ditch before itself being buried and forgotten in 1769. The little lanes and alleys branching off from the Fleet – Meal Yard, Goose Alley, Harp Alley, Turnagain Lane – are amongst the most squalid and deprived in London, reeking to high heaven as men and women cluster on the eastern bank to tan animal hides for boots and saddles.

With the fetid river burbling beneath your feet, cross the stone bridge, where you'll be eyed (as far as you can be) by some unsavoury characters operating grotty little shacks. Ned Ward evokes this pitiful market in the *London Spy*: 'We moved on till we came to Fleet Bridge, where nuts, gingerbreads, oranges and oysters lay, piled up in movable shops that run upon wheels, attended by ill-looking fellows, some with but one eye, and others without noses.' Best give them a wide berth and proceed onto the bustling grandeur of Ludgate Hill.

On your left sits the Fleet prison, London's oldest purpose-built gaol dating from the twelfth century, now specializing in the incarceration of debtors who, provided they can compensate the Keeper, may live anywhere in the paradoxically named 'Liberty of the Fleet', a square district bounded by Ludgate Hill, the Old Bailey, Fleet Lane and the river itself. It is also a hotspot for clandestine marriages performed, for the most part, by impoverished clergymen for a small fee and a bottle of wine in one of the area's forty or so 'marrying houses'. The Fleet has imprinted the whole area with something of a sleazy air.

Walk onto Ludgate, 'a wide and handsome [street] . . . entirely occupied by merchants' wares'. We're here to see a house that can lay a strong claim to being the cradle of modern journalism, a mere stone's throw from the spike where the head of the printer John Twyn was impaled just over half a century ago after he printed a thirty-two-page treatise which called for 'the people to execute the law of God upon wicked kings' – not his best move and, as it turned out, one of his last. These days, while printing seditious content is still unwise, the press enjoys more liberties and is becoming more inventive. The house is on your right, post-Fire, smartly built, next door to the King's Arms tavern that overlooks Fleet Ditch. It was here, in March 1702, that an enterprising publisher called Elizabeth Mallet produced Britain's first daily newspaper, the *Daily Courant*.

A bold and enterprising woman, Elizabeth Mallet had her finger on the commercial pulse of Fleet Street. On her husband's death in 1683, she threw herself into his trade – printing – taking on her son David as an apprentice and operating a printing house with two presses in the rank Black Horse Alley leading down to the Fleet. Over the next twenty-three years she operated from a number of addresses but, a true denizen of Fleet Street, she never strayed far from the slimy banks of the ditch. She demonstrated an excellent eye for the kind of personal stories that went down a storm with the public – stories that very rarely had a happy ending. She loved to publish accounts of the behaviour of condemned men and women in the moments after they were sentenced to death and, even more excitingly, the hours, minutes and seconds before they met their doom on the gibbet at Tyburn, the burning stake at Smithfield or Execution Dock at Wapping. Of William Charley, sentenced to death for stealing cloth from a warehouse, '[upon] his conviction he became exceedingly sad, imagining no mercy would be allowed him'; of Ann Scot, judicially slaughtered for stealing a flowered gown and satin petticoat from a house near St Dunstan's Church, she '[wrung] her hands and sigh[ed], saying she was the unhappiest woman alive wishing she had never been born'. Such are the little nuggets of voyeuristic titillation that elicit guilty fascination at human suffering, still a winning formula on Fleet Street in the twenty-first century.

For a time Elizabeth was the official publisher of the *Proceedings of the Old Bailey* and by the turn of the century, she also published the Ordinary (i.e. chaplain) of Newgate's moralizing accounts of the life, confessions and last dying speeches of criminals executed at Tyburn. We can assume that she built up a strong working relationship with the authors, shaping the content to maximize its commercial appeal. Sprinkled with biblical axioms, like many of her other publications, they adopt a rather pious and judgemental tone, rarely showing any flicker of sympathy for the condemned. One tells the story of Alice Milikin, like Elizabeth a single mother who arrived from the provinces to build herself a better life in London. Facing destitution, Alice turned to clipping coins to produce counterfeit currency. What sounds like a pretty trivial offence from a twenty-first-century standpoint counted as the highest treason in the eighteenth century, the penalty for which, for a woman, was to burn at the stake in Smithfield as the Protestant martyrs had done at the hands of Bloody Mary in the sixteenth century. For the pamphlet's author, this is precisely what Alice deserves for her 'wicked' and 'abominable' crime – grinding poverty is no excuse and only the flames of Smithfield can 'satisfy [her] excess in a sinful course of life'.

There are signs that, by the turn of the century, Elizabeth was interested in orientating her publishing business in a more highbrow direction. It's no surprise that she was inspired by the growing vogue for newspapers. After a few short-lived experiments with the medium, in March 1702 she did something no one, it seems, had ever thought of – or dared – doing before: launching a journal carrying political news on every single day of the week (except the Sabbath, of course). In such a crowded marketplace it was a risky proposition. But she had a plan. The *Courant* would fill its space by translating reports from a range of European gazettes (including from Scotland and Ireland) such as the *Paris Gazette*, *Amsterdam Courant*, *Leiden Gazette* and others: why bother to employ networks of costly correspondents when you could simply plagiarize the European press? As she declared in the first issue, the paper would be shorter, sharper and more accurate than its competitors, keeping its readers up-to-date with the very latest dramas from the theatre of European warfare. But Elizabeth's involvement was to prove fleeting. After a mere ten issues, she moved on to other projects, handing over the reins of production to Samuel Buckley, who steered the paper into profit. By the time of your visit, it is a flourishing double-sided sheet.

But don't just take my word for it. See for yourself.

Cross the road and walk up Ludgate Hill. As you go through Ludgate itself, note the statues of King Lud, the mythical founder of London, and Queen Elizabeth I. Have a good look to see if John Twyn's parboiled head is still up there.

Ahead of you, bathed in sunlight and seemingly with its own gravitational pull, is an iconic new feature of the London skyline – the magisterial, life-affirming cupola of the rebuilt St Paul's Cathedral; it's only been seven years since the final stone was laid. Take a good look at it and breathe in – it's good for the soul – then cut left into Cock Alley. Walk through to Stationers' Court, admiring the splendid new hall of the Stationers' Company on the left, then through to Amen Corner. The printing house of the *Daily Courant* is opposite the church, near Warwick Lane. Time to witness the churning of one of Fleet Street's inky turbines.

It's a small, low-ceilinged room, rather dark and dank, with creaking floorboards and an aroma of ink, moist paper and bodies caked in sweat. No one takes any notice of you as you walk in; there is a mountain of work to get through. Your attention is immediately drawn to the two wooden hand presses which, at six foot, loom somewhat over the bleary-eyed print-ers and compositors who are busy at work in greasy white overalls.

It's cumbersome work. Since the steam-powered printing press won't exist until the next century, the upper limit on what a newspaper printing house can produce on one wooden screw press is around 200 single-sided sheets per hour. This means that although some eighteenth-century weekly papers like the anti-government *Craftsman* and later on John Wilkes's radical *The North Briton* can sell in their respectable thousands, most papers, especially daily and tri-weekly papers for which the window of print is very narrow, are not exactly gigabuck prop-ositions (though there is a widespread assumption that each individual *copy* can be read by up to twenty people in coffee-houses and elsewhere, meaning readership is much higher than cold circulation data would suggest). Some papers are driven by ideology alone; others are propagandist rags funded by the government – if you think Tony Blair was obsessed with the portrayal of his government in the media, know that the first prime minister to live at number 10 Downing Street in 1735, Sir Robert Walpole, spent some £50,000, very crudely comparable to £11 million in 2015 terms, subsidizing the pro-government press over a ten-year period. Others are owned by committees of booksellers, keen to spread the risk of the £200 start-up cost. By 1716 the owner of the *Courant* is a certain Richard

Burleigh, a prolific purveyor of books, polemics, political poems, sermons and execution speeches – producing over fifty titles this year alone.

The staff and apprentices are racing to get the first page of tomorrow's *Daily Courant* – the news section – typeset and printed so they can get to the tavern at a reasonable hour. One compositor stands behind a tall wooden bureau, his eyes flitting between a messy handwritten script and a propped-up palette containing a grid of metal type. There are hundreds of versions of each character: letters, numbers, and punctuation marks, italics, Greek letters – all in many different sizes and various typefaces (or fonts to use the technical term). If any of these have been put back in the wrong place, the compositor's job becomes a complete nightmare and a storm of curses will descend upon the printing house.

The compositor takes the selected metal characters, or 'sorts', over to the press, and carefully clinks them into a wooden frame, or 'forme', ready to be slid underneath the press. With all the type inserted, the forme can weigh as much as a man.

The first page of the *Courant* has two columns of text and a large, resplendent title. Once these have been typeset, a second compositor or apprentice will appear with a pair of mushroom-shaped leather balls caked in a viscous substance made from soot, amber and linseed oil: ink, black as the night sky. It has to be rolled onto the metal type with great precision – there needs to be enough to print a strong impression but not too much to submerge the small gaps in characters like B, e and &. In a few minutes, the first impressions, which are likely to be riddled with errors, will be made and in preparation another printer is clamping a folio sheet into a thin metal frame ('the frisket') on the platen, which ultimately descends onto the inky type.

Printing is a delicate art, 'a chaos of chemicals, pressures, sequences and timings'. It's only now that you realize just how much you take for granted all the fonts that, at the click of a mouse, magically appear on your computer screen at home.

On a good day, the *Courant* might shift 700 copies; on a bad one, fewer than 500, scarcely enough to cover the costs of production. Newspaper sales usually soar at moments of political tension and crisis – such as this week, with all the rumours circulating about the impending execution of the Jacobite lords – but anticipating demand is still something of a dark and ruinous art, which is why the advertisement sections are so crucial as a supplementary source of income (for many papers, though not the *Courant*, they bring in more than 50 per cent of the revenue). The public don't just skim over the classified sections; they enjoy reading them as 'news from the little world, in the same manner that the foregoing parts of the paper are from the great' as Addison writes in the *Tatler*.

A number of people swarm about the room, trying to place notices and advertisements. At the back of the room sits a peri-wigged man at a table covered in foreign-language gazettes. He is poring over the scraps of handwritten paper, scowling. This is Richard Burleigh, the owner of the paper and someone who takes a keen interest in its contents. Every once in a while he gulps from a large flagon of red wine; it has proved something of a deep-rooted tradition on Fleet Street, right up to the 1980s, for copy to be written and edited in a state of mild to high intoxication. One medieval poem writes of 'that tippling street, distinguished by the name of Fleet, where tavern signs hang thicker far than trophies down at Westminster'.

An old woman with a mournful, wrinkled face, is telling a sob story about how her nephew, who can't walk properly, has absconded from the house of a stocking maker in Old Bedlam; if anyone returns him to her house near Aldgate, she will gladly offer a 10s reward. Also present is a finely dressed merchant, Mr Bird, advertising cognac brandy which he hopes to sell for 10s 6d a gallon from his house in the infamous Pudding Lane, and one Bernard Lintott, a Fleet Street bookseller, hoping his next hit will be *A General Table to all the Statutes from Magna Carta to the Year 1715*, listing all the monarchs on whose watch the laws were passed (a precursor perhaps of the historical ruler).

As the advertisers jockey for Mr Burleigh's attention, one of the printers marches over and slams down a proof of tomorrow's news section. Burleigh immediately stops what he is doing, whips out a pen and starts correcting it, tutting to himself every time he finds a mistake. After a couple of minutes he casts the corrected proof aside and resumes his conversations with the three individuals waving bits of paper at him. The printer who carried over the proof, meanwhile, has gone to assist those working on the other press on the new collected edition of something called the *Freeholder*, due out in a couple of days. Which gives you an opportunity to sneak a peek at tomorrow's news.

It opens with a vivid account of an earthquake in Algiers; next, a disturbing report from Vienna about a vast Turkish army amassing on the borders of Eastern Europe; then news on recent elections in Germany and so on. Reading early-eighteenth-century papers is a bit like flying in a hot-air balloon over the battlefields of Europe. Right at the end, there is a minuscule report from London on the current value of the stocks and shares but other than that, we only really hear about domestic affairs from the perspective of the *Scots Courant*, which reports on some aftershocks of the Jacobite rebellion in the Highlands. You may remember from your trip to the Grecian coffeehouse that most of London's other papers – the *Flying Post, Post Boy, Post Man, St James's Evening Post* – also favour foreign over domestic news, very unlike the news culture of twenty-first-century Britain. This is because domestic news spreads like lightning through the city's network of coffee-houses and taverns; foreign news is harder to acquire, so more valuable. It is the essay-papers and pamphlets that *do* engage in weighty yet witty political debate. Besides, Londoners are invested in ongoing and open-ended narratives, sometimes literally so – at the Royal Exchange, merchants like to gamble on the outcome of foreign news stories, although if they're caught they can be fined double the sum of the wager. More than anything, though, reading foreign news allows readers to peer into alien worlds, prompting them to reflect upon the nature of their own society, much like you have been doing on your travels.

Mr Burleigh looks up, meets your eyes. What business, prithee, have you rifling through his proofs? Stay calm and tell him you'd like to place an advertisement in tomorrow's *Courant*; you know you're cutting it a bit fine but you can give him 3s 6d for a good place. He grunts approval and picks up a pen. Tell him you've lost something valuable, something like a watch or a purse or a wife. Pack your notice full of detail, and offer a reward with no questions asked. Then make your way out, swiftly, and retire to the Black Horse for a brandy wine by the fireside.

Thursday, 23 February 1716

London's night of fire

A gentle, late-morning start. Make your way to Temple Bar, Christopher Wren's graceful, traffic-clogging archway wrought from Portland Stone replete with little dragons and sometimes the skewered heads of traitors.

Turn right up Sheer Lane. Take its sister street, Little Sheer Lane, heading west until you find an inconspicuous alleyway. At the end of it, down Serle Street, you can just make out the green leaves and painted wooden fences of Lincoln's Inn

Fields. Go into the alleyway, minding the uneven cobbles, and embrace the tranquillity of this little nook of the city. Tucked away on the right, set back from the alley, a dignified two-storey red-brick building suddenly reveals itself. It has a slate roof and steps leading up to a small portico that is flanked by casement windows.

Welcome to James Wood's Presbyterian meeting house, one of almost eighty new dissenters' chapels dotted around London and its suburbs, tokens of a more tolerant and sophisticated society. Dissenters are Protestants who, alienated by the incompleteness of the Reformation and vestiges of popery within the Anglican Church, have formed breakaway congregations to worship as their conscience dictates under the protection of the law. The most prominent are the Presbyterians – formerly known as Puritans – but there are also Independents, Quakers and Baptists, all with their own meeting places and beliefs. They remain barred from public and municipal office as well as the universities of Oxford and Cambridge, which Dudley Ryder, a dissenter himself, accordingly lambasts as resorts of pedants and pederasts.

Make your way into the chapel, quietly. Take a seat on one of the back pews; there's a sermon in progress but you'll find the congregants so immersed in their contemplations, you'll barely turn a head. You'll be struck by how spartan it is inside. Just wooden pews, wainscoting and the pulpit; the velvet-embroidered pulpit cushion is the only splash of colour in what Anglicans, rather unkindly, defame as 'the squalid sluttery of the Dissenting conventicle'.

The Presbyterians see any form of ornamentation – statues of the Virgin Mary, stained-glass windows, altar cloths and so on – as an idolatrous distraction; the seating, acoustics and lighting are all tailored to maximize the impact of the Word of God and nothing else. Daylight streams through the round-headed windows onto the Bible and there's a sounding board above the pulpit. Hymns are sometimes sung without organ accompaniment (though there might be a viol player to boost the bass) but they are hardly rousing – each individual line is read aloud by a minister, *then* sung.

They look so serene as they bow their heads in prayer but many of the worshippers gathered here today believe that God has predestined the greater part of humanity to bake in hell for all eternity while a tiny minority (them, they hope) have been earmarked for an afterlife of everlasting bliss. The godworthy ones are called the 'elect'; the damned the 'reprobate'. Following the thread of this Calvinist belief to its extreme conclusion, one branch of the Presbyterians believe that man's moral actions are essentially irrelevant since they have no bearing upon his destiny. But in practice most dissenters believe that 'a good tree cannot bring forth evil fruit', as the Gospel teaches, and far from being anarchic nihilists they interpret their own orderly and prosperous way of life as a sign that they are amongst the chosen ones.

For the younger generation of Presbyterians, though, this is all beginning to sound a bit staid. Many are coming to reject the bleak assumptions of high Calvinism and are moving towards a belief in the possibility of a general redemption of mankind, a message the Methodist John Wesley will preach to mass acclaim in twenty years' time. At his family home in Hackney one night, Dudley Ryder, ever an empirical thinker (except when it comes to his brazen political partisanship), puts it to his horrified father that the doctrine of predestination is 'directly contrary to the whole tenor and design of the Gospel which promises salvation to all who shall believe'. Ryder considers the difference between the Anglican Church and the dissenters' chapel 'very small and trifling', praying in the drabbest Hackney meeting house one day and then in the ethereal splendour of St Paul's the next. Eighteenth-century London can foster this liberal pick 'n' mix approach to religion. But it can also breed foaming zealots.

This is why so many of London's dissenting meeting houses are hidden away in back alleys: to avoid incurring the window-smashing wrath of the swivel-eyed Tory mob. They are fiercely hostile to the dissenters, whom they stigmatize as regicidal religious anarchists. It was a Puritan-dominated Parliament that pressed for the execution of Charles I then established a republican Commonwealth in the 1640s and 1650s in which radical sects like the Levellers and Fifth Monarchists flourished. The 'high church' Tories believe in protecting the sanctity of the established Anglican Church at all costs and are liable to be whipped into a frenzy should, say, a firebrand preacher take to the pulpit at St Paul's Cathedral and cry out that the Church is in mortal danger from enemies within. Which is precisely what happened in 1709 when a rabidly high-church, publicity-hungry demagogue called Dr Henry Sacheverell, who liked to terrify his servants with stories of hellfire, did that very thing. It was the anniversary of the Gunpowder Plot and he delivered an appropriately explosive ninety-minute sermon entitled 'The Perils of False Brethren', in which he lambasted the 'vipers in our bosom that scatter their pestilence at noon-day' – the dissenters, who worship at noon – gravely imperilling the Anglican Church. Illegally printed, his sermon became an instant bestseller, shifting tens of thousands of copies. But the next year he was put on trial at Westminster Hall by the pro-dissenter Whig government, which accused him of preaching against the Revolution of 1688. This turned out to be a terrible move.

Dr Sacheverell's three-week trial took place in early 1710. On each day the doctor processed from his lodgings in the Temple to New Palace Yard in Westminster in a fine carriage, trailed by a 3,000-strong mob to whom he extended his hand every so often to be kissed, like a king. After the hearings on 29 March, the crowd followed his coach back to his lodgings 'like clusters of bees' at around 6.30 p.m., seething through the gates of the Middle Temple. As the light died, they merged with a vanguard of supporters 'armed and arrayed in a warlike manner' with crowbars, axes, swords, clubs, hammers and bricks – this was a pre-planned uprising. Their target was the new Presbyterian meeting house of Dr Daniel Burgess (James Wood's predecessor), the ground-floor windows of which they had smashed with sticks the night before. They made the short journey across Fleet Street along Sheer Lane, just as you have done, and swirled into the courtyard, sending residents cowering for shelter.

The mob found the chapel completely unguarded in spite of promises made by the Secretary of State to Daniel Burgess's son the day before. The ground-floor windows were boarded up, but once the first man had clambered onto the portico and smashed a gallery window many others crept in after him. An hour later, an undercover dissenter was dismayed to find up to thirty people sinking axes into the roof, smashing the windows with hammers, wrenching out pews with crowbars and screaming the tribal cry of 'High Church and Sacheverell!' Perhaps wary of setting the neighbourhood on fire, the rioters hauled the guts of the meeting house up Serle Street to Lincoln's Inn Fields where pews, floorboards, wainscots, doors, window frames and tables were all heaped together, fodder for a giant bonfire. Just after eight o'clock it was alight. The mob pulled off their wigs and danced in joy as cushions, candlesticks and a grandfather clock were pitched into the flames. A high point was the burning of Dr Burgess's circular pulpit – alas, not with him in it. It was reported that he'd escaped by climbing out of a back window in his house and taking shelter with, of all people, a Catholic.

For the next three hours the flames shot into the London sky, attracting hundreds of people eager not to miss out on the excitement. One man, a pawnbroker, travelled all the way from Southwark in his night-gown. Empowered in their multitude and encountering no resistance whatsoever from the doddering watchmen and constables who were supposed to guard the streets, by 9.30 p.m. the mob had begun to splinter, seeking out fresh targets in other parts of the city in a scene a little prescient of the London riots of 2011. By 10 p.m. another bonfire was crackling away merrily at the top of Fetter Lane, on Holborn; this came courtesy of Mr Bradbury's Independent meeting house in New Street, the pews and pulpit of which were now flaming roundabouts for sedan chairs coming in and out of the City at Newgate. Soon, more bonfires blazed around Drury Lane, Leather Lane, Clerkenwell Green and Blackfriars. The wreckage of Taylor's Meeting House in Stable Yard went up in three separate bonfires in Hatton Garden – and so nearly did its builder, whom the mob wrenched from his bed. They pressed his nose to the flames, but in the end they only burned his nightcap. One dissenter dragged from Hamilton's meeting house in St John's Square in Clerkenwell wasn't so lucky. His skull was cracked in half with a spade; as his brains oozed out, the rioters danced around his limp body. 'High Church and Sacheverell! High Church and Sacheverell!'

It was only after rumours began circulating that the rebels were planning to attack the Bank of England and the town-houses of prominent politicians in the West End that the Secretary of State got his act together and took a sedan chair to see Queen Anne at St James's Palace, who, 'seized with a paleness and trembling', authorized the use of her personal horse and foot guards, potentially leaving her vulnerable. This intervention proved decisive, however, extinguishing much of the rioting overnight. The next day the crowds dispersed and the ringleaders were rounded up and arrested. But ultimately the judges were lenient. Dr Sacheverell received the lightest of light sentences – a three-year ban on preaching – and most rioters escaped with fairly modest fines; the last thing magistrates wanted was to inflame the mob once again.

The dissenters will never forget London's night of riot and fire and the Tories have found inventive ways of exculpating themselves. Dudley Ryder laments his Tory aunt and uncle's tendency to 'make black white and white black', laying the blame for the Sacheverell riots firmly at the door of London's glaziers who naturally sought to profit from so many smashed windows!

As you make your way out, take one last glance at the chapel's harmonious neoclassical architecture and remember that, in the London of 1716, violent impulses are always gushing beneath the surface of a seemingly polite and orderly society.

The sledgehammer of English justice

As you heave your way up Holborn Hill, your whalebone hoop skirt bursting out like a jellyfish or skirted velvet jacket and white stockings mottled with puddle water, you can only wish that you were looking at the world through the sash windows of another sedan chair, but sadly there are none in sight; on a day like today, you can understand why Dickens chose these swampy surroundings to have a Megalosaurus Rex appear on the first page of *Bleak House*, 'waddling like an elephantine lizard up Holborn Hill'. Holborn Bridge marks the north-westerly limit of the Great Fire's area of devastation. Here you'll see sprawling Tudor and Jacobean houses give way to more elegant, neoclassical brick buildings. As you climb Snow Hill, look to your right and gaze into the heart of the new City. It is a forest of Christopher Wren spires – almost fifty in all – wrought from silvery-grey Portland Stone, not quite gleaming new any more, assailed as they are by noxious sea-coal fumes.

Ugly Newgate confronts you. The prison is more expansive than its predecessor the Whit, but no less hellish; 'an emblem of hell itself and a kind of entrance to it', in the words of Daniel Defoe, who was incarcerated here in 1702. Its inmates have all, or will all, stand trial at the adjacent Sessions House, which is our next stop. Take a right down Old Bailey and trail the prison wall on your left; the court is about a minute's walk towards Ludgate. Today is a big day in the legal calendar. It's one of eight days reserved for the opening of the King's Commission of Oyer and Terminer (from old French, to listen and determine) and gaol delivery (that is, to clear Newgate by sending people home, to their grave, or to be punished). The Old Bailey is where people from the City of London and County of Middlesex are put on trial for felonies including murder, rape, sodomy, coin clipping but especially for a whole range of property crimes including burglary and robbery as well as some moral offences including fraud, forgery and libel. If you stay for the whole sessions, you will see dozens of lives smashed to pieces by the sledgehammer of English justice.

Described by the historian John Strype as a 'fair and stately building, very commodious, and with large galleries on both sides for spectators', the Sessions House in front of you is a three-storey brick building with six slender Doric columns bespeaking Italianate majesty. For many, it is the last civilized building they set foot in before they meet their maker. Immediately in front of the courthouse is the bail dock where defendants pace around nervously before being called to answer for their crimes. It is parcelled in by a brick wall sur-mounted with black spikes. But what's most striking is that from the outside, you can see straight into the courtroom; when the new Sessions House was designed in the early 1670s, the outside wall was omitted to increase ventilation and reduce the chances of anyone inside the court catching gaol fever from the prisoners who arrive fresh from the cesspit of Newgate. It is a good policy – in 1737 the courtroom will be walled in and thirteen years later at the notorious 'Black Sessions', sixty people will catch typhus and die, including two judges and the Lord Mayor.

Inside the courthouse, real-life drama and tragedy will unfold. So just as in a playhouse, 'groundlings' will cram into the courtyard outside and members of the public into the spectators' gallery, cheering and jeering and making their feelings clear at every stage in the proceedings, sometimes intimidating a jury to return a particular verdict.

There is a seat waiting for you in the spectators' gallery; go in.

From your vantage point, the courtroom looks familiar enough. The defendant (or prisoner, since the vast majority of those arrested on suspicion of a serious crime are sent straight to Newgate) stands at the bar or 'dock', the wind from the open-air yard whistling down their neck. Directly opposite, at the other end of the room, sit a row of solemn-faced judges underneath vast windows and a marble portico decorated with the sword of justice and the royal arms. Also present are scribes and witnesses. If better-off prisoners are in need of a reliable defence witness they can hire a professional witness for a reasonable fee – they gather outside the courtroom and are easily identified by the wisps of straw sticking out of their shoes, just as you saw in Westminster Hall back in medieval London.

The dock is decorated with sharp spikes. Above is an elevated rectangular mirror, shining light directly into the face of the prisoner: all the better for the jury to determine their guilt or innocence. The jury don't all sit together; they sit in two groups on either side of the court, as though umpiring a tennis match.

The chattering of the crowd dies down. Ashen faced, shivering and malnourished, a woman called Mary Tomlins from the parish of St Clement Danes shuffles to the stand, her eyes downcast after scanning the room and seeing neither family nor friend; like the other prisoners, she is encumbered with manacles and leg irons, smacking of guilt. This is a problem. An alarming feature of the eighteenth-century justice system – and there are many – is that there's no inbuilt assumption of innocence until guilt is proven; that idea would begin to gain traction only at the end of the century with the help of the progressive barrister William Garrow. Tomlins is indicted on two pickpocketing charges, a capital offence, even though the value of her alleged takings equated to £2 10s – approximately a sixth of a building labourer's annual wage; a month's dancing lessons; or, if you prefer modern-day comparisons, something in the region of £500. She is asked how she pleads: not guilty. There's really very little point entering a guilty plea – only very occasionally is it rewarded with a more lenient sentence – and she's in no mood to be pressed to death, so standing mute is off the table.

Mary Tomlins's first accuser, the shopkeeper Martha Richardson, steps forwards into the witness box. On the day of the theft, she claims, the prisoner followed one of her lodgers into her shop having spotted a gold watch she wanted to steal. But, missing her opportunity, she pickpocketed *her* instead. Richardson claims she accosted Tomlins, revealed how much money she had lost in front of the other customers, then forced her to empty her pockets, which contained that precise quantity of money. The accuser calls several witnesses to testify to the veracity of her story, which they do convincingly. Things are looking grim for Mary.

Like all prisoners, she is responsible for her own defence. There is no place here for the sophistry of lawyers; that, judges believe, would only obfuscate proceedings. They think that honest answers are more likely to flow from a spontaneous interrogation. (It isn't until the end of the eighteenth century that defence barristers will be employed.) The onus is all upon *her* to put on a convincing performance. When you hear the kind of hesitant, stuttering almost half-hearted answers she provides, you may wonder whether she realizes quite what is at stake here. But remember: she's been held in Newgate in exactly the kind of disgusting and degrading conditions you saw in Samuel Pepys's London since the time of her arrest (the last gaol delivery sessions were five weeks ago), and although she knows why she's been arrested, she has no foreknowledge of the exact wording of the indictment.

It was her own money she withdrew from her pocket, she alleges. There were forty other people in the shop at the time – one of *them* must have been the true thief. Through scrunched eyes the jury peer at her from both sides of the court.

She hardly fares better in her second indictment, put forward by the butcher Mrs Tibby, who claims that Mary thieved her of 9s 6d while she was chopping a leg and loin of mutton, of which three shilling pieces were misshapen, and hence easy to identify when she lured the prisoner back into the shop on the pretence of having found an even better slab of meat for her dinner. Mary Tomlins flatly denies all this but she doesn't call anyone to testify for her good nature and reputation, which is unfortunate since it weighs so heavily in the decision-making process of juries. Perhaps she hasn't been able to get anyone to turn up; they're under no legal or financial incentive to do so. In the blink of an eye, the trial is over. Mary must wait until Saturday to learn her fate.

Meanwhile the court has to get through the rest of its eighty-six cases. In the eighteenth century, courts rattle through as many as twenty trials in the same day. And don't think those on trial for their lives will be afforded any more time than a bigamist. Naturally, the jury have all been taking meticulous notes, not snoozing or daydreaming or the like.

At the end of the sessions, one of the judges sums up each case. Occasionally he might give little winks and nods as to the guilt or innocence of the parties, but gone are the days when juries returning an unsatisfactory verdict could have the words 'I WILL have a positive verdict or you shall starve for it!' screamed in their faces, as happened in 1670 during the trial of the Quaker William Penn, founder of Pennsylvania. That said, the decision-making process isn't exactly played out in an ideal working environment: 'The jury then retire into a room,' says César, 'where they have no light and no food, and here they must remain until they are unanimous as to whether the accused is guilty or innocent.'

Once the verdict is read, the Recorder muses for a while then delivers the sentence like a thunderbolt. Punishments fall into the short, sharp and visceral variety – or they're eternal. There are three main options: hanging, public whipping or branding on the hand with a red-hot iron. Any crimes that are seen to endanger life or threaten the stability of the economy are one-way tickets to Tyburn. These include murder, highway robbery, housebreaking and counterfeiting coins; also some moral crimes like rape and sodomy, though convictions for these are much rarer. In these sessions, there are some no-hopers – Matthew Chester stole a mare worth £8 then used it to commit two highway robberies, galloping off with various goods including a gold ring and a further horse: he is a dead man. Then there's the team of burglars who broke into a house at night and stole £50 worth of hats: dead men. If you commit a moral crime such as bigamy or libel, you can expect a fine, a spell in the pillory and a term in a workhouse, but again, convictions for these crimes are not as common.

Anyone guilty of 'petit treason' – that is, killing your master – can expect the same fate as the Protestant martyrs in the reign of Bloody Mary. (Not too long after your visit, Catherine Hayes got her husband drunk and murdered him, then had two of her lovers chop him up and sprinkle him into a pond in Marylebone. His head they booted into the Thames, but it bobbed up the next day. Resourcefully, the authorities displayed it on a wooden pole in St Margaret's churchyard so the victim could be identified, a novel form of crime poster. Hayes was caught, convicted and became the last woman in England to be scorched alive. Female coiners – those who attempt to counterfeit currency – can expect the same fiery punishment. Steal goods worth more than 40s (crudely put, around £440 today) and you are also in grave danger (no pun intended) of the gallows. The next most serious crime is grand larceny – generally the theft of goods worth up to 40s, including pickpocketing. Technically this also carries the death penalty – and indeed, shockingly, some people are executed for it – but with the crucial, life-saving qualifier that it's a 'clergyable' offence.

This is a hangover from the Middle Ages, when priests could ask to be sentenced by an ecclesiastical court (which dished out much softer sentences) by proving their literacy via a recital of Psalm 51, the 'neck verse' beginning, fittingly, 'O God, have mercy upon me, according to thine heartfelt mercifulness'. By the eighteenth century 'benefit of the clergy', as it is known, is extended to anyone – clergy or no – who can read aloud the neck verse or another verse from a New Testament printed in a large Gothic font. If they read it satisfactorily, their death sentence is commuted to a small 'F' scar (for felon) stamped on their palm by a red-hot iron; only since 1697 have women enjoyed equal rights with men as regards benefit of the clergy.

What constitutes satisfactory reading is very much at the judge's discretion. Merciful judges could choose to accept even the most brazen of mumbles as proof of literacy. They could choose, too, to ignore previous brandings on prisoners (technically, benefit of the clergy could only be granted once). Equally, nothing is stopping vengeful or sadistic judges from picking two Bible verses at random, and insisting on nothing less than a pitch perfect, Ciceronian delivery, thereby condemning the semi-literate and illiterate to death for stealing, say, an embroidered waistcoat.

The final major punishment, for petit larceny (stealing property valued at a shilling or less – something like £10 in twenty-first century money) – will earn you a public whipping, though these crimes don't tend to be prosecuted in the Old Bailey. Magistrates prefer to send malefactors to Bridewell House of Correction. However, to save prisoners from the gallows, kind-hearted juries sometimes 'downvalue' the goods stolen to a shilling, so that a whipping – not an execution – is the outcome.

It is unfortunate for the defendants gathered here today that the criminal justice system has been made even more savage and retributive in the last two decades. Since 1690, many new capital offences have been added to the statute books. Now you can be hanged for daylight robbery and housebreaking (1691), counterfeiting coins (1697), shoplifting goods worth more than 5s – perhaps as little as £55 today (1699), and thieving your master's households of goods worth more than 40s. And here's the kicker. With the exception of the Shoplifting

Act, none of these are 'clergyable' offences, so anyone found guilty of these crimes could well be hanged. In the absence of a centralized, uniformed and effective police force, this savage criminal justice system has been put in place to protect the interests of the property-owning classes whose prosperity has swelled following a prolonged economic boom from around 1660, and who constitute the majority of jurors and every single one of the magistrates.

Remarkably, in the next few decades, the criminal law will become even more severe. After 1723 you could be hanged for cutting down a tree illegally or stealing a sheep. In some respects the law now is much harsher than it was in medieval London. In the fourteenth century, anyone taking part in a riotous assembly could be sentenced to a year and a day in gaol; after the Riot Act of 1714, however, the sentence could be death without benefit of the clergy.

Who or what is responsible for this turning of the screw? In large part, people like Elizabeth Mallet, the press. Crime reporting – often in the form of ballads and short pamphlets – had traditionally been romantic, lurid and quasi-fictional. From the late seventeenth century, though, which saw the rise of the periodical press, journalism, while sometimes still sensationalist, became much more accurate. Now there are sobering and detailed accounts of the proceedings of the Old Bailey and brief moralizing autobiographies of executed criminals in the Ordinary of Newgate's monthly *Account*. Some chaplains could be callous. Some time later, in the 1770s, the Ordinary of Newgate, John Vilette, accompanied a young boy in the execution cart to the gallows at Tyburn. Right before the execution, someone else confessed to the crime, raising expectations of reprieve, to which Vilette told the executioner that this was no time to worry about details of this kind. Setting an example to the public was of paramount importance, he argued; the guilt or innocence of the condemned was neither here nor there. Luckily for the boy, the under-sheriff disagreed.

So crime reporting, coupled with the never-ending influx of near destitute migrants to plug London's high mortality rates, is fuelling a powerful *perception* of an inexorable tide of rising crime and immorality. Cue alarmist calls to be ever tougher. The title of the 1701 pamphlet 'Hanging Not Punishment Enough' says it all. In the eyes of the eighteenth-century elites, criminal behaviour stems not from dire social and economic circumstance but squarely from moral weakness, personal depravity and innate sinfulness of the individual, and there is no Dr Barnardo around to tell people otherwise.

If you returned in a couple of days to watch the sentences being handed out, you'd see the City of London and Middlesex juries leave the room to confer, then file back in to deliver their verdicts in two separate batches. Of the eighty-six defendants, you'd see eighteen slump in their chains or make hopeless, watery eye contact with relatives as they are awarded the sentence of death. Twenty would receive benefit of the clergy. You'll see a court official sink a red-hot poker onto their palms. Twenty-one will be sentenced to be whipped through the streets of London; four to pay a fine, stand the pillory and suffer a brief spell of confinement. The remaining twenty-three, to their palpable relief, will be acquitted for immediate and unconditional release. The jury will downvalue some goods, and thus lives will be spared for porridge pots but not fine hats, for a periwig worth 15s but not one worth four times as much, for bacon but not several yards of muslin and cambric linen, for a horse saddle but not eight bushels of white corn. In a burgeoning consumerist society, you might conclude, a greater value is placed on things than people.

And as for Mary Tomlins, on trial for pickpocketing? Guilty. Usually this would carry the death penalty but she pleads her belly, hoping this will get her off the hook. A jury of matrons agree that she is indeed pregnant. The English justice system is merciful and takes such things into account. The solution? She will be reprieved until her baby is born. Then she will be killed.

For those like Mary sent back down to their cells in chains to await the call of the bells of St Sepulchre's, there is one last, desperate hope: a royal pardon. Those without prior convictions and whose crimes are not understood to have imperilled human life stand a reasonably good chance of being reprieved by a cabinet committee. Once the committee has reached its decision, a 'dead writ' is sent to Newgate with a sinister black 'H' scrawled next to the names of those who are to hang and alternative punishments or pardons for the reprieved. These cabinet reprieves are something of a tonic to the savagery of the justice system; between 1714 and 1767, approximately 50 per cent of all death sentences are reprieved at cabinet. But from 1717, many of these pardons would come with such pernicious strings attached that for many they are scarcely better – and for some even worse – than death itself: transportation.

'Draining the nation of its offensive rubbish'

If you were to revisit the Old Bailey next year, in 1717, you'd find the punishments of branding and whipping, never much of a deterrent effect in the eyes of magistrates, superseded by transportation to the American colonies. Increasingly, the elites didn't like to see too many people executed en masse at Tyburn as this bespeaks a Catholic-style authoritarianism incompatible with notions of English liberty. Transportation on the other hand was a perfect way of 'draining the nation of its offensive rubbish without taking away their lives', as a pamphlet from 1731 bluntly put it. Fewer people will be sentenced to death over the next fifty years but tens of thousands of Londoners – over two-thirds of felons, in fact – will be wrenched from their families, herded across the Atlantic and all but enslaved on the American plantations for seven years, fourteen years, or for life. Many for offences that, in our own time, would merit no more than a slap on the wrist at the police station, or a small fine.

On transportation days, final memories of London are likely to have been sour. With a single night's notice, precluding any farewells with family whom they might never see again, transports were chained into a coffle – 'a line of animals or slaves fastened or driven along together' – and made to shuffle their way, two by two, from Newgate to lighters at Blackfriars waiting to transport them to the ocean-faring vessels down-river. This spectacle brought coaches and sedan chairs to a halt and piqued the interest of people starting their day's work, who delighted in taunting and pelting them.

Sometimes there were farewell scenes at Blackfriars. One coffled Londoner was surprised to see his old landlord waiting for him at Blackfriars Stairs. 'I am very sorry to see you trans-ported,' he told him. In his shackled state, the convict somehow managed to reach out a hand, craving a touch of human warmth, perhaps, as seven years' servitude beckoned. 'Not so familiar as that!' snapped back the landlord. 'I think it is ten thousand pities you was not hanged!' at which his former ten-ant understandably hurled a bottle of gin in his face.

It can be hard to square the cruel excesses of the Old Bailey with the praise heaped upon it by foreign writers. Many of the French *philosophes*, particularly Voltaire and Montesquieu, admired the English justice system, heralding it as a paragon of fairness. And what's not to like? It has as its centrepiece habeas corpus, meaning that everyone has the right to a trial, their guilt determined by a jury drawn from their peers in full public view. Nothing like that would appear in France for over seventy years (although habeas corpus is temporarily suspended owing to the Jacobite insurrection).

When you return to the Black Horse for supper, you see a copy of the *Daily Courant* lying on the table. You turn to the advertisement section. The third notice reads:

> Lost out of a person's pocket at Guildhall, on Wednesday the 8th instant in the Evening, a silver minute watch, the maker's name (Wightman) on the Dial Plate, with a silver chain and a triangular steel seal to it. Whoever brings it to Steele's Coffee House in Bread Street, shall have 40s Rewards, and no questions asked.

Nicely done. At common board, you also overhear that the king was displeased by the Lords' address to save the condemned peers – but many people think this is just a tactic, and that they will, ultimately, be reprieved.

Friday, 24 February 1716

'The world in epitome': the Royal Exchange

After a nice lie-in, soaking up the sounds of the city, you need to get yourself to Cornhill, one of the main commercial thoroughfares of the City, to view the pumping heart of the British economy. Why not walk up the Strand, Fleet Street and Cheapside, which César de Saussure found some of the best streets in Europe for window shopping?

When you reach the mouth of Exchange Alley you'll see, looming resplendent in the sunshine, the high arches,

Corinthian columns, and three-storey bell tower (which gives Wren's spires a run for their money) of the 'spacious and handsome' Royal Exchange. Inspired by the great *bourse* at Antwerp, the original exchange was opened in 1569 'for the more facile expediting the affair of negotiation', on the initiative of the Tudor financier Thomas Gresham. It is perched on one of the highest points in the city and if you gaze up at the dome at the top of the bell tower, you will be rewarded with the sight of a gilt brass weathervane shaped like a grasshopper, the emblem of the Gresham family. Note too the sculpted emblems of the four corners of the globe rising from behind the balustrade on your right.

The bells summon merchants to trade only twice per day: for High 'Change, at noon, and Low 'Change, at six o'clock in the evening. It is thought that these rules, which are strictly enforced, will focus minds, accelerate deals and deliver serious and productive negotiation rather than idle speculation and loitering (though there is plenty of that too).

High 'Change is underway. Get ready to go in.

According to Ned Ward, the entrance pillars swarm with 'memorandums of old age' selling 'glass eyes for the blind, ivory teeth for broken mouths, and spectacles for the weak sighted'. Ignore them and walk towards the main archway. Emanating from within is 'an incessant buzz, like the murmurs of a distant ocean'. It's getting louder. You are about to walk straight into the powerhouse of Britain's commercial empire, a vast entrepôt of global trade.

Get ready.

As you emerge onto the trading floor, you'll see 'the world in epitome' immersed in commerce, striking deals. With a commonplace book in one hand and a pipe in the other, merchants in their richly coloured velvet jackets and felt cockhats swarm about the pillars, craning their necks to read pinned-up advertisements and 'price currents' showing the value of goods, commodities and shares; they scan the room for useful acquaintances, pace about nervously, hold little dogs on leashes, nod at friends, call for notaries, listen in to conversations, whip out bills of exchange and flit between small groups in an ever-changing kaleidoscope of trade. In the centre of the piazza is an equestrian statue of Charles II, a rock around which a sea of commerce swirls, testament to the mutually beneficial and reciprocal relationship between the state and the merchants. Watching over this scrum from niches in the upper storey are statues – some in pretty poor condition – of past and present kings and queens of England; some of the alcoves are empty, awaiting future monarchs while King William III and Queen Mary II, who ruled together, are squeezed into the same one.

In front of you is a finely pebbled trading court, open to the elements, with a colonnade of almost thirty arches sheltering a marble pavement with black-and-white tiles, its chessboard connotations highly apt for an arena where so much is at stake; where great fortunes are exchanged on a daily basis. Plumes of tobacco smoke waft into the luxury shops and stalls in the upper gallery and beyond into the heavens. If you've visited Rome it may remind you of the Pantheon, but here only one god is worshipped: Mammon.

For the Anglophile *philosophe* Voltaire, the pursuit of wealth is a force of great tolerance and humanity. Exiled to London in the 1720s, he wrote of the Royal Exchange: 'there the Jew, the Mahometan, and the Christian transact together, as though they all professed the same religion, and give the name of infidel to none but bankrupts'. And for Mr Spectator himself 'there is no place in town which I so love to frequent as the Royal Exchange', making as it does the metropolis 'a kind of emporium for the whole earth ... knit[ting] mankind together in a mutual intercourse ...

distributing the gifts of nature, finding work for the poor, adding wealth to the rich, and magnificence to the great'. Reputation is everything on the Exchange's piazza. Flash, ostentatious dress is discouraged since it is seen to belie the honesty and equanimity consonant with successful trade, much of which is conducted on credit (this is not quite the machismo, uber-individualist world of *Wall Street*).

The columns of the colonnade mark the points where merchants and wholesalers specializing in particular commodities can be found. You can circumnavigate the whole world of global trade in a matter of minutes. Along these walks you will see domestic and overseas merchants open conversations with suppliers, buyers soliciting goods and commodities, notaries drawing up contracts (and doubling up as translators), ship captains offering their services, and sometimes brokers coordinating all this, oiling the wheels. On the south-western side of the building you'll find some very prosperous merchants sealing deals to transport spices and tobacco at the East India Walk and the Virginia Walk. And if you venture into the centre, you'll find yourself jostled by wine merchants from the Canary Walk (named after the Canary Islands, the source of canary wine) assailed by the conversations of grocers and druggists, and eyed up by some stockbrokers.

Although many of the brokers have forsaken the Exchange for the coffeehouses of Exchange Alley after punitive regulatory legislation was introduced in 1697 limiting their numbers to a hundred, requiring them to pay a bond of good behaviour and restricting their commission to a risible one-eighth of one per cent of any deal, some remain, but they have a dubious reputation, sometimes spreading false news in an effort to manipulate the price of stock.

There is other shady activity. People like to gamble on the outcome of foreign sieges and battles, as we have heard, particularly during wartime, when there is a slump in trade, and often against their own country. There is also a nice line in corrupting the electorate. During the reign of George I's predecessor, Queen Anne, reports circulated that brokers were 'stockjobbing elections' by auctioning rotten boroughs to the highest bidder on the trading floor, who could then return two MPs to the House of Commons at each general election.

Don't linger by the Barbados or Jamaica Walks for too long; according to Ned Ward, they form a 'Kidnappers' Walk'. Fittingly, it is adjacent to the Druggists' Walk. Watch out that you're not taken to a nearby tavern, plied with spiked rum, then carried off to the American plantations in the dead of night (hence the term 'spirited away', which entered the English language as European colonization of North America gathered pace).

Ned Ward, who was no more prejudiced towards foreigners than most Englishmen, captures the Exchange's multicultural milieu with gusto: at High 'Change he has to shove his way through

A crowd of bumfirking Italians . . . grunting monsters . . . with swinish looks [and] effeminate waists and buttocks like a Flanders mare . . . my friend told me these were the Dutchmen, the water rats of Europe . . . a parcel of lank-haired formalists, in flat crowned hats and short cloaks, walking with as much state and gravity as a snail over a leaf of cabbage . . . these, my friend told me, were Spaniards . . . they stink as strong of garlic as a bologna sausage . . . [England's] neighbouring antics [the French], who talk more with their hands and their heads than with their tongues . . . and sit as gracefully on an Exchange bench, as if in a great saddle [and] lean, carrionly creatures, with reddish hair and freckly faces, very much given to scratching and shrugging . . . these, I found, were a compound of

Scotch and Irish, who looked as if they rather came to seek for business, than dispatch any.

He might as well have been climbing the Tower of Babel.

As the tocsin sounds, marking the end of High 'Change, the plan is to go into Exchange Alley to watch a candlelit auction at Garraway's coffeehouse. But there's a slight problem – you can't get in. A vast crowd of people is pouring out of the narrow mouth of the alley. They are all heading to Tower Hill. The Earl of Derwentwater and another Jacobite lord, it seems, are to be executed this afternoon.

It's bound to be entertaining.

The block of death

At Tower Hill, a square, fenced-off scaffold rises from a sea of vulturish spectators. A magnificent ring of horseguards surrounds the death block. Opposite the scaffold, the Tower broods in its dark *majesté* from behind its moat, gulls swirling and crowing about its Norman turrets. In the houses overlooking the green, people are crammed onto balconies and stuffed into the upper storeys, jostling for the best view. In the crowds, pamphlet sellers, pippin hawkers and little dogs leap about. The spectators are excitable, thrusting forwards to get a better view; little children stare with wide gaping eyes from the shoulders of their parents – for many, this is their first execution, a moment they'll remember for the rest of their lives.

Hidden in the crowds is a sweating, panting Dudley Ryder. Earlier today his maid in the Temple shared with him a rumour that the king had reprieved the rebel lords for forty days; 'I could not give much credit to that,' he recalled later, 'knowing the Tories love to deceive themselves with agreeable news. I resolved therefore to go immediately into the City and know the truth of it.' At his brother's in Bishopsgate Street he learned, to his relief, that the execution was still on, and imminent! Finally, he will get to watch the beheading he's been so looking forward to, of the pernicious Jacobite wretch James Radcliffe. He can't wait to discuss it with the learned company in the Grecian later this evening. It's going to be quite an event. No one has been executed here for thirty-one years.

The first person to die on this blood-soaked green – killed during the Peasants' Revolt – was Sir Robert Hales, the official responsible for enforcing the hated poll tax. Over a hundred more would follow – Sir Thomas More, Anne Boleyn's brother George Boleyn, Edward Seymour the Duke of Somerset (and builder of Somerset House), Archbishop Laud, and now the young earl – butchered not by violent peasants but by the state. And sometimes they really were butchered. As he is escorted out of his coach, James Radcliffe will be hoping against hope he doesn't repeat the experience of the Duke of Monmouth in 1685 at whose execution a drunken Jack Ketch, the royal executioner, botched the job. It ultimately took five strokes to sever the head (he lost interest and tried to give up half-way through, eventually having to complete the job with a knife). At an earlier Jack Ketch beheading, of Lord Russell in 1683, he received a large tip of ten guineas from his victim in an early instance of what Kelly Grovier has described as 'severance pay'. It failed – Russell perished in a fountain of blood after multiple blows. Lord Lovat, the last person to be executed here, in 1747, was to find he had a clutch of unexpected co-passengers in Charon's boat to the Underworld after a scaffold holding a thousand people collapsed at his beheading, killing twelve.

A hackney coach approaches the scaffold. The young earl

steps out. He is of athletic build and seems young. His eyes are sad. He is brought onto the stage, where he is saluted by several officers. Then he kneels in prayer. After his death, his head and body will be wrapped in black cloth, put in the coach and driven back to the Tower in a gruesome mirror-image of his arrival.

On his mother's side, he is the grandson of Charles II and Moll Davies. He grew up in exile in St Germain in France, an intimate of the Old Pretender, son of the exiled King James II. As an intransigent Catholic Jacobite with Stuart blood, he is just the kind of person the new regime wants shot of. Given his Catholicism, there is no priest by his side, but there is a sheriff of London, a few other officials and the executioner with his axe.

He makes a brief speech, frantically scribbled down by hacks in the crowds who will send it to press later today, interspersed with their remarks, even though many of them can't hear him properly.

He proclaims he's an innocent man, walking to his death with his head held high, guilty of nothing besides serving Britain's true, divinely appointed ruler, King James III, may God bless his soul.

He pitches his knees onto the wood and lowers his head onto the cold block. He closes his eyes. He spreads his arms. Looming behind him, feet far apart, is the executioner. He raises the axe. In the crowd, husbands and wives, grandparents and small children shoot each other quick, lively glances before cranking their heads back. Hoisted behind the executioner's head, the axe flashes in the sunlight. A hush descends on the crowd.

Then down it plunges, slicing through the young man's flesh, spinal cord and throat like butter. His head plops to the ground like an apple then dribbles away from the pathetic stem of his body like a teary globule. The executioner grabs the spurting head by both cheeks:

'Here is the head of a traitor! God bless King George!'

Epilogue: echoes of Dudley Ryder's London

The eighteenth century was the period when cities began to look recognizably modern, and in spite of Hitler's bombs and massive redevelopment programmes in the twentieth century, you don't have to walk too far in London to see an eighteenth-century house. This is particularly the case in the West End, still as upmarket as ever, with house prices in May-fair amongst the highest in the world. Perhaps the finest example of a complete Georgian square is Bedford Square in Bloomsbury, off Tottenham Court Road, but there is also much to admire in St James's Square, Manchester Square in Maryle-bone and Gray's Inn Fields in Holborn. A brilliant starting point would be Dr Johnson's beautifully preserved townhouse at 17 Gough Square, an architectural gem in a maze of alleys off Fleet Street. *Early* Georgian houses, though, from the days when Dudley Ryder was writing his diary, are fewer and farther between.

My personal favourites are Meard Street in Soho, laid out in the 1720s with an engraved white street sign from 1732, whose bricks are of the redder hue that characterized earlier post-Fire and Queen Anne houses. The beguiling Fournier Street in Spi-talfields has one of the most attractive parades of Georgian townhouses in Britain, many dating from the 1720s and subse-quently occupied by Huguenot silk weavers. Pickering Place in St James's is London's smallest public square, and one of the few places still to use gas-lit lamps. The houses were laid out in the 1730s and some are now occupied by the famous wine merchants Berry Brothers and Rudd. A tradition reports that this is the site of the last public duel fought in London, but this seems improbable since it would have been just about the most dangerous place for such a thing to take place (for the residents of the houses, that is).

Not until 1770 was the tide of public visitors to Bethlem stemmed. Ironically, the measure proved disastrous for many of the inmates, who, sequestered from the outside world, were more vulnerable than ever to abuses and neglect. In 1814 a humanitarian Quaker called Edward Wakefield advocated the reform of lunatic asylums and made harrowing reports of 'dog kennels' in which semi-naked men and women were chained to the walls, including an American marine who'd remained collared to the same iron rod for more than a dozen years. When the asylum was rebuilt in St George's Fields in Southwark, it was run according to higher ethical standards; it still exists in the twenty-first century – in Beckenham, south London, where the mentally ill are kept firmly out of sight.

Elsewhere, as much is lost as survives. London is dotted with eighteenth-century taverns but sadly none of the original coffeehouses have survived the passage of time. Many of them evolved into clubs, hotels and taverns from the later eighteenth century; others crumbled into oblivion, although the George Tavern at 213 Strand operates from within essentially the same building as the George coffeehouse, a haunt of wits and lawyers in the mid-eighteenth century, albeit with a mock-Tudor frontage added later; the Grecian was remodelled as a pub in 1843. Button's coffeehouse in Covent Garden is now a Starbucks. Not even a blue plaque marks the spot – but you can find them on the sites of Lloyd's on Lombard Street, Garraway's and Jonathan's in Exchange Alley and the Grecian in Devereux Court. To soak up something of the dusky, candlelit atmosphere of a Georgian coffeehouse, try the Jerusalem Tavern in Clerkenwell, or the George and Vulture in Cornhill.

A cluster of original street signs survive – Smith's Square (1726) and Cowley Street (1722) in Westminster, 'Chigwell Streate' in Wapping (1678) and Yorke Street (1636), now renamed Tavistock Street, in Covent Garden. Stone shop signs carved into niches of buildings crop up from time to time but the original painted and sculpted shop signs are much more elusive. The best place to see an approximation of them is Lombard Street in the City, where you'll find Edwardian reconstructions of the golden Gresham grasshopper and a rather fetching sign of a cat and fiddle, amongst others. Sadly none of the jelly houses and brothels of Covent Garden remain (to the best of my knowledge). You can see a public sedan chair and poles from around 1780 in the London Transport Museum and an earlier one, from around 1700, in the Museum of London. They look sturdier and sleeker than you might imagine.

Fleet Street is a sad shadow of its former self; the editorial and printing offices of the national papers have been replaced by law firms, chain restaurants and investment banks. Some of the early taverns, though, do survive in all their musty oak glory. No trip to Fleet Street would be complete without stopping in at the Cheshire Cheese, a haunt of Dr Johnson, but there is also the Old Bell towards Ludgate. Gog and Magog still keep the hours by the church of St Dunstan in the west. St Bride's church graces the other end of the street and remains the spiritual home of journalism, with people from the highest echelons of the media industries returning there to get married, christen their children and be remembered at funerals. The Fleet now, of course, runs underground; Farringdon Street and Farringdon Road follow its trajectory. You can still hear it burbling below if you put your ear to the gutter in Ray Street, outside the Coach and Horses Pub. There is a plaque marking the approximate site of Elizabeth

Mallet's house when she launched the *Daily Courant*, though it is on the wrong side of the street. Further up, a plaque marks the site of Ludgate, near Ye Olde London, a ghastly pub on the site of the London Coffee House. The Presbyterian Meeting House near Lincoln's Inn Fields has been obliterated by a giant concrete structure but other dissenters' meeting houses can be found dotted around Stoke Newington and Hackney.

You can still watch trials from the galleries of the rebuilt Old Bailey – for free. The present building is early twentieth century. The Royal Exchange still dominates Cornhill. Its third incarnation, opened in 1844, features a grasshopper weather vane leaping from the roof. But the building has been reorientated; its frontage now looks towards Cheapside, not the mouth of Exchange Alley. Its classical architecture is far too grand for what goes on inside – not trade any more but shopping, oyster-slurping and champagne drinking for wealthy financiers. Finally, at Tower Hill, there is a light-green plaque near the site of the scaffold 'to commemorate the tragic history and in many cases the martyrdom of those who for the sake of their faith, country or ideals staked their lives and lost'. (I'm not sure Dudley Ryder would agree with this encomium.) Some of the most notable beheadees are mentioned, including James Radcliffe, 3rd Earl of Derwentwater.

Falling Back to Earth

Time now to return to your own world. The time machine has been pretty generous to you so far. Just imagine where you *could* have landed: Bermondsey during the Blitz; *Lundenwic* during the Viking assaults of the ninth century; the ghostly walled city after the Romans withdrew in the late fifth century, roamed by feral beasts; the year Queen Boudica burned the whole thing to the ground. Or even an underwater London of the not too distant future.

What you've seen has regrettably but necessarily been fragmentary, nothing like a comprehensive panorama. There are so many other worlds we could have visited if only we'd had the time – Roman London, the London of Dr Johnson and his black cat Hodge, or the Swinging Sixties.

You have experienced six different years in London's history – 1390, 1603, 1665, 1716, 1884 and 1957 – each with its own unique flavour. We landed first in the theatrical city of Shakespeare, hot blooded but eager to demonstrate man's dominion over nature and inferior peoples, with its knot gardens, tobacco houses and *Golden Hinde* museum – inquisitive too, holding up a secular mirror to humanity in the timbered playhouses each afternoon. Shakespeare's London was very much a city of dominance and discovery. The contrast when we jumped back to the violent and insecure medieval city, in thrall to the teachings of the Church and focused on the afterlife, gave us a sense of the radical changes that took place as the Renaissance and Reformation swept through Europe. Then there was the Boschian spectacle of 1665, a city devastated by its twin nemeses plague

447

and fire just as it began to spread its tentacles, encroach on the countryside and 'expel the rural deities'.

And then Victorian London! The imperial megalopolis, a city of contrasts and paradoxes: self-avowedly a great moral leader yet knee-deep in porn, a scientific powerhouse yet obsessed with freak shows, and with manufactured, commodified entertainment to mollify the masses. The London of the late 1950s was finally re-emerging from the wasteland of the Blitz and beginning to reach for the skies, still drab and austere in places but slowly turning to colour in places, as in Soho and Chelsea, where things were beginning to swing, paving the way for the 1960s. Finally, we looped back to the crucible of the recognizably modern city, convivial and commercial Georgian London with its coffeehouses, global trading piazzas and an embryonic mass media. Modernity may have been mid-construction but the city's dark underbelly was still much in evidence. Raw social tensions gushed beneath the surface of 'polite' society and the empire was being assembled, in part with the aid of slavery. Human life continued to be valued cheaply, or at least more cheaply than petticoats and silk handkerchiefs.

And now that you're back in twenty-first century London, how does it seem to you, in light of your adventures? It is something of a commonplace to accuse historians of allowing their present-day experiences and concerns to shape their perceptions of the past. But in your case, it's the other way round: your time in the past may well affect how you perceive the present-day city. Perhaps you will see a high-rise council estate in a new light. Lament the dreary anonymity of Starbucks compared with the conviviality and companionship of an eighteenth-century coffeehouse. See Covent Garden as the embodiment of the birth pangs of an urban revolution rather than a tired tourist trap. Savour London's nightlife even as the memory of the strict medieval curfew hangs over you. Regret what little use is made of the Thames these days. Be inspired to detect the mood in the air and launch an era-defining entrepreneurial venture, like Mary Quant. Think of e-cigarette bars as an evolution of a much older tradition rather than something new, harking back to the quasi-religious inhalations of the Tudor tobacco houses. Pause to reflect at the base of the concrete spike at the southern end of London Bridge, casting your mind back for a moment to the Keeper of the Heads, strumming his lute amidst the grinning skulls. Buy yourself a hawk. Start a jelly house. Think of reality television as a modern-day Bedlam. Consider how London has always thrived on immigration. Wonder whether the city would deal with another deadly outbreak of contagion – Ebola fever, for example – more competently than it did the Great Plague.

Whichever parallels you wish to draw, wherever you roam, whether in twenty-first-century Bloomsbury or seventeenth-century Bankside, there is always the sense that there's a fresh discovery waiting just around the corner, another portal into an alien world. It is this that makes wandering the streets of London such a euphoric and rewarding odyssey.

Notes

As far as we know, no one has ever actually managed to travel back in time. The book, therefore, of necessity incorporates some elements of historical fiction, particularly in the passages where the time traveller interacts with people from the past. It is my hope that the reader will grant me a degree of artistic licence in this regard. But in the main, this is a work of popular history and my evocations of London at various stages in its history are grounded as far as possible in fact – and so in the notes below, and in the further reading essay at the end of the book, I have taken the liberty of referencing my sources and clarifying my thinking where I feel it might be helpful.

Chapter One: A Whirlwind Tour of Shakespearean London

p. 9: *offensively out-of-tune bagpipes accompanied by an ungodly shrieking . . .* see: Joseph strutt, *The Sports and Pastimes of the People of England* (1810), pp. 229–30

p. 11: *the mourning period for the late Queen Elizabeth . . .* Elizabeth died on 24 March 1603.

p. 15: *In 1554 one such bear had the last laugh: breaking free from his stake, he dived into the crowd and bit off a man's leg . . .* John Strype, *Ecclesiastical Memorials Relating Chiefly to Religion and the Reformation of it* (1722), vol. 3, pt 1, p. 327. The unfortunate man, a servant, died three days later.

p. 16: *Some form of animal baiting has been taking place in London since at least the twelfth century . . .* It is mentioned in the chronicler William Fitzstephen's 'Description of the Most Noble City of

London', written in the late twelfth century, and transcribed into John Stow's *Survey of London* (1598). See the 1842 edition of John Stow, *A Survey of London Written in the Year 1598* (1598, revised 1603), p. 35.

p. 19: *a camel going about his day's business on London Bridge* . . . This is reported by Thomas Platter in 1599: 'in one house on the Thames bridge I also beheld a large live camel'. *The Journal of Two Travellers in Elizabethan and Early Stuart England: Thomas Platter and Horatio Busino*, ed. P. Razell (1995), p. 35.

p. 19: *a dozen liverymen removing their caps every time their master's horse stops to urinate* . . . This weird custom is described by Alessandro Magno, who observed how servants would remove their caps if their master – or any of his horses – stopped to urinate, and put them back on again once he or they had finished. 'The London Journal of Alessandro Magno 1562', ed. Caroline Barron, Christopher Coleman and Claire Gobbi in *The London Journal* 9:2 (1983), 146.

p. 21: *'the single most disciplined and authoritative director of the city's affairs'* . . . Peter Ackroyd, *London: The Biography* (2001), p. 91.

p. 23: *'thou shalt commit adultery'* . . . *The Holy Bible Containing the Old Testament and the New* (1631), Exodus 20.14; Ray Boston *The Essential Fleet Street* (1990) p.22

p. 27: *'the very children in school took a pipe of tobacco instead of breakfast'* . . . Walter Besant, *London in the Time of the Tudors* (1904), p. 285.

p. 27: *'holy herb'* . . . It seems almost too good to be true, but this term was in currency at the time. See, for example *The Woman in the Moon* by William Lilly (1597), which contains the line 'Gather me balm and cooling violets / And of our holy herb *nicotian*'.

p. 27: *chroniclers and pamphleteers counted 7,000 such places* . . . The idea that there were 7,000 tobacco houses comes from Barnaby Rich, *The Honestie of this Age* (1614), p. 39. And he's not sure that there weren't *more* than 7,000, citing 'credible' but unattributed reports.

p. 29: *building labourers earn only around 8d per day; building craftsmen, around a shilling* . . . The information that appears throughout the book on the wages of building labourers and building craftsmen is taken from E. H. Phelps Brown and Sheila V. Hopkins, 'Seven Centuries of Building Wages', *Economica* 22:87 (August 1955), 195–206. That tobacco cost 3d a pipeful comes courtesy of Andrew Gurr, *The Shakespearean Stage, 1574–1642* (1992), p. 264.

p. 31: *James increases the tax on tobacco by 4,000 per cent*... Eric Burns, *The Smoke of the Gods: A Social History of Tobacco* (2009), p. 47.

p. 37: *It draws upon the earlier tradition of the painted floor labyrinth*... On the history of mazes and labyrinths, see Nigel Pennick, *Mazes and Labyrinths* (1990).

p. 38: *'when you seem farthest from your destination is when you suddenly arrive'*... Rebecca Solnit, *Wanderlust: A History of Walking* (2001), p. 70.

p. 39: *'Rapists, Anabaptists, libertines, drunkards, common women'*... Lisa Ferraro Parmelee, 'Printers, Patrons, Readers and Spies: Importation of French Propaganda in Late Elizabethan England', *Sixteenth Century Journal* 25 (1994), 853–7.

p. 40: *'That darksome street': London Bridge*... 'I remember well the street on London Bridge, narrow, darksome, and dangerous to passengers from the multitude of carriages: frequent arches of wretches'. This recollection is Thomas Pennant's, in *Some Account of London* (1790).

p. 42: *'silver streaming Thames'*... Edmund Spenser, *Prothalamion* (1596).

p. 43: *a sort of Shakespearean Bond Street*... Bill Bryson, *Shakespeare: The World as a Stage* (2007), p. 50.

p. 45: *'Humpty Dumpty of nightmare'*... David Starkey, *The Reign of Henry VIII: Personalities and Politics* (2002), p. 100.

p. 45: *a visiting Icelander describes how all eating houses on the bridge have a trapdoor in the floor*... *The Life of Jón Ólafsson, Traveller to India*, Hakluyt Society (1923), p. 28.

p. 51: *the annual wage of the kind of carpenter who might have helped build his ship*... In his *Time Traveller's Guide to Elizabethan England* (2012), Ian Mortimer reveals that a carpenter and other skilled labourers might have received up to 10d per day (without food and drink) though it's unlikely such people would have been in work all year around.

p. 54: *The playhouse is open for business now that the official mourning period for the late queen . . . is over . . .* Following the death of Queen Elizabeth on 24 March 1603, all the playhouses shut for a period of mourning. They reopened in May only for a second, much longer closure to begin on 26 May owing to a surge in plague deaths. So here the time traveller is witnessing one of the last plays to be performed before the playhouses reopen in the spring of 1604.

p. 54: *takes it into the 'box office' to smash it open . . .* Neil MacGregor, *Shakespeare's Restless World* (2012), p. 21.

p. 56: *The higher one's social status, the higher one's hat . . . ibid.,* p.64

p. 57: *'a gorgeous playing-place erected in the fields' . . .* The preacher John Stockwood, quoted in *The Plays and Poems of William Shakespeare,* ed. R. C. and J. Rivington (1821), p. 53.

p. 60: *'Kill! Kill! Kill!' . . .* Peter Ackroyd, *Shakespeare: The Biography* (2005), p. 338.

p. 61: *'but steal my thunder' . . .* Thomas Whincop, *Scanderbeg, Or, Love and Liberty: A Tragedy . . . to which are added a List of all the Dramatic Authors, with some account of their lives* (1747), p. 215. There are a number of different versions of John Dennis's exact wording; 'My God! The villains will play my thunder but not my plays!' being another. *Brewer's Dictionary of Phrase and Fable,* 14th edn, ed. Ivor H. Evans (1989).

Chapter Two: A Descent into Medieval London

p. 73: *At eight o'clock each night a curfew is sounded by the churches of . . .* A. R. Myers, *London in the Age of Chaucer* (1988), p. 72. The four listed churches replaced the bells of St Martin Le Grand, which had earlier signalled curfew. The main gates were shut at sunset whereas the wicket gates closed as curfew sounded.

p. 74: *the Spital Field*... This is how it appears on the so-called Agas Map of 1561. It takes its name from the medieval priory and hospital of St Mary Spital to the west of the fields, near the City bars.

p. 75: *The next biggest city in England is York*... Ian Mortimer, *The Time Traveller's Guide to Medieval England* (2008), p.10.

p. 76: *Sadly no literary panoramas of London that would be of any use survive from the fourteenth century*... Somewhat inevitably, the sources for Medieval London are somewhat less abundant than for some of the other time periods we will be visiting. I have sometimes had to rely upon quotations from the earlier and later Middle Ages to evoke the city.

p. 76: *'Behold! I warn you,' writes the Winchester monk Richard of Devizes*... *The Chronicle of Richard of Devizes concerning the deeds of Richard the First* (London, 1841), p. 60.

p. 76: *'Amongst the noble and celebrated cities of the world'*... William Fitzstephen, 'Description of the Most Noble City of London', in John Stow, *Survey of London* (1842), p. 208.

p. 77: *In 1321, an esquire careering through Thames Street on his way to the Tower nearly knocked down a mother and child*... Myers, *Chaucer's London* p.102.

p. 77: *One winter's night in 1322*... Quoted in Barbara A. Hanawalt, *Growing Up in Medieval London: The Experience of Childhood in History* (1995), p. 30.

p. 78: *an old woman ... dribbling all sorts of lurid slander and sexual scandal into the cell*... 'It is rare these days to find any recluse alone before whose window does not sit an old garrulous woman, often a rumour-monger, who occupies the anchoress with stories and feeds her with scandal and slander... Aelred, *De Institutis*, quoted in Ann Warren, *Anchorites and their Patrons in Medieval England*, (1985), p. 108. Aelred, the abbot of a Cistercian monastery, composed his *Rule* around 1160.

p. 78: *the Cornhill shopkeepers, who are apparently deeply unhappy about the court's preparations for some great event at Smithfield* . . . For the hated practice of purveyance, see: Ronald Fritze and William Robison, *Historical Dictionary of Late Medieval England, 1272–1485* (2002), pp. 452–3; W. R. Jones, 'Purveyance for War and the Community of the Realm in Late Medieval England', *Albion* 7 (1975), 300–317. Richard II faced petitions against purveyance in 1383 and 1384.

p. 80: *He pictures himself, barefoot as he is today* . . . Details of the 'enclosure ceremonies' are given in most works on anchorites and anchoresses. See: Warren, *Anchorites*, pp. 92–8.

p. 81: *'scrape up earth every day out of the grave in which they shall rot'* . . . *Ancrene Riwle*, trans. M. R. Salu (1990), p. 51. The *Riwle*, also known as the *Ancrene Wisse*, was written for three freshly immured anchoresses around 1250.

p. 81: *There are around a dozen anchorholds dotted around London* . . . Charles Pendrill, *Wanderings in Medieval London* (1925), pp. 213–14.

p. 82: *'like a drug that has the sweetness of drink'* . . . Aelred, *De Institutis*, quoted in Warren, *Anchorites*, p. 108.

p. 84: *Gropecunt Lane* . . . For some educated speculation by a senior curator at the Museum of London on what Gropecunt Lane was like, see: Peter Silverton, *Filthy English: The How, Why, When And What Of Everyday Swearing* (Portobello Books), pp. 53–4. Recently someone submitted an e-petition to HM Government to reinstate all the Gropecunt Lanes in England (there were many). It failed.

p. 85: *In 1332 a pig snuck into a shop and bit a newborn baby to death* . . . Myers, *Chaucer's London*, p. 19.

p. 85: *They get 4d for every pig they exterminate* . . . Ian Mortimer, *The Time Traveller's Guide to Medieval England* (2009), p. 18.

p. 90: *Erkenwald* . . . Much of this section is indebted to an eye-opening article by Eamon Duffy: 'St Erkenwald: London's Cathedral Saint', in *The Medieval English Cathedral: Papers in*

Honour of Pamela Tudor-Craig: Proceeding of the 1998 Harlaxton Symposium (2003), pp. 150–67.

p. 90: *'preferred to seek out the solitude of caves'* . . . *'Vita Sancti Erkenwaldi'* in *The Saint of London: The Life and Miracles of St. Erkenwald*, ed. and trans. E. Gordon Whatley (Medieval and Renaissance Texts and Studies, 1989). It is though that the *Vita* was written around 1000.

p. 91: *as concocted and recounted in the Miracula* . . . The *Miracles of St Erkenwald* were penned around 1140 and are included in *Saint of London*, ed. E. Gordon Whatley. For further examples of Erkenwald's poetic justice, see miracle 12, in which a pelterer refuses to honour Erkenwald's feast day, for which he is blinded with his own blade; miracle 2, in which another feast-day shirker trips over an ominously lurking half-buried skull, bangs his own skull and dies; and miracle 17, in which Erkenwald himself turns up and proceeds to thrash a painter who has dishonoured his feast day with his pastoral staff.

p. 92: *a clergyman is composing an alliterative poem about St Erkenwald in the English vernacular* . . . If you want to read it in the original Middle English, see *A Book of Middle English*, ed. J. A. Burrow and Thorlac Turville-Petre. Out of concern for the flow of the section, I have relied upon a good translation of the poem into modern English prose: 'A Translation of the Middle English "St Erkenwald"', unpublished MA thesis by Christopher Cameron, presented to the Division of English at Emporia State University in 1993.

p. 93: *'pressing existential interest for every man and woman in late medieval England'* . . . Duffy, 'St Erkenwald', 165.

p. 94: *Chantry chapels* . . . This section has greatly benefited from Marie Hélène Rousseau, *Saving the Souls of Medieval London: Perpetual Chantries at St Paul's* (2011).

p. 96: *Roger Holme* . . . *has recently hired no fewer than seven chantry priests to sing Masses in St Paul's* . . . He was the major canon and executor who shared the chantry of his dead friend, Adam de Bury. He also provided on-site accommodation for the seven chantry priests within the colleges. Rousseau, *Souls*, p. 19.

p. 99: *a monk at Westminster Abbey composed a set of arguments 'for and against'* ... Gervase Rosser, 'Sanctuary and Social Negotiation in Medieval England', in John Blair and Brian Golding (eds.), *The Cloister and the World* (1996), p. 71.

p. 99: *John Frowe of Lincoln, fired by an old grudge, stalked a mason* ... Alfred Kempe, *Historical Notices of the Collegiate Church or Royal Free Chapel and Sanctuary of St Martin-le-Grand* (1825), p. 129.

p. 100: *In 1430, a soldier called Knight was languishing in Newgate prison* ... Stow, *Survey*, p. 115.

p. 102: *'A youth must have seen his blood flow and felt his cheek crack under the blow of his adversary'* ... Roger of Hoveden, writing in the early twelfth century, cited in John Marshall Carter, *Medieval Games: Sports and Recreations in Feudal Society* (1992), p. 32.

p. 103: the following evocation is based in part upon Froissart's *Chroniques*. See: *Sir J. Froissart's chronicles of England, France, and the adjoining countries: From the latter part of the reign of Edward II. to the coronation of Henry IV*, vol. 4, trans. T. Johnes (1804), p. 527. There is very little else on the Smithfield Joust of 1390, and I have thought it expedient to base some parts of my account on Rosamund Mitchell, *The Medieval Tournament: The Story of the Tournament at Smithfield on 11 June 1467* (1958).

p. 105: *'I thought I was queen here, but now I see there are thousands of them!'* ... Quoted in E. Jane Burns, *Courtly Love Undressed* (2002), p. 37.

p. 105: *Regarding what you can wear, they are detailed and unequivocal* ... There is a very detailed list of what certain people in society can and cannot wear according to the sumptuary laws in Mortimer, *Medieval England*, pp. 103-104.

p. 106: *'it [is] scarce possible to distinguish the poor from the rich'* ... *The Parliamentary or Constitutional History of England: Being a Faithful Account of All the Most Remarkable Transactions in Parliament* (1751), vol. 1, p. 441.

p. 110: *your whole suit of armour, not including helmet, lance or shield and chainmail can weigh as much as sixty pounds* . . . Mitchell, *Tournament at Smithfield*, p. 16.

p. 110: *England is moving towards a post-feudal society* . . . See for example: Carter, *Games*, p. 32.

p. 111: *they dig puddles in the earth, whence (so one theory goes) its name* . . . Stow, *Survey*, p. 136.

p. 112: *from the Old French* estuve, *'stove', since they were originally bathhouses* . . . Martha Carlin, *Medieval Southwark* (1996), p. 211.

p. 113: *Codpiece Lane, Sluts' Hole, Cuckold Court* . . . E. J. Burford, *Bawds and Lodgings* (1976).

p. 114: *This game is known as queek, and is popular* . . . McLean, *English at Play*, p. 105.

p. 115: *'Sire, God you keep!'* . . . The sample dialogue in this section is all taken from *Dialogues in French and English. By William Caxton. Adapted from a fourteenth-century book of dialogues in French and Flemish*, ed. H. Bradley (1900).

p. 116: I am grateful to Ian Mortimer for his panorama of medieval accommodation in his *Medieval England*, pp. 143–53.

p. 116: *one fine riverside mansion between the Tower of London and Billingsgate* . . . Myers, *Chaucer's London*, p. 29.

p. 120: *a bewitching manuscript illustration depicting the lengthy incarceration of the Duke of Orléans in the fifteenth century* . . . There are many versions online, for instance: http://viintage.com/wp-content/uploads/public-domain-images-first-valentines-greeting-card-poems-charles-of-orleans.jpg.

p. 123: *the first documented case of torture at the Tower is still some fifty years off* . . . Nigel Jones, *Tower: An Epic History of the Tower of London* (2011), pp. 8, 117; G. Abbott, *The Tortures of the Tower of London* (1986), p. 7.

p. 124: *No fewer than 350,960 squirrel skins* . . . Myers, *Chaucer*, p. 53.

p. 124: *a mini Noah's Ark beached in the south-west corner of the Tower* . . . A compelling account of London's embryonic zoo is Daniel

Hahn, *The Tower Menagerie: Being the Amazing True Story of the Royal Collection of Wild and Ferocious Beasts* (2003).

p. 126: *'eats and drinks with a trunk'* . . . These are the words of Matthew Paris, who'd travelled up especially from his monastery in St Albans to see the elephant, which he later drew. Jones, *Tower*, p. 22, which also quotes the king's command regarding the Norwegian polar bear.

p. 129: *The loriners, painters and joiners turned up armed to the teeth and proceeded to attack the saddlers* . . . Charles Pendrill, *London Life in the 14th Century* (1925), pp. 137–9.

p. 129: *with one fishmonger trying to chop off His Worship's head* . . . Ibid., p. 140.

p. 130: *One royal proclamation laments (in Latin) its 'deep and muddy' condition* . . . William John Loftie, *Memorials of the Savoy: The Palace: The Hospital: The Chapel* (1878), p. 43.

p. 133: *the Savoy was a prime target for the followers of Wat Tyler in the Peasants' Revolt* . . . A good modern account of the Peasants Revolt is Dan Jones, *Summer of Blood: The Peasants' Revolt of 1381* (2010).

p. 135: *an ancient flood-prone eyot which evolved from a sand bar in the River Thames over 4,000 years ago* . . . Robert Shepherd, *Westminster: A Biography from Earliest Times to the Present* (2012), p. 4.

p. 140: *'like a nought in arithmetic, that marks a place but has no value in itself'* . . . Gervase Rosser, *Medieval Westminster* (1989), p. 39.

p. 141: *he was placed on an ox hide and dragged to the gallows by six horses as the devils pranced about, taunting and beating him* . . . Shepherd, *Westminster*, p. 71.

p. 141: *will be dethronement by his magnates the first time he appears underneath it in 1399* . . . John Steane, *The Archaeology of the Medieval English Monarchy* (1998), p. 76.

p. 142: *'but for lack of money, I might not speed'* . . . The poem is online but for a printed edition see *Historical Poems of the XIVth and XVth Centuries*, ed. R. H. Robbins (1959), pp. 150–52.

p. 142: *'gorgeous pride' alongside 'so much wretchedness'* . . . Cited in Rosser, *Medieval Westminster*, p. 221.

p. 144: *'we have sent you a hawk and two falcons, two shields and two lances'* . . . Robin Oggins, *The Kings and Their Hawks: Falconry in Medieval England* (2004), p. 38.

p. 145: *surviving medieval treatises on falconry mention 111 separate diseases and distempers afflicting the birds* . . . Ibid., p. 103.

p. 146: *moods, moreover, could affect the weather conditions the falcons would have to face on the hunt* . . . Ibid., p. 18.

p. 147: *a late-fourteenth-century poem called 'The Parliament of the Three Ages'* . . . Ibid., p. 34.

p. 148: *the flesh of a blind puppy for a weak hawk* . . . Ibid., p. 2.

p. 151: *sometimes coroners can be sadistic* . . . In 1307 the constituent parts of a husband-and-wife murdering duo were assigned Dover and Portsmouth, respectively.

p. 151: *of felons being given mere days to walk hundreds of miles* . . . John Kipernol from East Anglia was ordered to walk 170 miles in four days. John Bellamy, *Crime and Public Order in the Later Middle Ages* (1973), p. 113.

p. 151: *you might find a mob trailing you menacingly until you 'stray' from the main road* . . . Rosser, 'Sanctuary', p. 69. In one example, a posse trailed a Hertfordshire labourer abjuring the realm until he 'strayed' from the main road and 'on the hue and suit of the whole vill he was beheaded by the township of Houghton'.

p. 151: *you are now legally dead* . . . Ibid., p. 64.

pp. 151–2: *you must every day paddle into the sea, either up to your knees or, as some sources would have it, neck, and scream out three times* . . . Freeman, 'And He Abjured the Realm', p. 296; Bellamy, *Crime and Public Order*, p. 113; Shoemaker, *Sanctuary and Crime*, p. 120.

p. 152: *'it is not unamusing to hear, how the women and children lament over the misfortune of these exiles'* . . . *A relation, or rather A true account, of the island of England: with sundry particulars of the customs of these people, and of the royal revenues under King Henry the Seventh, about the year 1500*, trans. Charlotte Sneyd (1847), p. 35.

Chapter Three: A Mournful Walk through Plague-Struck London

p. 163: *Mount Mills* . . . I am grateful to Peter Ackroyd for revealing the significance of this seemingly unremarkable corner of London. Ackroyd, *London: The Biography* (2001), p. 204.

p. 165: *In July nearly 6,000 deaths were attributed to the plague* . . . The best source for the weekly Bills of Mortality is *London's Dreadful Visitation: or, a collection of all the Bills of Mortality for this present year (1665)*, which can be found online via the Wellcome Library: http://wellcomelibrary.org/player/b20663717#?asi=0&ai=0.

p. 166: *to almost 400,000 in 1650* . . . Roy Porter, *London: A Social History*, p. 131. However, *The Rise of the English Town, 1650–1850* by Christopher Chalklin (2001) places the figure at 375,000 in 1650 (on p. 5) as does *The Tudor and Stuart Town 1530–1688: A Reader in English Urban History* by Jonathan Barry (1990).

p. 168: *as it does in rarer cases of pneumonic* . . . Although it's generally acknowledged by historians and scientists that both bubonic and pneumonic plague were to blame for the 1665 epidemic, there is some disagreement about which was the more prominent. Most histories of the plague portray bubonic as the dominant strain but others point to the speed with which the disease ripped through London, suggestive, in their eyes, of a contagion that was principally airborne. These theories, which are not ungrounded in archaeological evidence, relate mainly to the Black Death of 1348–50 but have obvious implications for the Great Plague 300 years later. See: www.theguardian.com/science/2014/mar/29/black-death-not-spread-rat-fleas-london-plague.

p. 168: *'this disease [is] making us more cruel to one another than we are to dogs'* . . . Pepys, *Diary*, 22 August 1665.

p. 168: *happily visiting up to forty plague victims a day* . . . This comes from an advertisement Boghurst himself placed in the *Intelligencer* on 31 July 1665.

p. 169: *'razed out [the] hearts' of Londoners'* . . . *The City Remembrancer* (1769).

p. 171: *'persons in their last agonies'* . . . Quoted in Evelyn Lord, *The Great Plague: A People's History* (2014), p. 80.

p. 172: *'cosmic fart'* . . . Liza Picard, *Restoration London: Everyday Life in the 1660s* (1997), p. 100.

p. 172: *'First. All sins in general'* . . . William Boghurst, *Loimographia: An Account of the Great Plague of London in 1665* (1666).

p. 173: *to blow up their watchman with gunpowder* . . . Daniel Defoe, *A Journal of the Plague Year* (2003), p. 51. Of course, some of these stories may be untrue or exaggerated out of all proportion – but they are at the very least the kinds of stories that were circulating in London during the plague.

p. 177: *'Good in all cases, much above the rest'* . . . This is adapted from an impersonation of a shady apothecary in Ned Ward, *The London Spy*, ed. Kenneth Fenwick (1955), p. 10.

p. 178: *a little leather-bound book brimming with thousands of medicinal, cosmetic and gastronomic recipes she had concocted in her still room and kitchen to maintain the health of her household* . . . The recipes that follow are taken from the following manuscript books of receipts in the British Library: Margaret Baker, Sloane MS 2485; Elizabeth Digby, Egerton MS 2197; Mary Glover, ADD MS 57944; Lady Ranelagh (Katherine Jones), Sloane MS 1367; Mary Doggett, ADD MS 47944.

p. 183: *you can make out hundreds of ships lying in rows of two or three spanning the river* . . . Defoe, *Journal*, p. 108.

p. 186: *London is a far cry from the pomp and prestige of places like Rome, Turin and Vienna* . . . I am grateful to Roy Porter for this idea. Porter, *London*, p. 96.

p. 191: *you could buy six carriage horses for the same price – or three coaches* . . . See Picard, *Restoration London*, p. 147.

p. 193: *'God has given you one face, and you make yourselves another'* . . . *Hamlet*, III.i. 142–44

p. 194: *'eyes like stars or the sun'* . . . Farah Karim-Cooper, *Cosmetics in Shakespearean and Renaissance Drama* (2006), p. 37.

p. 195: *You might be surprised to see that double chins are also at a premium* . . . Richard Corson, *Fashions in Make-Up from Ancient to Modern Times* (1972), p.160.

p. 197: *handsome young man with long curly hair* . . . This description is based on a woodcut of 1645 showing just such a young man hawking accessories from a basket, on which is written 'here be your new fashions mistress'.

p. 197: *'In England, the young, old, handsome, ugly, are all bespatch'd till they are bed-rid'* . . . M. Misson's *Memoirs and Observations in His Travels over England*, trans. J. Ozell (1719), p. 214.

p. 198: *according to one authority on fashion* . . . R. Carson, *Fashions in Make-Up* (1972), p. 167.

p. 201: *'Glad am I to say that they were hissed, hooted, and pippin-pelted'* . . . These are the words of the puritan Thomas Blande from a splenetic letter quoted in Andrew Gurr, *Playgoing in Shakespeare's London* (1936), p. 247.

p. 201: *The first female actress to appear on stage* . . . See Pamela Allen Brown and Peter Parolin (eds.), *Women Players in England 1500–1660* (2008).

p. 202: *These allow male audience members to be gratified by a sex scene without infringing upon the moral virtue of the female character* . . . Elizabeth Woodrough, *Women in European Theatre* (1995), pp. 14–20.

p. 203: *after spiking Davis's cakes with laxative* . . . See, for example, Elizabeth Abbott, *Mistresses: A History of the Other Woman* (2012), p. 72.

p. 205: *offering chocolate 'at reasonable rates' as early as 1652* . . . It was previously thought that chocolate was first sold to the public in

1657; the handbill for *Chocolate or, An Indian Drink*, however, suggests that Londoners' love affair with chocolate began in 1652 – the same year coffee was first publicly sold.

p. 206: *'twill make old women young and fresh'* . . . *Chocolate: or, An Indian Drink by the wise and Moderate use whereof, Health is pre served, Sicknesse Diverted, and Cured, especially the Plague of the Guts* (1652), trans. James Wadsworth.

p. 206: *'as strong in the back as a lion'* . . . From a comic dialogue between two Islington milk maids who tell tales of how chocolate makes their boyfriends better lovers. *The Coffee-Man's Granado incorporating some merry passages between Peg and Cis, two merry milk-maids of Islington upon the rare virtues of CHOCOLATE* (1663).

p. 208: *'they lie like swine'* . . . Captain James Turner, quoted in Anthony Babington, *The English Bastille: A History of Newgate Gaol and Prison Conditions in Britain, 1188–1902* (1971), p. 56.

p. 210: *'I saw the heads when they were brought up to be boiled'* . . . These are the reminiscences of Thomas Elwood. William Allen, *Friends Library: History of the Life of Thomas Ellwood* (1836), p. 190.

p. 211: *'the quintessence of disparagement'* . . . Alexander Smith, *A Complete History of the Lives and Robberies of the Most Notorious Highwaymen, Footpads, Shoplifts and Cheats of Both Sexes* ed. Arthur Hayward (2002), p. 108.

p. 211: *'a troop of Hell Cats'* . . . *Memoirs of the Right Villainous Jack Hall* (1717), cited in Smith, *Robberies*, x.

p. 214: *'witness real agony'* . . . *Punch or the London Charivari*, vol. 2 (1841), p. 240. In the mid-eighteenth century, James Boswell describes a young seaman, Paul Lewis, attending his condemned sermon. 'A genteel, spirited young fellow. He was dressed in a white coat and blue silk vest with his hair neatly queued and a silver-laced hat . . . Poor fellow! I really took a great concern for him and wished to relieve him. He walked firmly and with a good air, with his chains rattling upon him to the chapel.'

Boswell's London Journal, 1762–1763, ed. Frederick Pottle (2004), pp. 251–2.

p. 216: *The figure in the window pushes out a shrouded lump tied to a rope* . . . Defoe, *Journal*, p. 173.

p. 218: *The poor piper* . . . Ibid., p. 88–89.

p. 219: *'piled up like faggots in a stack'* . . . Joseph Hall, *The Works of Joseph Hall, with some account of his life and suffering, written by himself* (1837), p. 223.

p. 219: *'came and threw themselves in'* . . . Defoe, *Journal*, p. 60.

p. 221: *'out of [the] dark and smoky laboratories'* . . . Robert Boyle, *The Sceptical Chemist: or Chemico-physical doubts and paradoxes, touching the experiments* (1679).

p. 222: *'Differences of opinion cause no manner of resentment'* . . . Samuel Sorbière, *A Voyage to England: Containing Many Things Relating to the State of Learning, Religion, and Other Curiosities of that Kingdom* (1709), p. 37.

p. 224: *'An Arcadia beyond Moorfields'* . . . *The Diary of Dudley Ryder, 1715–1716*, ed. William Matthews (1939), p. 4.

pp. 225–6: *The villagers are taking it in turns to grease the tail of a pig then swing it around their heads* . . . Margaret Willes (ed.), *Hackney: An Uncommon History in Five Parts* (2012), p. 59. This cruel tradition lasted from the seventeenth century into the eighteenth and possibly the nineteenth.

p. 231: *the Great Dog Massacre of 1665* . . . I am indebted to Mark Jenner, 'The Great Dog Massacre', in W. G. Naphy and P. Roberts (eds.), *Fear in Early Modern Society* (1997), pp. 44–62.

p. 235: *'I could not help seeing the innocent blood of this exotic flowing in a plentiful stream'* . . . *The Camden Miscellany*, vol. 2 (1853), p. 11.

p. 235: *'Then, then the city did shake indeed, and the inhabitants did tremble'* . . . Thomas Vincent, *God's Terrible Voice in the City: Wherein are Set Forth the Sound of the Voice, in a Narration of the Two Dreadful Judgements of Plague and Fire, Inflicted Upon the City of London; in the Years 1665, and 1666* (1811), p. 44.

p. 237: *'glowing with fiery redness, so as no horse, nor man, was able to tread on them'* . . . This account of a mini-apocalypse at St Paul's comes from John Evelyn's diary: *The Diary of John Evelyn*, ed. Guy de la Bédoyère (1995), 4 September 1666.

Chapter Four: Depravity and Wonder on a Tour of Victorian London

p. 250: *'the grind and howl of machinery, railways shooting above houses and soon to be beneath them'* . . . Quoted in Jennifer Speake (ed.), *Literature of Travel and Exploration: An Encyclopedia* (2003), p. 739.

p. 252: *'The most vile street in the civilized world'* . . . I am grateful to Jerry White for alerting me to the sleazy history of Holywell Street and Wych Street. Jerry White, *London in the 19th Century: 'A human awful wonder of God'* (2007), pp. 318–20.

p. 252: *a 'foul sink of iniquity', a place where 'dirt and darkness meet and make mortal compact' or, in the words of* The Times, *'the most vile street in the civilized world'* . . . *Stories from Scotland Yard as Told by Inspector Moser*, ed. Charles Rideal (1890), p. 36; *Punch*, 9 January 1856; correspondent to *The Times*, cited in Lynda Nead, *Victorian Babylon: People, Streets and Images in Nineteenth-century London* (2000), pp. 164–5.

p. 255: Index Librorum Prohibitorum . . . *Forbidden Books of the Victorians: Henry Spencer Ashbee's Bibliographies of Erotica*, ed. Peter Fryer (1970).

p. 258: *'while I fucked her, I hated her'; 'her cunt constricted'* . . . *My Secret Life*, vol. 4, ch. 3; vol. 5, ch. 3. The full text of this epic romp is available online: http://www.my-secret-life.com/.

p. 259: *In 1880 a police inspector went undercover in search of a family-run mail-order enterprise* . . . Rideal (ed.), *Inspector Moser*, pp. 36–45.

p. 260: *One melancholic, end-of-the-century painting depicts the sun setting over a forlorn Wych Street* . . . I haven't been able to source this but it can be seen online: http://partleton.co.uk/WychStreet1901.jpg.

p. 262: *As of 1883, 15 morning dailies, 9 evening papers and no fewer than 383 weekly publications* ... White, *London in the 19th Century*, p. 231.

p. 263: *'enough to make you believe that some gigantic spider has spun a web over your head'* ... Max O'Rell, *John Bull and his Daughters* (1893), p. 21.

p. 263: *To other observers, the Victorian city is 'the infernal Wen', 'the monster city' and even 'the human awful wonder of God'* ... William Cobbett, *Rural Rides* (1830), p. 507; Henry Mayhew, *The Criminal Prisons of London and Scenes of Prison Life* (1862), p. 9. In the case of the latter, looking down at London from a hot-air balloon, Mayhew writes: 'It was impossible to tell where the monster city began or ended, for the buildings stretched not only to the horizon on either side, but far away into the distance, where, owing to the coming shades of evening and the dense fumes from the million chimneys, the town seemed to blend into the sky, so that there was no distinguishing earth from heaven.' A beautiful, lyrical description.

p. 264: *areas that Roy Porter would wittily label 'stuccovia'* ... Porter, *London*, p. 250.

p. 265: *'after an hour's walking one ... can understand suicide'* ... Hippolyte Taine, *Notes on England*, ed. and trans. Edward Hyams (1957), p. 9.

p. 267: *in fact, the population's average life span will have risen by 50 per cent by 1901* ... Stephen Halliday, *The Great Filth: The War against Disease in Victorian England* (2007), p. 4.

p. 268: *The touring of poverty-stricken districts is called slumming* ... Seth Koven, *Slumming: Sexual and Social Politics in Victorian London* (2004).

p. 269: *even the social investigator Beatrix Potter confessed to feeling 'a certain weird romance' for the slums* ... Ibid., p. 183.

p. 270: *'The streets were filled with a new and different race of people'* ... Jack London, *The People of the Abyss* (1904), p. 7.

p. 270: *two in five of the 4,800 houses that had sprung up in East Dulwich for tradesmen and clerks lay empty* . . . Porter, *London*, p. 250.

p. 274: *'tall chimneys vomiting clouds of black smoke'* . . . Henry Mayhew, *London Labour and the London Poor: A Cyclopædia of the Condition and Earnings of Those that Will Work, Those that Cannot Work, and Those that Will Not Work*, vol. 3 (1861), p. 302.

p. 276: *'then begins the scuffling and scrambling'* . . . Ibid., p. 310.

p. 277: *it is Thomas Barnardo who is the age's leading philanthropic entrepreneur* . . . John Herridge Batt, *Dr Barnardo: The Foster Father of 'Nobody's Children'* (1904); Koven, *Slumming*.

p. 282: *'a bag of spongy, fungous-looking skin'* . . . Frederick Treves, *The Elephant Man and Other Reminiscences* (1923), p. 4.

pp. 284–7: *the African Leopard Boy . . . the creature cowering before your eyes* . . . I am indebted to Nadja Durbach's *Spectacle of Deformity: Freak Shows and Modern British Culture* (2009) for this section. On the Leopard Boy, see p. 30.

p. 285: *a young Portuguese man with 'two complete and well-formed penises'* . . . Lisa Kochanek, 'Reframing the Freak: from Sideshow to Science', *Victorian Periodicals Review* 30:3, 1997.

p. 287: *'to see dwarfs, giants, fat-women, and monstrosities at the freak shows'* . . . Cited in Durbach, *Spectacle of Deformity*, p. 39.

p. 289: *'Who really exploited poor Joseph?'* . . . Tom Norman, *The Penny Showman: Memoirs of Tom Norman 'Silver King'* (1925), p. 110.

p. 290: *'Lighthouses, my boy!'* . . . Arthur Conan Doyle, *The Penguin Complete Sherlock Holmes* (2009), p. 456.

p. 292: *Board School laryngitis* . . . Carol Adams, *Ordinary Lives* (1982), p. 41.

p. 293: *'filthy, dirty . . . sickly looking'* . . . W. E Marsden, *Unequal Education Provision in England and Wales: The Nineteenth-Century Roots* (1987), p. 164.

p. 295: *There is no eastbound and westbound, only 'up' (towards the City and beyond) and 'down'* . . . Andrew Martin, *Underground, Overground: A Passenger's History of the Tube* (2012), p. 35.

p. 297: *'I had my first experience of Hades to-day'* . . . Christian Wolmar, *The Subterranean Railway: How the London Underground was Built and How it Changed the City Forever* (2004), p. 113.

pp. 303–6: *A man with a blacked-up face appears . . . the raison d'être of music hall* . . . I should clarify that I do not have any evidence that the acts described in this section ever appeared on the same bill, rather it is a composite of the kind of acts that were performed at the Canterbury as gleaned from music hall programmes, newspaper reports and secondary works on the history of the music hall. I am particularly indebted to *Lambeth and Music Hall: A Treasury of Music Hall Memorabilia*, compiled by Eva O'Rourke (1977); John Major, *My Old Man: A Personal History of the Music Hall* (2012); *The Canterbury Theatre of Varieties and its Associations* (1878).

p. 304: *cooking an omelette in mid-air* . . . Michael Diamond, *Victorian Sensation* (2003), p.264.

p. 306: *Time now for some songs* . . . A rich collection of music-hall songbooks can be found in the British Library.

p. 307: *'I'm sure I can't think what the world's coming to'* . . . The sheet music for 'It's Wealy a Dweadful Affair' (*c.*1885) can be found in the British Library, written by J. B. Geoghegan and composed and sung by Harry Liston.

p. 310: *They want to mollify the music halls* . . . I am grateful to Fern Riddell, who directed me towards her brief history of the music halls blog post: http://thevictorianist.blogspot.co.uk/2012/09/a-brief-history-of-music-halls-or-why.html.

p. 311: *'tasty, trippy, twiggy, timely, telling, tender, tempting, toothsome, transcendent, trim, tactical, twinkling, tricksy, triumphal and tantalizing'* . . . Graham Nown, *When the World Was Young: Lost Empires* (1986), p. 112.

Chapter Five: London Rising: A Tour of the Blitzed City

p. 321: *Love Lane, where, in creaky chambers, medieval prostitutes plied their trade* . . . In John Stow's *Survey*, he claims this street was 'so called of wantons', p. 111.

p. 323: *'There are shades of barbarism in twentieth-century Europe'* . . . Norman Davis, *Europe: A History* (1997), p. 897.

p. 323: *almost 30,000 civilians were killed in London by bombs and rockets between 1940 and 1945* . . . Jerry White cites a death toll of 29,890 civilians from bombs and rockets. Jerry White, *London in the 20th Century* (Random House, 2008), p. 38.

p. 323: *'London will be one vast raving bedlam'* . . . These are the words of Major General J. F. C. Fuller, though it is often misattributed to, bizarrely, Bertrand Russell. Leo Mellor, *Reading the Ruins: Modernism, Bombsites and British Culture* (2011), p. 17.

p. 325: *beyond that there has been very little progress at rebuilding* . . . Even a decade after the end of the war, progress at rebuilding was very slow, as Nikolaus Pevsner makes clear in *The Buildings of England, London 1: The City of London* (1957).

p. 330: *This is the rosebay willowherb* . . . H. V. Morton, *In Search of London* (1951), pp. 43–4.

p. 333: *look like the surface of the moon* . . . In 1944 the novelist Elizabeth Bowen wrote, 'London looked like the moon's capital . . . shallow, cratered, extinct.' Quoted in White, *London in the 20th Century*, p. 39.

p. 333: *around 116,000 irreparably and almost 288,000 seriously* . . . Ibid., p. 146.

p. 335: *This is the Blemundsbury block, one of the first – if not the first* . . . According to the Museum of London website, 'this was the first block of flats in London to reach 10 storeys. It was designed in 1948–9 by Hening & Chitty for Holborn Metropolitan Borough Council,' a statement reflected in other academic and popular histories. A handful of other high-rises existed outside central London before Blemundsbury opened in 1949: the White City Estate in Hammersmith opened in the 1930s; the Woodberry Down Estate in Manor House opened in 1948, with some eight-storey blocks; the Churchill Garden Estate began construction in 1946. The ground-breaking Spa Green Estate in Finsbury was built in 1946–9 but wasn't completed until 1950, and it rose to only eight storeys although the other blocks opened at around the same time, perhaps even before Blemundsbury.

p. 336: *And then there's the ground* ... Herbert Wright, *London High* (2006), p. 14.

p. 337: *By housing people in identical collective dwellings – or 'machine-homes' as he called them* ... I have benefited from Lynsey Hansley's lucid and intelligent distillation of Le Corbusier's ideas in her heartfelt and eye-opening *Estates: An Intimate History* (2007).

p. 339: *'We felt like King and Queen'* ... ILEA, Education Resources for Older People, *Woodberry Down Memories: The History of an LCC Housing Estate* (1989), p. 40.

p. 341: *'a great burbling, wheezing, spluttering monster'* ... These are the words of author John Sutherland, quoted in Antony Clayton, *London's Coffee Houses: A Stimulating Story* (2003), p. 146.

p. 347: *'A thousand rocket bombs would not batter it down'* ... George Orwell, *Nineteen Eighty-Four* (2003), p. 32.

p. 353: *the Circle Line cocktail party* ... Shawn Levy, *Ready, Steady, Go: Swinging London and the Invention of Cool* (2003), p. 49.

p. 357: *A small woman with short brown hair, an angular jaw and sharp cheek-bones appears* ... The following interaction and indeed much of this section is based upon passages in Mary Quant's inspiring and uplifting autobiography, which captures the zeitgeist of a city restless for change: *Quant by Quant* (1966).

Chapter Six: Four Days in Dudley Ryder's London

p. 371: *'you quit all the hurry and bustle of the City in Fleet Street and the Strand, and all at once find yourself in a pleasant academical retreat'* . . . These are the words of Dr Hugh Blair, a Scottish preacher and renowned literary critic, quoted by James Boswell in his *London Journal*, entry for 6 April 1763. Dr Blair came to town in the spring of 1763, with Boswell as his guide. *Boswell's London Journal*, ed. Frederick Pottle (2004), p. 234.

p. 374: *'to make a coffeehouse out of a woman's cunt'* . . . Francis Grose, *A Classical Dictionary of the Vulgar Tongue*, (1785), unpaginated. The full entry reads 'COFFEE HOUSE. A necessary house. To make a coffee-house of a woman's ****; to go in and out and spend nothing.'

p. 375: *the long-suffering coffeehouse cat, in whose mind a plot seems to be forming to spend a penny of his own in the bubbling coffee cauldron* . . . In *Knavery of all Trades* (1664), a cat defecates in the coffee cauldron, at which the amused coffee man's apprentice comments, 'Oh sir let it boil well, a dog or cats turd is as good as the berry itself.' I am grateful to Markman Ellis who quotes this in his *The Coffee-House: A Cultural History* (2004), p. 116–17.

p. 379: *the dissection of a dolphin* . . . Most historians of coffeehouses claim that the dolphin that strayed into the Thames was dissected *inside* the Grecian coffeehouse. Perhaps it was, but the only evidence for it, a diary entry for 12 June 1712 written by the antiquarian and fellow of the Royal Society Ralph Thoresby, suggests otherwise. 'Attended the Royal Society,' he writes, 'where I found Dr Douglas dissecting a dolphin, lately caught in the Thames, where were present the President, Sir Isaac Newton, both the Secretaries, the two professors from Oxford, Dr Halley and Keil, with others whose company we after enjoyed at the Grecian Coffee-House.' At this stage, the Royal Society met in Crane Court, off Fleet Street, and its members are known to have decamped to the Grecian, which was nearby, afterwards for a more informal gathering. In my view, the diary entry is referring to two separate places, though it's entirely possible they brought the dissected dolphin along to the Grecian for further discussion after their formal meeting wound down.

p. 380: *'nothing certain . . . one report contradicting another'* . . . This is how the Mancunian poet and shorthand entrepreneur John Byrom describes the culture of news in London on 28 April 1748, but it's equally true of thirty years earlier. *The Private Journal and Literary Remains of John Byrom*, ed. R. Parkinson, 4 vols., Chetham Society Remains, vol. 4 (1857), p. 438.

p. 385: *'a very fine elephant was led across the Thames'* . . . The elephant story is reported in a couple of provincial newspapers but seems quite conspicuously absent in both the London press (from what I could find) and *Frostiana: Or A History of the Frozen Thames* (1814), written for the specific purpose of chronicling all the wondrous activity on the ice. It would not have been beyond the wit of provincial journalists simply to make it up.

p. 386: *at least 550 and possibly several thousand coffeehouses all over London* . . . Contemporary estimates of coffeehouses ranged wildly from 550 to 8,000. The London Directories of 1734 counted 551 official London coffeehouses, excepting the many unlicensed ones. But the coffeehouse boom had peaked by this point. If we imagine that there were around 1,000 then we shan't go too far wrong.

p. 386: *a Latin coffeehouse operated by Hogarth's father* . . . An advertisement in the *Post Man* newspaper in January 1704 reads: 'At Hogarth's Coffeehouse in St John's Gate . . . there will meet daily some learned gentlemen, who speak Latin readily, where any Gentleman that is either skilled in that language, or desirous to perfect himself in speaking thereof, will be welcome. The Master of the House, in the absence of others, being always ready to entertain Gentlemen in the Latin tongue.' The

Hogarth family seem to have lived in one of the rooms in the old gate, perhaps above the coffee room. Theirs was neither the first nor the last Latin coffeehouse. A pamphlet from 1662 refers to 'the Latine coffee house near the stocks [market]' in Cornhill and in 1710 the German traveller Zacharias von Uffenbach reports that 'in the evening we drove to the so-called Latin coffee-house near St Paul's Cathedral to see an auction of books': *London in 1710: From the Travels of Zacharias von Uffenbach*, ed. W. H. Quarrel and Margaret Mare (1934).

p. 387: *'the internet in a cup'* . . . *The Economist*, 18 December 2003.

p. 388: *'this great and monstrous thing'* . . . Daniel Defoe, *A Tour Through the Whole Island of Great Britain*, vol. 1 (1724), p. 325.

p. 388: *'I found myself in the strangest forest,' wrote one American visitor* . . . The words are John Dickinson's, quoted in Peter Clark, *British Clubs and Societies 1580–1800: The Origins of an Associational World* (2000), p. 157.

pp. 390–1: *In a poem by the Restoration debauchee Lord Rochester, a libertine and his mistress both covet their pretty young link boy* . . . 'The Disabled Debauchee', *The Complete Poems of John Wilmot, Earl of Rochester*, ed. David Vieth (2002), p. 116. It was written around 1675.

p. 393: *a perfume-making factory in Stoke Newington* . . . Katherine Frank, *Crusoe: Daniel Defoe, Robert Knox and the Creation of a Myth* (2011) pp. 63–4.

p. 394: *A correspondent to the* Spectator . . . *Spectator*, 2 April 1711. This issue was penned by Joseph Addison.

p. 396: *the 'Square of Venus'* . . . According to a writer in 1776, quoted in *An Eighteenth Century Journal*, ed. John Hampden (1940), p. 334.

p. 396: *Blind fiddlers are in high demand as they're perfect for orgies* . . . Jerry White, *London in the 18th Century: A Great and Monstrous Thing* (2012), p. 342.

p. 397: *'this gang of aristocratic thugs like to attack old women, seal them in hogsheads, and roll them down streets'* . . . *Walking the Streets of*

Eighteenth-Century London: John Gay's Trivia, ed. Susan Whyman and Clare Brant (2007), p. 125.

p. 400: *John Evelyn admits 'stepping into Bedlam'* . . . *Diary of John Evelyn*, 21 April 1657.

p. 401: *softer reds and pinks were in vogue* . . . White, *London in the 18th Century*, p. 5.

p. 403: *'an abode for those who have fallen out of wit'* . . . These are the words of William Gregory, Mayor of London, written in a manuscript in 1451, quoted in Catharine Arnold, *Bedlam: London and its Mad* (2009), p. 36.

p. 409: *'Lament, ye heroes, who frequent the wars,' proclaims a mock-heroic poem* . . . Anon., 'On the Death of Old Bennet the News-Crier' (1708), printed in Roger Lonsdale, ed., *The New Oxford Book of Eighteenth-Century Verse* (2009), p. 78.

p. 413: *a multi-tiered wedding cake with layers of diminishing size, just like the spire* . . . It is unclear when this story first captured the public imagination. It doesn't appear in any of the main newspapers, is probably apocryphal, and circulated by word of mouth (hence the apprentices are talking about it in the public house).

p. 420: *'a chaos of chemicals, pressures, sequences and timings'* . . . John Man, *The Gutenberg Revolution* (2002), p. 138.

p. 420: *A number of people swarm about the room, trying to place notices and advertisements* . . . All the advertisements that we glimpse being placed appear in the *Daily Courant* of Wednesday, 22 February 1716. I would concede that some of the customers might have sent errand boys or even messages in the penny post rather than turning up in person. The price of placing an advertisement in the *Daily Courant* was 3s 6d in 1725, when John Byrom placed one. Byrom, *Journal*.

p. 422: *at the Royal Exchange, merchants like to gamble on the outcome of foreign news stories* . . . I am grateful to Dr Perry Gauci for this point, which he makes in his *Emporium of the World: The Merchants of London, 1660–1880* (2007), p. 54.

p. 424: *each individual line is read aloud by a minister,* then *sung* . . . Duncan Coomer, *English Dissent Under the Early Hanoverians* (1946), p. 42.

p. 427: *One man, a pawnbroker, travelled all the way from Southwark in his night-gown* . . . Geoffrey Holmes, *The Trial of Dr Sacheverell* (1973), For the section on the Sacheverell riots I am indebted to Geoffrey Holmes's account.

p. 429: *the sledgehammer of English Justice* . . . My understanding of the criminal justice system is shaped in particular by John Beattie, *Policing and Punishment in London, 1660–1720* (2001), a fascinating work.

p. 430: *wisps of straw sticking out of their shoes* . . . H.van Schevikhoven *Forensic Anecdotes* (1882), p.282.

p. 431: *a woman called Mary Tomlins from the parish of St Clement Danes shuffles to the stand* . . . The dramatizations here are based on the *Proceedings on the King's Commission of the Peace, and Oyer and Terminer, and Gaol-Delivery of Newgate, held for the City of London, and County of Middlesex, on 22–26 February 1716.* These are freely available online at the Proceedings of the Old Bailey website: http://www.oldbaileyonline.org/.

p. 436: *John Vilette, accompanied a young boy in the execution cart to the gallows at Tyburn* . . . This story is told in James Boswell, *Life of Johnson*, ed. R. Chapman (1980), p. 1319 and mentioned too in Vic Gatrell, *The Hanging Tree: Execution and the English People, 1770–1868* (1994), p. 383.

p. 441: *the original exchange was opened in 1569 'for the more facile expediting the affair of negotiation'* . . . Edward Hatton, *The New View of London*, vol. 2 (1708), p. 617, on which there is also a diagram of all the various walks on the floor of the Royal Exchange.

p. 446: *an early instance of what Kelly Grovier has described as 'severance pay'* . . . Kelly Grovier, *The Gaol: The Story of Newgate – London's Most Notorious Prison* (2008), p. 74.

Further Reading

General histories

The literature on the history of London is as infinite and overwhelming as the city itself. To list everything here would be an absurd and fruitless endeavour and impossible within the space available. Parts of the foregoing chapters are based on primary sources (as attested by the endnotes) but since I have relied upon so many secondary sources, it would be ungracious of me not to list some of the principal works to which I'm indebted here. I hope they will also provide starting points for any readers who might wish to pursue any of the topics in more detail.

For general histories of London from the Roman period to the late twentieth or twenty-first century, Roy Porter provides an eloquent, concise and well-paced account in his *London: A Social History* (1994), which is complemented beautifully by Peter Ackroyd's magisterial *London: the Biography*, a felt and poetic impression of a city he clearly loves. Of interest too is Stephen Inwood's *A History of London* (1998) and *The London Encyclopaedia*, 3rd edn, ed. Ben Weinreb, Christopher Hibbert, Julia Keay and John Keay (2008), while Ed Glinert's topographically arranged *The London Compendium* (2003) is a masterpiece of concision and wit.

I do not claim to have invented historical time travel – far from it. For other second-person accounts of Old London, written for immediacy in the present tense, see Norman Lloyd Williams, *Tudor London Visited* (1991); Richard Tames, *Shakespeare's London on Five Groats a Day* (2009); the children's book *London: A Time Traveller's Guide* by Moira Butterfield (2013) and, of course, the brilliantly researched *Time Traveller's*

Guide to Medieval England (2009) and *Time Traveller's Guide to Elizabethan England* (2012), by Ian Mortimer. Sections of Liza Picard's books on London, cited below, also take the form of walking tours set in the past.

Shakespearean London

An invaluable portrait of the city on the cusp of the seventeenth century is John Stow, *A Survey of London, Written in the Year 1598* (1598, revised 1603).

Travellers' journals, though they are sometimes prone to exaggeration, provide a clear and compelling picture of many aspects of Shakespearean London: *The Journals of Two Travellers in Elizabethan and Early Stuart England: Thomas Platter and Horatio Busino*, ed. P. Razell (1994); Paul Hentzner, *A Journey into England* (1598); *The Diary of Henry Machyn, 1550–63*, ed. J. G. Nichols, Camden Society 42 (1848). There is also a useful compilation: *England as seen by foreigners in the days of Elizabeth and James I*, ed. W. B. Rye (1865). For overviews of the social history of the period, see Liza Picard, *Elizabeth's London: Everyday Life in Elizabethan London* (2003) and Stephen Porter, *Shakespeare's London: Everyday Life in London, 1580–1616* (2009). To delve into the mental universe of contemporaries through the prism of surviving objects and artefacts, see Neil MacGregor, *Shakespeare's Restless World* (2013).

The *Civitas Londinium* map of London (known as the Agas map), first printed from woodblocks around 1560, has been inordinately useful. A brilliant, zoomable edition is freely available online at http://mapoflondon.uvic.ca/LOND3.htm.

On **bull and bear baiting**, most of this is cobbled together from vivid contemporary and near-contemporary eyewitness accounts but see also Martin Holmes, *Elizabethan London* (1969); Hannah Velten, *Beastly London: A History of Animals in the City* (2013); Giles Dawson, *London's Bull-Baiting and Bear-Baiting Arena in 1562* (1964); Joseph

Quincy Adams, *Shakespearean Playhouses* (1917); and contemporary panoramas and maps.

On the mastiff dog, see John Caius, *De Canibus Britannicis* (1570).

On the **booksellers of Paul's Churchyard**, an invaluable guide, replete with detailed map, is Peter Blayney, *The Bookshops in Paul's Cross Churchyard* (1990). For the book trade in general, see H. S. Bennett, *English Books and their Readers 1603–1640* (1970). On the life and work of Wynkyn de Worde, see the slim *Wynkyn de Worde, Father of Fleet Street* (1960) by James Moran; H. S. Bennett, *English Books & Readers, 1475–1557: being a study in the history of the book trade from Caxton to the incorporation of the Stationers' Company* (1952); Ray Boston, *The Essential Fleet Street* (1990).

If you want to immerse yourself in **the soundscape of pre-industrial cities**, look no further than Bruce Smith, *The Acoustic World of Early Modern England* (1999). It includes musical notation for street hawkers' cries and a chapter on the acoustics of the Globe playhouse.

Though there may have been as many as 7,000 **Tudor and Jacobean tobacco houses**, there has never been a comprehensive study of them. However, they feature in Eric Burns's excellently readable *The Smoke of the Gods* (2007) and, a century before, the prolific Walter Besant made a series of startling claims in his *London in the Time of the Tudors* (1904). See also Sandra Bell, *The Subject of Smoke: Tobacco and Early Modern England* (2010).

The arrival of tobacco triggered a slew of polemical pamphlets for and against the 'holy herb'. I have drawn upon: King James I, *A Counterblaste to Tobacco* (1604); Barnaby Rich, *The Honestie of this Age* (1614); Anthony Chute, *Tabaco* (1595); the fantastically titled *Tobacco Battered and the Pipes Shattered* by Joshua Sylvester (1633); and 'Philaretes', *Work for Chimney Sweepers; Or, a Warning for Tobacconists* (1602), for a modern medical analysis of which – one that reflects well on Philaretes – see 'Tobacco or Health: An Elizabethan Doctor Speaks', *Health Education Research* 20:1 (2005). And don't miss C. Tatman, *The Archaeology of the Clay Tobacco Pipe* (1995).

On the **Drapers' Garden**, see in particular Penelope Harding, *A History of the Drapers' Company* (1989) and Liza Picard, *Elizabeth's London* (2003). On the history and philosophy of Tudor and Jacobean gardens more generally, I have particularly enjoyed *London's Pride: The Glorious History of the Capital's Gardens*, ed. Mireille Galinou; C. Paul Christianson, *The Riverside Gardens of Thomas More's London* (2005); Roy Strong, *The Renaissance Garden in England* (1970) and Rebecca Solnit's amazing *Wanderlust: A History of Walking* (2001). Some contemporary texts have also been useful: Thomas Hill, *The Gardener's Labyrinth* (1577) and John Schofield, *The London Surveys of Ralph Treswell* (1987) to name but two.

For **Old London Bridge**, see Peter Jackson, *London Bridge: A Visual History*, burbling with eyewitness accounts and brimming with contemporary and modern illustrations. For a full and pleasingly digressive account, consult Patricia Pierce, *Old London Bridge* (2001). Contemporary and near-contemporary illustrations are invaluable in bringing the old bridge to life, particularly Anthony van den Wyngaerde's *Panorama of London* (*c.*1544), Claes Janszoon Visscher's 1616 engraving, John Norden, *A View of the East Side of London Bridge* (1600), Claude de Jongh, *View of London Bridge* (*c.*1632), Wenceslaus Hollar's achingly beautiful *Long View of London from Bankside* (1647 – and also available as an iPad app called 'London in 1647') and William Hogarth, *Marriage à la mode*, episode six, in which a caricatured depiction of Old London Bridge can be glimpsed through the window.

On the ***Golden Hinde*** in Deptford, see the History of Deptford via British History Online (from the *Survey of London* (1878)) and the usual clutch of travellers' testimonies from the works cited above. Enjoyable accounts of Drake's circumnavigation of the world have flowed from the pens of John Sugden, *Sir Francis Drake* (1990) and George Malcom Thomson, *Sir Francis Drake* (1972). For a survey of what life was like on the ocean wave, see Juliet Gardiner and Michael J. Allen (eds.), *Before the Mast: Life and Death aboard the Mary Rose* (Archaeology of the Mary Rose, vol. 4, 2005).

On **Shakespeare's life and the birth of the Globe**, I have found particularly compelling James Shapiro, *1599: A Year in the Life of William Shakespeare* (2005); Bill Bryson, *Shakespeare: The World as a Stage* (2007); and Peter Ackroyd, *Shakespeare: The Biography* (2005). For my evocation of playgoing in Shakespearean London I am indebted to Andrew Gurr, *Playgoing in Shakespeare's London* (1987); Alexander Leggatt, *Jacobean Public Theatre* (1992); and Andrew Gurr and Mariko Ichikawa, *Staging in Shakespeare's Theatres* (2000).

Medieval London

Eyewitness accounts are few and far between, though there is, of course, Chaucer's *Canterbury Tales*, of which many editions exist, and also *London Lickpenny*, often attributed to John Lydgate and composed, it is believed, in the early fifteenth century.

Of the general secondary works on medieval London, a heavy-going and (thanks to multiple typesetting errors) confusing read – but a valuable one – is A. Myers, *London in the Age of Chaucer* (1972); its portrait of the medieval city is complemented by Charles Pendrill, *Wanderings in Medieval London* (1928) and his *London Life in the Fourteenth Century* (1925), as well as the lively and lengthy Walter Besant, *Medieval London* (2 vols, 1906). There are a handful of sourcebooks, of which I'd recommend G. G. Coulton, *Social Life in Britain from the Conquest to Reformation* (1918) and *Memorials of London and London Life in the 13th, 14th and 15th Centuries* (1868), ed. Henry Riley.

No detailed maps survive, but you can get a good sense of the medieval city from the Panorama of 1543 by the Flemish artist Anton van den Wyngaerde, though much monastic land, so intrinsic a feature of medieval London, had been pillaged by that point. For an excellent online edition, see www.panoramaofthethames.com/pott/wyngaerde-pan/.

On **anchorites and anchoresses**, see Ann Warren, *Anchorites and their Patrons in Medieval England* (1985); Charles Pendrill, *Wanderings in Medieval London* (1925); Walter Besant, *Medieval London* (1906); Hugh White (trans.), *Ancrene Wisse: Guide for Anchoresses* (1993); Mari Hughes-Edwards, *Reading Medieval Anchoritism: Ideology and Spiritual Practices* (2012); Liz Herbert McAvoy (ed.), *Anchorite Traditions of Medieval Europe* (2010), many of which have chilling manuscript illustrations of anchorites and anchoresses in their cells.

On **Old St Paul's**, see the informative, if dry, G. Cobb, *The Old Churches of London* (1942) and G. H. Cook, *Old St Paul's Cathedral* (1955); an older work but more readable is William Benham, *Old St Paul's* (1902). All these draw upon William Dugdale, *History of St Paul's Cathedral in London* (1658), illustrated by Wenceslaus Hollar.

For London's forgotten saint, **Erkenwald**, in addition to the primary sources listed in the endnotes, see in particular: Eamon Duffy, 'St Erkenwald: London's Cathedral Saint', in *The Medieval English Cathedral: Papers in Honour of Pamela Tudor-Craig: Proceedings of the 1998 Harlaxton Symposium* (2003). The same author's *The Stripping of the Altars* (2005) paints a convincing portrait of the vibrancy of late-medieval religion, a useful corrective to all the Reformation histories that are inclined to portray it as corrupt, superficial and out of touch. There is a comprehensive study of the chantry chapels of Old St Paul's: Marie-Helene Rousseau, *Saving the Souls of Medieval London: Perpetual Chantries at St Paul's Cathedral, c. 1200–1548* (2011). For St Paul's as a hub of social interaction, see L. Cowie, 'Paul's Walk until the Great Fire', *History Today* 24 (1974).

For **St Martin's Le Grand and sanctuaries in general**, I have found enlightening: Jessica Freeman, 'And he abjured the realm of England, never to return', in *Freedom of Movement in the Middle Ages: Proceedings of the 2003 Harlaxton Symposium* (2007); John Bellamy, *Crime and Public Order in the Later Middle Ages* (1973); Gervase Rosser, 'Sanctuary and Social Negotiation in Medieval England', in John Blair and Brian Golding (eds.), *The Cloister and the World* (1996); Karl

Shoemaker, *Sanctuary and Crime in the Middle Ages* (2011) and Shannon McSheffrey, 'Stranger Artisans and the London Sanctuary of St Martin le Grand', *Journal of Medieval and Early Modern Studies* 43:3 (2013) and her fascinating 'Sanctuary and the Legal Topography of Pre-Reformation London', *Law and History Review* 27:3 (2009). She also has written a book on the history of sanctuaries in the London area (forthcoming).

Jousting still inspires much historical interest. In addition to Froissart and other primary sources, I have drawn upon: Sheila Linenbaum, 'The Smithfield Tournament of 1390', *Journal of Medieval and Renaissance Studies* 20 (1990); John Marshall Carter, *Medieval Games: Sports and Recreations in Feudal Society* (1992); Juliet Barker, *The Tournament in England: 1100–1400* (1986). More focused on the tournament is David Crouch, *The Rise of the Joust* (2005). It is also covered in Teresa Mclean, *The English at Play in the Middle Ages* (1983), which is fascinating for medieval sports and games in general.

For developments in **medieval fashion and the sumptuary laws**, I am indebted to E. Jane Burns, *Courtly Love Undressed* (2002) and Margaret Scott, *Medieval Dress and Fashion* (2007). See also Myers, *London in the Age of Chaucer*.

On **food and drink**, see Martha Carlin, *Food and Eating in Medieval Europe* (1996) and her '"What say you to a piece of beef and mustard?" The Evolution of Public Dining in Medieval and Tudor London', *Huntingdon Library Quarterly* 71:1 (2008); David Brandon and Alan Brooke, *Bankside: London's Original District of Sin* (2011); and Ian Mortimer, *The Time Traveller's Guide to Medieval England* (2009).

The Tower continues to fascinate tourists and historians alike. A pacey, wide-ranging history can be found in the form of Nigel Jones, *Tower: An Epic History of the Tower of London*, but see also D. Diehl and M. P. Donnelly, *Tales from the Tower of London* (2004) and G. Abbott, *The Tortures of the Tower of London* (1986). The London historian Stephen Porter has also written *The Tower of London: The Biography* (2013).

The history of **London's guilds and livery halls** can be very dry and detailed but summaries can be found in Myers, *London in the Age of Chaucer*; Porter, *London: A Social History*; Inwood, *A History of London* and particularly Pendrill, *Wanderings*. For longer studies, try William Herbert, *The History of the Twelve Great Livery Companies of London* (1968) and George Unwin, *The Guilds and Companies of London* (1908). Matthew Davies and Ann Saunders, *The History of the Merchant Taylors' Company* (2004) is an informative case study.

An imperfect but rewarding way of getting a feel for the riverside palaces and mansions of **the Strand** is to consult sixteenth- and seventeenth-century maps, as listed above. But they are also explored in: Wilberforce Jenkinson, *The Royal & Bishops' Palaces in Old London* (1921); Myers, *London in the Age of Chaucer*; Nigel Jones, *Tower*. See also the entry for the Strand in British History Online (part of the *Survey of London*, written in 1878).

Medieval **Westminster** is surveyed in great detail in Gervase Rosser, *Medieval Westminster* (1989) and brought to life in Robert Shepherd, *Westminster: A Biography from Earliest Times to the Present* (2012); see too Dorian Gerhold, *Westminster Hall: Nine Hundred Years of History* (1999). Elsewhere, much can be gleaned from the general works cited above.

For the history of **the Royal Mews** at Charing Cross, see Robin Oggins, *The Kings and their Hawks: Falconry in Medieval England* (2004), his 'Falconry and Medieval Social Status', *Mediaevalalia* 12 (1989); and Tony Hunt, *Three Anglo-Norman Treaties on Falconry* (2009).

Plague-struck London

To get to grips with life during the Restoration, see Liza Picard, *Restoration London: Everyday Life in the 1660s* (1997) and the less effervescent but still useful Stephen Porter, *Pepys's London: Everyday Life in London 1650–1703* (2011).

The best map of the city for this period is An Exact Delineation of the Cities of London and Westminster and the Suburbs Thereof by Richard Newcourt: www.bl.uk/onlinegallery/onlineex/crace/a/zoomify87874.html.

On **the Great Plague**, a great deal has been written. Any study of London's year of hell should begin with Samuel Pepys's diary, of which many versions exist, including online, and, in spite of its historical fiction status, Defoe's *A Journal of the Plague Year*, which can't be equalled for vividness and immediacy (though this is an illusion since it was written almost sixty years after the events depicted). I have been working from the Cynthia Wall edition, published in 2003. The other primary sources I have used are listed in the endnotes. From the secondary literature, I have drawn upon: James Leasor, *The Plague and the Fire* (1962); Stephen Porter, *The Great Plague* (1999); A. Lloyd Moote and Dorothy C. Moote, *The Great Plague: The Story of London's Most Deadly Year* (2004); Paul Slack, *The Impact of the Plague in Tudor and Stuart England* (1985); and, though it evokes the Cambridge experience, Evelyn Lord, *The Great Plague: A People's History* (2014).

Most of the gruesome and outlandish recipes listed in the visit to **the apothecary's shop** are drawn from manuscript 'books of receipts' (recipe books) kept in the British Library, as detailed in the endnotes, but I have also consulted Henrietta Maria, *The Queen's Closet Opened* (1655); Lynette Hunter, *Women, Science and Medicine: 1500–1700* (1997); Thomas Dawson, *The Good Housewife's Jewel* (1596–7); Betty S. Travitsky and Anne Lake (eds.), *The Early Modern Englishwoman: A Facsimile Library of Essential Works*, series 3, vol. 3 (2008) and, in the secondary literature, Edith Snook, *Women, Beauty and Power in Early Modern England* (2011).

Specifically on apothecaries, see Louise Curth, *From Physick to Pharmacology* (2006) and W. S. C. Copeman, *The Worshipful Society of Apothecaries of London: A History, 1617–1967* (1967).

On **the rise of Covent Garden**, see John Richardson, *Covent Garden Past* (1995); Porter, *London: A Social History*; Vic Gatrell, *The First*

Bohemians: Life and Art in London's Golden Age (2013); Reginald Jacobs, *Covent Garden: Its Romance and History* (1913).

The **history of cosmetics** – powder, perfume, paint, patches and hair dye – is a substantive field and I have mined for information: Farah Karim-Cooper, *Cosmetics in Shakespearean and Renaissance Drama* (2006); R. Corson, *Fashions in Make Up: From Ancient to Modern Times* (1972); Valerie Steele, *Encyclopedia of Clothing and Fashion* (2005); Patricia Phillippy, *Painting Women: Cosmetics, Canvases and Early Modern Culture* (2006); Maggie Angeloglou, *A History of Make-Up* (1970).

There is not much specifically on **the first Theatre Royal on Bridges Street** (or Drury Lane), but on female actresses, see Joanne Lafler, 'Theatre and the Female Presence', in Joseph Donohue (ed.), *The Cambridge History of British Theatre*, vol. 2: *1660 to 1895* (2004); Sophie Tomlinson, *Women on Stage in Stuart Drama* (2005); Katharine Maus, '"Playhouse Flesh and Blood": Sexual Ideology and the Restoration Actress', *English Literary History* 46 (1979); Walter Macqueen-Pope, *Ladies First: The Story of Woman's Conquest of the British Stage* (1952); Elizabeth Howe, 'A State of Undress. The First English Actresses on Stage: 1660–1700', in her *Women in European Theatre* (1995). There are many biographies of Nell Gwyn; I enjoyed Charles Beauclerk's *Nell Gwyn: Mistress to a King* (2005) and Roy MacGregor-Hastie, *Nell Gwyn* (1987).

The great St James's chocolate houses like Ozinda's, the Cocoa Tree and White's did not yet exist in 1665 but for a delightful **history of chocolate**, which touches upon the arrival of chocolate in London, why not treat yourself to Sophie and Michael D. Coe, *The True History of Chocolate* (2013).

There is a wide literature that delights in conveying the horror and misery of **Newgate Prison** in its various incarnations through the century. The morbid voyeur may well relish as I did: Kelly Grovier, *The Gaol: The Story of Newgate – London's Most Notorious Prison* (2008), which was serialized on BBC Radio 4; Donald Rumbelow, *The Triple Tree: Newgate, Tyburn, and the Old Bailey* (1982); Anthony Babington, *The English Bastille: A History of Newgate Gaol and Prison Conditions in*

Britain, 1188–1902 (1971); Stephen Halliday, *Newgate: London's Prototype of Hell* (2013).

On the birth of the **Royal Society**, there is some great material in Jenny Uglow, *A Gambling Man: Charles II's Restoration Game* (2010), but for full studies see Lisa Jardine, *Ingenious Pursuits: Building the Scientific Revolution* (1999); and Michael Hunter, *Establishing the New Science: The Experience of the Early Royal Society* (1989). Much can be found too in biographies of Newton, Hooke, Wren and Boyle.

A classic and well-illustrated study of the rich history of **Hackney** is William Robinson, *The History and Antiquities of the Parish of Hackney* (1842) but see the more recent publication from the Hackney society, Margaret Willes (ed.), *Hackney: An Uncommon History* (2012), which recreates the world of Hackney, Stoke Newington and Shoreditch every hundred years from 1612 to 2012. It gets a poetic, psycho-geographical treatment in Iain Sinclair, *Hackney, that Rose-Red Empire: A Confidential Report* (2009), which links past and present effortlessly.

Culls of dogs, cats and to a much more limited extent rats are covered in most general histories of the plague, but on the **massacres of dogs**, the authority is Mark Jenner, 'The Great Dog Massacre', in W. G. Naphy and P. Roberts (eds.), *Fear in Early Modern Society* (1997).

The Great Fire blazes a trail through any book on Pepysian London and is frequently a convenient (if misleading) epilogue to Great Plague tomes. I have relied upon primary sources as referenced in the text and endnotes and some of the general works cited above rather than any particular source.

Victorian London

For general portraits of Victorian London, see K. Baedeker, *London and its Environs: A Handbook for Travellers* (1900); Liza Picard, *Victorian*

London: The Life of a City 1840–1870 (2005); Peter Cunningham, *A Handbook for London* (1849).

Compulsory reading is also Jerry White, *London in the 19th Century* (2011). See also Judith Flanders, *The Victorian City: Everyday Life in Dickens' London* (2012). A formidable online resource, with links to a wide range of Victorian maps, is Lee Jackson's *Dictionary of Victorian London*: www.victorianlondon.org/index-2012.htm.

A great article on foreigners' perceptions of Victorian London is Joseph de Sapio, '"A reign of steam": Continental Perceptions of Modernity in Victorian London, 1840–1900', *The London Journal* 37:1 (2012).

Dickens is, of course, one of the richest sources for London life. Though not used much in the chapter, I have relied upon *Sketches by Boz* (1837) and *Bleak House* (1853).

On **the emergence of parks** as sites of moral refreshment in the Victorian city, see Neil Macmaster, 'The Battle for Mousehold Heath, 1857–1884: "Popular Politics" and the Victorian Public Park', *Past and Present* 127 (1990).

On **Holywell Street and Victorian pornography**, see Iain McCalman, *Radical Underworld* (1988); Lynda Nead, *Victorian Babylon* (2000); and Simon Popple, 'Photography, Vice and the Moral Dilemma in Victorian Britain', *Early Popular Visual Culture* 3:2 (2005); also Deborah Lutz, *Pleasure Bound* (2011). For transgressive sexual attitudes and behaviour, a classic study is Steven Marcus, *The Other Victorians* (1966). There are a handful of photographs of Holywell Street and Wynch Street in their twilight online.

For **the Whitechapel slums and slumming**, see Jack London, *The People of the Abyss* (1903); Seth Koven, *Slumming: Sexual and Social Politics in Victorian London* (2004); Drew Gray, *London's Shadows: The Dark Side of the Victorian City* (2010); John Batt, *Dr Barnardo, The Foster Father of Nobody's Children* (1904); J. Wesley Bready, *Doctor Barnardo: Physician, Pioneer, Prophet* (1932).

On London's **docks and wharves**, see White, *London in the 19th Century*; Fiona Rule, *London's Docklands: A History of a Lost Quarter*

(2012); Glinert, *Compendium*; Hippolyte Taine, *Notes on England* (1872); and, of course, Henry Mayhew, *London Labour and the London Poor* (1851). For an historical flight of fancy taking **Mr Jamrach's tiger** as its launch pad, there is Carol Birch, *Jamrach's Menagerie* (2011), nominated for the Man Booker Prize.

The classic account of the **Elephant Man** remains Michael Howell and Peter Ford, *The True History of the Elephant Man* (1980, updated 1992). See also John Treves's account in his *The Elephant Man and Other Reminiscences* (1923). For the **wider culture of freak shows**, an excellent starting point is Nadja Durbach, *Spectacle of Deformity: Freak Shows and Modern British Culture* (2009); also L. A. Kochanek, 'Reframing the Freak: From Sideshow to Science', *Victorian Periodicals Review* 30:3 (1997). On specific exhibits, see Nadja Durbach, '"Skinless Wonders": Body Worlds and the Victorian Freak Show', *Journal of the History of Medicine* 69 (2014) and Janet Browne and Sharon Messenger, 'Victorian Spectacle: Julia Pastrana, The Bearded and Hairy Female', *Endeavour* 27:4 (2003).

For **the birth of the London Underground**, a very enjoyable account is Andrew Martin, *Underground, Overground: A Passenger's History of the Tube* (2012). See also Christian Wolmar, *The Subterranean Railway: How the London Underground was Built and How It Changed the City Forever* (2009).

On **music halls**, see John Major, *My Old Man: A Personal History of the Music Hall* (2012); Richard Anthony Baker, *British Music Hall* (2005); Anon., *The Canterbury Theatre of Varieties and its Associations* (1878); *Lambeth and Music Hall: A Treasury of Music Hall Memorabilia*, comp. Eva O'Rourke (1977); W. Macqueen-Pope, *The Melodies Linger On* (1950); Raymond Mander, *British Music Hall: A Story in Pictures* (1965); George Speaight, *Bawdy Songs of the Early Music Hall* (1977); and Anon., *The Music Hall Songster* (1893). For two of the most famous music hall performers see Mary Tich and Richard Findlater, *Little Tich* (1979) and Daniel Farson, *Marie Lloyd and Music Hall* (1972).

1950s London

For overviews of 1950s London, I would recommend the highly readable Dominic Sandbrook, *Never Had It So Good: A History of Britain from Suez to the Beatles* (2005); Jerry White, *London in the 20th Century* (2008); Anthony Jones, *London: Photographs* (1958) and Peter Lewis, *The Fifties* (1978).

The literature on **the London Blitz** is, as you'd expect, enormous. I would like to register my debt of obligation to the following, all of which excel at providing vivid, eyewitness accounts of the destruction: Joanna Mack and Steve Humphries, *London at War* (1985); Basil Woon, *Hell Came to London: A Reportage of the Blitz During 14 Days* (1941); Juliet Gardiner, *The Blitz: The British Under Attack* (2010); Amy Helen Bell (ed.), *London Was Ours: Diaries and Memoirs of the London Blitz* (2008); Gavin Mortimer, *The Longest Night: The Bombing of London on May 10 1941* (2006). Also useful were: Porter, *London*, H. V. Morton, *In Search of London* (1951), and Nikolaus Pevsner, *The Buildings of England, London 1: The City of London* (1957). To really understand the damage you really need to immerse yourself in photographs of bombed streets online or in print, such as Gavin Mortimer, *The Blitz: An Illustrated History* (2010), which digs up some shocking images from the archive of the *Daily Mirror*.

My account of **London's high-rise experiment** is informed by White, *London in the 20th Century*; Herbert Wright, *London High* (2006); John Grindrod, *Concretopia: A Journey Around the Rebuilding of Postwar Britain* (2014); John Burnett, *A Social History of Housing, 1815–1985* (1986). For a more personal account, see Lynsey Hanley, *Estates: An Intimate History* (2007) – it's a wonderful read.

For **the espresso bars of 1950s Soho**, see Antony Clayton, *London's Coffee Houses: A Stimulating Story* (2003) and Markman Ellis, *The Coffee House: A Cultural History* (2011). To see the 1950s coffee bars in all their Formica glory, you can watch on YouTube an episode of the documentary series *Look at Life* (shown in cinemas in the 1950s and 1960s) which features some of the most famous ones: https://www.youtube.com/watch?v=rW5Oi_gXodk.

For **Soho** itself, see Richard Tames, *Soho Past* (1994) and Judith Summers, *Soho: A History of London's Most Colourful Neighbourhood* (1989).

For **Senate House and Orwell's Ministry of Truth**, see Negley Harte, *The University of London: An Illustrated History* (1986); Richard Simpson, 'Classicism and Modernity: The University of London's Senate House', *Bulletin of the Institute of Classical Studies* 43 (1999); and, of course, George Orwell, *Nineteen Eighty-Four* (1949).

The best way to learn about **Mary Quant and her Chelsea Bazaar** is straight from the horse's mouth, so see Mary Quant, *Quant by Quant* (1966) and also her later memoir *My Autobiography* (2012). Many surveys of the countercultural Swinging Sixties track back to the late 1950s too in a way that I have found useful, such as Shawn Levy, *Ready, Steady, Go: Swinging London and the Invention of Cool* (2003). See also Barry Miles, *London Calling: A Counter-Cultural History of London since 1945* (2010); Ernestine Carter, *Magic Names of Fashion* (1980); and Simon Rycroft, *Swinging City: A Cultural Geography of London 1950–1974* (2012).

Early Georgian London

Though its sheer heft may make you groan, it's well, well worth reading Jerry White, *London in the 18th Century: A Great and Monstrous Thing* (2012). Liza Picard, *Dr Johnson's London* (2000) is a treasure trove of minute detail about the practicalities of how people actually lived while Lucy Inglis, *Georgian London: Into the Streets* (2013) succeeds in showing the human face of Georgian London.

Eyewitness accounts of eighteenth-century London are manifold. For travellers' reports, see *A Foreign View of England in the Reigns of George I and George II: The Letters of Monsieur César de Saussure*, ed. Madame Van Muyden (1902) and *London in 1710: From the Travels of Zacharias von Uffenbach*, ed. W. H. Quarrel and Margaret Mare (1934). The scurrilous hack and tavern keeper Ned Ward revels in reviling all things metropolitan in *The London Spy*, ed. Kenneth Fenwick (1955). And two obscure but helpful diaries complementing Dudley Ryder's are: *The Private Journal and Literary Remains of John Byrom*, ed. R. Parkinson, 4 vols., Chetham Society Remains (1854–7), 32, 34, 40, 44; and *Secret Comment: The Diaries of Gertrude Savile, 1721–1757*, ed. A. Savile (1997). See also Edward Hatton, *A New View of London* (1708) and John Strype, *A Survey of the Cities of London and Westminster* (1720), which updates John Stow's earlier *Survey of London*. And no visit to eighteenth-century London would be complete without reading *Boswell's London Journal, 1762–1763*, ed. Frederick Pottle (2004).

I have also relied heavily upon contemporary newspapers, many of which belong to the British Library's Burney Collection and have been digitized.

One of the best ways of travelling back to the eighteenth century is to explore John Rocque's amazingly detailed 1746 map, which is freely available online at www.locatinglondon.org/.

For the history of **London's coffeehouses**, see Clayton, *Stimulating Story*; Ellis, *Coffee House*; Brian Cowan, *The Social Life of Coffee: The Emergence of the British Coffeehouse* (2005) and on the London experience specifically, my own *The Lost World of the London Coffeehouse*, published in limited edition by Idler Books (2013). There is a scholarly study of the Grecian coffeehouse: Jonathan Harris, 'The Grecian Coffeehouse and Political Debate in London, 1688–1714', *The London Journal* 25:1 (2000). You may also like to join one of Unreal City Audio's immersive coffeehouse tours in the City each month.

The full shorthand diary of **Dudley Ryder** remains unpublished, but around two-thirds of it appeared in 1939, along with an informative introduction. See *The Diary of Dudley Ryder, 1715–1716*, ed. William Matthews (1939). The diary really allows the reader to get inside the head of an early-eighteenth-century bourgeois.

On the **frost fairs**, see G. Davis, *Frostiana: or A History of the Frozen Thames* (1814); Ian Currie, *Frosts, Freezes and Fairs: The Chronicles of the Frozen Thames* (2002); Nicholas Reed, *Frost Fairs on the Frozen Thames* (2002) – all with magical illustrations. See also Peter Ackroyd, *Thames: The Sacred River* (2008) and Helen Humphreys, *The Frozen Thames* (2012), which tells forty icy tales – one for each time the Thames froze over. My evocation is also based on contemporary newspaper reports.

For a lengthy compendium of London's old **shop signs**, the authority is Bryant Lillywhite, *London Signs: A Reference Book of London Signs from Earliest Times to about the mid-Nineteenth century* (1972), but see too Liza Picard, *Restoration London: Everyday Life in the 1660s* (1997); Ambrose Heal, *The Signboards of Old London Shops* (1947); and for some stunning photographs of shop signs that survived into the age of the camera, see the Gentle Author, *Spitalfields Life*, 5 October 2011, available online at http://spitalfieldslife.com/2011/10/05/the-signs-of-old-london/.

For Georgian **Covent Garden**, see Gatrell, *First Bohemians*; Dan Cruickshank, *The Secret History of Georgian London: How the Wages of Sin Shaped the Capital* (2010) and, of course, *Harris's List of Covent Garden Ladies: Sex in the City in Georgian Britain*, ed. Hallie Rubenhold (2005), which contains 'the funniest, rudest and most bizarre entries'.

To get to grips with how **sedan chairs** worked, see Geoffrey Wilson, *Poles Apart: The Public Sedans of Bygone London* (2002).

On the horrors of **Bethlem** and attitudes towards mental illness, see Catherine Arnold, *Bedlam* (2008); Jonathan Andrews and Andrew Scull, *Undertaker of the Mind: John Monro and Mad-Doctoring in Eighteenth-Century England* (2001); Edward Geoffrey O'Donoghue, *The Story of Bethlehem Hospital* (1914); Roy Porter, *A Social History of Madness: Stories of the Insane* (1996); David Russell, *Scenes from Bedlam*

(1997); Nikolai Karamzin, *Letters of a Russian Traveller*, ed. Andrew Kahn (2003).

On **Fleet Street** see Alan Brooke, *Fleet Street, the Story of a Street* (2012); Bob Clarke, *From Grub Street to Fleet Street: An Illustrated History of English Newspapers to 1899* (2004); Ray Boston, *The Essential Fleet Street: Its History and Influence* (1990). On the news mania of the early eighteenth century, see Hannah Barker, *Newspapers, Politics and English Society, 1695–1855* (2000) and early issues of the *Tatler* and *Spectator* written by Joseph Addison and Richard Steele.

My evocation of a **newspaper office** has been shaped by M. Handover, *Printing in London from 1476 to Modern Times* (1960); Ellic Howe, *The London Compositor: Documents Relating to the Wages, Working Conditions and Customs of the London Printing Trade, 1785–1900* (1947); Michael Harris, *London Newspapers in the Age of Walpole* (1987). For a witty popular history of the invention of movable printing in fifteenth-century Germany, look no further than John Man, *The Gutenberg Revolution* (2002).

For understanding the beliefs and culture of **the dissenters**, we have Duncan Coomer, *English Dissent Under the Early Hanoverians* (1946) and the authoritative work on **the Sacheverell riots of 1710** remains Geoffrey Holmes, *The Trial of Dr Sacheverell* (1973), to which my narrative is indebted.

To get to grips with the **criminal justice system** in all its savage complexity, I would recommend the lengthy but lucid John Beattie, *Policing and Punishment in London, 1660–1720* (2001) as well as an older work, William Hooper, *The History of Newgate and the Old Bailey* (1935) and Bernard O'Donnell, *The Old Bailey and its Trials* (1950). For a more polemical work exploring the relationship between capital punishment and capitalism, see Peter Linebaugh, *The London Hanged: Crime and Civil Society in the Eighteenth Century* (2003). On **transportation**, one fascinating work, not strictly within our period but serviceable for our purposes is A. Roger Ekirch, *Bound for America: The Transportation of British Convicts to the Colonies, 1718–1775* (1987).

The workings of the **Royal Exchange** are laid bare in Perry Gauci, *Emporium of the World* (2007) and Natasha Glaisyer, *The Culture of Commerce in England, 1660–1720* (2006) as well as the eyewitness accounts listed above.

And most studies of the Tower of London, including those cited above, feature the execution site at Tower Hill.